Hagstrom®

Fairfield County Atlas

FOURTH LARGE SCALE EDITION

Cover Photo of East Norwalk Harbor and Veterans Memorial Park by Michael Warren

Fairfield County

Key Map

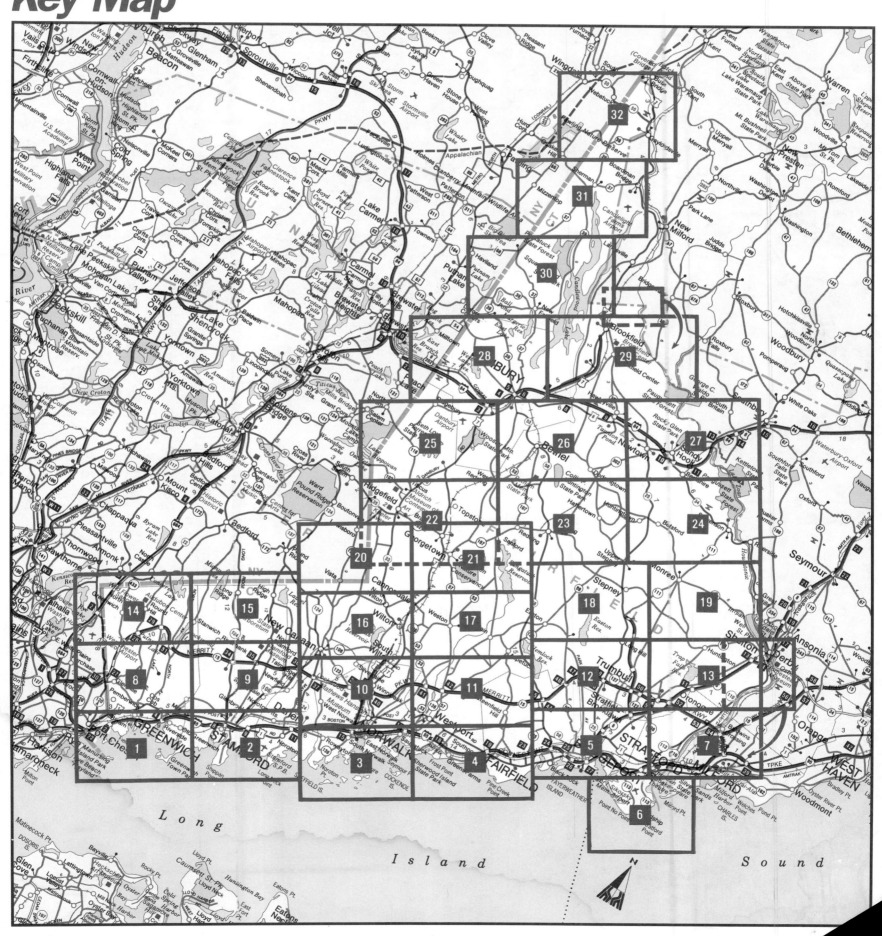

Fairfield County

Main Through Routes

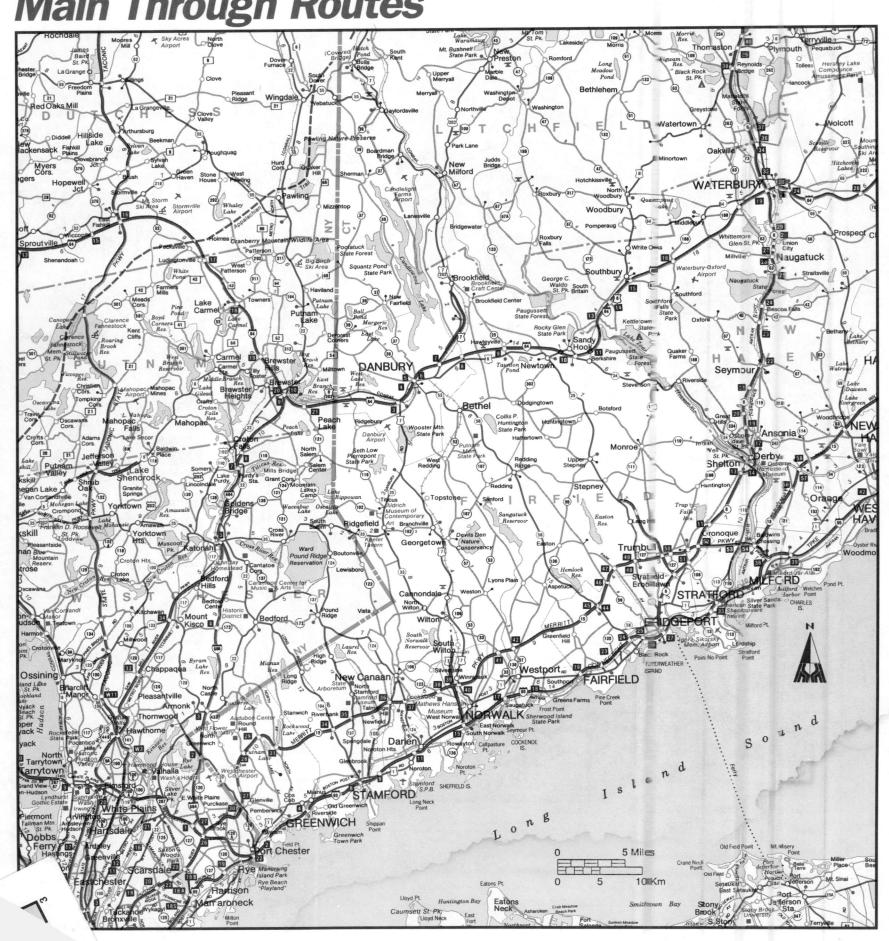

Fairfield County

at a Glance

Fairfield County (Population 829,786) occupies 659 square miles in the southwestern corner of Connecticut. The county contains attractive suburban homes as well as established cities. Service and manufacturing industries provide employment for the majority of residents, and the county enjoys both a low unemployment rate and the highest per capita income in the state. Many of its residential towns along the Long Island Sound are among the best known and most desirable places to live.

Along with the production of helicopters and other aircraft, the county's highly developed industrial economy includes the manufacturing of sophisticated electronics, specialized machinery and equipment. Fairfield County is also home to many corporate headquarters (ranked third nationally as a location of choice by Fortune 500 companies). A large number of research and development laboratories draw on a reserve of highly trained personnel and skilled labor. It is served by three large electric power companies and a number of smaller utility companies.

The county's scenic beauty, charming old towns and cities provide an ideal environment for suburban living and easy access to New York City, where many of its citizens are employed. It is linked to New York by Metro North Commuter Railroad, and to the entire country by Amtrak. Bridgeport offers scheduled air service from the Igor Sikorsky Memorial Airport to New York and cities throughout New England. Major destinations are served by neighboring Westchester County and Bradley International Airports. Passenger and car ferry service runs between Bridgeport and Port Jefferson, Long Island.

Population Statistics

Municipality	Area* (Sq. Miles)	Population** 1994 estimate	Map No.
Bethel	17.0	17,939	26, 29
Bridgeport	17.5	136,693	5, 6, 7, 12
Brookfield	19.8	14,526	29, 30
Danbury	44.0	66,464	25, 26, 28, 29, 30
Darien	13.7	19,108	2, 3, 9, 10
Easton	28.8	6,499	12, 17, 18
Fairfield	30.6	52,988	4, 5, 11, 12
Greenwich	50.6	57,816	1, 2, 8, 9, 14, 15
Monroe	26.4	17,773	18, 19, 24
New Canaan	23.3	18,538	9, 10, 15, 16, 20
New Fairfield	25.3	13,109	30
Newtown	60.4	20,920	23, 24, 26, 27, 29
Norwalk	27.7	79,106	3, 10, 11
Redding	32.2	8,095	22, 23, 25
Ridgefield	34.8	21,560	22, 25, 28
Shelton	31.4	36,058	7, 13, 19
Sherman	23.5	2,994	31, 32
Stamford	39.9	109,950	2, 9, 15
Stratford	18.7	47,743	5, 6, 7, 13
Trumbull	23.5	31,814	12, 13, 18, 19
Weston	20.8	9,068	17, 21
Westport	22.4	24,708	3, 4, 11
Wilton	26.8	16,317	16, 17, 20, 21
Total	**659.1**	**829,786**	

Sources: *Connecticut State Register and Manual 1995
**Connecticut Dept. of Health Services

Government Guide

Municipality	Location	Telephone*
Bethel	5 Library Pl., Bethel 06801	794-8505
Bridgeport	45 Lyon Ter., Bridgeport 06604	576-7207
Brookfield	Pocono Rd., Brookfield 06804	775-7313
Danbury	155 Deer Hill Av., Danbury 06810	797-4531
Darien	2 Renshaw Rd., Darien 06820	656-7307
Easton	225 Center Rd., Easton 06612	268-6291
Fairfield	611 Old Post Rd., Fairfield 06430	256-3000
Greenwich	101 Fieldpoint Rd., Greenwich 06836	622-7700
Monroe	7 Fan Hill Rd., Monroe 06468	452-5417
New Canaan	77 Main St., New Canaan 06840	972-2323
New Fairfield	4 Brush Hill Rd., New Fairfield 06812	746-8110
Newtown	45 Main St., Newtown 06470	270-4200
Norwalk	125 East Av., Norwalk 06856	854-7747
Redding	100 Hill Rd., Redding 06875	938-2377
Ridgefield	400 Main St., Ridgefield 06877	431-2785
Shelton	54 Hill St., Shelton 06484	924-1555
Sherman	9 Rte. 39 North, Sherman 06784	(860) 354-5281
Stamford	888 Washington Blvd., Stamford 06904	977-4056
Stratford	2725 Main St., Stratford 06497	385-4020
Trumbull	5866 Main St., Trumbull 06611	452-5035
Weston	56 Norfield Rd., Weston 06883	222-2616
Westport	110 Myrtle Av., Westport 06881	226-831
Wilton	238 Danbury Rd., Wilton 06897	834-8

Note: *Area code is 203 unless otherwise noted

Fairfield County

State Parks and Recreation Guide

Pootatuck State Forest-1,055 acres-Undeveloped forest, features fishing, hunting, hiking, and winter sports. Located in New Fairfield.

Squantz Pond State Park-172 acres-Park features boating, swimming, fishing, hiking, picnicking, and winter sports. Located in New Fairfield.

Wooster Mountain State Park-324 acres-Undeveloped park, features skeet. Located in Danbury.

Seth Low Pierrepont State Park-305 acres-Undeveloped park, features hiking and winter sports. Located in Ridgefield.

Putnam Memorial State Park-183 acres-Park features fishing, hiking, picnicking, and a museum. Located in Redding.

Paugussett State Forest-1,935 acres-Undeveloped forest, features fishing, hunting, and hiking. Located in Newtown.

Rocky Glen State Park-41 acres-Undeveloped park, features hiking. Located in Newtown.

Collis P. Huntington State Park-878 acres-Park features fishing, hiking, and winter sports. Located in Redding.

Indian Well State Park-153 acres-Park features boating, swimming, fishing, hiking, and picnicking. Located in Shelton.

Sherwood Island State Park-234 acres-Park features swimming, fishing and picnicking. Located in Westport.

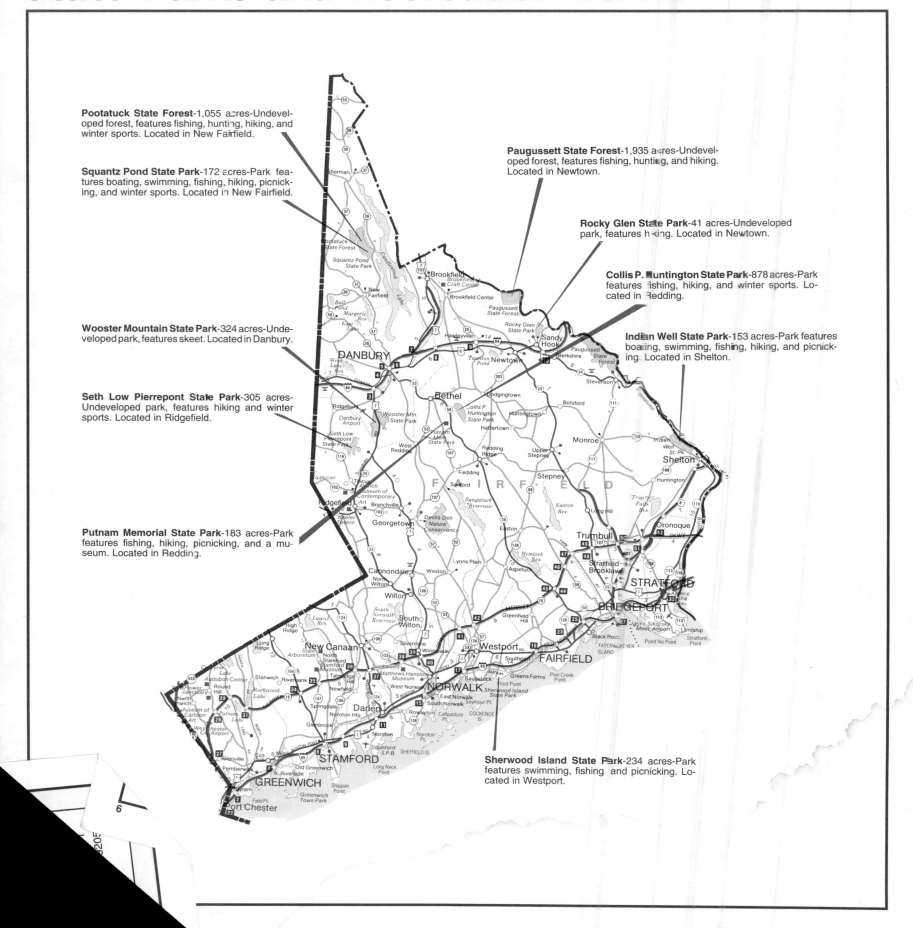

Fairfield County

Index to Places

1
A
B

PEMBERWICK PARK

(Deliveries from Greenwich P.O.)

06831

G R E E N

Port Chester

10573

Port Chester Sta.

25

06830

Greenwich

JHS

Greenwich Sta.

CONNECTICUT

95

Bruce Park

Grass Island

Byram Park

Rich Is.

BYRAM HARBOR

Indian Harbor Y.C.

SMITH COVE

INDIAN HARBOR

Brush Is.

Mead Pt.

Shore Is.

Belle Haven Club

Belle Haven

Field Pt.

Tweed Is.

Hawthorne Beach (PVT)

26
Byram Pt.

Calf Islands

Bowers Is.

Ferry to Little Captain's Island (Island Beach) (June thru Sept.)

L O N G   I S L A N D   S O U N D

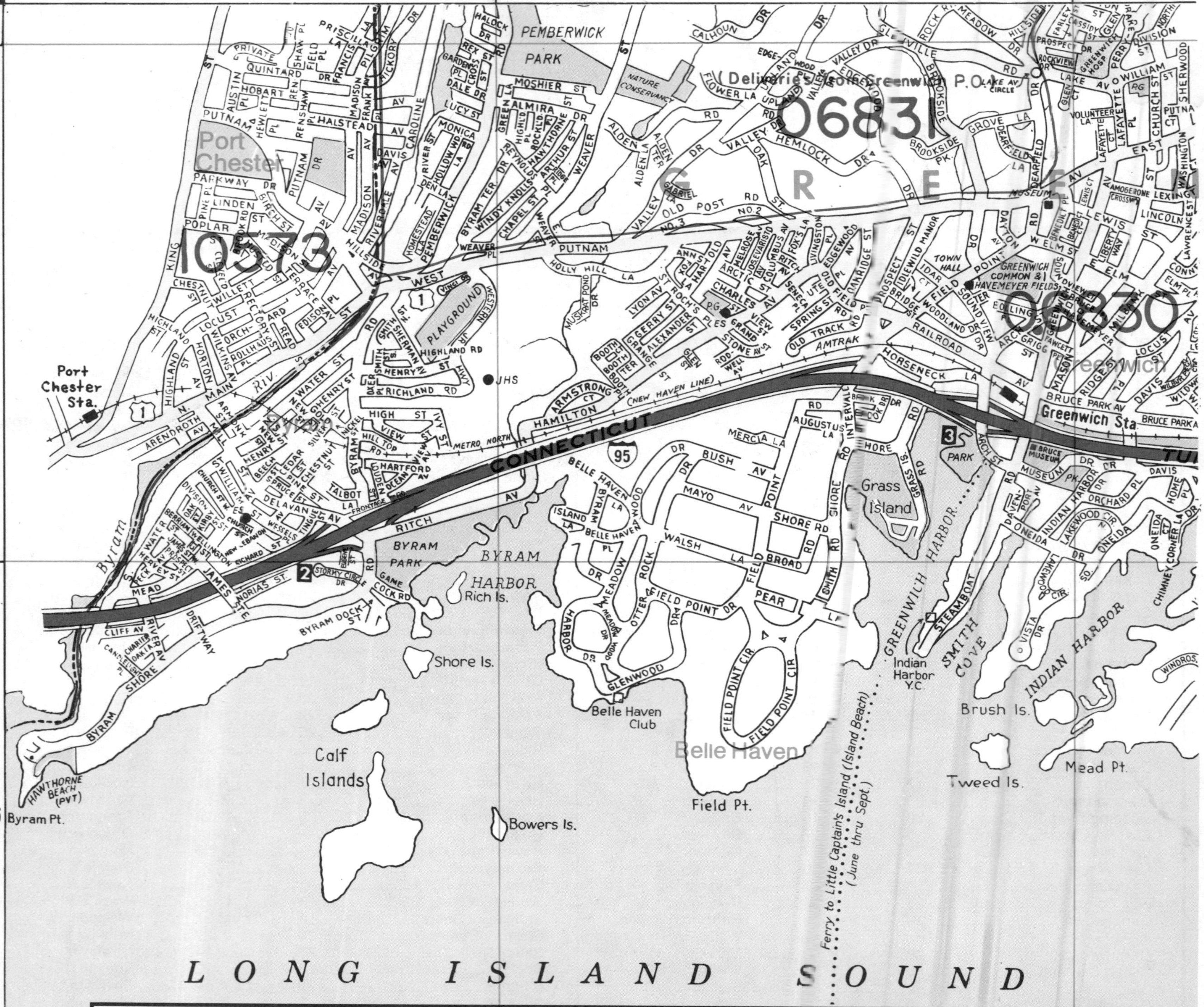

Legend for Street Maps

Symbol	Description		Symbol	Description		Symbol	Description
	Main Highways/Limited Access			State Boundaries			Cemeteries
	Main Through Roads			County Boundaries			Points of Interest
	Unimproved Roads			City and Town Boundaries			Airports
U.S. 1 / Interstate 95 / State 33	Highway Symbols			Borough Boundaries			Hospitals
12	Interchange Numbers		06902	Zip Code Numbers and Boundaries			Yacht Clubs
	Merritt Parkway			Parks			Post Office Stations
Freight Only / Passenger	Railroad Lines and Stations			Golf & Country Clubs		ES MS JHS HS	Elementary Schools Middle Schools Junior High Schools High Schools
						TH	Town Hall

Maps 1 to 21 Scales (Approximate) 1:24,000 • 1" = 2,000 Feet

0 — 5,000 Feet

0 — 1,000 Meters

Maps 22 to 32 Scales (Approximate) 1:32,000 • 1" = 2,700 Feet

0 — 5,000 Feet

0 — 1,000 Meters

A
B

C · D · 1

GREENWICH

06807

06878

06870

06820

CONN. TPKE.

Cos Cob Sta.

Riverside, Sta.

Old Greenwich Sta.

COS COB HARBOR

Riverside Yacht Club

The Milbrook Club

Innis Arden Golf Club

UNION CEM.

BRUCE PARK

Park Is.

Horse Is.

Saw Is.

Goose Is.

Diving Island

Bluff Is.

Salt Rock

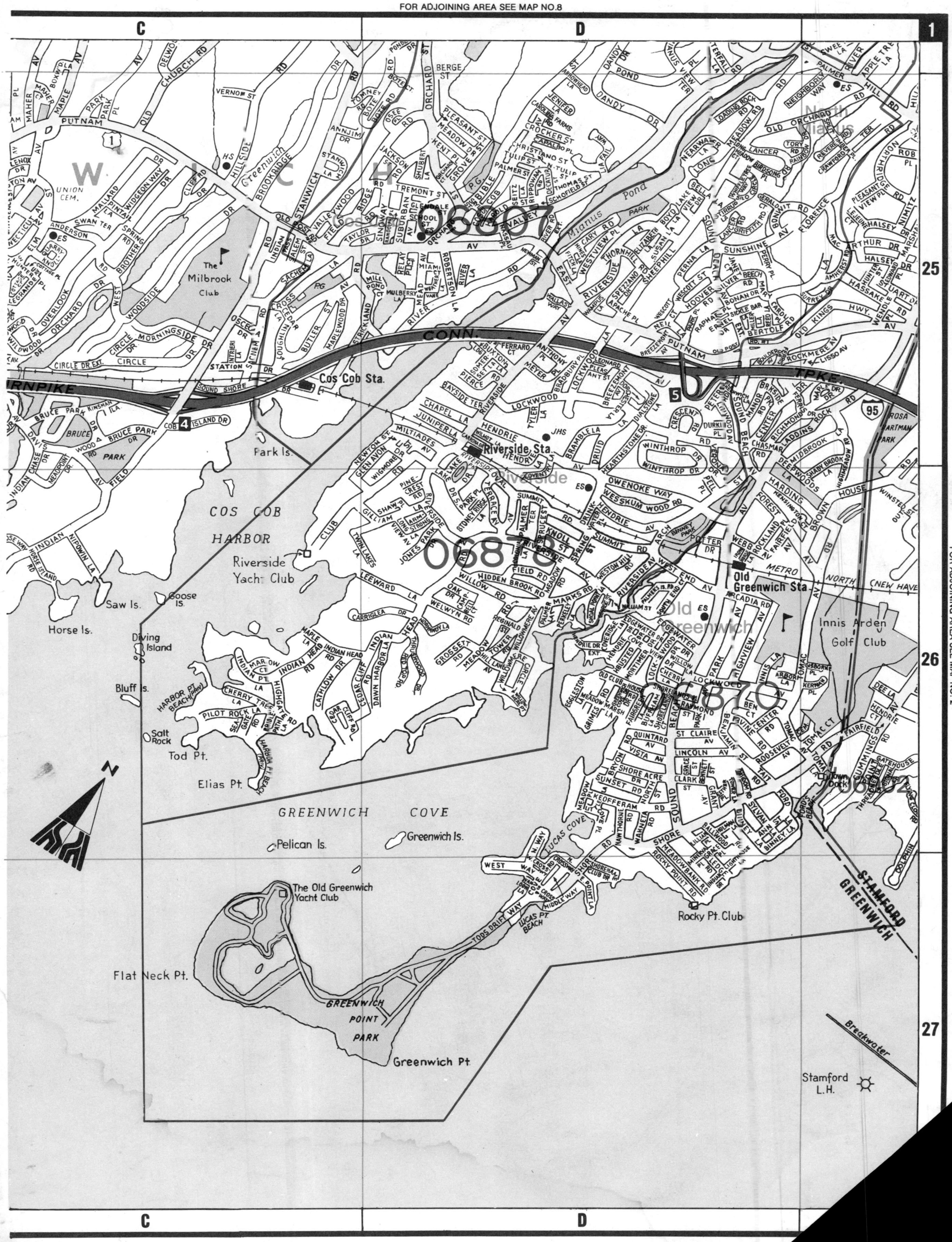

Tod Pt.

Elias Pt.

GREENWICH COVE

Pelican Is.

Greenwich Is.

The Old Greenwich Yacht Club

Flat Neck Pt.

GREENWICH POINT PARK

Greenwich Pt.

Rocky Pt. Club

Lucas Pt. Beach

Stamford L.H.

STAMFORD GREENWICH

Breakwater

North Mianus

Mianus Pond

SOUND

25 · 26 · 27

E   F

25

26

27

06870

06905

06906

06901

06902

E. Gaynor Brennan Golf Course

SCALZI PARK

STATE OF CONN. WRIGHT TECH SCHOOL

RIDGEWAY PLAZA

GLENBROOK SHOPPING AREA

St. JOSEPH MED. CENTER

STAMFORD HOSP.

LATHAM PARK

Downtown Stamford

PUTNAM

Innis Arden Golf Club

WEST BRANCH

EAST BRANCH

WOODLAND CEM.

KOSCIUSZKO PARK

Ponus Yacht Club

Southfield Village

CUMMINGS PARK

Halloween Yacht Club

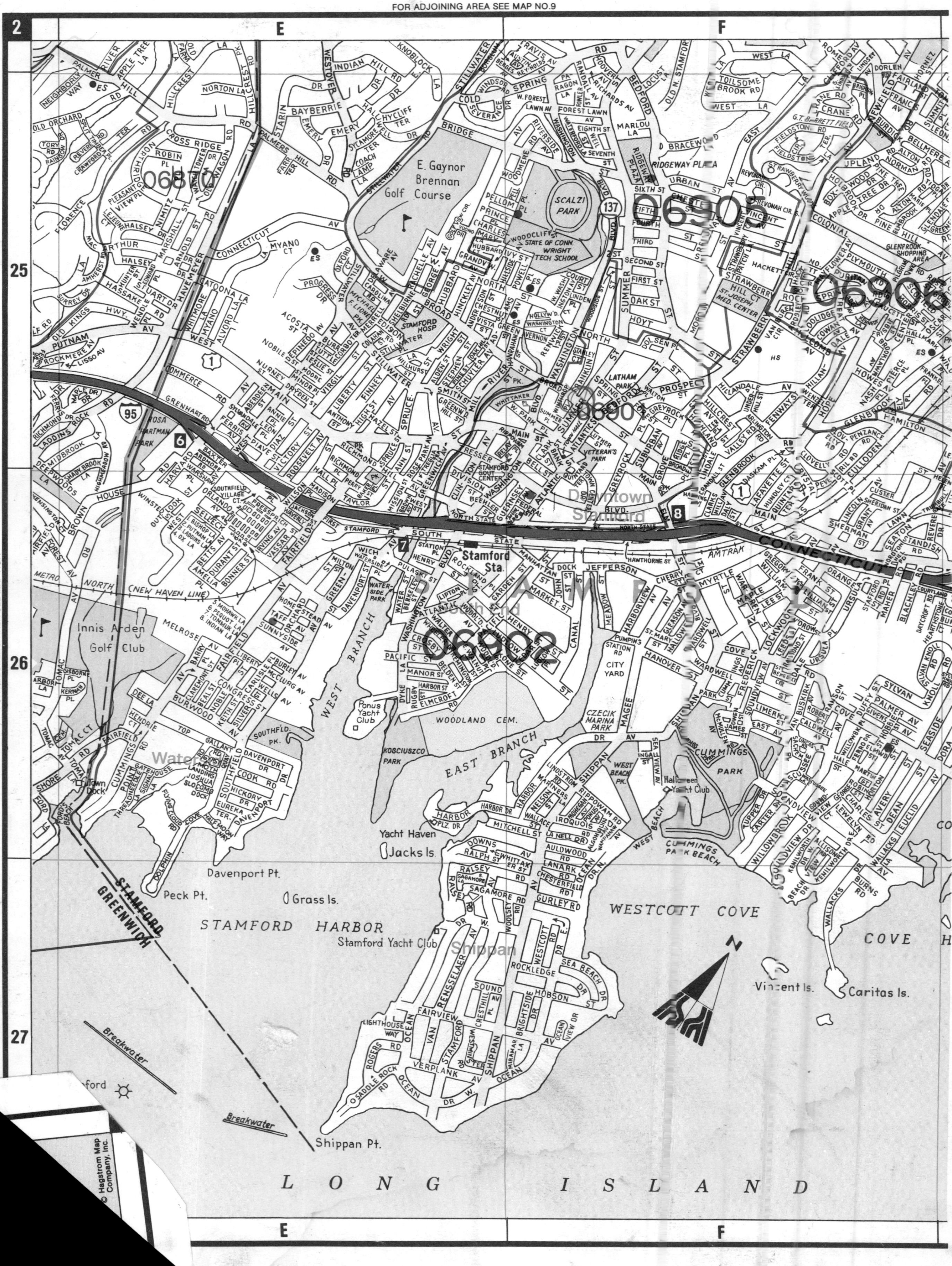

Czecik Marina Park

City Yard

West Beach Pk.

CUMMINGS PARK BEACH

Stamford Sta.

Veteran's Park

STAMFORD GREENWICH

Waterside

Town Dock

Yacht Haven

Jacks Is.

Davenport Pt.

Peck Pt.

Grass Is.

STAMFORD HARBOR

Stamford Yacht Club

Shippan

WESTCOTT COVE

COVE

Vincent Is.

Caritas Is.

Breakwater

Breakwater

Shippan Pt.

L O N G   I S L A N D

CONNECTICUT

AMTRAK

(NEW HAVEN LINE)

G H 2

C

Wee Burn Country Club

Ox Ridge Hunt Club

Country Club of Darien

DARIEN

STAMFORD

Metro-North (New Canaan Branch)

Glenbrook Sta.

WOODLAND PARK

Darien HS

HIGH SCHOOL

Noroton Heights

06820

D. Nick Frate Park

95

TURNPIKE

Noroton Hts. Sta.

McGuane Field

Darien Sta.

Darien J.C.

New Haven Line

METRO NORTH

AMTRAK

Baker Park

Spring Grove Cemetery

Mather Fields

Tokeneke

Noroton

HOLLY POND

Cove Is.

Brush Is.

Noroton

Gorhams Pond

Darien River

Goodwives River

Weed Beach Park

Neck

STAMFORD
DARIEN

HARBOR

SCOTT'S COVE

Great Is.

Pear Tree Point Beach

Pratt Is.

Ned Is.

Hay Is.

Contentment Is.

SHENNAMERE RD

Butlers Is.

Prices Pt.

DARIEN
NORWALK

Long Neck Pt.

Fish Islands

© Hagstrom Map Company, Inc.

G H 2

3 J K

CHERRY LAWN PARK
MEADOWBROOK
APPLE TREE LA

06820
DARIEN
SELLECKS WOODS

NORWALK

06854

06853

Rowayton Sta.
Rowayton

Streets Pond

MS PARK

McMAHON H.S. ROBINS PARK

S. Norwalk Sta.

THE MARITIME CENTER NORWALK

VETERANS MEMORIAL PARK

E. NORWALK HARBOR

Ischoda Yacht Club
South Norwalk Boat Club
Fitch

NORWALK HARBOR

Harborview

Gregory Pt.
Peach Is.
Shore and Country Club

Springwood Park

Village Cr.

Norwalk Yacht Club

Wilson Cove

Wilson Pt.

Bell Is. Cr.
St. James Pl.
Cox Pl.
Fillow Ct.
Cliff Pl.
Plant Ct.
Bell Island
HARBOR PL.
ROCKY POINT RD
PARK AV
PARK CT

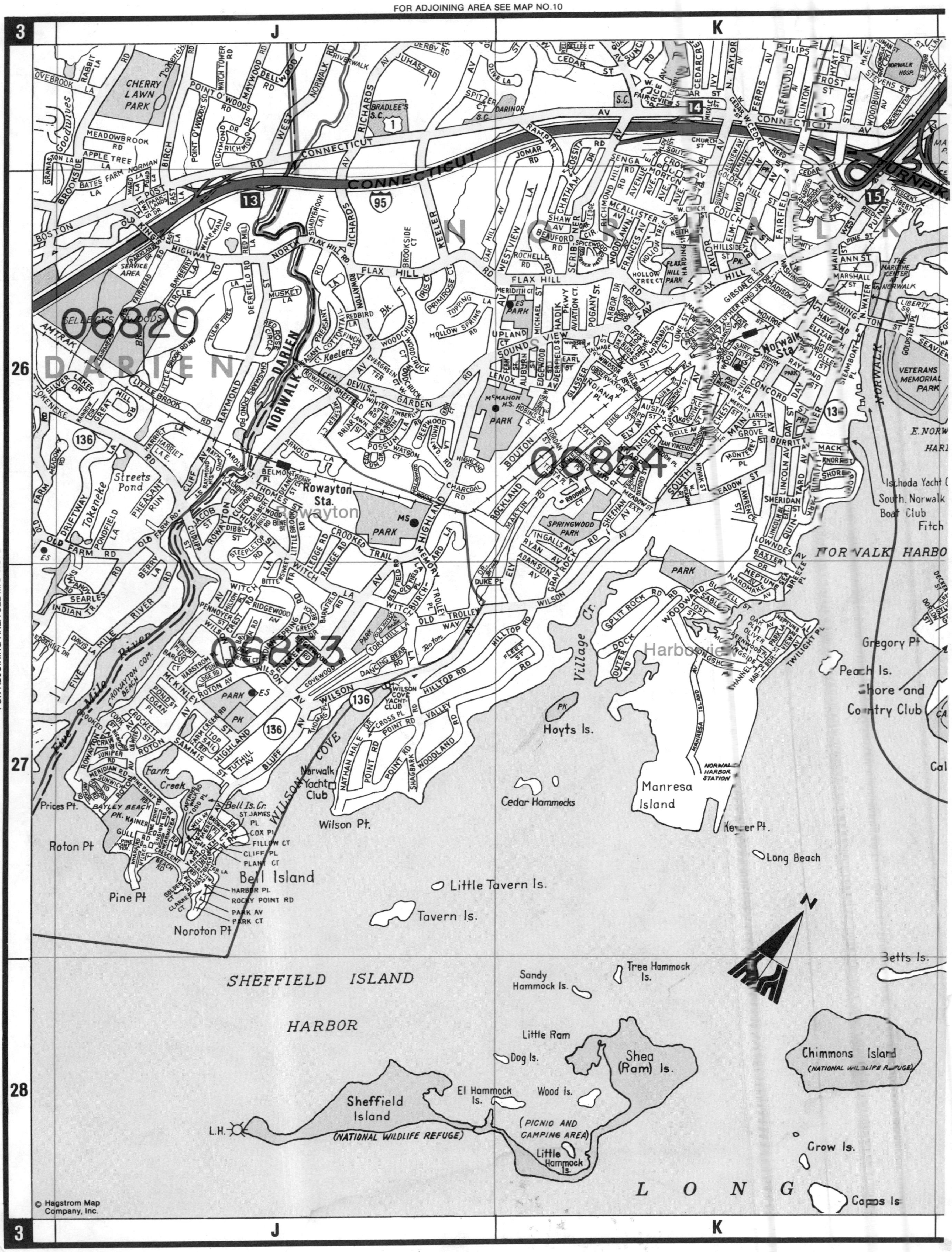

Roton Pt
Pine Pt
Prices Pt.
Bayley Beach Pk. Kainer

Noroton Pt.

Little Tavern Is.
Tavern Is.

Hoyts Is.
Cedar Hammocks

Manresa Island

NORWALK HARBOR STATION

Keeler Pt.
Long Beach

Betts Is.

SHEFFIELD ISLAND

HARBOR

Sandy Hammock Is.
Tree Hammock Is.

Little Ram
Dog Is.
Shea (Ram) Is.

Chimmons Island
(NATIONAL WILDLIFE REFUGE)

Sheffield Island
(NATIONAL WILDLIFE REFUGE)
L.H.
El Hammock Is.
Wood Is.
(PICNIC AND CAMPING AREA)
Little Hammock Is.

Crow Is.

LONG

Copas Is

CONNECTICUT

95
13
15
TURNPIKE
1

© Hagstrom Map Company, Inc.

3 J K

12

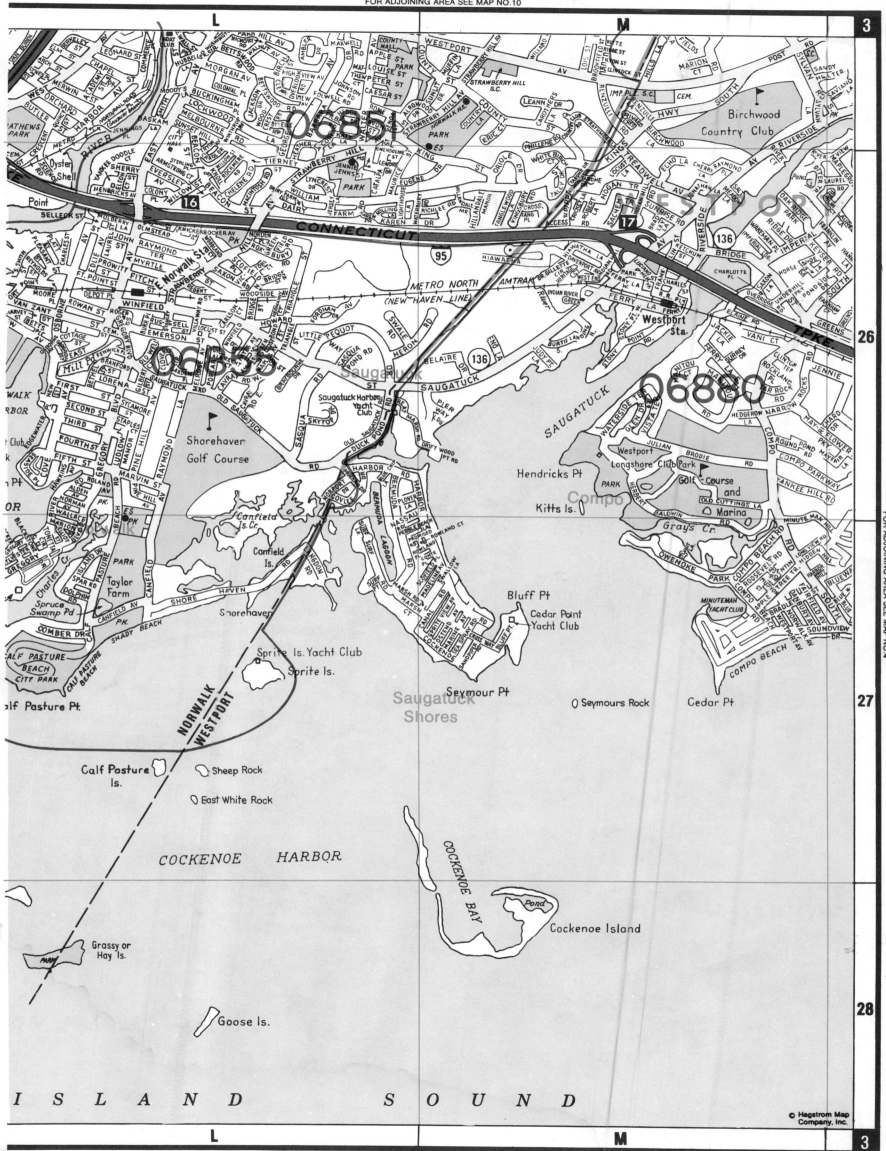

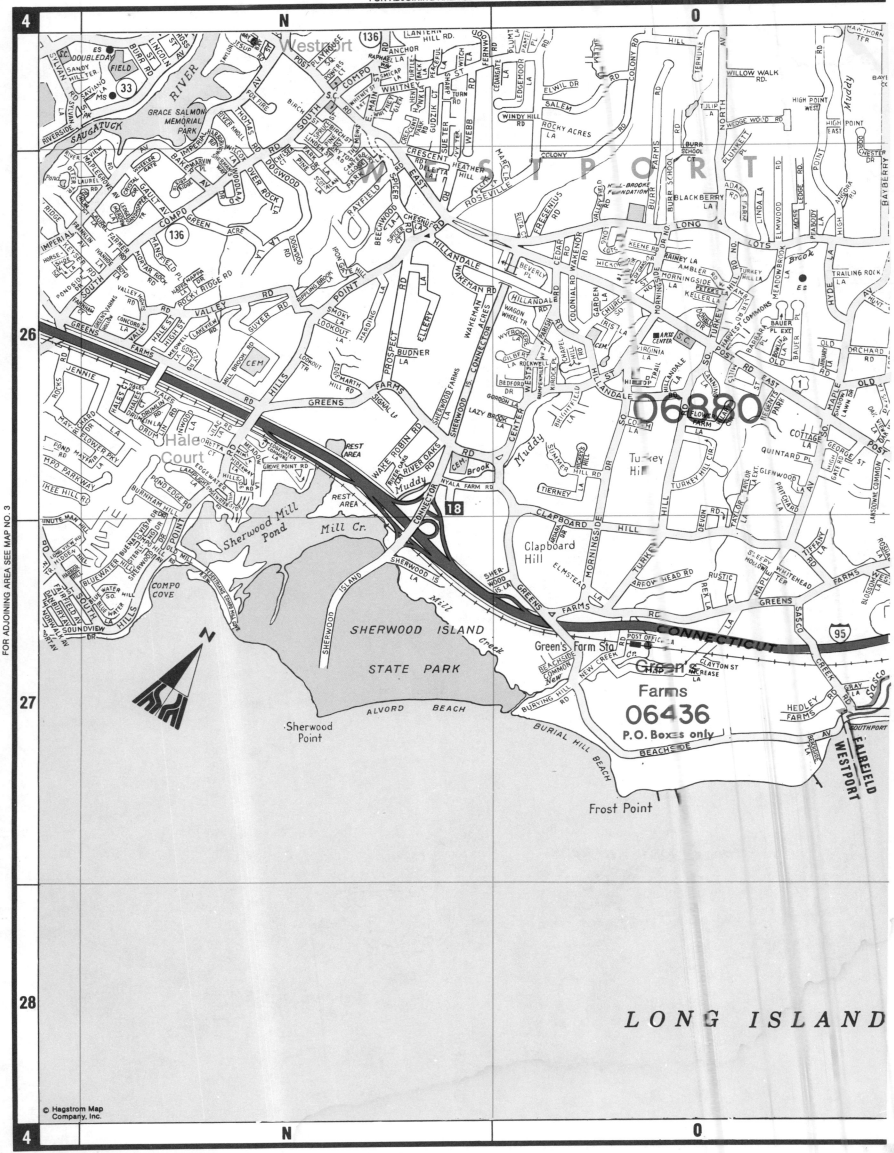

SHERWOOD ISLAND STATE PARK

06880

Green's Farms 06436
P.O. Boxes only

LONG ISLAND

Frost Point

© Hagstrom Map Company, Inc.

FAIRFIELD

06490

06430

Greenfield Hill

OAK LAWN CEM.

FAIRFIELD UNIVERSITY

Round Hill

Osborne Hill

Fairfield County Hunt Club

Banks Pond

Mill Hill

Perrys Millpond

Mill Plain

Southport

Southport Sta.

METRO NORTH (NEW HAVEN LINE)

AMTRAK

Fairfield Sta

Country Club Beach

Country Club of Fairfield

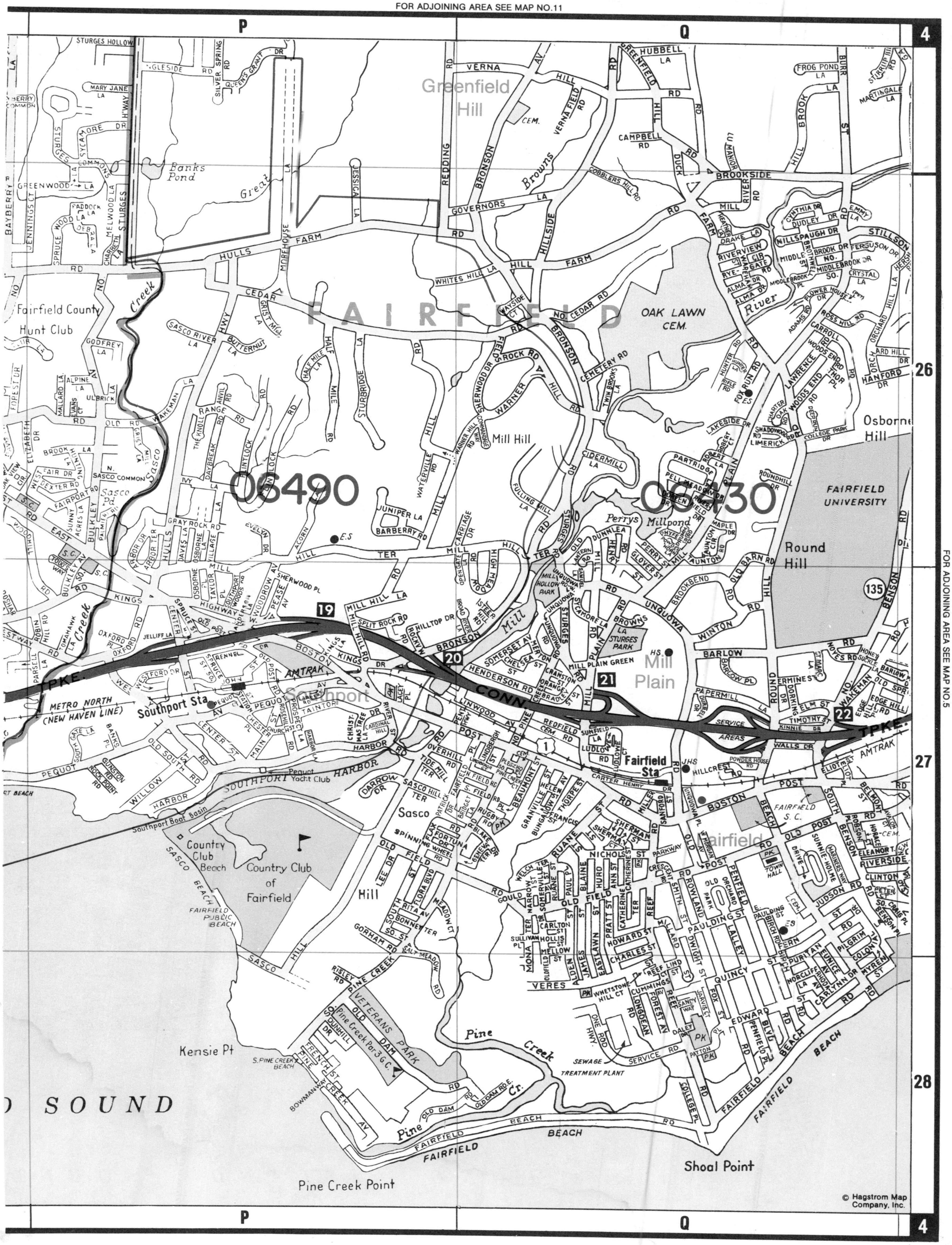

Fairfield Public Beach

Southport Yacht Club

Southport Boat Basin

Sasco

Kensie Pt

Pine Creek Par 3 G.C.

S. Pine Creek Beach

Veterans Park

Sewage Treatment Plant

Pine Creek

Fairfield Beach

SOUND

Pine Creek Point

Shoal Point

CONN. TPKE.

19 20 21 22

135

© Hagstrom Map Company, Inc.

FOR ADJOINING AREA SEE MAP NO.12

FOR ADJOINING AREA SEE MAP NO.4

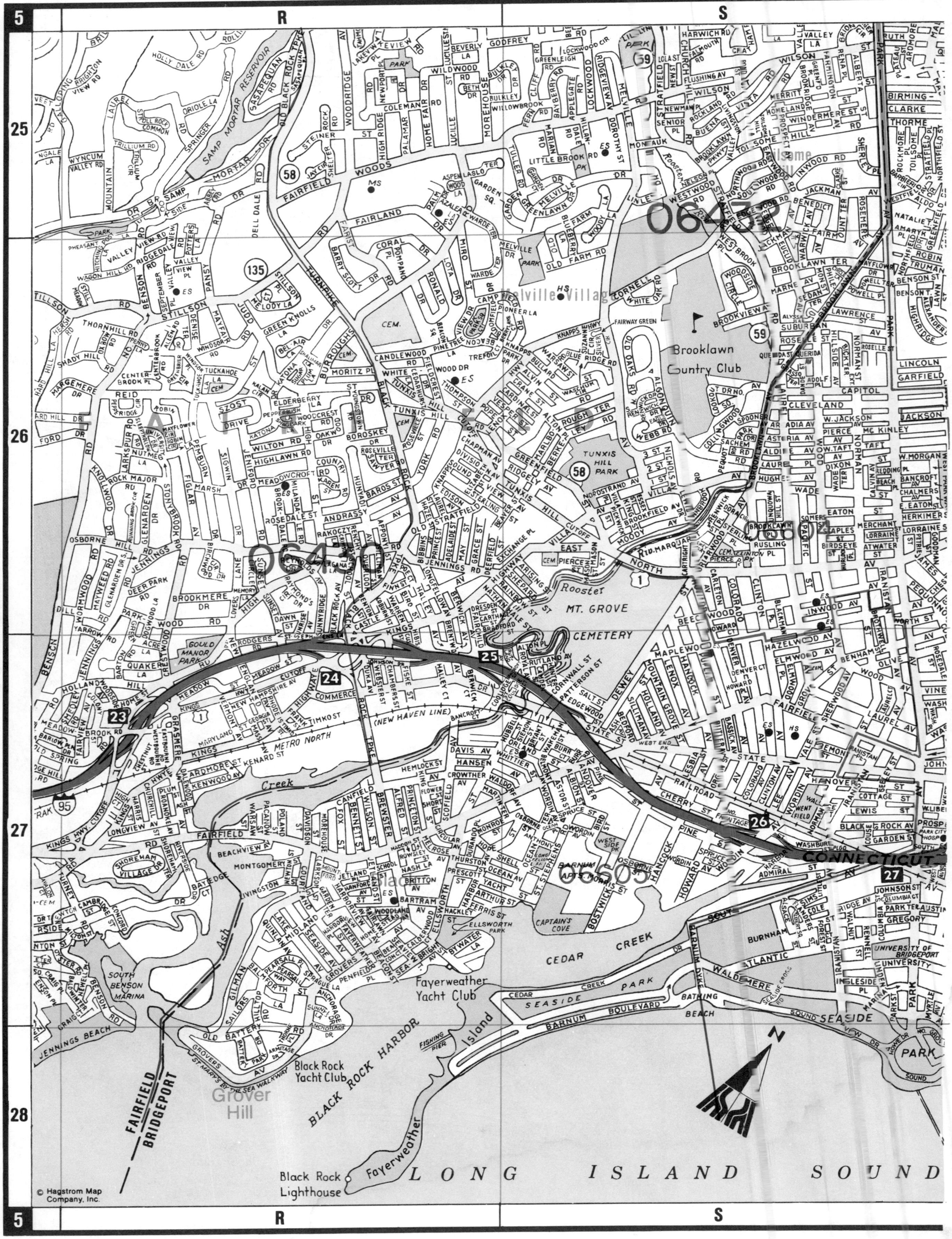

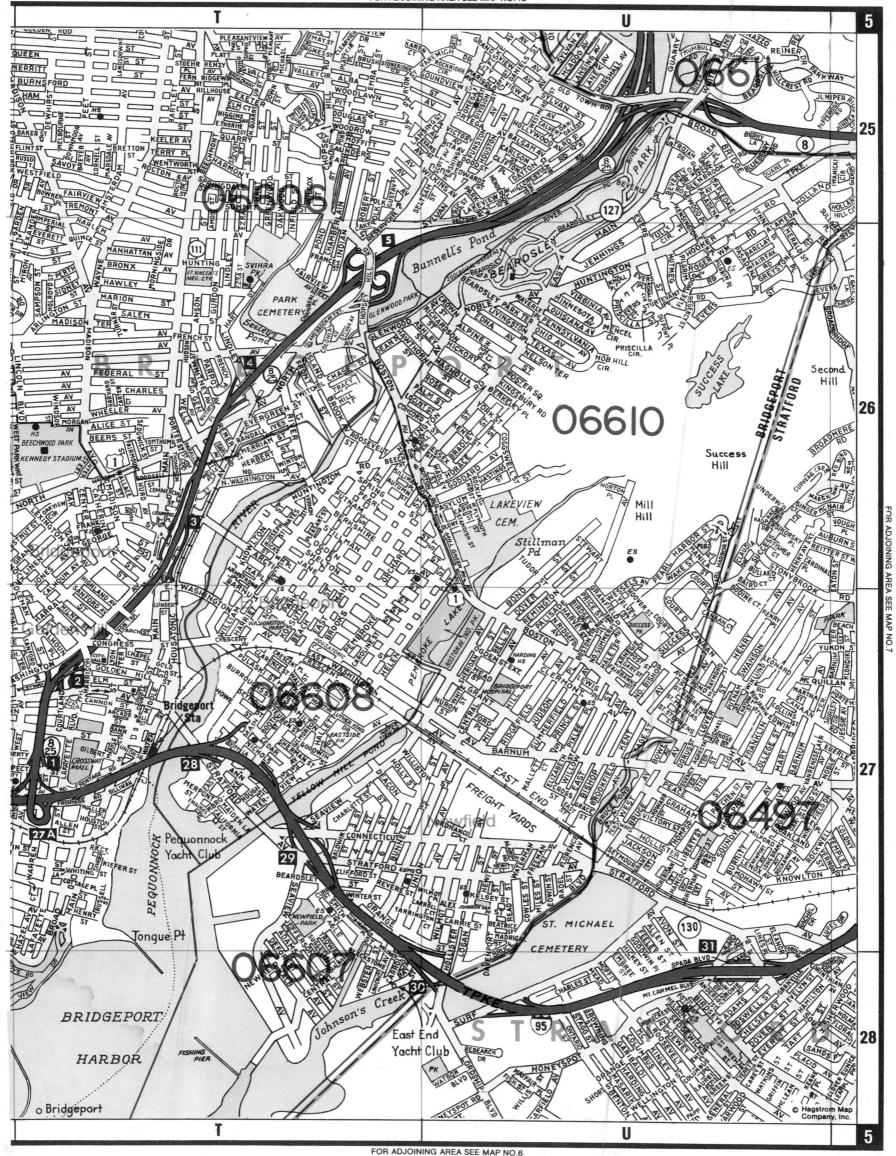

6

T

U

FOR ADJOINING AREA SEE MAP NO.5

06608

06610

CONNECTICUT

27

06604

Bridgeport Sta.

Pequonnock Yacht Club

28

29

Tongue Pt

06607

Newfield

CONNECTICUT

STRATFORD

St. MICHAEL CEMETERY

130

31

95

CONNECTICUT

BRIDGEPORT

HARBOR

Fishing Pier

o Bridgeport Light

Ferry to Port Jefferson L.I.

SEASIDE PARK

PLEASURE BEACH (PARK)

LONG BEACH

GUT

Johnson's Creek

East End Yacht Club

Bridgeport / Stratford

S T R A T F O

Great Meadows

113

IGOR I. SIKORSKY

(BRIDGEPORT MU

Lordship

Point No Point

L O N G   I S L A N D

27

28

29

© Hagstrom Map Company, Inc.

6

T

U

V   W

27

06497

Stratford Center

Stratford Sta.

Stratford HS

TPKE.

(NEW HAVEN LINE)   AMTRAK

95

FAIRFIELD / NEW HAVEN CO CO

Carting Island

Peacock Island

River

110

33

32

130

113

113

Pootatuck Yacht Club Goose I.

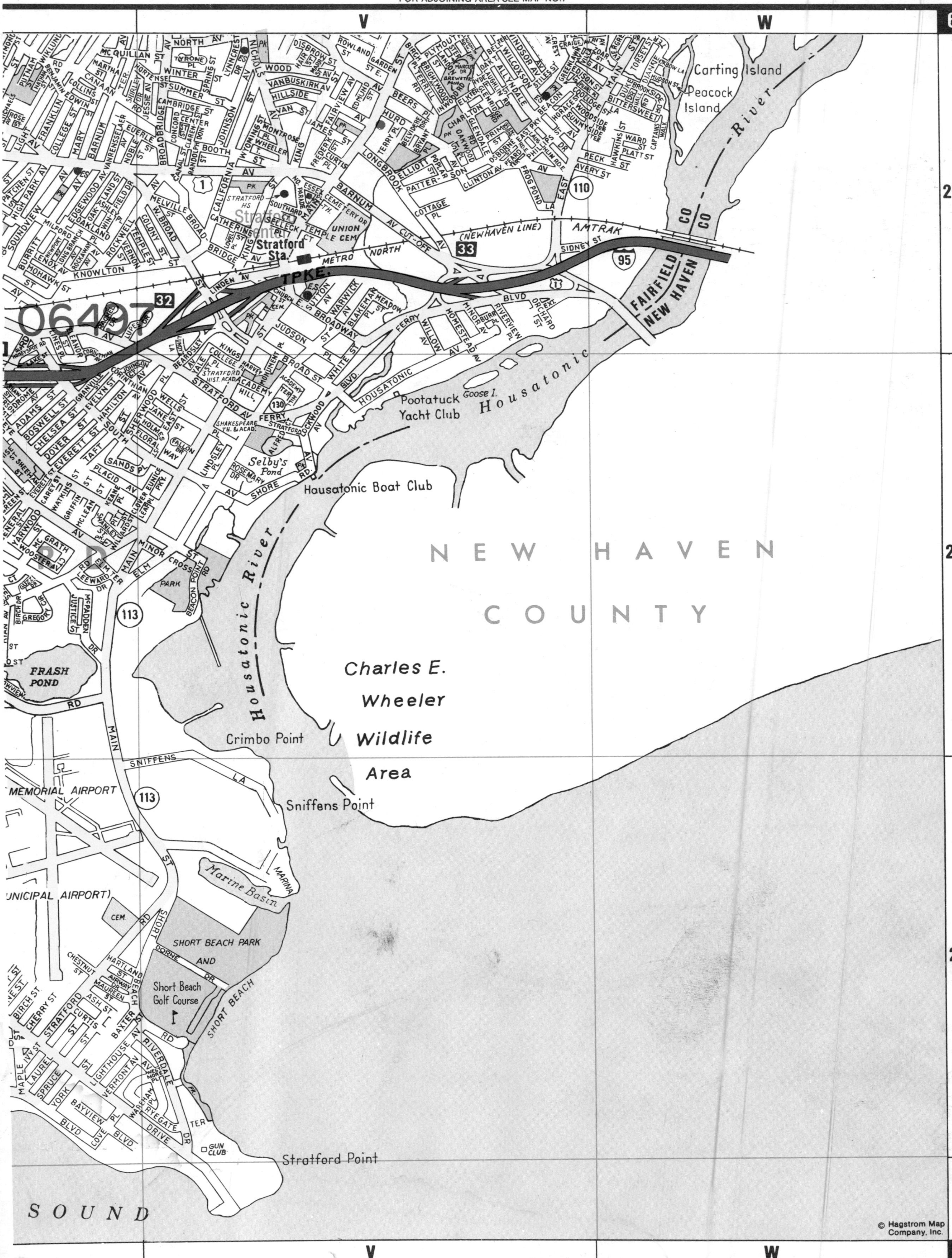

Housatonic

Housatonic Boat Club

Selby's Pond

Housatonic River

NEW HAVEN

COUNTY

Charles E.

Wheeler

Wildlife

Area

Crimbo Point

Sniffens Point

FRASH POND

MEMORIAL AIRPORT

(MUNICIPAL AIRPORT)

Marine Basin

CEM

Short Beach Park

Short Beach

Short Beach Golf Course

GUN CLUB

Stratford Point

S O U N D

28

29

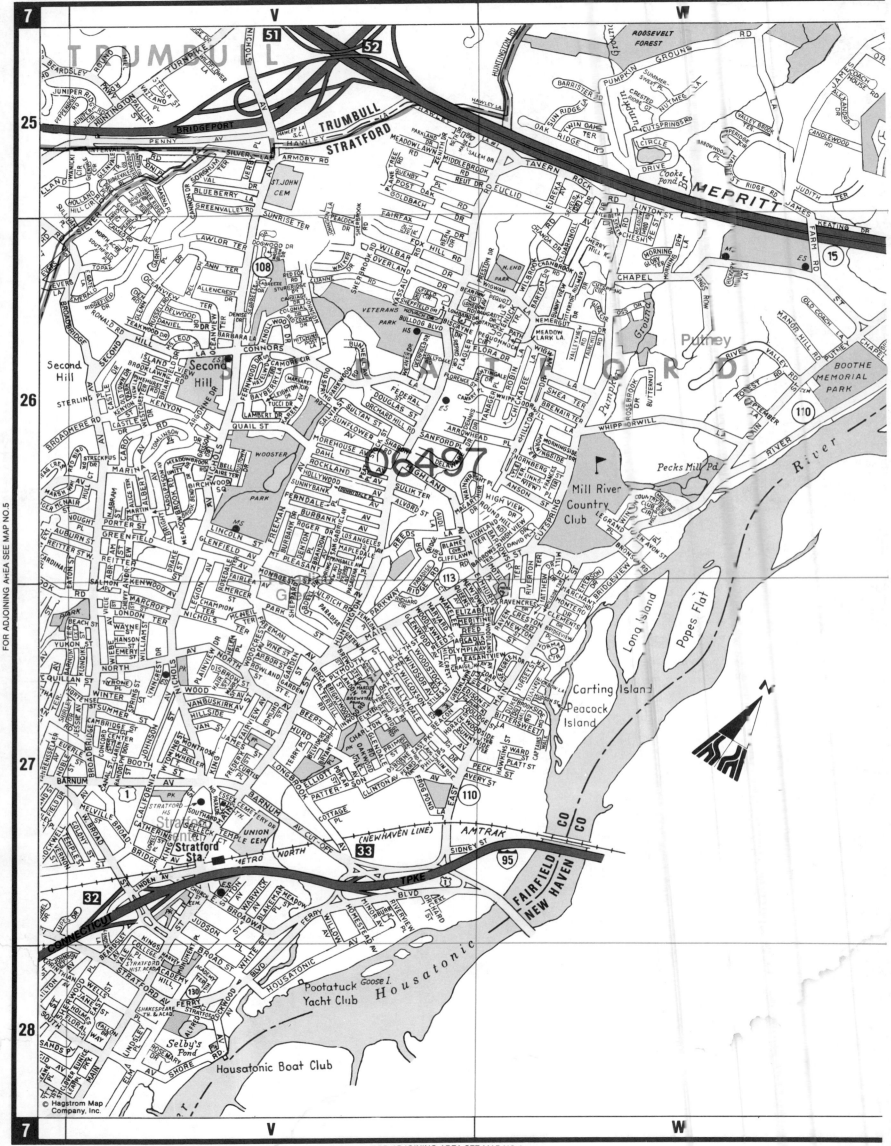

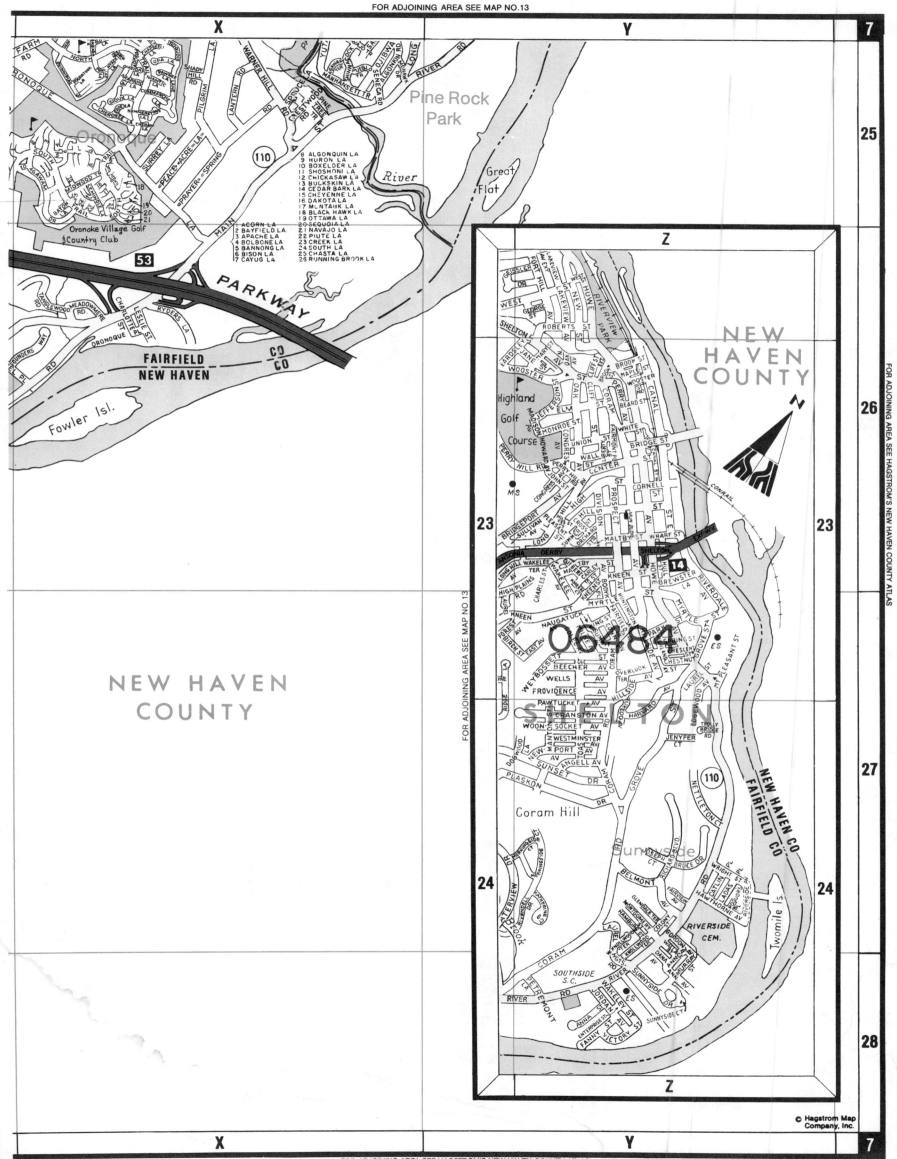

8

| A | B |

22

LINCOLN AV

FAIRVIEW COUNTRY CLUB

NATURE CONSERVANCY

Wilcox Pond

INDIAN KNOLL PL

HYCLIFF RD

RIVERVILLE RD

PARKWAY

QUAIL RD

BRYNWOOD LA

15

PEEPERS HOLLOW

Riversville

SHERWOOD

120 A

NUTMEG LA

ALEC TEMPLETON LA

MERRITT

THUNDER MOUNTAIN RD

HEBREW CEMETERY

ROUND HILL CLUB RD

CLAPBO

SABINE FARM RD

23

WILLOW RUN RD

HETTIEFRED RD

HEATHER DR

BOWMAN DR

STONEHEDGE DR N.

ANDERSON HILL RD

MANSION PL

RINCARD TER

NY CT

COUNTY

BOWMAN DR

CHOCTAW LA

STONEHEDGE

BLIND BROOK LA

Toll Gate Pond

SADDLE RIDGE RD

MEMORY LA

ORCHARD HILL

MAYFAIR LA

Round Hill Club

G R E E E

LISMORE LA

SHEFFIELD RD

FORT HILLS RD

WILD FLOWER TR

PUT RD

EDSON LA

BLANCHARD RD

BALLIWICK RD

PECKSLAND RD

MAYFAIR LA

FRENCH RD

COUNTY

KING E. LAWN LA

SERVICE AREA

27

15

WOODS MGR

ELSKIP LA

DUNCAN LA

BATTIWICK

HARKIM

MEADOW RD

ZACCHEUS MEAD LA

VINEYARD LA

ROUND HILL RD

GLEN RIDGE RD

SHADY

DOUGLAS DR

TAMARACK PL

E. BYWAY

LESLIE AV

MAIDEN LA

ANGELUS DR

RIVERVILLE RD

Glenville

ES

06831

(Deliveries from Greenwich P.O.)

ASHTON DR

FOX RUN

RAPIDS LA

WINDABOUT DR

WALSH CT

GLENVILLE

HUNT

RIVER

ETTL LA

HIGHVIEW

BANKS

GLENVILLE ST

WESTERN GREENWICH CIVIC CENTER (PARK)

KANDAHAR RD

GLENVILLE RD

SIDNEY LANIER LA

AMIDWOOD DR

Horseneck

DEER LA

FAIRVIEW TER

PEMBERWICK RD

MURIEL PL

HAWTHORNE ST

LINDEN PL

HOMESTEAD RD

GREY ROCK DR

INDIAN SPRING RD

MIDWOOD DR

WOODSIDE DR

DEERPARK RD

NEDLEY LA

BISHOP DR NO.

BISHOP DR

GREEN LANTERN LA

BUENA VISTA

BENDERS DR

COBBLE STONE RD

TREE TOP TER

HOBART DR

HUNTZINGER DR

CALHOUN

WITHERALL DR

LAUDER WAY

DEERPARK RD

WESTCHESTER FAIRFIELD

GREENWICH HILLS DR

CARTRIDGE DR

CONCORD ST

DEEP GORGE RD

THISTLE LA

FLINTLOCK RD

ANGUS RD

RIDGEWAY

PRESCOTT ST

EVERGREEN RD

FIELD CLUB OF GREENWICH

LAKE CHAPMAN

COMLY AV

120 A

BURDSALL DR

NICHOLAS AV

POWELL ST

MITCHELL

FLETCHER

MORGAN ST

UPLAND

STRAWBRIDGE LA

EAST LYON FARM DR

ANGUS LA

GLENVILLE DR

ROCK RIDGE

Rock Ridge

MIDWOOD RD

CARLETON

SKYLARK RD

EVERGREEN RD

10573

UPLAND RD

PRISCILLA LA

FAIRVIEW

RENSHAW LA

FRANCIS DR

FIELD PL

HICKORY

REX ST

HALOCK DR

UPLAND

EAST LYON FARM DR

CALHOUN

EDGE-WOOD PL

UPLAND RD

VALLEY DR

VALLERA

BROOKSIDE DR

GLENVILLE

PROSPECT DR

LAKE AV

PERRY

DIVISION

WILLIAM ST

NORTHFIELD

Pemberwick

PEMBERWICK PARK

MOSHIER ST

NATURE CONSERVANCY

FLOWER LA

UPLAND

VALLEY DR

HEMLOCK DR

MEADOW

HILL

CASSIDY

PRIVATE RD

QUINTARD

AUSTIN

HOBART

MADISON AV

RENSHAW

FRANK AV

HALSTEAD AV

CAROLINE

LUCY ST

MONICA

ALMIRA DR

HAWTHORNE ST

ARTHUR ST

WEAVER

ALDEN RD

OAK ST

VALLEY DR

VALLEY RD

BROOKSIDE PK

LAFAYETTE CT

VOLUNTEER LA

EAST CHURCH ST

LEXING

PUTNAM

LINCOLN

LEWIS

WASHINGTON ST

Port Chester

PARKWAY DR

LINDEN AV

POPLAR ST

KING ST

BROOK ST

MADISON AV

RIVERDALE AV

PUTNAM DR

HOMESTEAD

PEMBERWICK RD

BYRAM TER

WINDY KNOLLS DR

CHAPEL ST

REYNOLDS ST

GABRIEL

OLD POST RD NO.3

WEAVER

PUTNAM

GREENWICH CROSSWAY

MASON ST

© Hagstrom Map Company, Inc.

8

| A | B |

C   D   8

22

06831

MERRITT

PARKWAY

Burning Tree C.C.

PUTNAM LAKE

23

GREENWICH

06830

Putnam Cemetery

St. Mary's Cem.

Greenwich Country Club

Bolling Pond

Lake

06807

North Mianus

24

Montgomery Pinetum

Cos Cob Pond

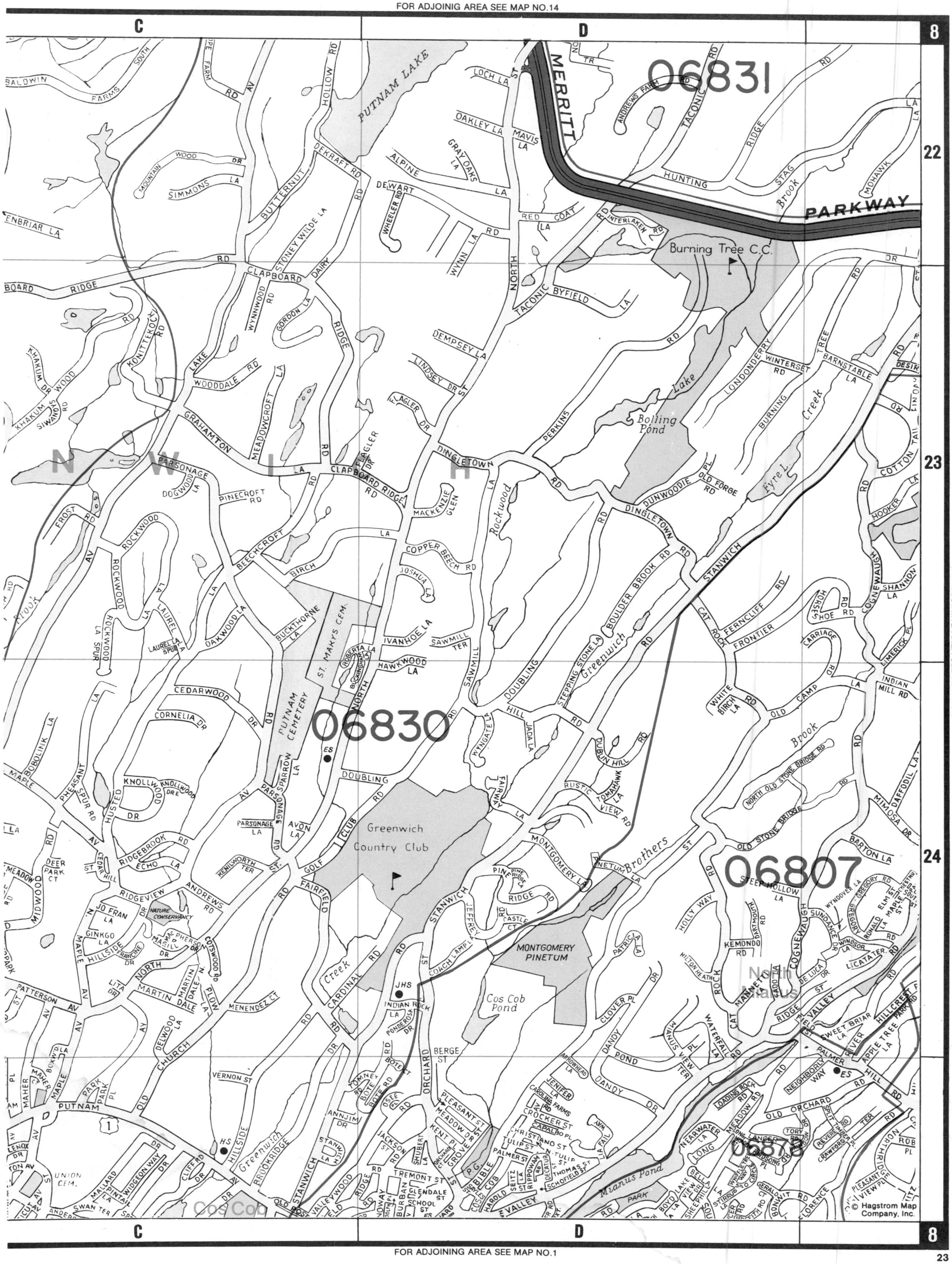

FOR ADJOINING AREA SEE MAP NO.9

06878

Mianus Pond

Cos Cob

© Hagstrom Map Company, Inc.

C   D   8

9 E F

22

06831

MERRITT

15

CARRINGTON DR.

MOHAWK

Newman Mills Park

Altschul Pond

East River

PARKWAY

06830

Londonderry

Guinea

Greenwich Creek

Barnstable

Desiree Dr.

Rock Maple Rd.

Juniper Hill Rd.

Cedge Brook Rd.

Mianus Glen

Thunder Hill Dr.

Cow Path Dr.

33

Barclay

Willoughby Rd.

Smoke Hill Dr.

Flint Rd.

Fawnfield Rd.

Constance La.

Hardesty

Midrocks Dr.

104

Dogwood

Northwood La.

Lynam Rd.

Jeffrey La.

Briarwood

Four Brook Cir.

23

Fyre Lk.

Stanwich

Cotton Tail La.

Hooker Rd.

Mianus River State Park

Mill Brook Rd. W.

High Line Ter. So.

Walter La.

Roxbury

CEM.

Munko Dr.

Doolittle

MacArthur La.

Parkenmer Rd.

Dee Hill Rd.

15

Holts Ice Pd.

MERRITT

34

Wire Mill Rd.

Vineyard La.

Maltbie Av.

Rippowam River

Loughran Av.

Timber

Cedar Heights

Crystal Lake Rd.

Barnes Rd.

137

06902

Fort Stamford Pk.

Nathan Hale Dr.

Cogswell Dr.

Westover

Merriebrook La.

General Waterbury La.

Long Close

Akbar

MacGregor

West Hill La.

West Hill Rd.

104

West Hill H.S.

Drum Hill La.

Westwood Pl.

Hartswood

Ayres Dr.

Nichols

Swamscott Rd.

Belaire Dr.

06807

Benenson Dr.

Serenity La.

Azalea

West Glen Dr.

Bank

West La.

Carriage Dr.

Carriage Dr. S.

Stony Brook Dr.

Greenleaf Dr.

Skyview

Stanton La.

Westwood

Greentree Dr.

Skyview Dr.

Three Lakes Dr.

Cooper Pond

Long Ridge Rd.

Woodway Rd.

Stone Wall La.

24

Daffodil La.

Mimosa

Gregory Rd.

Elm St.

Walnut St.

Mianus Rd.

Westover Av.

Stark

Wesgate Dr.

Blueberry Dr.

Stillview Rd.

River Hill Dr.

Rippowam

104

Stillwater Pond

137

Silver Hill La.

Kensington

High Clear Dr.

Unity Rd.

Valley

Hillcrest Park

Apple Tree La.

Summit Ridge

Victoria Rd.

Westview

West Knobloch

Hemlock

Wyndover La.

Paul St.

E. Gaynor Brennan Golf Course

Old Barn Rd.

Barn Rd. N.

Long Ridge Rd.

Oaklawn Av.

Colonial Cemeteries Inc.

Newfield Av.

Port Mianus

Old Orchard

Cross Ridge

06877

Palmers Hill Rd.

Bayberrie Dr.

Emery

Coach Lamp La.

Stillwater Av.

Cold Spring Rd.

W. Forest

Forest Lawn

Ridgeway Plaza

Scalzi Park

137

Bedford

West La.

Toilsome Brook Rd.

Crane Rd.

Newfield

Upland Rd.

© Hagstrom Map Company, Inc.

GREENWICH / STAMFORD

24

9 E F

FOR ADJOINING AREA SEE MAP NO.8

G H 9

22

23

24

9

06903

06840

06905

06907

06820

06906

NEW CANAAN

STAMFORD

DARIEN

Springdale

Belltown

Newfield

Talmadge Hill

NORTH STAMFORD RES.

BIRD SANCTUARY

STAMFORD MUSEUM

Bendels Pd.

Poorhouse

Sterling Farms Golf Club

Woodway Country Club

Woodway Park

Wee Burn Country Club

Ox Ridge Hunt Club

Country Club of Darien

Springdale Sta.

Talmadge Hill Sta.

St. John's Cem.

Grand Central S.

PARKWAY

METRO NORTH

(NEW CANAAN BRANCH)

Jelliff Mill

Waveny Park

River

137 35 15 106 36 124

© Hagstrom Map Company, Inc.

G H 9

25

10   J   K

23

24

25

06840

06850

06820

06854

NEW CANAAN

NORWALK

DARIEN

W. Norwalk

MERRITT

PARKWAY

NEW CANAAN NORWALK

Marvin Ridge

Clapboard Hill

Guthrie Pd.

Wardwell Pd.

Guild Brook

BIRD SANCT.

WAVENY PARK

Country Club of Darien

Mathers Pond

Cherry Lawn Park

Kiwanis Park

Oak Hills Park

Golf Course

St. Johns Cemetery

Hebrew Cem.

Holy Ghost Fathers Pond

Hites Pd.

Norwalk Technical Community College

Norwalk Hosp.

New Canaan H.S.

Five Mile River

Goodwives River

Metro North

106   124   37   15   31   123   13   95   14   1   15

CONNECTICUT AV

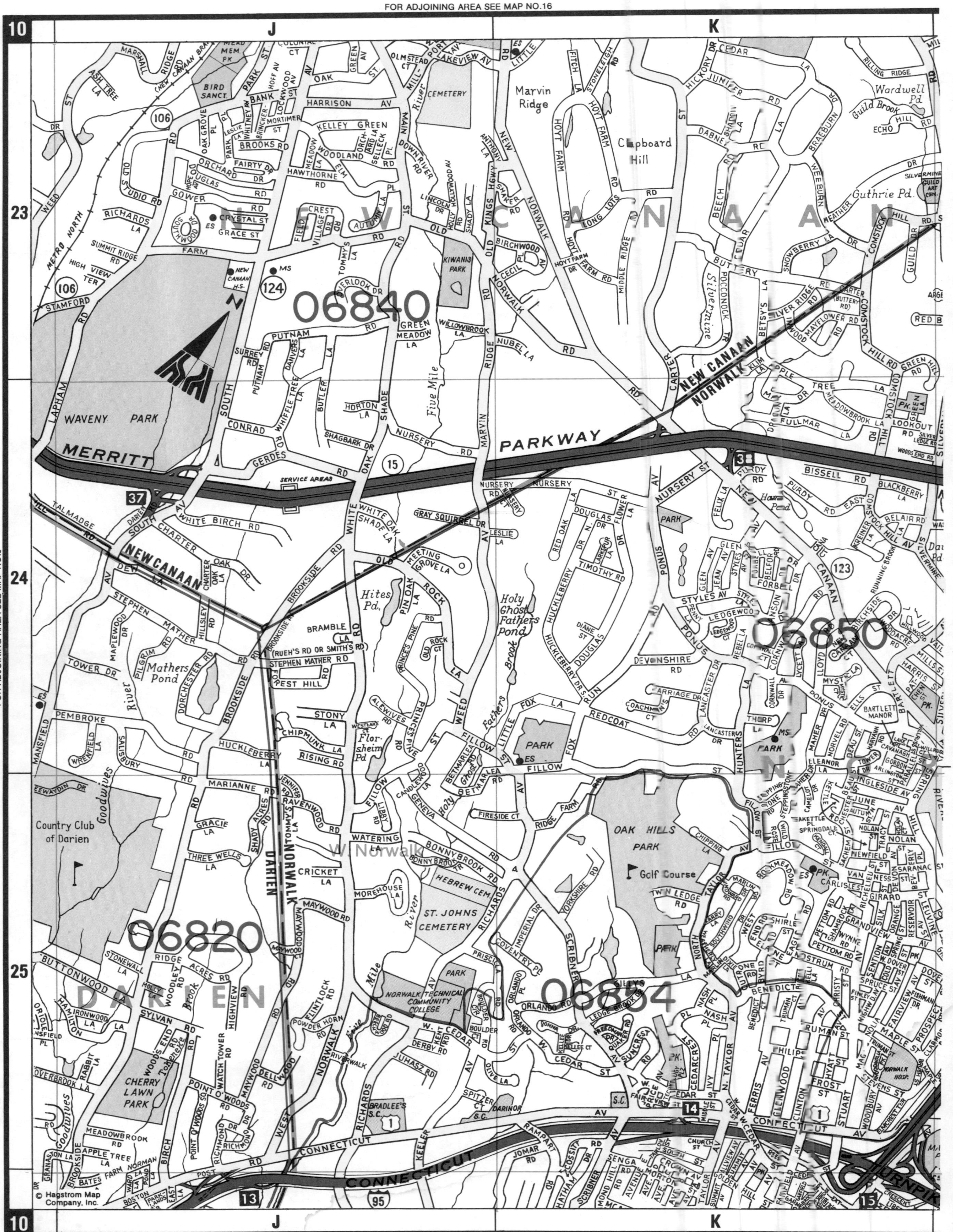

FOR ADJOINING AREA SEE MAP NO.9

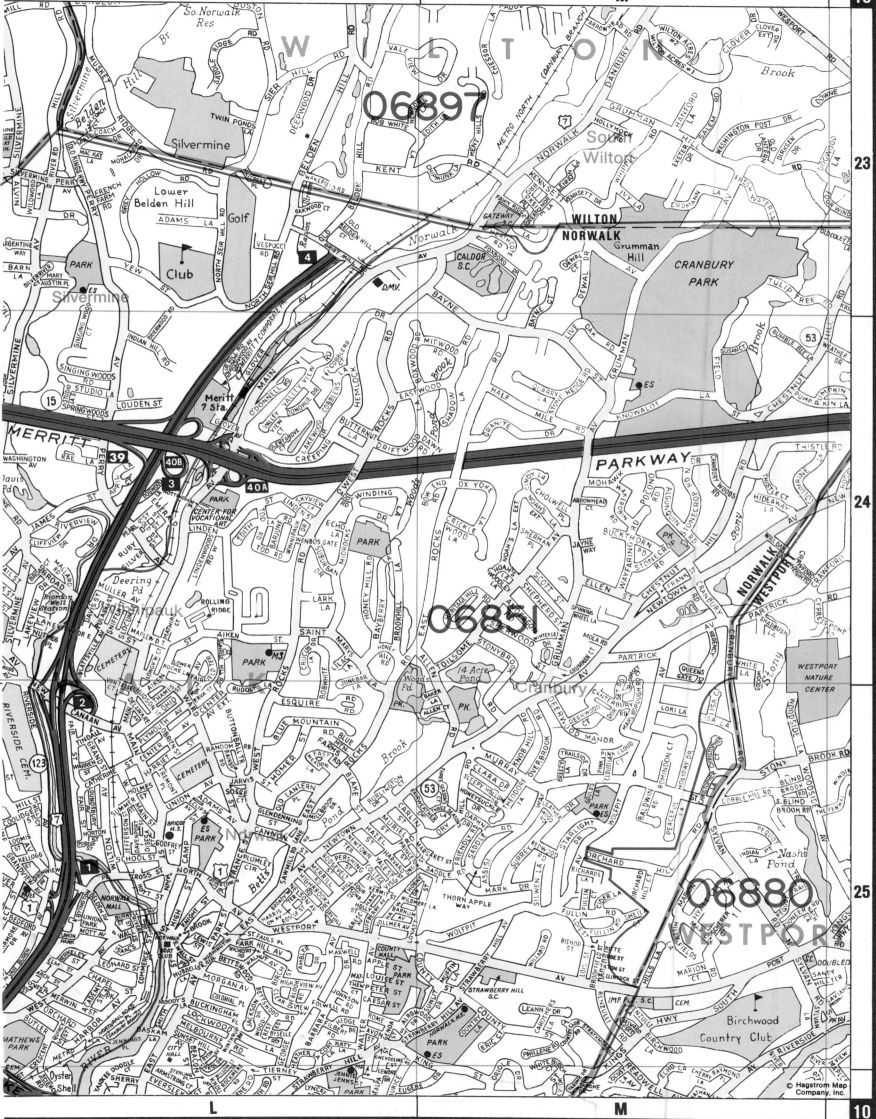

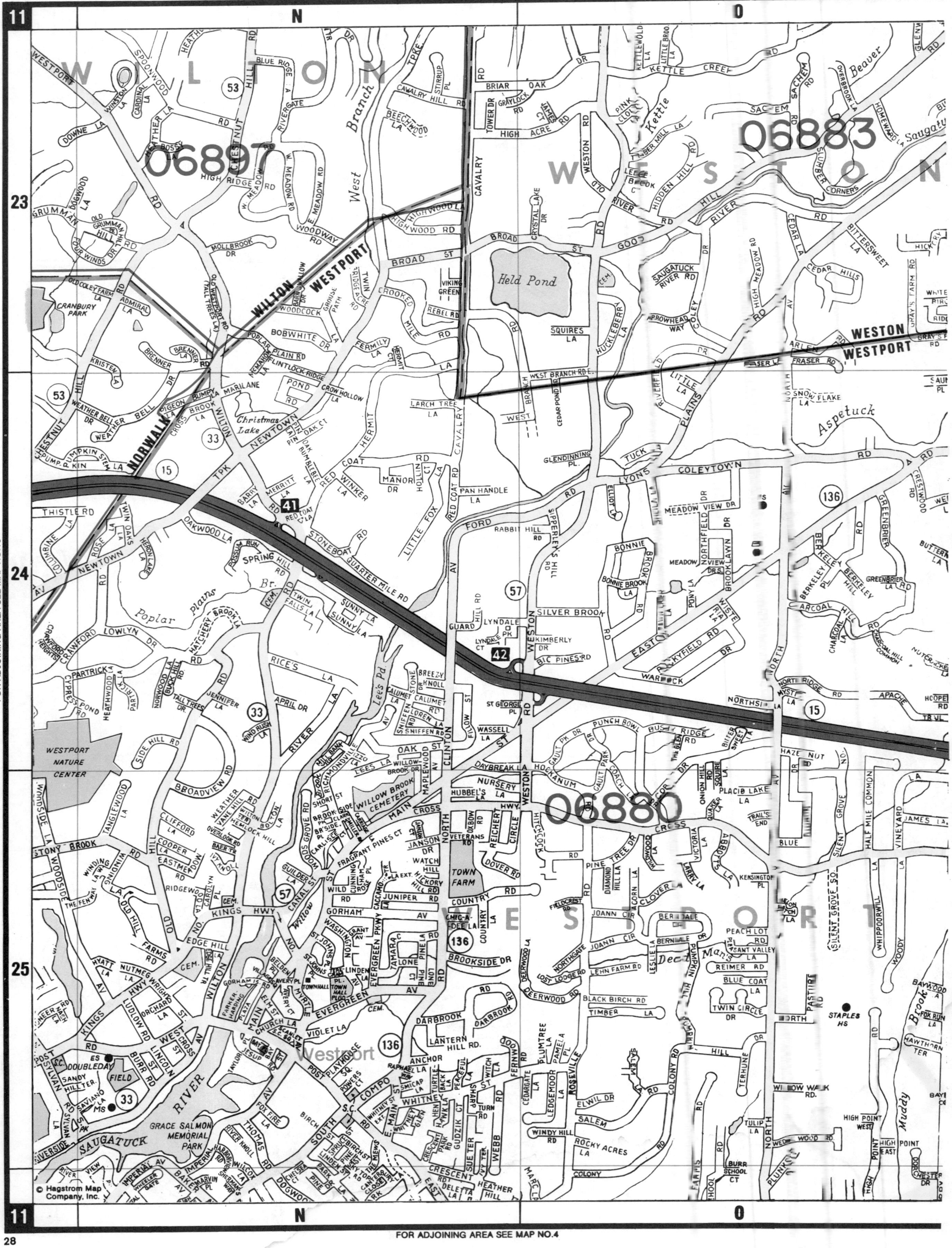

FOR ADJOINING AREA SEE MAP NO.10

W I L T O N

WESTPORT

WILTON

06897

06883

W E S T O N

WESTON
WESTPORT

WESTON
WESTPORT

06880

W E S T P O R T

NORWALK

Westport

Held Pond

Cranbury Park

Westport Nature Center

Christmas Lake

Grace Salmon Memorial Park

Willow Brook Cemetery

Town Farm

Staples HS

Aspetuck

Saugatuck River

Poplar Plains

Rices La

Kings Hwy

Post Rd

Main St

Compo

Viking Green

© Hagstrom Map Company, Inc.

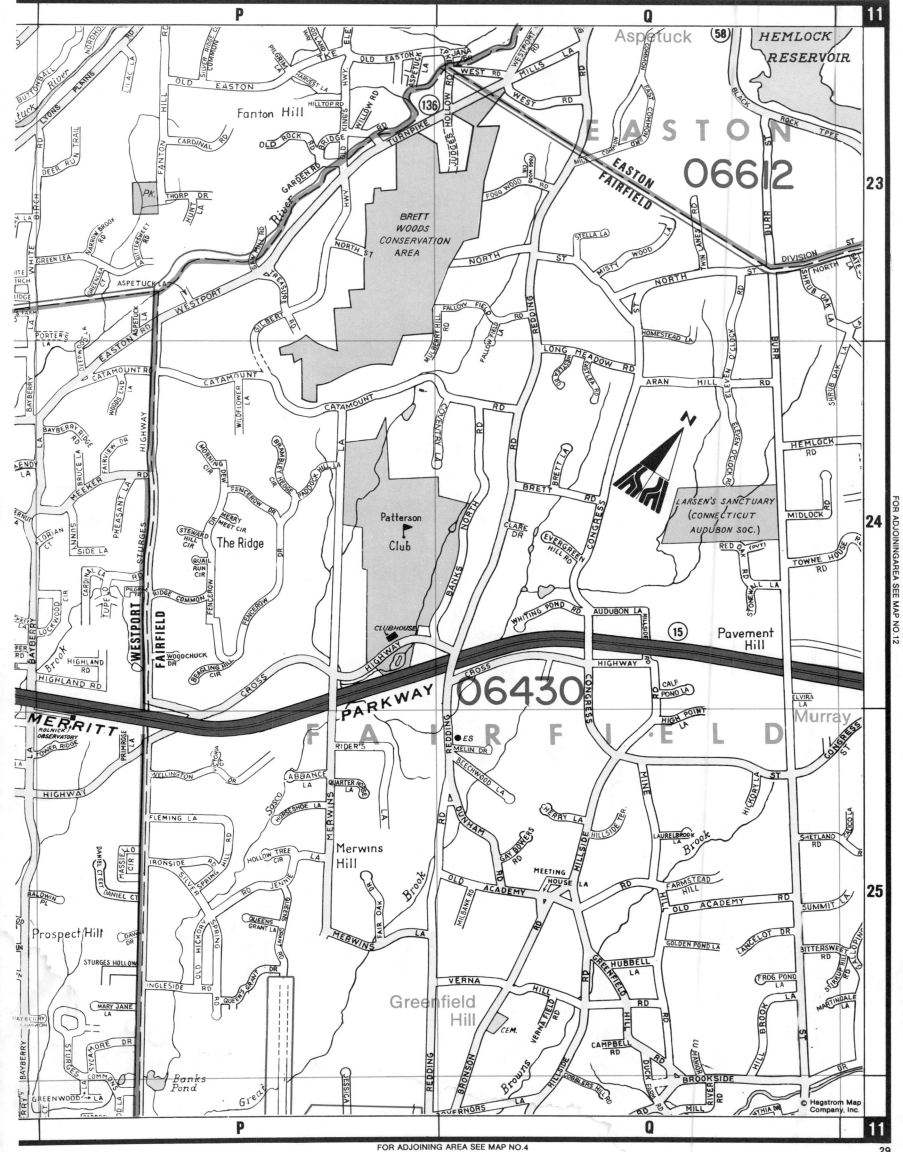

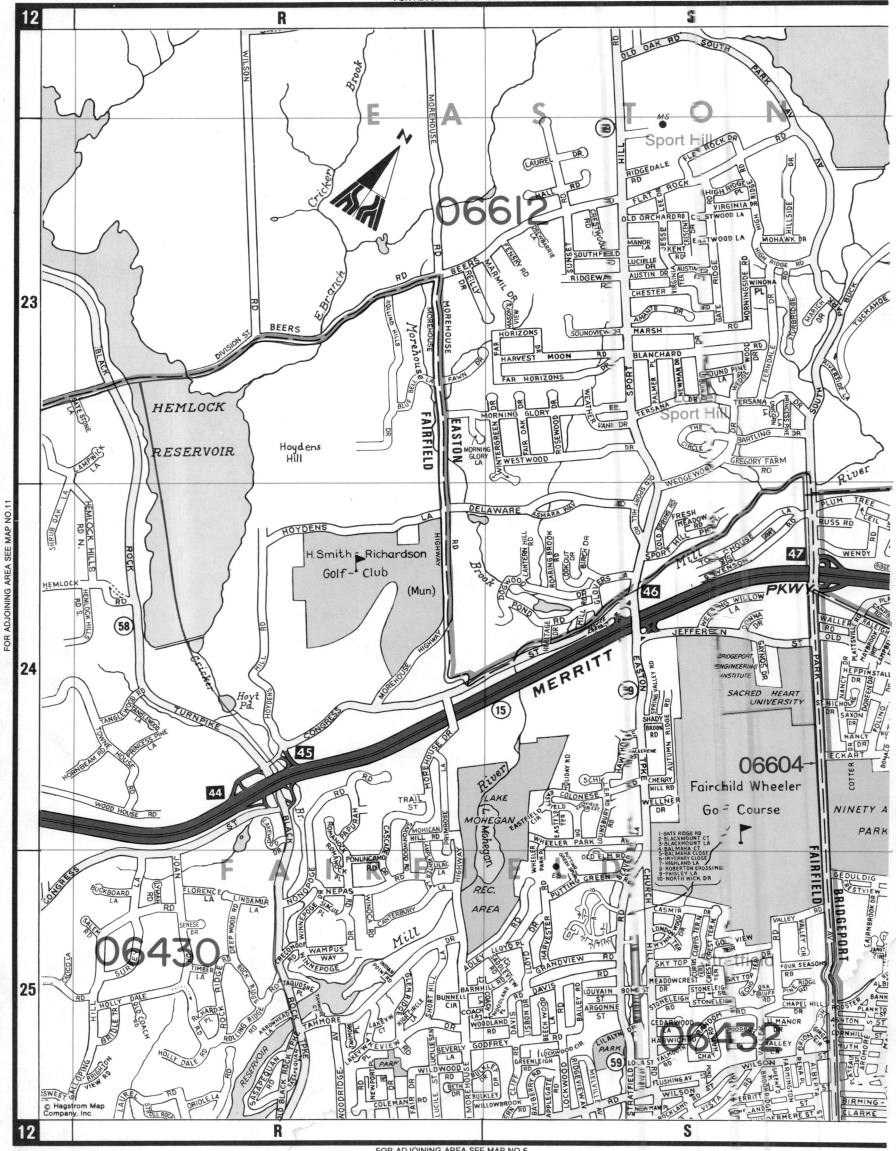

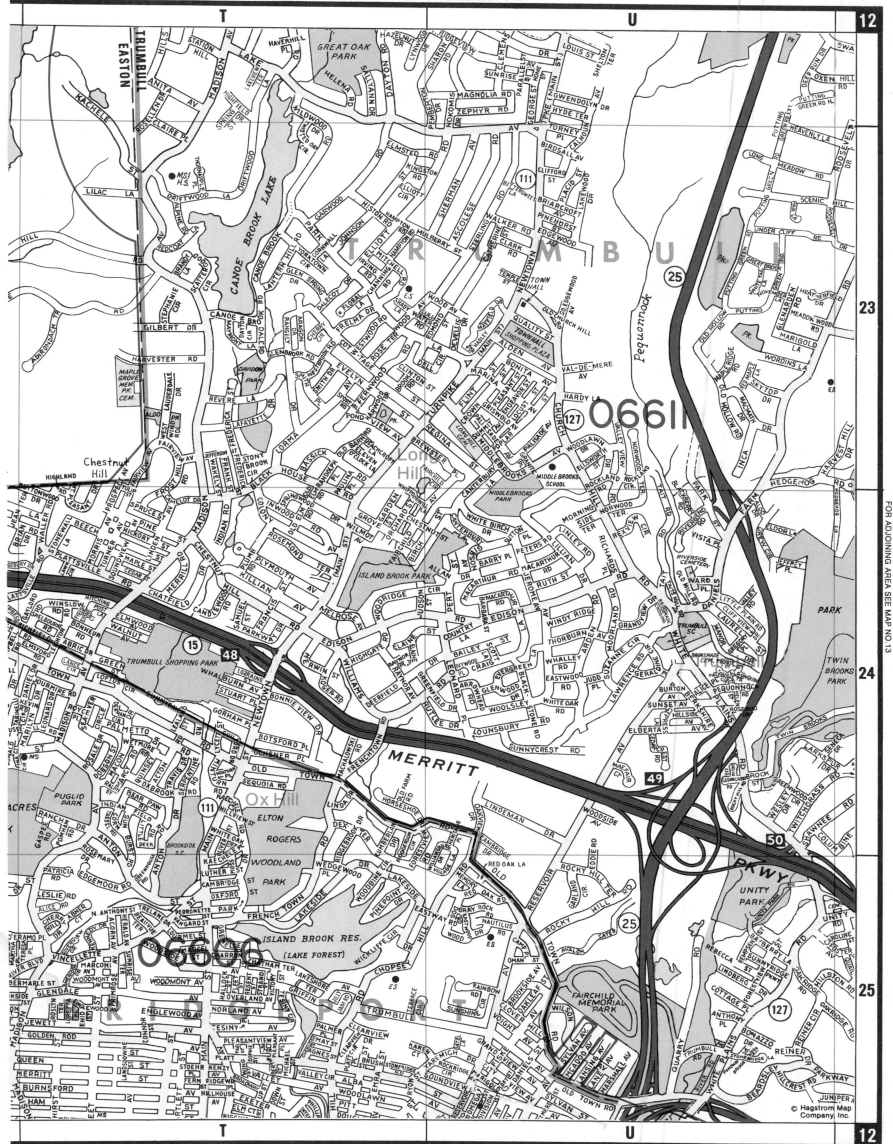

© Hagstrom Map Company, Inc.

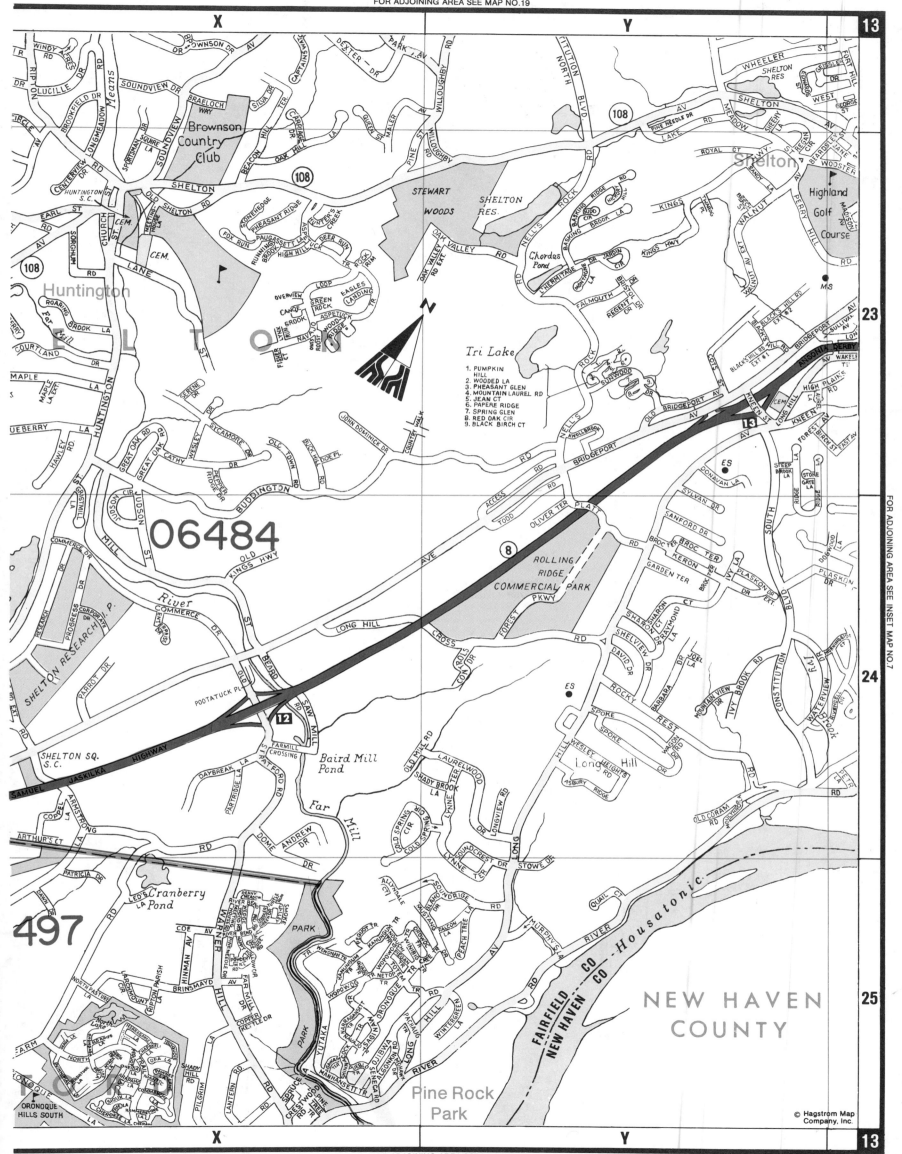

14
A
3

20

AMERICAN LA. NO.

NEW ST

MORTON LA

KING ST

KING ST

AMERICAN LA SO.

684

NATURE CONSERVANCY

MARK TR

NATURE CONSERVANCY

STERLING

Tamarack Country Club

CARPENTERS BROOK RD

RD

CUTLER

BEDFORD

JEFFERSON RD

STILES

DR

LA.

L. Mead

AUDUBON CENTER OF GREENWICH

LOCUST

JOHN

DWIGHT

RICHMOND

11TH

RD

LANGHORNE

Carringb Pond

GATEWAY LA.

AUDUBON LA

WHITNEY DR

BEDFORD

River

LAPHAM RD

RIVERSVILLE ST

JOHN

120

NY CT

2

120

Quaker Ridge

North Greenwich

NATURE CONSERVANCY

QUAKER

LA

NORTH

OLD

Bruce Memorial Golf Club (Mun.)

Wooley Pond

TRACY TER

AUDUBON FAIRCHILD GARDENS

PORCHUCK

MILL

Brui

CLIFFDALE

HERONVIEW

LAUB POND RD

FAIRCHILD LA

RYE LAKE AV

WESTCHESTER COUNTY AIRPORT

WESTCHESTER COUNTY

FAIRFIELD COUNTY

KING ST

Bruce Memorial Golf Club

SELDON LA

(Mun.)

NATURE CONSERVANCY

CORRIGAN LA

QUAKER RIDGE RD

HARD CRABBLE RD

PORCHUCK RD

East

28

CHATEAU RIDGE DR

Fairview Country Club

HYCLIFF RD

RIVERSVILLE RD

MERRITT

BRYNWOOD LA

SANDY LA

22

Byram

NATURE CONSERVANCY

INDIAN KNOLL PL

QUAIL RD

SABINE FARM RD

ROBERTSON DR

GREE

Wilcox Pond

PEEPERS HOLLOW

15

G

Riversville

LINCOLN AV

ALEC TEMPLETON LA

NUTMEG DR

AV

ROUND HILL CLUB RD

CLAPB

120 A

SHERWOOD

THUNDER MOUNTAIN RD

HEBREW CEMETERY

© Hagstrom Map Company, Inc.

14
A
B

C D 14

WESTCHESTER COUNTY NY
FAIRFIELD COUNTY CT

Branch

East

20

CONVERSE LAKE

Banksville

HURLINGHAM

CHITWICK POND RD

CREAMER HILL RD

EDGAR RD

GASTON FARM RD

PARTRIDGE HILL LA

CLIFTON FARM LA

MT LAUREL DR

CONDRAY PK DR LA

GUARDS

FARWELL LA

SUMNER RD

HILL RD

AIKEN RD

CLOSE RD

Wilshire Pd.

WILSHIRE RD

LAKE AV

UPPER CROSS

NORTH ST

HEKMA RD

PARTRIDGE HOLLOW RD

LAFRIENTZ LA

BUCKFIELD ST

ROUND HILL RD

MERRY LA

CONYERS LA

Brook

Pond

FARM RD

DR

Stanwich Club

Closes Pond

N

BURYING HILL RD

TOPPING RD

Topping Pond

LAKE AV

LOWER CROSS

ES

Pond

21

Round Hill

BITTER SWEET LA

HIGHLAND FARM RD

Converse

MILLS RD

N. STANWICH RD

CAMERON DR

ingtons

MOORELAND LA

CHERRY RD

HILL RD

VALLEY

BAYBERRY LA

RD

REYNWOOD MANOR

Brook

06831
(Deliveries from Greenwich P.O.)

TOWN PARKLAND

TACONIC RD

ROUND HILL RD

OLD MILL RD

CONVERSE

Brook

PADDOCK DR

OLD MILL RD NORTH

WYCKHAM HILL LA

Horseneck

NORTH ST STANWICH RD

CROWN

Pond

29

HUCKLEBERRY LA

TINKER LA

PARKWAY

SKYRIDGE RD

SPRING HOUSE RD

WILL MERRY LA

OLD MILL AV

LAKE AV

ROCKWOOD LAKE

TACONIC RD

BIRCHWOOD

GATE FIELD DR

HEDGEROW LA

RD

31

STALLION TR

BALDWIN FARMS NORTH

COVER LA

ROGER DR

HOPE FARM RD

Putnam Lake

LOCH LA

ANDREWS FARM RD

HUNTING RIDGE RD

STAG LA

BALDWIN FARMS SOUTH

HOLLOW RD

06830

OAKLEY LA

MAVIS LA

GRAY OAKS LA

ALPINE LA

Stag Brook

MOHAWK LA

E E N W I C H

COUNTAIN WOOD DR

SIMMONS LA

BUTTERNUT LA

DEKRAFT RD

DEWART RD

WHEELER RD

RED COAT LA

INTERLAKEN RD

Burning Tree C.C.

22

ENBRIAR LA

STONEY WILDE LA

WYNWOOD RD

DAIRY LA

GORDON LA

CLAPBOARD RD

WYNN RD

NORTH ST

TACONIC BYFIELD LA

LONDONDERRY

BURNING TREE RD

BOARD RIDGE RD

© Hagstrom Map Company, Inc.

FOR ADJOINING AREA SEE MAP NO.15

C D 14

15   E   F

20

WESTCHESTER
FAIRFIELD

Banksville

Grays Pond

Grays Pd.

Stanwich Club

SAMUEL J. BARGH (GREENWICH WATER CO.) RESERVOIR

Long Ridge

104

21

GREENWICH
STAMFORD

06831
(Deliveries from Greenwich P.O.)

06903

104

Bear Rock Pd.

Mianus

22

Altschul Pond

Newman Mills Park

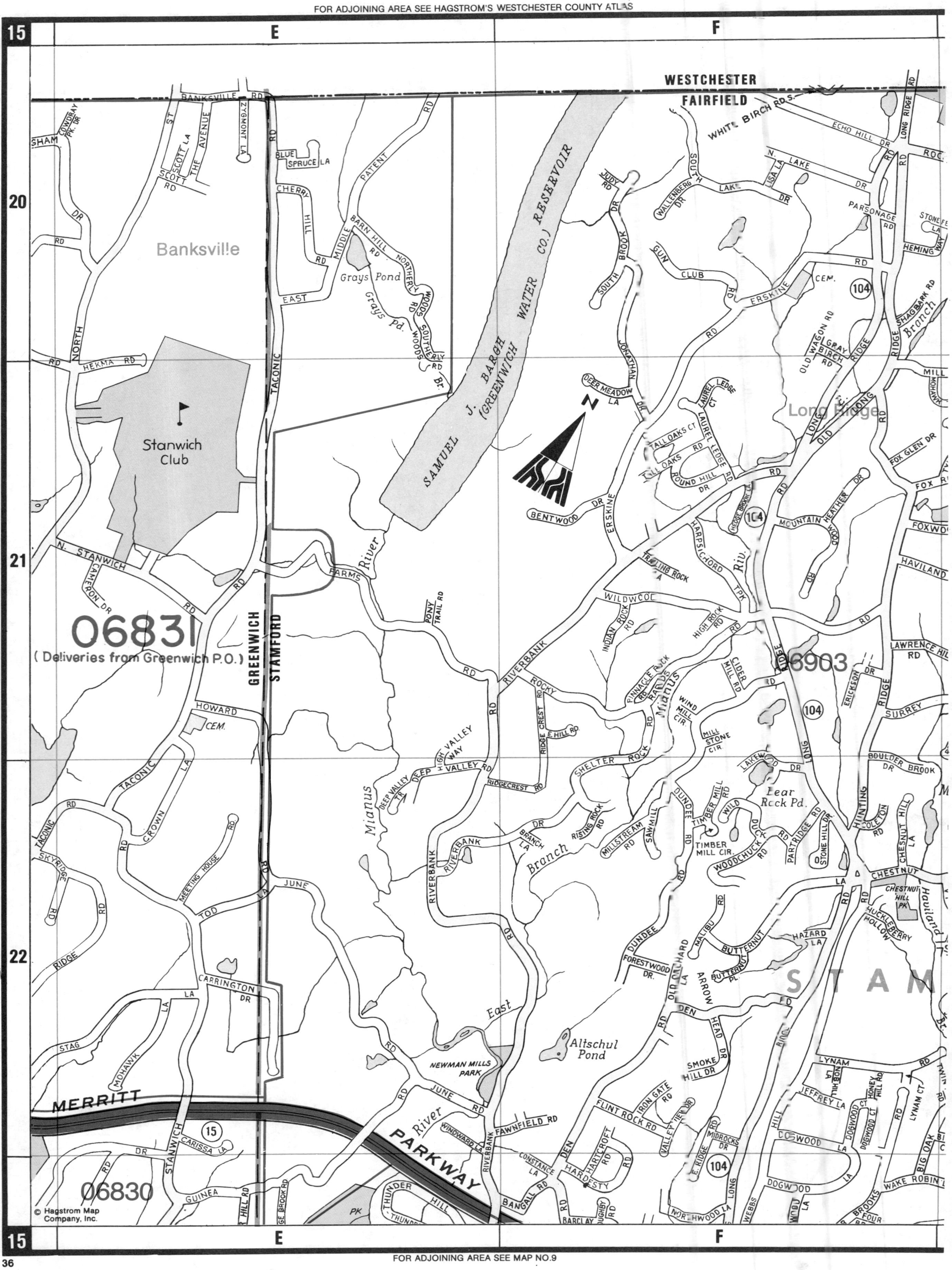

STAM

MERRITT

15

PARKWAY

104

06830

© Hagstrom Map
Company, Inc.

15   E   F

COUNTY
COUNTY

NY
CT

20

21

22

15
G | H

FOR ADJOINING AREA SEE MAP NO.20 | FOR ADJOINING AREA SEE MAP NO.16

Rockrimmon Country Club
Mianus River
Winslow Dr
RIMMON
Pond View La
Orient Lodge Ponds
Rock Meadow La
Delwood Rd
Tanglewood La
Boulderol Rd
Country Club Rd
Coventry Rd
Rolling Ridge Rd
Fairway
Greens Cir
Craig Ct
Riding Stable Tr
Sally Ann La
Black Rock Rd
Heroy Recreation Area
Trinity Pass
Lost District Ridge
Alan La
Pequot La
Hunters Creek
Proprietors La
White Fall La
Squire's La

Mayapple Rd
McIntosh Rd
Apple Valley Rd
Winesap La
Crab Apple Pl
Black Twig Pl
Russet Rd
High Ridge Rd
CEM
Flora Pl
Spring Hill La
Laurel Hill La
Bonny Glen Rd
Class La
Trinity
LAUREL RESERVOIR
PONUS RIDGE RD
Dans H'way
Lakewind Rd
River Wind Rd

Blackberry La
Happy Hill Rd
Blackberry Dr
Breezy Hill Rd
Mile Valley La
Mill Springs La
Ridge Brook Dr
Shady La
Merri-Land Rd
N. Briar Brae Rd
Briar Brae Rd Conn
Ingleside
Shady Knoll Dr
Spring Hill La E
Reservoir La
Woodbine Rd
Fernwood Dr
Rippowam River
Tobis La
Rippowam Rd
Ramhorne Rd

06903
Saddle Hill La
Briar Brook Rd
Rock Ridge Rd
Briarwood La
Doris La
West Mountain Tr
Eliot La
Alexandra Dr
Sunset Rd
Settler's Tr
Hickory Ridge Rd
Bracchi Dr
Cricket La
Lake Pond Rd
Woodbine Rd
Bittersweet La
Quails Tr
Clearview La
Collins Pd.
Stonehenge Dr
Woodridge
Sherwood La
Wellesley Dr

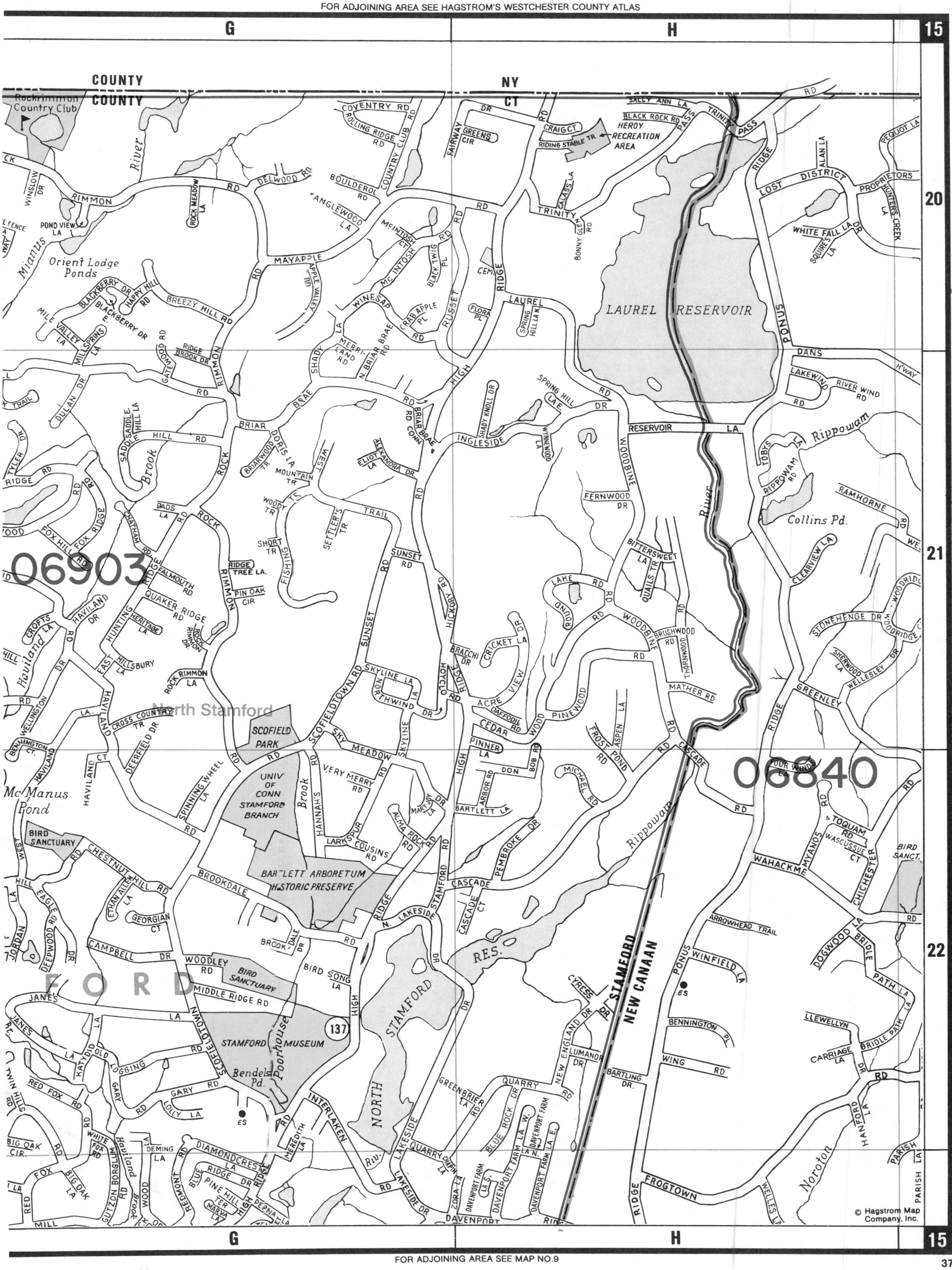

Fox Hill Fox Ridge
Tyler Rd
Ridge
Chatham La
Dads La
Rock Rd
Short Tr
Ridge Tree La
Pin Oak Cir
Fishing Trail
Woody Tr
Skyline La
Northwind Dr
Acre View
Daffodil
Wood Pinewood Rd
Thornwood Rd
Mather Rd
Greenley Ridge
Cascade

Haviland La
Crofts La
Falmouth Rd
Quaker Ridge Rd
Heritage La
Rock Rimmon La
East Hillsbury La
Cross Country Tr
Deerfield Dr
North Stamford
SCOFIELD PARK
Scofieldtown Rd
Sky Meadow
Skyline La
Cedar
Pinner La
High
Frost Pond Rd
Aspen La
06840
Four Winds

McManus Pond
Bennington Ct
Haviland Ct
Haviland Rd
Spinning Wheel Rd
UNIV OF CONN STAMFORD BRANCH
Brook
Hannah's Rd
Very Merry Rd
Larkspur La
Cousins Rd
Alma Rock Rd
Marion Dr
Bartlett La
Arbor Rd
Don Bob Rd
Michael Rd
Rippowam
STAMFORD
NEW CANAAN
Wahackme
Mianos Rd
Toquam Rd
Wascussue Ct
Bird Sanct.

Bird Sanctuary
Chestnut Hill Rd
Ethan Allen Rd
Georgian Ct
Brookdale
Ridge
N. Lakeside
Stamford
Cascade Ct
Cascade
Pembroke Dr
Arrowhead Trail
Dogwood La
Bridle Path La

West Rd
Eagle La
Jordan La
Deepwood La
Campbell Dr
Woodley Rd
Bird Sanctuary
Middle Ridge Rd
Bird Song La
Brookdale Rd
RES.
STAMFORD RES.
Cyress Dr
New England Dr
PONUS
Winfield La
ES
Bennington B
Llewellyn La
Carriage La
Bridle Path Rd

FORD
Janes La
Red Fox Rd
Katydid Old Logging
Gary Rd
Lolly La
STAMFORD MUSEUM
137
Poorhouse Rd
Bendels Pd.
ES
NORTH
N. Lakeside
High
Greenbrier La
Blue Rock Dr
Quarry
New England Dr
Lumanor Dr
Bartling Dr
Wing Rd
Hanford Rd
Parish La

Big Oak Cir
White Fox Rd
Fox La
Red Fox
Big Oak La
Gutzon Borglum Rd
Redmont Rd
Diamondcrest La
Ridge Dr
Pine Hill Rd
Deming Rd
Meredith Rd
Interlaken Rd
Lakeside Dr
Davenport Farm La
Davenport
Quarry
FROGTOWN
Noroton
Welles La
Parish La

© Hagstrom Map Company, Inc.

16   J   K

06840

N E W C A N A A N

New Canaan Nature Center

124

Country Club of New Canaan

Smith Ridge

Ruscoe Ridge

Pine Hill

Canoe Hill

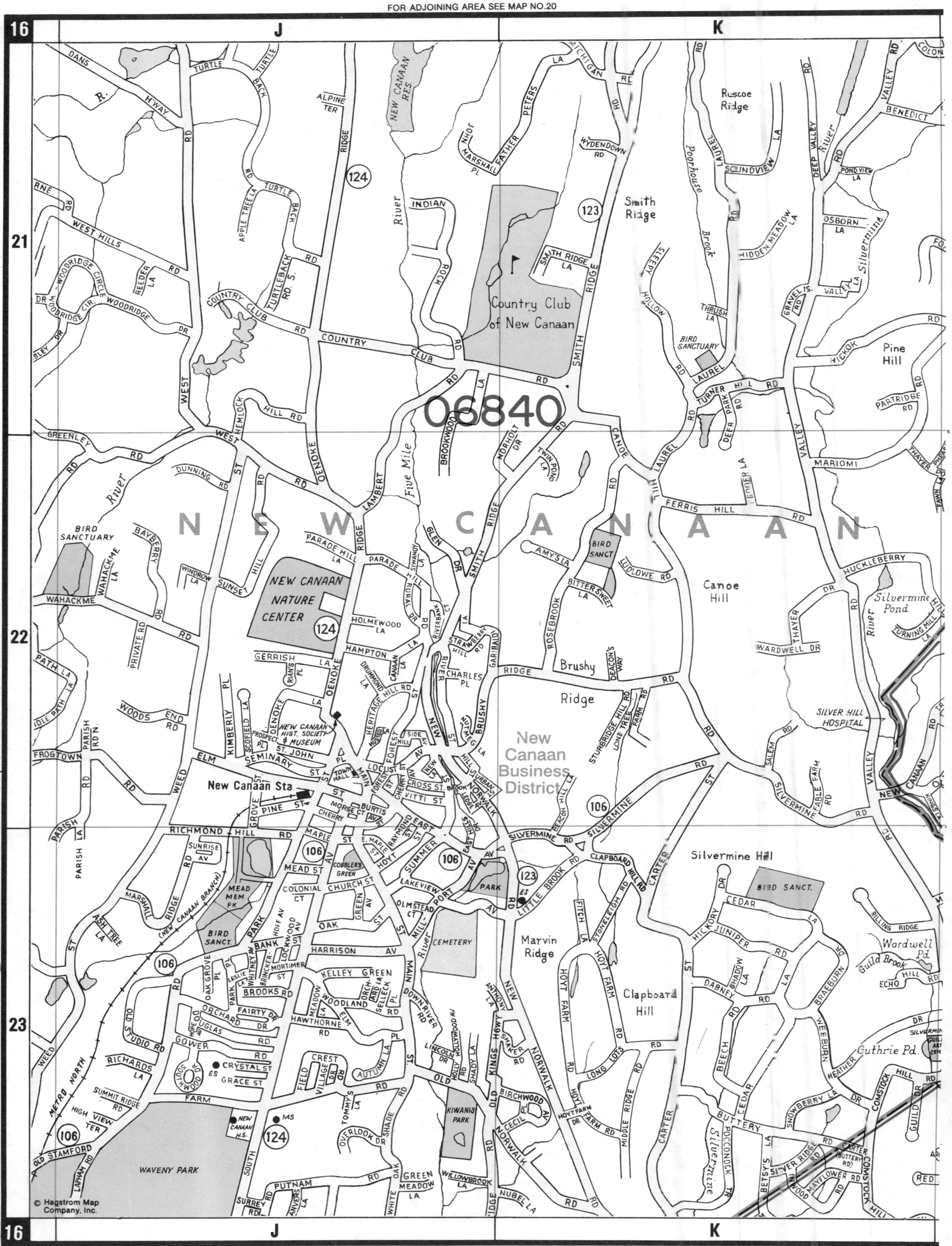

Silvermine Pond

Silver Hill Hospital

Brushy Ridge

New Canaan Business District

New Canaan Hist. Society & Museum

New Canaan Sta.

Bird Sanctuary

Mead Mem. Pk.

Silvermine Hill

Marvin Ridge

Clapboard Hill

Wardwell Pd.

Guthrie Pd.

Cemetery

Kiwanis Park

Waveny Park

New Canaan H.S.

Green Meadow La

21

22

23

106

123

124

123

106

124

106

16   J   K

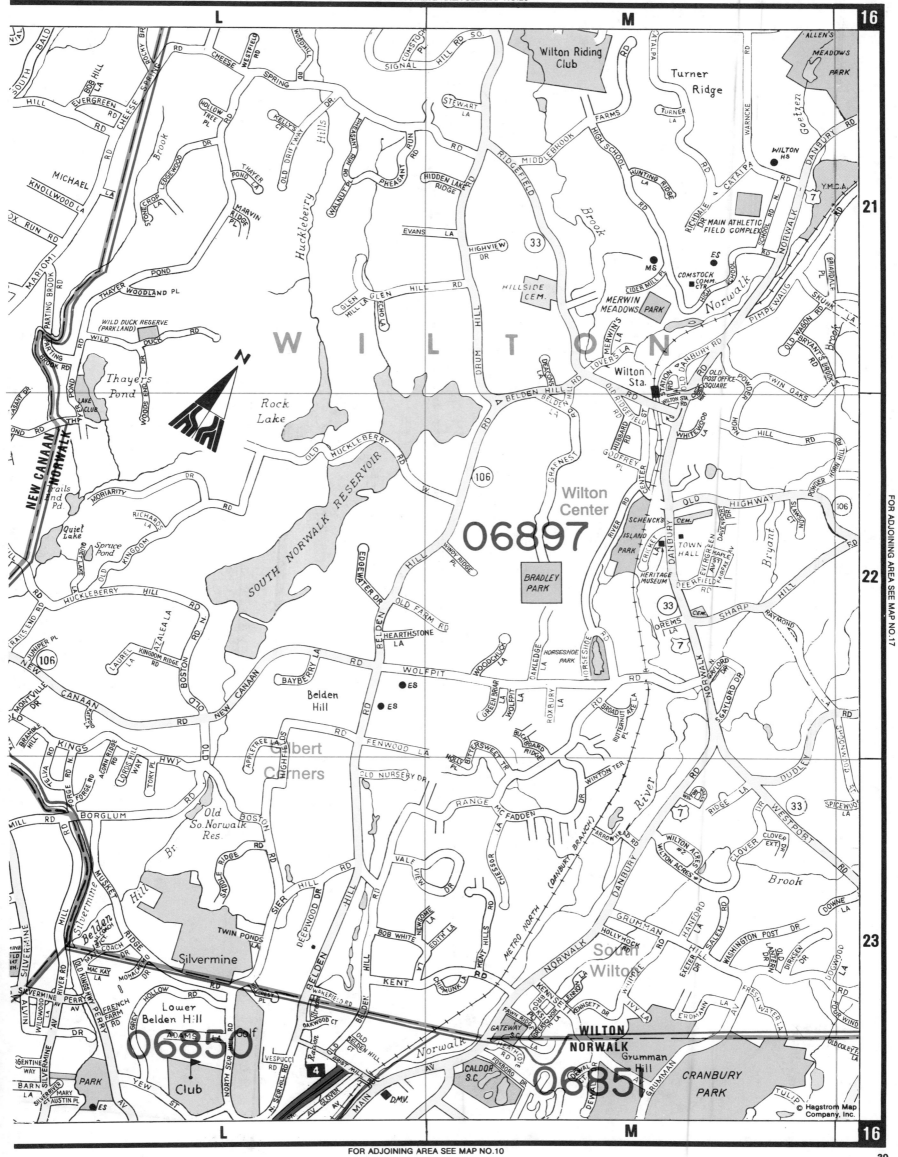

06897

Wilton Center

BRADLEY PARK

06850

06851

WILTON
NORWALK

© Hagstrom Map
Company, Inc.

17   N   O

ALLEN'S MEADOWS PARK
CEM.
River
Cannondale Sta.
DANBURY
CANNON RD
NORWALK
Goetzel
Brook
SPRING BROOK LA
COBBLESTONE
Y.M.C.A.
7
PIMPEWAUG
BRIARDALE
SKUNK
Bryant's Brook
BRYANT'S BROOK RD

CANNONDALE RD
BROOKWOOD LA
SHINNECOCK PL
ROSCREA PL
TRAILS END RD
(TRAIL'S END RD SPUR)
TRAIL'S END RD
TRAIL'S END RD
SCATACOOK TR
PENT RD
PILOT HILL RD
OLD ORCHARD DR
PINE FIELD
OLD FIELD LA
DILLON PASS
WEDGES FIELD
TURNPIKE
WALDEN WOODS
North
River

SEELEY RD
CANNON RD
BLACK ALDER
Brook
WILTON WESTON
MARSHALL LA
HERITAGE
LANGNER
GODFREY
MOUNTAINVIEW
GLORY RD
GEORGETOWN
NOVEMBER
OCTOBER DR
SEPTEMBER
MICHAELS WAY
53

21

Rolling Hills Country Club
Sturges Ridge
CROSSWICKS RIDGE RD
RIDGE RD
SKUNK END
AMBLER LA
SPRUCE DR
HYLAND DR
ORCHARD DR
LEE ALLEN LA
SPRING VALLEY RD
WHITE OAK LA
HILLSIDE
LAKESIDE DR
STILLWATER LA
SCRIBNER PARK
HART
NORTH CALVIN RD
57

W I L T O N

DUCK POND PL
FRIENDLEE LA
BUCKINGHAM RIDGE
LIBERTY ST
PEPPERIDGE LA
HENRY AUSTIN DR
PINE RIDGE
BHASKING RIDGE RD
Boone
RIDGEWOOD RD
SHADOW LA
POWDER HORN HILL
PARISH RD
OLD HIGHWAY
106
HURLBUTT RD
SHARP HILL
CALVIN ST
COLEY RD
LITTLE FOX LA
CALVIN RD
OVERIDGE LA
HAWTHORNE LA
COBBS MILL RD
OLD MILL
River
Newtown
WATERBURY ST
Cobbs Mill Pond
TOBACCO RD
HILLSIDE RD S
GEORGE
NIMROD FARM RD
ADAM'S WAY
WOOD HILL RD
SCHOOL PATH RD
SCHOOL RD
CRICKET LA
WILLOW DR
HYDE RIDGE RD
Beaver Brook Lake
WESTON HS
WILDWOOD
HYDE
SALEM RD
HIGHWAY
BIRCH HILL RD
ROGUES RIDGE

06897

06883

22

CHERRY HILL
CHERRY LANE PK.
Chestnut Brook
RAYMOND LA
BANKS DR
POND ST
CEDAR RD
CAPTAIN'S
STONEBRIDGE LA
TWIN BROOK LA
STONEBRIDGE RD
LORING LA (PVT)
TOPFIELD RD
LITTLEBROOK RD
JACKSON RD
MORAND LA
DUDLEY
SPOONWOOD RD
Chestnut Hill
RIVER GATE
PILGRIM TR
Saugatuck
NEWTOWN TPKE
NORFIELD
53
TOWN HALL
LIBRARY
ES
NORFIELD RD
HEDGEROW COMMON
WOODS DEER PATH
NORFIELD
WOODCHUCK HILL RD
TIMOTHY RD
HIDDEN MEADOW
57
JOANNE
WESTON
Creek
KETTLE CREEK
NORFIELD
BENEDICT LA
CURIOSITY LA
LITTLE BROOK LA
Davidson Pond
FARRELL
Van Syp
PARADE GROUND CT
STEEP HILL
Beaver Brook

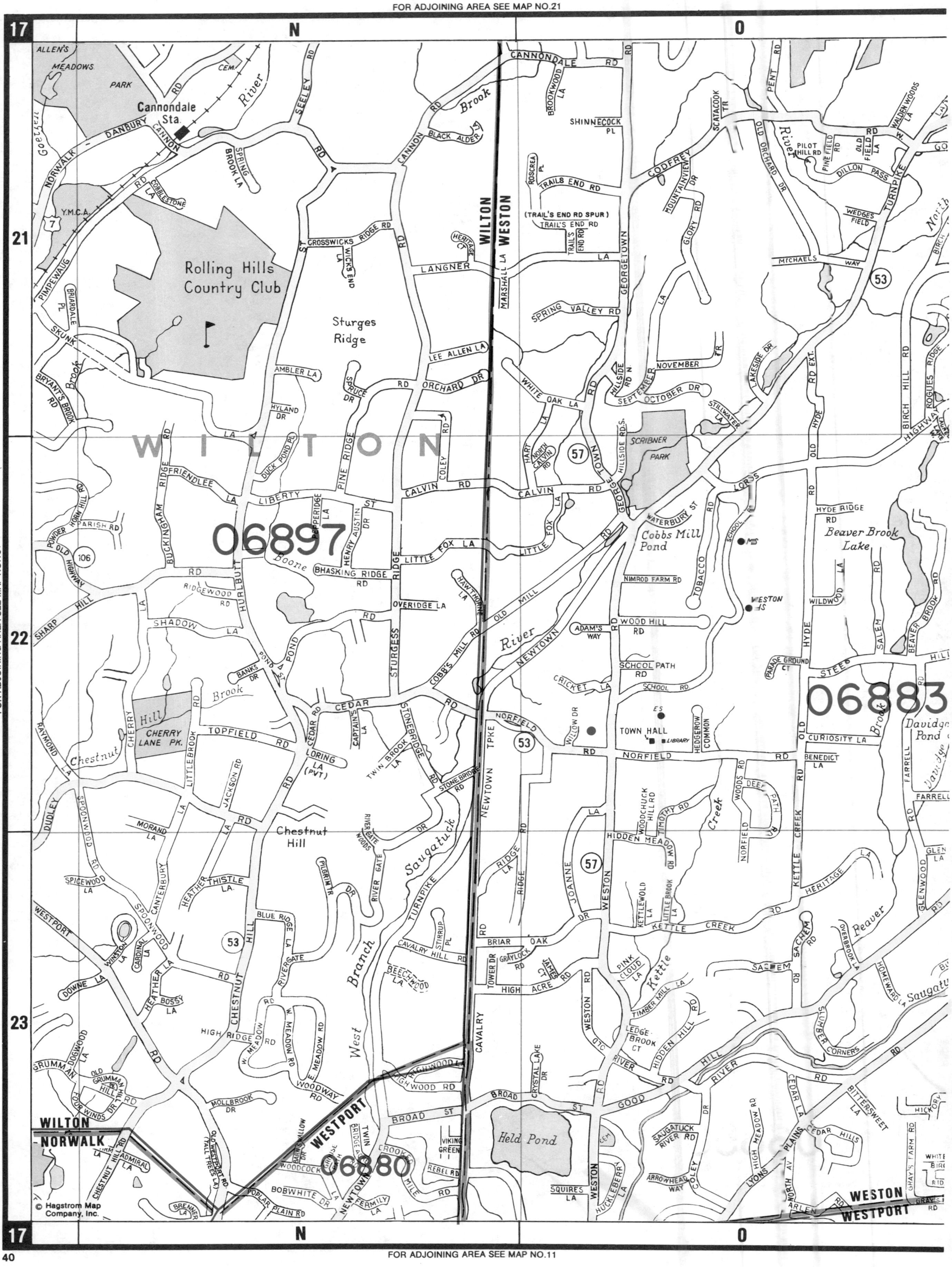

West Branch

23

SPICEWOOD LA
HEATHER LA
THISTLE LA
BLUE RIDGE LA
CANTERBURY
CARDINAL LA
WINSTON
DOWNE LA
BOSSY LA
HIGH RIDGE RD
CHESTNUT HILL RD
W. MEADOW RD
W. MEADOW RD
RIVERGATE
53
STIRRUP PL
CAVALRY HILL RD
BEECHWOOD LA
Saugatuck
TURNPIKE
RIDGE LA
BRIAR OAK RD
TOWER DR
GRAYLOCK RD
HIGH ACRE RD
CAVALRY
WESTON RD
PINK CLOUD LA
KETTLEWOLD
LEDGE BROOK CT
HIDDEN HILL RD
TIMBER MILL LA
KETTLE CREEK
SACHEM RD
OVERBROOK LA
HOMEWARD LA
Saugatuck
GLEN

WILTON NORWALK
GRUMMAN HILL RD
OLD GRUMMAN HILL RD
FOUR WINDS DR
CHESTNUT HILL RD
ADMIRAL LA
MOLLBROOK DR
WILLOW
WESTPORT
WOODCOCK
TWIN RIDGE LA
NEWTOWN
BOBWHITE DR
POPLAR PLAIN RD
BRENNER
06880
VIKING GREEN
REBEL RD
BROAD ST
BROAD
Held Pond
CRYSTAL LAKE DR
SQUIRES LA
HUCKLEBERRY LA
GOOD
River
ARROWHEAD WAY
SAUGATUCK RIVER RD
LYONS PLAINS
NORTH AV
HIGH MEADOW RD
CEDAR HILLS
COLEY RD
GRAY'S FARM RD
BITTERSWEET LA
HICKORY
WESTON WESTPORT

17   N   O

© Hagstrom Map Company, Inc.

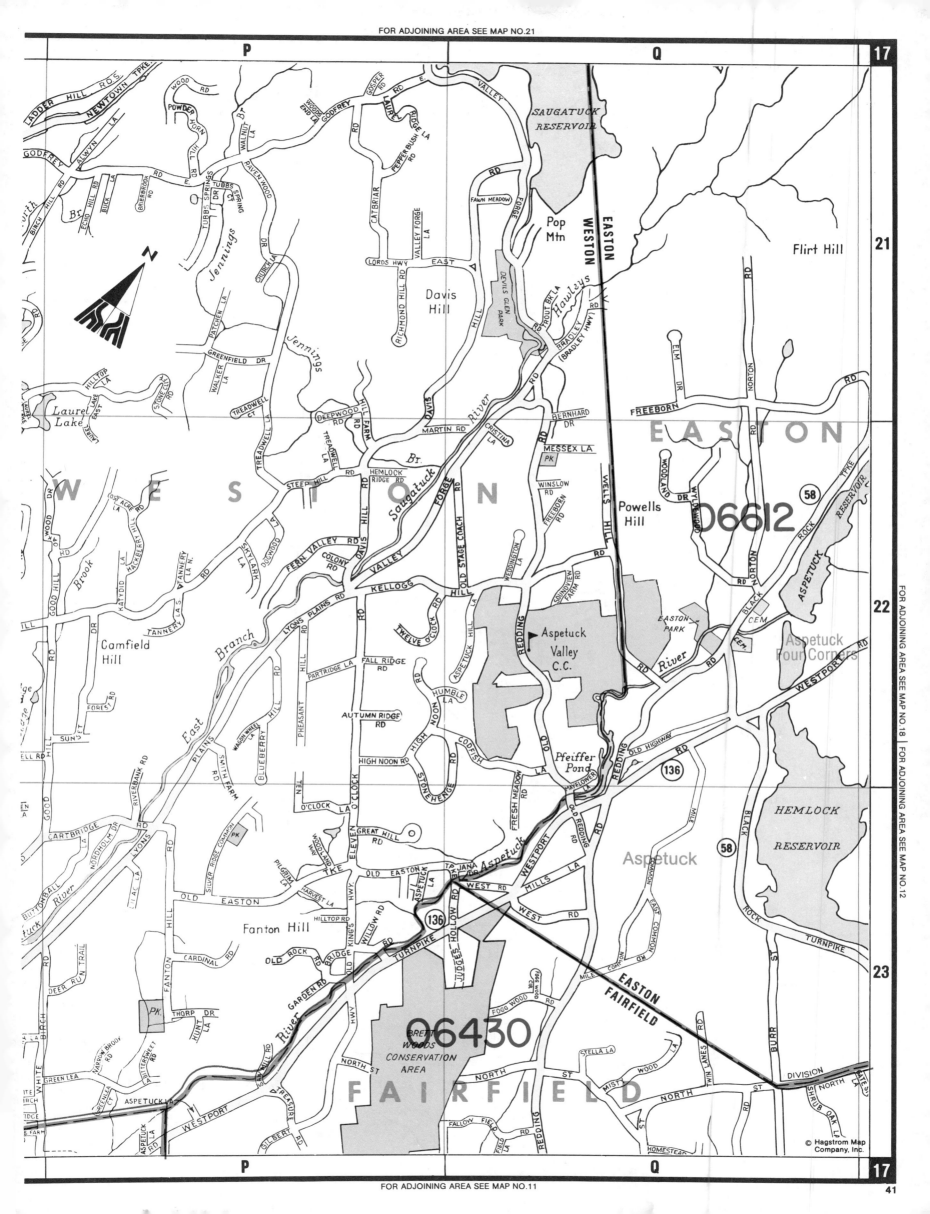

18

R

S

FEDDING EASTON

OLD INDIAN CEM.

Livermore Pond

CEM.

ROCK

HOUSE

EASTON RD

NORTH

Tateduck

SHERW

58

River

VALLEY

LEDGENAI RD

VISTA

WOOD END DR

DR

CEM

RD

SHERWOOD

Patterson

PARK

20

Connecticut Golf Course

COUNTRY CLUB LA

STAPLES RD

TURNPIKE

Brook

TRANQUILITY DR SWEET BRIAR

BALLWALL RD

SUNNY RIDGE

MARTIN LA

SUNNY RIDGE LA

RD

Br.

DEERFIELD DR

BOHUS LA

WIMBLEDON

59

River

ROCK VALLEY

HILL

STAPLES

CEDAR HILL LA

BIBBONS

CEDAR HILL

RD

EVERETT

SANFORD DR AV

TODDS WAY

BLACK

SILVER

HONEYSUCKLE LA

HILL

BIBBONS LA

BIBBONS RD

RD

UNION CEM.

STEPNEY

CHURCH

ALGONQUIN LA

BURROUGHS

NORTH

BAYBERRY

LA

21

Aspetuck

06612

DAIRY LA

ORCHARD

RD

136

MEADOW DR

RIDGE DR

BROOK SIDE DR

IOETTA

WOOD

HILL

KNOLLCREST RD

RC

PARK

RD

JAMESTOWN

DEEPWOOD RD

R

LOBDELL LA

ANDREWS

59

PHEASANT LA

BARROWS RD

STONE'S THROW

CENTER

RESERVOIR

WESTPORT

MOREHOUSE

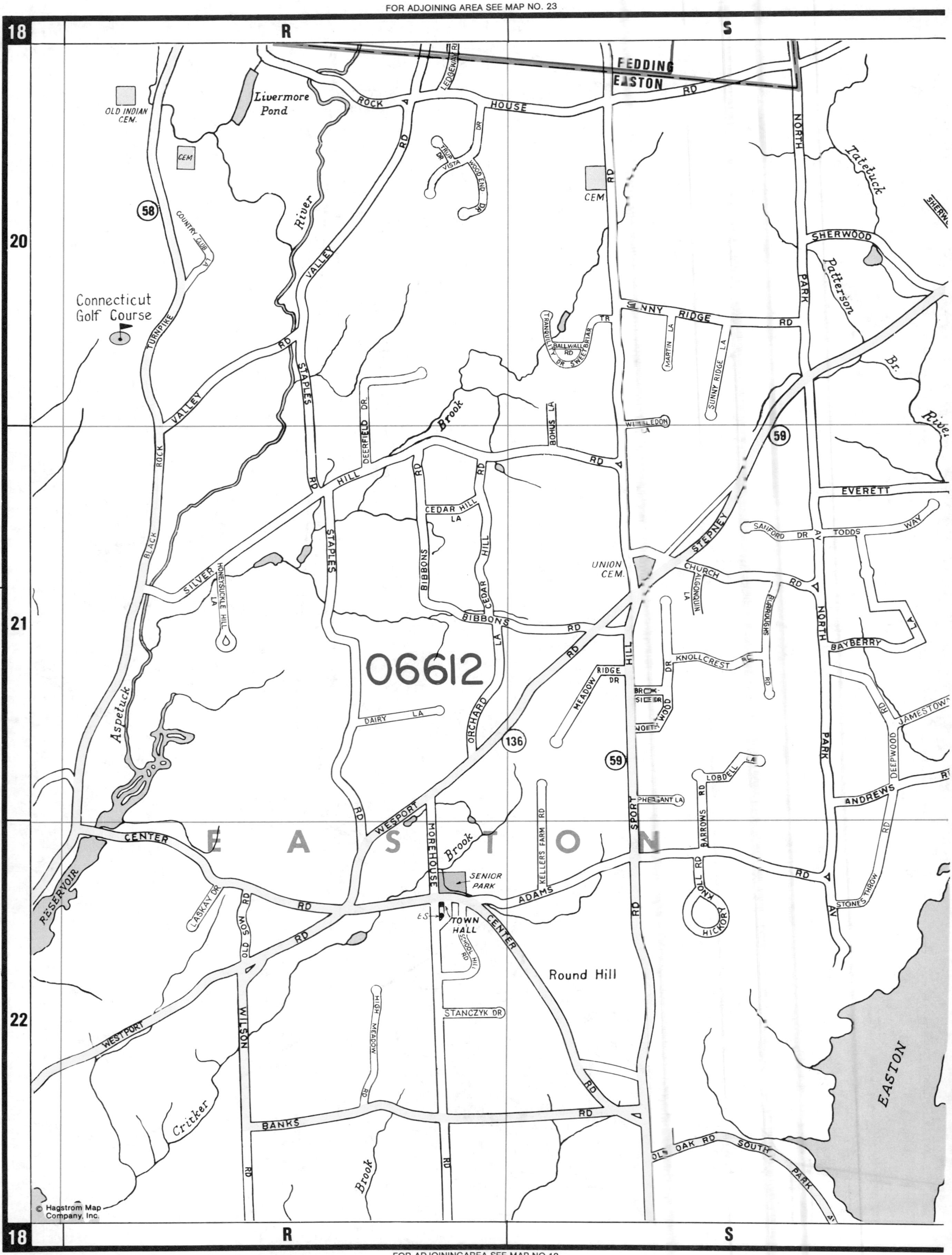

Brook

KELLERS FARM RD

SPORT

RD

KNOLL RD

HICKORY

KNOLL

AV

LASKAY DR

OLD SOW RD

RD

ES

TOWN HALL

SCHOOL HILL RD

ADAMS

CENTER RD

Round Hill

22

WESTPORT

WILSON

HIGH MEADOW RD

STANCZYK DR

RD

Critker

BANKS RD

RD

Brook

RD

RD

OAK RD

SOUTH

PARK

AV

© Hagstrom Map Company, Inc.

EASTON

18

R

S

42

FOR ADJOINING AREA SEE MAP NO. 23

T
U
18
20
21
22
MONROE
TRUMBULL
EASTON
Stepney
06468
06611
Hirams Hill
Rock Raymond
North Farrar
RESERVOIR
WILLIAM E. WOLFE PARK
INDUSTRIAL PARK
TASHUA KNOLLS GOLF COURSE
OLD MINE PARK
INDIAN LEDGE PARK
GREAT OAK PARK
Pequonnock River
Mill River
Chub Br.
Spring Br.
Kaatz Pond
PITKIN HOLLOW
59
25
111
© Hagstrom Map Company, Inc.

FOR ADJOINING AREA SEE MAP NO.19

FOR ADJOINING AREA SEE MAP NO.12

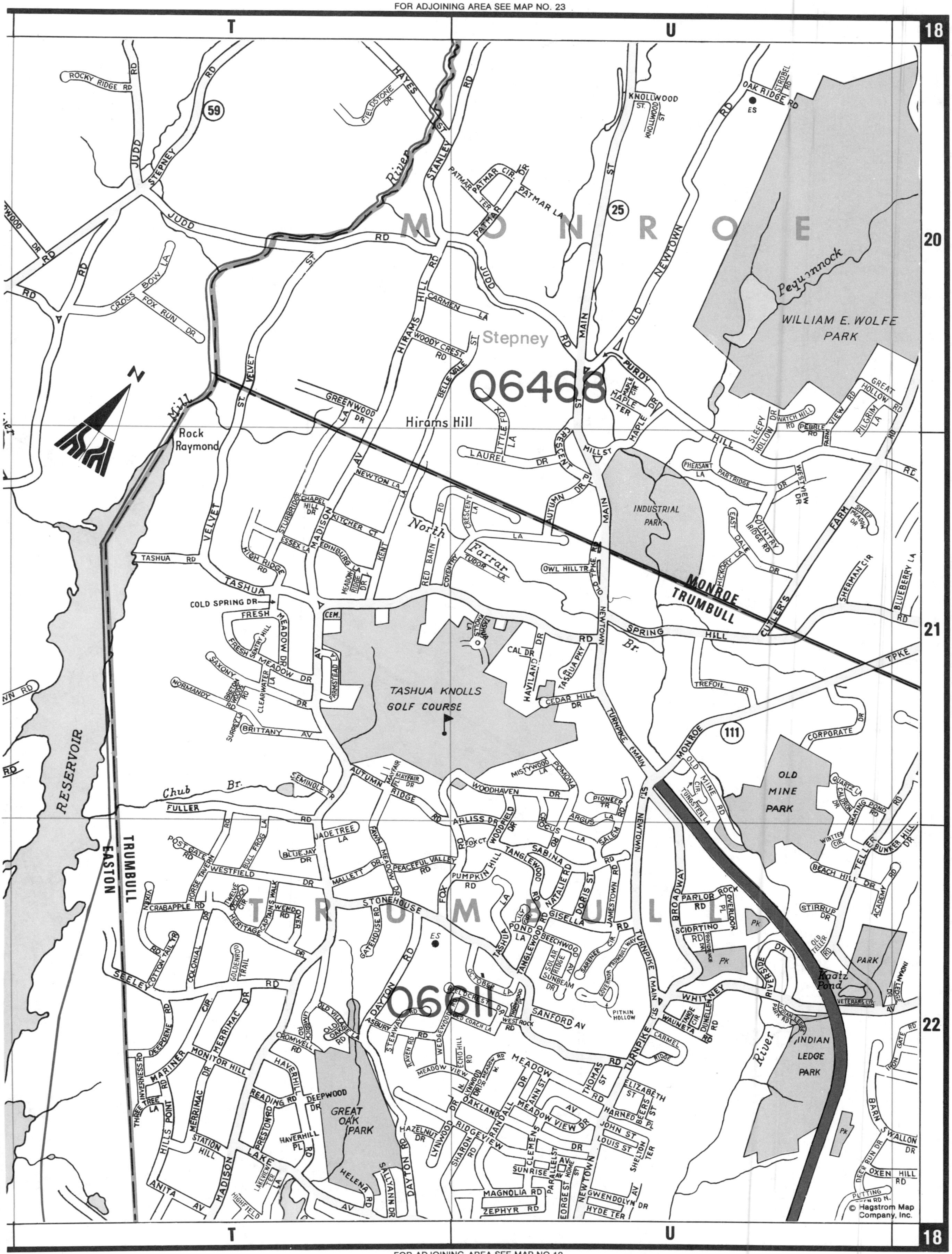

19 V W

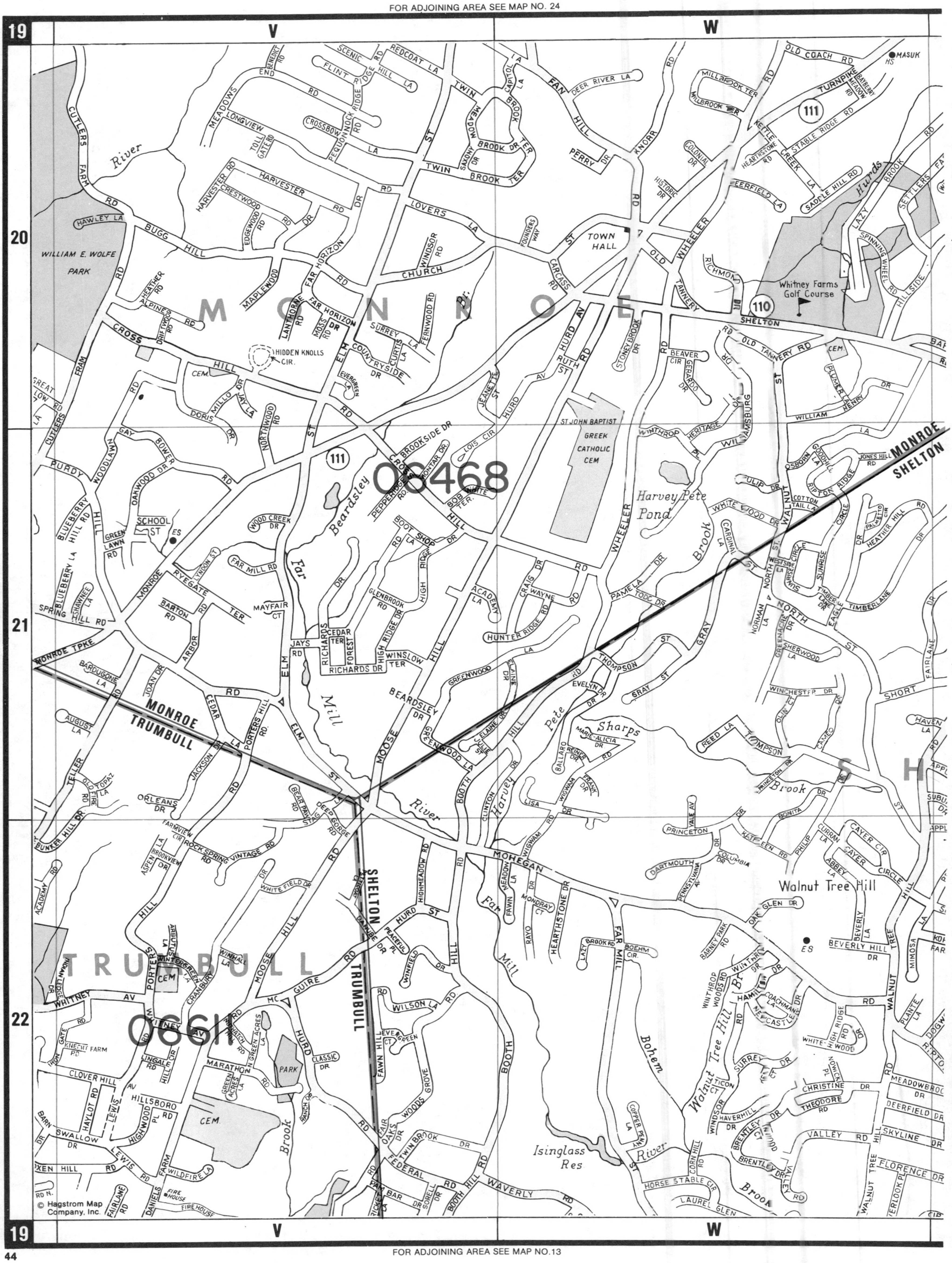

FOR ADJOINING AREA SEE MAP NO.18

MONROE

06468

MONROE
TRUMBULL

T R U M B U L L

06611

MONROE
SHELTON

S H

SHELTON
TRUMBULL

William E. Wolfe Park

Whitney Farms Golf Course

St John Baptist Greek Catholic Cem

Harvey Pete Pond

Walnut Tree Hill

Isinglass Res

Town Hall

© Hagstrom Map Company, Inc.

20

21

22

19 V W

X   Y   19

20

FOR ADJOINING AREA SEE HAGSTROM'S NEW HAVEN COUNTY ATLAS

21

22

19

06484

S H E L T O N

Lower White Hills

White Hills

Upper White Hills

MEANS BROOK RESERVOIR

Means Brook

INDIAN WELL STATE PARK

Housatonic River

FAIRFIELD CO / NEW HAVEN CO

WHITE HILLS RECREATION AREA

WHITE HILLS S.C.

SHELTON HS

SHELTON RES

Indian Hole Brook

Upper White Hills Brook

Street / place labels:

Brook, SUMMER VIEW DR, YANKEE HILL, CAMELOT LA, SQUIRE RD, WEBB CTR, VISTA DR, MEGHAN CT, MEGHAN, DICKINSON DR, WHITTIER, THOREAU DR, BRYANT LA, N. HILLSIDE LA, HIGHFIELD DR, OLD CASTLE DR, HAMLET LA, CAMELOT DR, SWENDSEN RD, ELLIOT DR, STEPHEN DR, BIG HORN LA, REVERE RD, VISTA DR, SHELTER ROCK DR, WEBSTER, LITTLE PRINCESS WENONAH, HIAWATHA TRL, PRINCESS WENONAH DR, OKENUCK WAY, COMMUNITY, BOULDER PATH, ROUNDHILL, Brook

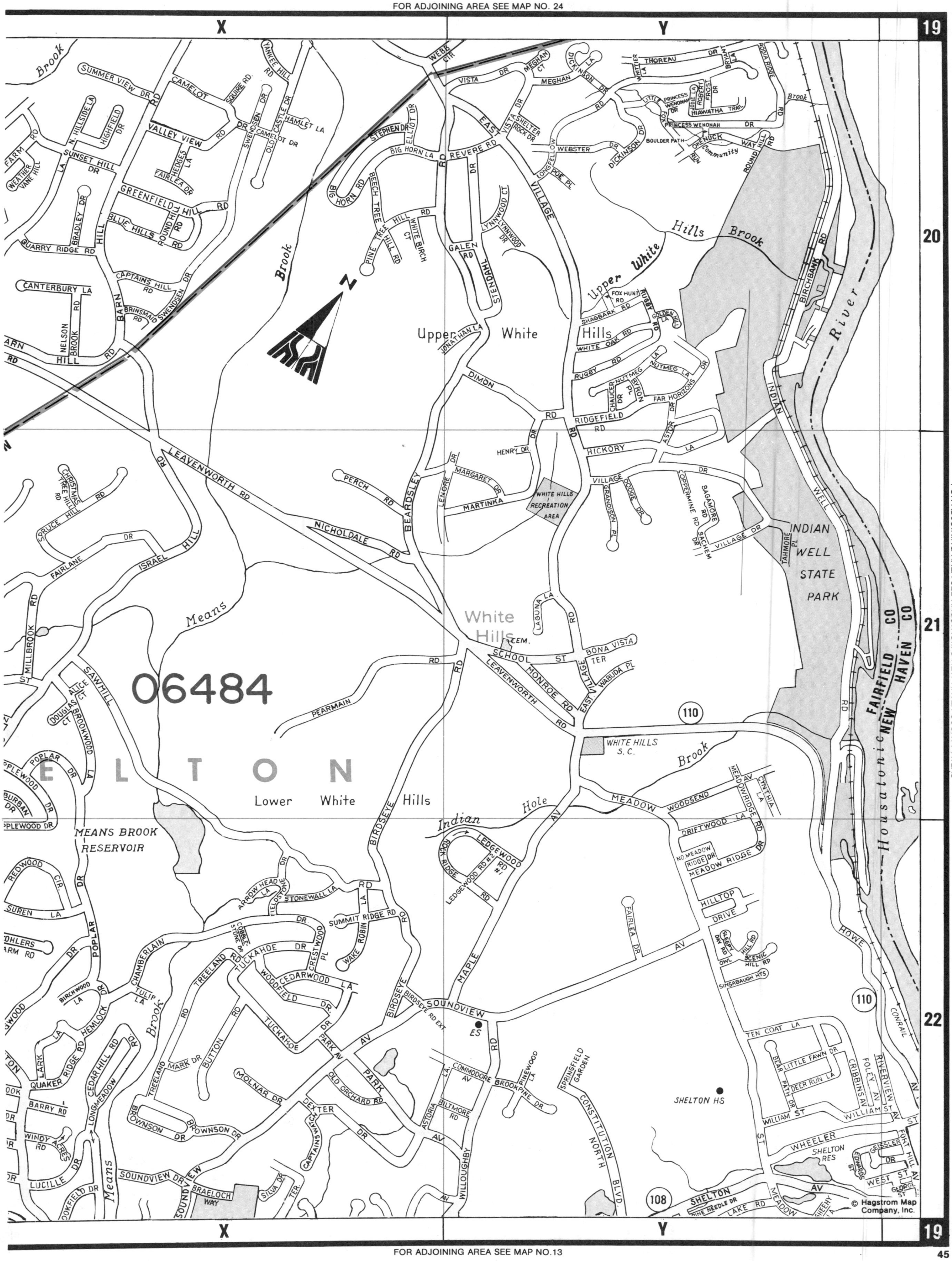

WEATHER VANE HILL LA, SUNSET HILL DR, FAIRLEA DR, HEDGES LA, BEECH TREE HILL RD, PINE TREE HILL RD, WHITE BIRCH CT, GALEN RD, LYNNWOOD CT, LYNNWOOD DR, VILLAGE RD, FOX HUNT RD, RUGBY RD, GOLDEN HILL, SHAGBARK RD, WHITE OAK RD, RUGBY RD, NUTMEG DR, NUTMEG LA, CHAUCER DR, BYRON DR, FAR HORIZONS, BRINSMAID RD, SWENDSEN DR, CAPTAINS HILL RD, BARN, NELSON RD, BROOK, CANTERBURY LA

GREENFIELD HILL RD, BLUE HILLS, ROUND HILL RD, QUARRY RIDGE RD, BRADLEY DR, BARN HILL, LEAVENWORTH RD, NICHOLDALE RD, MEANS, CHRISTMAS TREE HILL RD, SPRUCE HILL, FAIRLANE RD, ISRAEL HILL, MILLBROOK ST, SAWMILL, DOUGLAS CT, ALICE CT, BROOKWOOD DR, SUBURBAN DR, POPLAR, APPLEWOOD DR, REDWOOD CIR, SUREN LA, KOHLERS FARM RD, BIRCHWOOD DR, TULIP LA, CHAMBERLAIN, TREELAND RD, TUCKAHOE RD, WOODFIELD DR, CEDARWOOD LA, CRESTWOOD DR, WAKE ROBIN RD, SUMMIT RIDGE RD, ARROW HEAD LA, FIELDS END, STONEWALL LA, COBBLE STONE DR, BIRDSEYE RD, BIRDSEYE RD EXT, LEDGEWOOD RD, LEDGEWOOD RIDGE RD, MAPLE AV, SOUNDVIEW, MEADOW, WOODSEND, DRIFTWOOD LA, CYNTHIA, MEADOWRIDGE RD, NO MEADOW RIDGE DR, MEADOW RIDGE DR, HILLTOP DRIVE, FAIRLEA DR, SLEEPY OWL RD, SCENIC HILL RD, KELLY RD, SINSABAUGH HTS, TEN COAT LA, BEAR, LITTLE FAWN DR, DEER RUN LA, FOLEY AV, CRIBBINS AV, RIVERVIEW AV, WILLIAM ST, GEISSLER DR, FORT HILL, HOWE AV, CONRAIL

NICHOLDALE RD, BEARDSLEY RD, PERCH RD, MARGARET DR, LENORE DR, MARTINKA, HENRY DR, DIMON RD, JONATHAN LA, STENDAHL RD, RIDGEFIELD RD, HICKORY RD, DODGE DR, GRANDSON DR, ASTOR LA, COPPERMINE RD, SAGAMORE RD, SACHEM DR I, VILLAGE DR, TAHMORE PL, LAGUNA LA, CEM., SCHOOL ST, MONROE RD, EAST VILLAGE, BONA VISTA TER, WARLUDA PL, LEAVENWORTH RD, PEARMAIN, BIRDSEYE, 110, INDIAN WELL RD

MAPLE AV, PARK AV, BUTTON DR, MARK DR, MOLNAR DR, TREELAND, TUCKAHOE RD, CEDAR HILL RD, HEMLOCK, RIDGE RD, LARK LA, QUAKER, LONGMEADOW, BARRY RD, LUCILLE DR, WINDY ACRES RD, SOUNDVIEW DR, BRAELOCH WAY, SILVA DR, TER, WILLOUGHBY AV, DEXTER DR, OLD ORCHARD DR, CAPTAINS WAY, BROWNSON DR, BILTMORE RD, ASTORIA, COMMODORE AV, BROOKPINE DR, PINEWOOD LA, SPRINGFIELD GARDEN, CONSTITUTION NORTH BLVD, 108, SHELTON, PINE NEEDLE DR, LAKE RD, WHEELER, WILLIAM ST, GEORGE, WEST ST, WHEN, MEADOW

ES

Ⓗ 110   Ⓗ 108

© Hagstrom Map Company, Inc.

FOR ADJOINING AREA SEE HAGSTROM'S WESTCHESTER COUNTY ATLAS

FOR ADJOINING AREA SEE HAGSTROM'S WESTCHESTER COUNTY ATLAS

FOR ADJOINING AREA SEE MAP NO.15

20
J
K
19
20
21
WESTCHESTER
COUNTY
FAIRFIELD
COUNTY
NY
CT
PUDDIN HILL RD
SISCOWIT RESERVOIR
124
PINNEY
BARNEGAT RD
JONATHAN RD
PEQUOT LA.
PROPRIETORS CROSSING
HUNTERS CREEK LA
LOST DISTRICT DR.
ST GEORGE LA
Sellecks Corners
LOUISES LA
RD
LOGAN RD
BOWERY RD
LUKES WOOD RD
WAKEMAN RD
OGDEN RD
ROCKY NOOK RD
MICHIGAN RD
06840
123
SHERIDAN DR
CROSS RIDGE RD
JOHN D. MILNE RESERVOIR
BRISCOE RD
NORTH WILTON RD
NORTH
JENNIFER LA
RIDGE RD
GRUPES RESERVOIR
COLON
WEST RD
TURTLE BACK LA W.
TURTLE BACK LA E.
Lockwood Pd.
DANS R. H'WAY
TURTLE BACK RD
ALPINE TER
RIDGE
NEW CANAAN RES
PETERS LA
FATHER PETERS
JOHN MARSHALL PL
MICHIGAN RD
SMITH RIDGE
NORTH WILTON
Ruscoe Ridge
VALLEY
BENEDICT
NEW CANAAN
WYDENDOWN RD
Poorhouse Brook
LAUREL RD
SOUNDVIEW LA
DEEP VALLEY
River
POND VIEW LA
RAMHORNE RD
WEST HILLS RD
APPLE TREE LA
TURTLE BACK RD
OENOKE RIDGE
River
INDIAN
ROCK RD
123
Smith Ridge
HIDDEN MEADOW LA
OSBORN LA.
Silvermine
WOODRIDGE CIRCLE
DR
WOODRIDGE CIR.
WOODRIDGE DR
REEDER LA
TURTLEBACK RD. S.
COUNTRY CLUB RD
SMITH RIDGE LA
Country Club of New Canaan
SMITH RIDGE
SLEEPY HOLLOW RD
THRUSH LA
LAUREL
GRAVEL RD
IS.
VALLEY
HICKOK RD
© Hagstrom Map Company, Inc.

FOR ADJOINING AREA SEE MAP NO.16

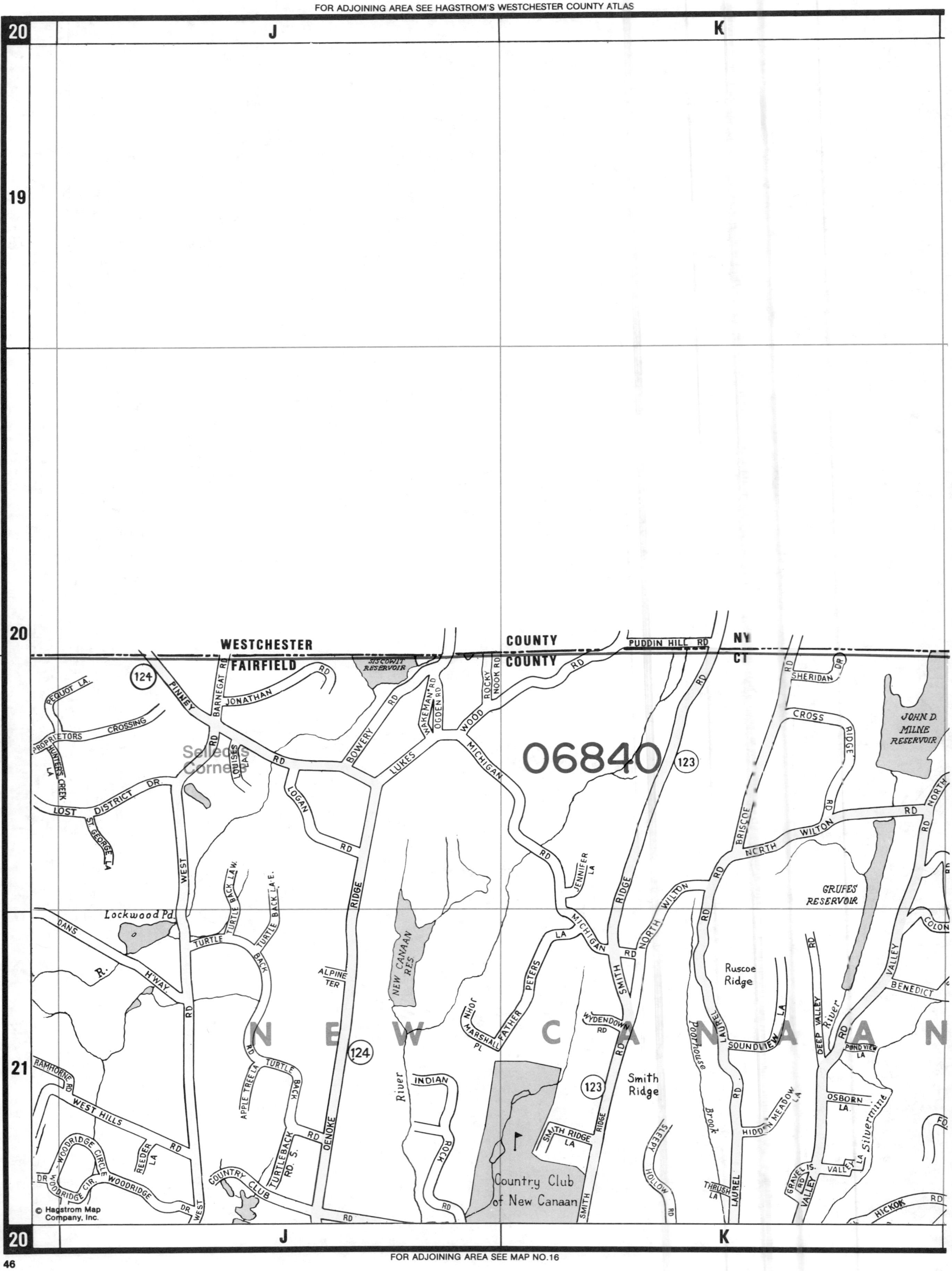

FOR ADJOINING AREA SEE MAP NO. 22

L
M
20
19
20
21
RIDGEFIELD
WILTON
NY
CT
WESTCHESTER COUNTY
FAIRFIELD COUNTY
N
06897
North Wilton
WILTON
Quarry Head Park
Bald Hill
Hendersons Pond
Kent Pond
Mullens Pond
STREETS POND
TOWN FOREST
ALLEN'S MEADOWS PARK
Wilton Riding Club
Turner Ridge
WILTON HS
MS
ES
MAIN ATHLETIC FIELD COMPLEX
COMSTOCK COMM. CTR.
HILLSIDE CEM.
MERWIN MEADOWS PARK
Y.M.C.A.
Silver Spring Cr.
Silvermine
River
Spectacle Brook
Comstock Br.
Comstock Branch
East
Mullens Br.
Comstock
Brook
Norwalk
Huckleberry Hills
Goetzen
SUGARBUSH CT
SPRING RD
SILVER SPRING RD
SCARLET OAK DR
MAYFLOWER DR
WEEBURN LA
FULLIN LA
LITTLE FLOWER LA (PVT)
LYNLEE LA
ROBIN LA
KELLOGG DR
KELLOGG HILL PL
BLUEBERRY HILL PL
WILTON WOODS RD
LONGMEADOWS RD
SNOWBERRY LA
FOX RUN
SPECTACLE LA
DEER RUN RD
FAWN PL
ANTLER LA
GILLY LA
PELHAM LA
DARK POND TR
QUARRY WAY
TURTLE HEAD
TURTLEBACK RD
TEAPOT HILL RD
WHIPSTICK RD
TITO LA
NOD HILL RD
BREED'S HILL PL
BOAS LA
RUSCOE RD
MILLSTONE RD
RIDGEFIELD RD
TANNER'S DR
GREY ROCKS RD
HICKORY HILL RD
LENOX LA
BALD HILL PL
BALD HILL RD
VISTA RD
LINDEN TREE
COACHMANS PL
NUTMEG LA
CARRIAGE DR
KEELERS RIDGE RD
HILLBROOK RD
SHAGBARK PL
BRANCH BROOK RD
LAVILLA PL
PIPER'S
MARK'S TR
CHARTER OAK RD
SPRUCE MEADOW CT
RYDERS LA
MULLENS HILL
ST. JOHNS RD
COLLINWOOD RD
CHICKEN ST
JOURNEY'S END RD
DANFORTH DR
LANTERN RIDGE RD
BALD HILL
WILDWOOD DR
WILTON RD
DE FOREST RD
GROUND PINE RD
WILLOWBROOK PL
CEM
CROFOOT RD
ABBOTT LA
ROSSIMUR CT
OLMSTEAD HILL RD
NOD HILL RD
ENGLISH DR
RIDING CLUB RD
TUPNER RIDGE CT
HEMMELSKAMP RD
WREN THICKET
SURREY GLEN
DE FOREST LA
FOREST LA
ROCKY NECK RD
ROCKY BROOK RD
SIGNAL HILL RD
SIGNAL HILL RD SO.
COMSTOCK PL
CATALPA RD
WARNCKE RD
WESTFIELD RD
WOODHILL RD
SOUTH BALD HILL RD
BOB HILL LA
EVERGREEN RD
CHEESE SPRING RD
HILL RD
SPRING
KELLY'S CT
OLD DRIFTWAY
PHEASANT RUN RD
STEWART RD
STEWART LA
MIDDLEBROOK FARMS
HIGH SCHOOL RD
TURNER LA
HUNTING RIDGE LA
HOLLOW TREE RD
HOLLOW TREE PL
LEDGEWOOD DR
THAYER POND LA
STONECROP LA
MARVIN RIDGE PL
HIDDEN LAKE RIDGE
WALNUT PL
MICHAEL LA
KNOLLWOOD LA
FOX RUN RD
MARIOMI RD
BROOK RD
THAYER POND RD
WOODLAND PL
EVANS LA
HIGHVIEW DR
GLEN HILL RD
DRUM HILL RD
CIDER MILL PL
KICHDALE DR
SCHOOL RD N.
DANBURY RD
NORWALK RD
PIMPEWAUG RD
BRIARDALE PL
33
7
© Hagstrom Map Company, Inc.

FOR ADJOINING AREA SEE MAP NO.21

FOR ADJOINING AREA SEE MAP NO.16

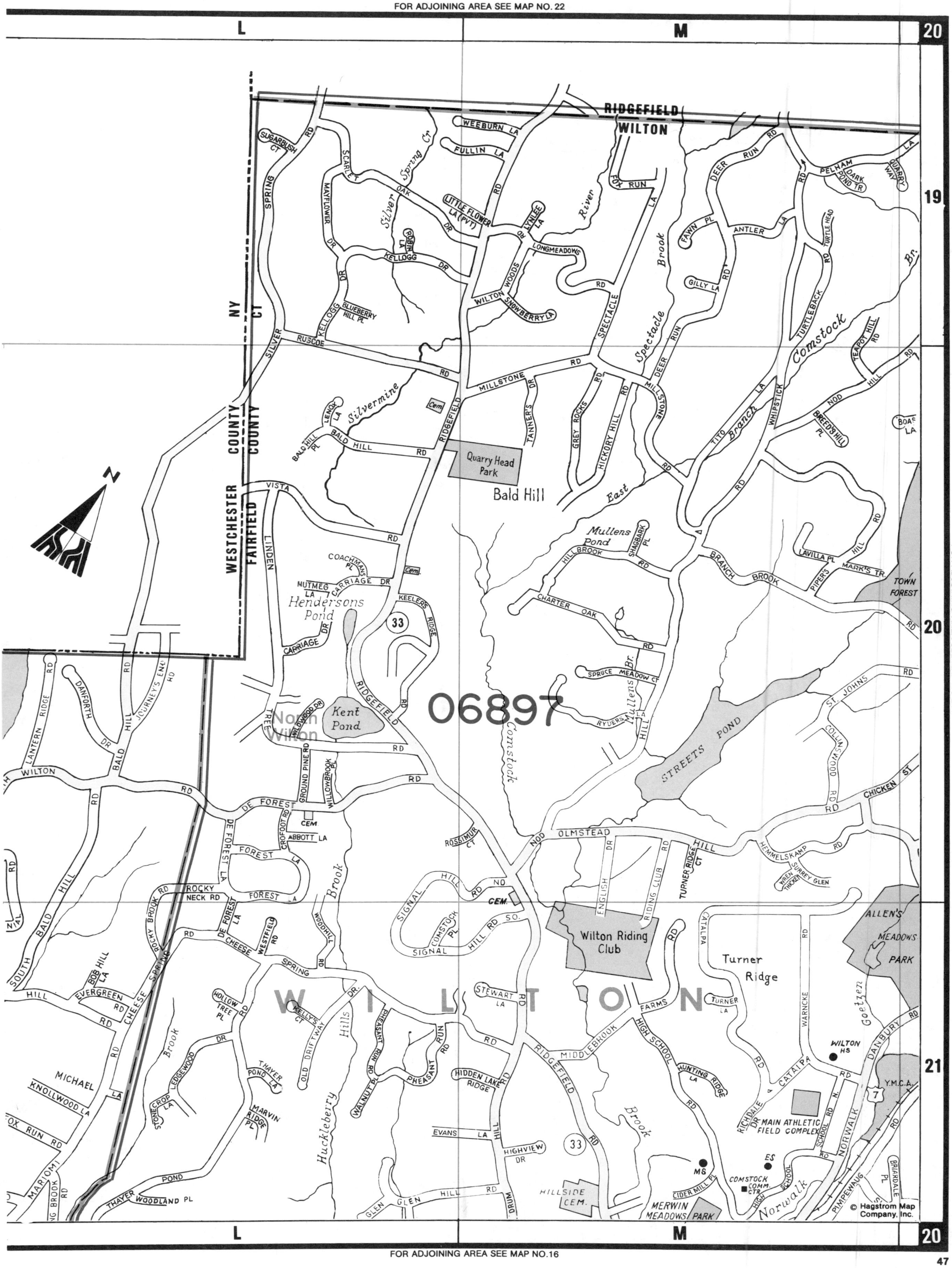

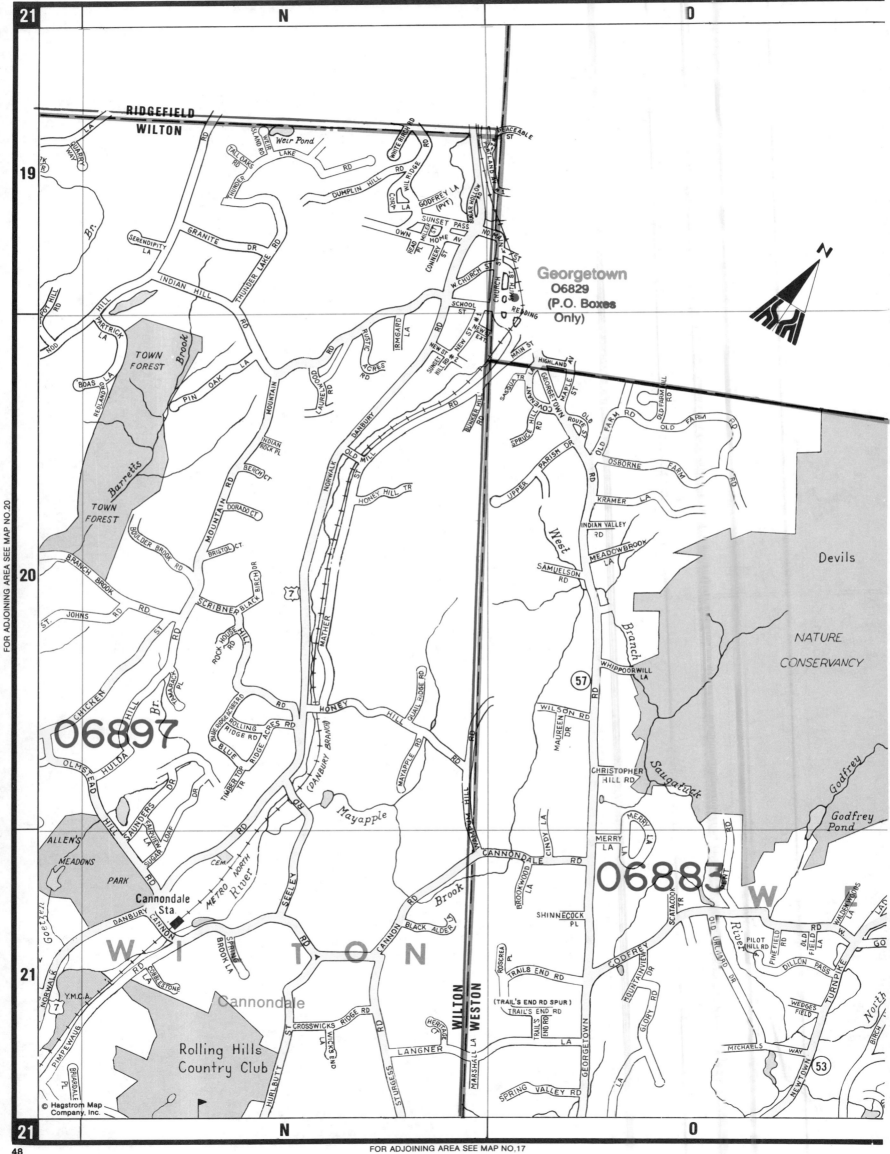

N

O

RIDGEFIELD
WILTON

Weir Pond

Georgetown
06829
(P.O. Boxes
Only)

N

TOWN
FOREST

Brook

TOWN
FOREST

Barretts

20

Devils

NATURE

CONSERVANCY

06897

57

Saugatuck

Godfrey

Godfrey
Pond

06883

Mayapple

River

Brook

ALLEN'S
MEADOWS
PARK

Cannondale
Sta.

W I L T O N

WILTON
WESTON

W   E

S

Rolling Hills
Country Club

Cannondale

Y.M.C.A.

7

(TRAIL'S END RD SPUR)
TRAIL'S END RD

North

53

© Hagstrom Map
Company, Inc.

N

O

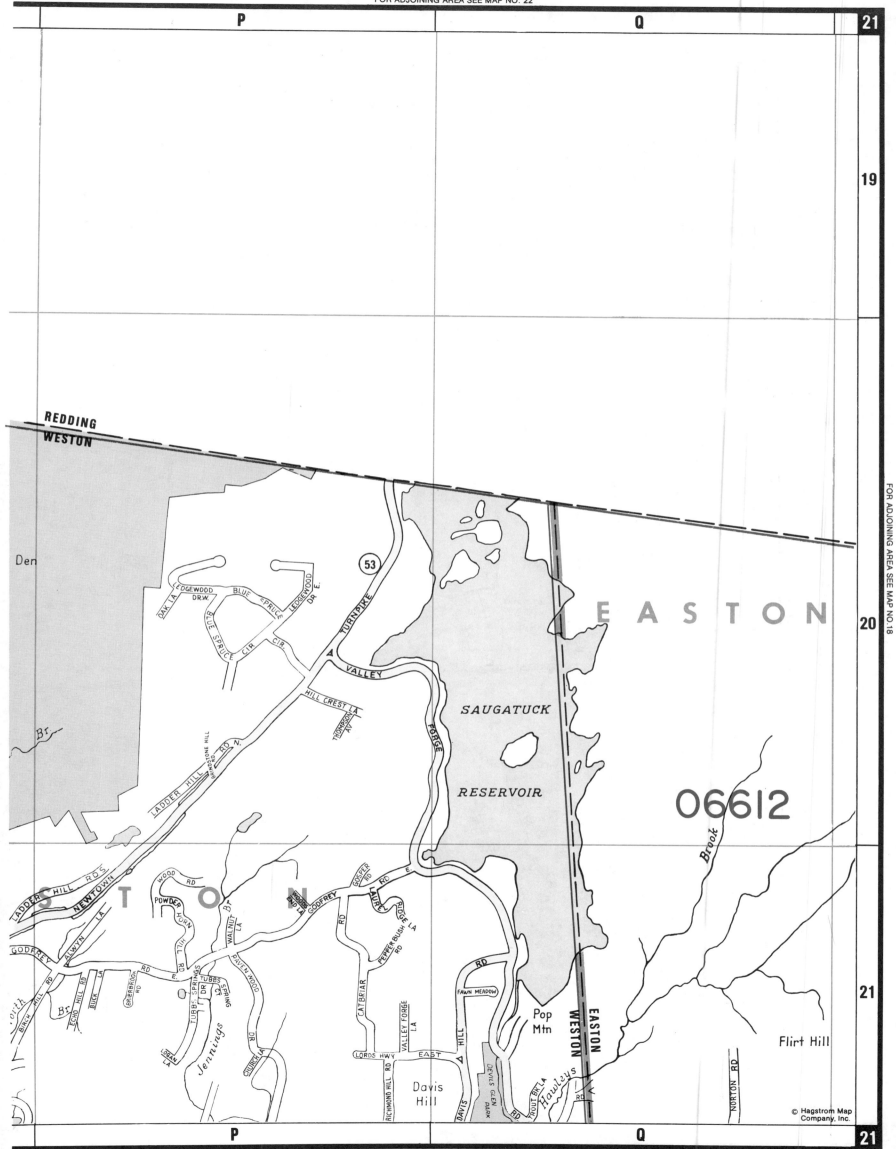

P   Q   21

19

REDDING
WESTON

Den

53

EASTON

LEDGEWOOD DR.W.
OAK LA.
BLUE SPRUCE
LEDGEWOOD DR. E.
BLUE SPRUCE CIR.
BLUE SPRUCE CIR.

TURNPIKE

VALLEY

HILL CREST LA.
THOMPSON AV.

LADDER HILL RD. N.
GRINDSTONE HILL

FORGE

SAUGATUCK

RESERVOIR

06612

Br.

20

LADDER HILL RD.

NEWTOWN
WESTON
LADDER HILL RDS.
WOOD RD.
POWDER HORN HILL RD.
WALNUT LA.
WOODS END LA.
GODFREY RD.
GOSPER RD.
LAUREL RD. E.
PEPPER BUSH LA.

GODFREY
ALLWYN LA.
BUCK LA.
BRIERBROOK RD.
ECHO HILL RD.
BIRCH HILL RD.
North Br.
TUBBS SPRINGS DR.
TUBBS SPRING CT.
RAVEN WOOD
DR.
CHURCH LA.
LOGAN LA.
Jennings
CATBRIAR
VALLEY FORGE LA.
RICHMOND HILL RD.
LORDS HWY.
EAST
Davis
Hill
DAVIS HILL RD.
FAWN MEADOW
DEVILS GLEN PARK
Pop
Mtn
TROUT BK LA.
EASTON
WESTON
Hawleys
RD. LA.

Brook

Flirt Hill

NORTON RD.

© Hagstrom Map
Company, Inc.

21

P   Q   21

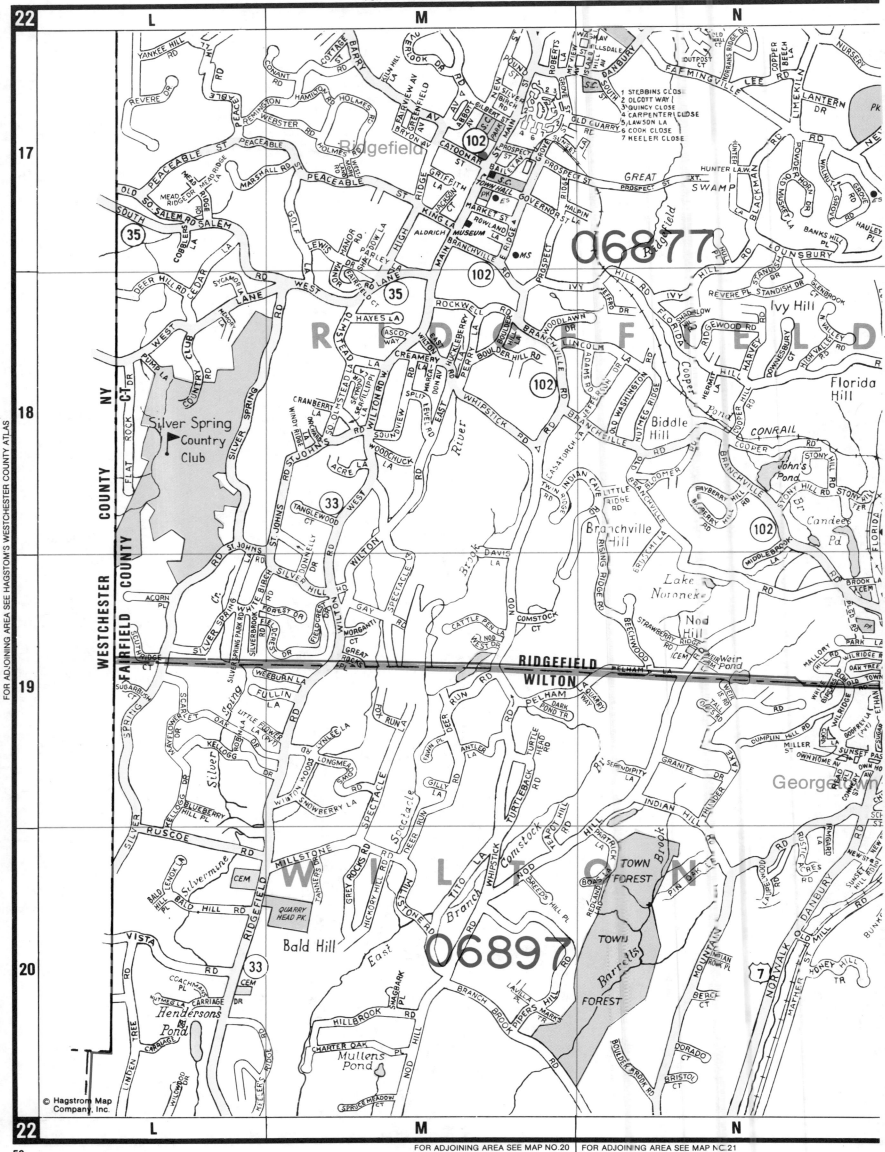

O P Q 22

ROLLING HILLS RD
WHITEWOOD HOLLOW CT
FIRE HILL LA
RIVERSIDE DR
LONGVIEW DR
DRUID LA
OLD STONE CT
BOBBY'S CT
ROCK LEDGE RD
PICKETT RD
SIMPAUG TPKE
METRO NORTH TPKE
STATION RD
SIDE CUT RD
REDDING RD
LIMEKILN RD
ROB RIDER RD
WHORTLEBERRY RD
COSTA LA
MARCHANT RD
Brook
53
GALLOWS HILL RD
EAST FARM LA
LOST MINE PL
FULLING MILL LA
GRIFFIN HILL
Umpawaug Pond
CHALBURN CLOSE
CHESTNUT WOODS RD
Huckleberry Swamp
GUARDHOUSE DR
BRICK SCHOOL DR
KIMBERLY DR
COSTA LA
MOUN
SAUNDERS
CAINS HILL RD
TOPSTONE RD
ALLEN HIGHWAY
CHALBURN RD
BAYBERY LA
TOPSTONE
Topstone Mtn.
Steichens Ponds
JEREMIAH SANFORD RD
Pond
Saugatuck
TANNERY HILL
DRUMMER RD
RD
17

RICHARDSON DR
ASHBEE LA
WILKINSON RD
7
Topstone
TOP LEDGE RD
SIMPAUG
TOPSTONE PARK
Blackmans
Umpawaug Hill
RIDGE RD
WH BIRCH RD
DUCK RUN RD
MARLI LA
LOUNSBURY LA
Millers Pond
ETHAN ALLEN HIGHWAY
OLD SERGEANT'S LA
OLD REDDING RD
REDDING RD
FIRE TOWER RD
BARRETT LA
GRANITE RD
ARCHERS LA
UMPAWAUG RD
Cem.
MS RD
BEAUILES RD
OLD STAGECOACH RD
WINDING BROOK LA
WINDING BROOK CT
OAK LA
ES
GREAT
18

HICKORY LA
RD
FLORIDA LA
LAUREL HILL RD
ES
METRO NORTH (Danbury Branch)
MOUNTAIN LAUREL LA
SEVENTY ACRE RD
MINE HILL RD
Fire Lookout
Windy Hill
DIAMOND HILL RD
FOX RUN RD
Br.
MARK TWAIN RD
HILL RD
GREAT PASTURE RD
DAN BEARD LA
LONETOWN RD
Redding Center
TOWN HALL
CEM.
R E D D I N G
Brook
INDIAN HILL RD
MALLORY LA
Moffitts
06896
Diamond Hill
107
MAILCOACH RD
DEER HILL RD
SHADY LA
CEM.
DRY RIVER CT
19

Branchville
DEPOT RD
ETHAN ALLEN HWY
Branchville Sta.
PINE MOUNTAIN RD
HILLSIDE LA
Pecks Pd
PEACEABLE RD
PINE MOUNTAIN RD
BENNETT ST
PARSONS RD
UMPAWAUG RD
LOCKWOOD RD
LITTLE BOSTON RD
APPLE LA
Br
Crook
MORRILL RD
LEE LA
DAYTON RD
GLEN HILL RD
Br
GLEN RD
Redding Glen
TURNPIKE
HEMLOCK TR
SHERMAN TPKE

SUGAR HOLLOW RD
ETHAN ALLEN HWY
PORTLAND HILL RD
Gilbert
Perrys Pd
BLUEBERRY HILL RD
107
CONNARY LA
GOODSELL HILL RD
BEEHOLM RD
FARM RD
Nob
REDDING RD
WAYSIDE RD
DORETHY RD
Huckleberry Hill
ORCHARD RD
Crook
LEDGEWOOD RD
Nob
SAUGATUCK
OLD DIAMOND RD
TUDOR RD
NEWTOWN TPKE

PORTLAND RD
Factory Pond
NO MALL
BROOKSIDE
REDDING AV
CHURCH ST
MAIN ST
06829
(P.O. Boxes only)
Gilbert Hill
FARVIEW FARM RD
JOHN APPLEGATE RD
FARVIEW RD
THANKFUL BRADLEY RD
Goodsell Hill
COVERLY RD
53
RES.

NEW ST
SCHOOL ST
SASQUA TR
COVENANT LA
GEORGE TOWN RD
OLD FARM RD
OLD FARM HILL RD
REDDING
WESTON
EASTON

UPPER PARISH DR
SPRUCE
57
KRAMER LA
OSBORNE FARM RD
W E S T O N
NEWTOWN TPKE
20

INDIAN VALLEY RD
DEVILS DEN NATURE CONSERVANCY
06883
SAMUELSON RD
MEADOWBROOK LA

© Hagstrom Map Company, Inc.

O P Q 22

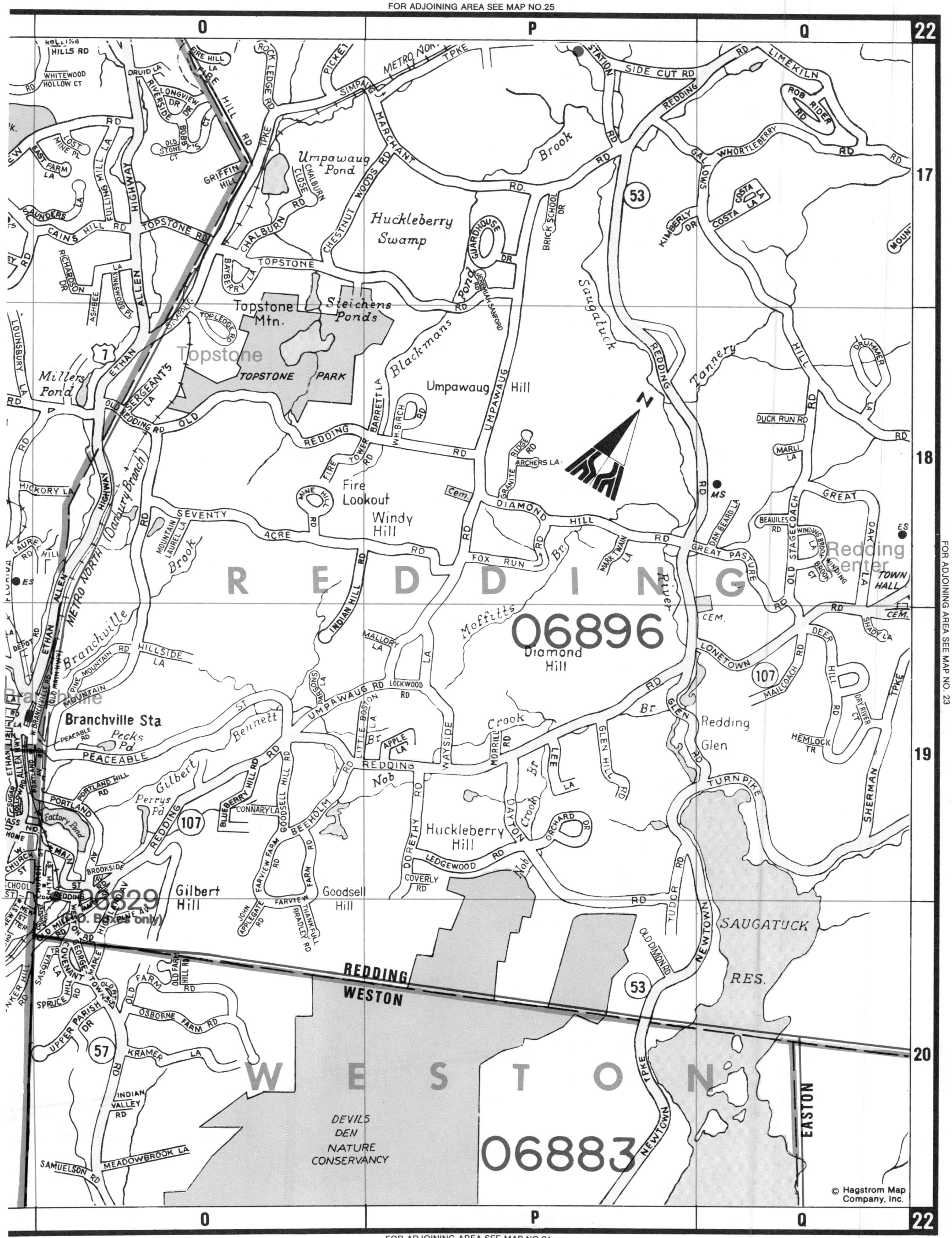

FOR ADJOINING AREA SEE MAP NO. 23

23

P   Q   R

BETHEL
REDDING

17

58

Putnam Lake

PUTNAM MEMORIAL STATE PARK

Brook

SIDE CUT RD

LIMEKILN RD

ROB RIDER RD

53

MARCHANT

STATION RD

REDDING RD

GALLOWS HILL RD

WHORTLEBERRY

BRICK SCHOOL DR

KIMBERLY DR

COSTA LA

MOUNTAINVIEW

OVERLOOK LA

RIDGEWOOD DR

CEM

PUTNAM

07

BARTRAM DR

OVERLOOK AV

PUTNAM AV

MUSKET LA

BLACK ROCK

PARK RD

POCAHONTAS

WAGON WHEEL

RED COAT LA

VAN CAMPEN LA

WILLIAMS RD

SUNSET HILL

BIRNAM WOOD RD

DODD

PUTNAM HILL DR

58

PHEASANT RIDGE

OLD PHEASANT RIDGE RD

SUNNY VIEW DR

Couch Hill

SUNSET HILL RD

Saugatuck

Tannery Brook

UMPANYWAUG

Brook

DRUMMER LA

Redding Country Club

LONETOWN RD

JOHN READ RD

DAHLIA LA

18

R E D D I N G

DUCK RUN RD

MARLI LA

GREAT

NEWELL RD

DEACON ABBOTT RD

DEACON ABBOTT RD S.

OLD FIELD

HIGH RIDGE RD

HIGH RIDGE RD

LITTLE RIVER LA

SULLIVAN

MIDDLEBROOK

HOPEWELL

TPKE

Five Points

58

DIAMOND HILL RD

ARCHERS LA

WHITE RIDGE RD

DAN BEARD LA

MARK TWAIN LA

MS

BEAUILES RD

OLD STAGECOACH RD

WINDING BROOK CT

OAK LA

ES

Redding Center

TOWN HALL

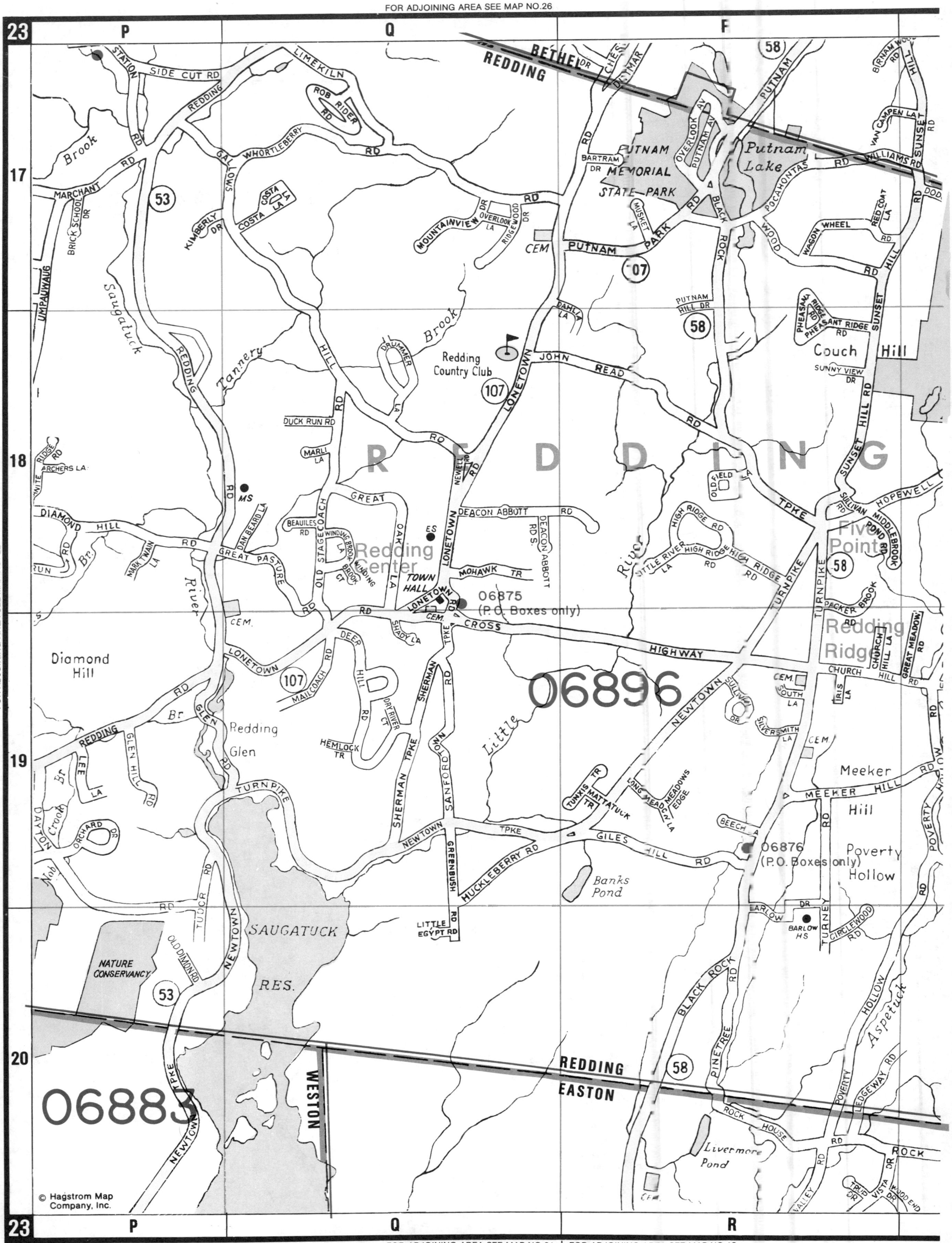

LONETOWN RD

MOHAWK TR

06875
(P.O. Boxes only)

River

CHURCH HILL

CEM

IRIS LA

CHURCH SOUTH LA

SILVERSMITH LA

Redding Ridge

GREAT MEADOW

Diamond Hill

GREAT PASTURE

CEM

LONETOWN RD

DEER RD

SHADY LA

LONETOWN TPKE

CROSS

HIGHWAY

06896

NEWTOWN

SULLIVAN DR

CEM

19

REDDING RD

GLEN HILL RD

LEE LA

GLEN BR

Redding Glen

107

MAILCOACH RD

HEMLOCK TR

DRY RIVER CT

SHERMAN TPKE

SANFORD

Little River

NEWTOWN

Meeker Hill

MEEKER HILL RD

BEECH LA

06876
(P.O. Boxes only)

Poverty Hollow

POVERTY RD

CROOK BR

DAYTON

ORCHARD DR

NOB

TURNPIKE

NEW TOWN TPKE

GREENBUSH RD

HUCKLEBERRY RD

GILES HILL RD

Banks Pond

TUNXIS TR

MATTATUCK TR

LONG MEADOWS

MEADOWS EDGE

BARLOW DR

BARLOW HS

CIRCLEWOOD RD

TURNEY

BLACK ROCK RD

SAUGATUCK RES.

TUDOR RD

OLD DIMOND RD

Nature Conservancy

53

LITTLE EGYPT RD

PINETREE RD

POVERTY HOLLOW RD

LEDGEWAY RD

Aspetuck

20

06883

NEWTOWN TPKE

WESTON

REDDING
EASTON

58

ROCK HOUSE RD

Livermore Pond

VALLEY RD

VISTA DR

WOOD END

CEM

© Hagstrom Map Company, Inc.

23

P   Q   R

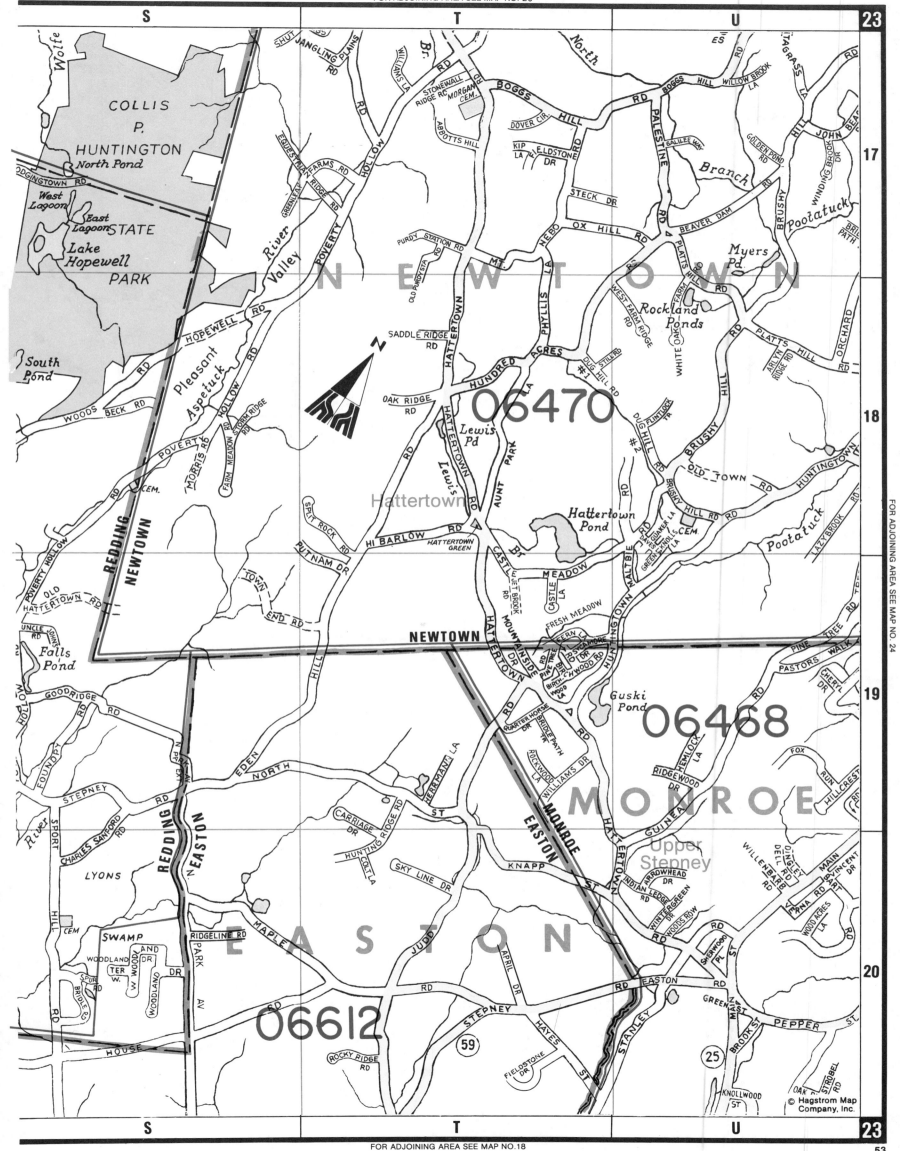

06470

06468

06612

MONROE

NEWTOWN

EASTON

REDDING

Upper Stepney

Hattertown

COLLIS P. HUNTINGTON STATE PARK

Lake Hopewell

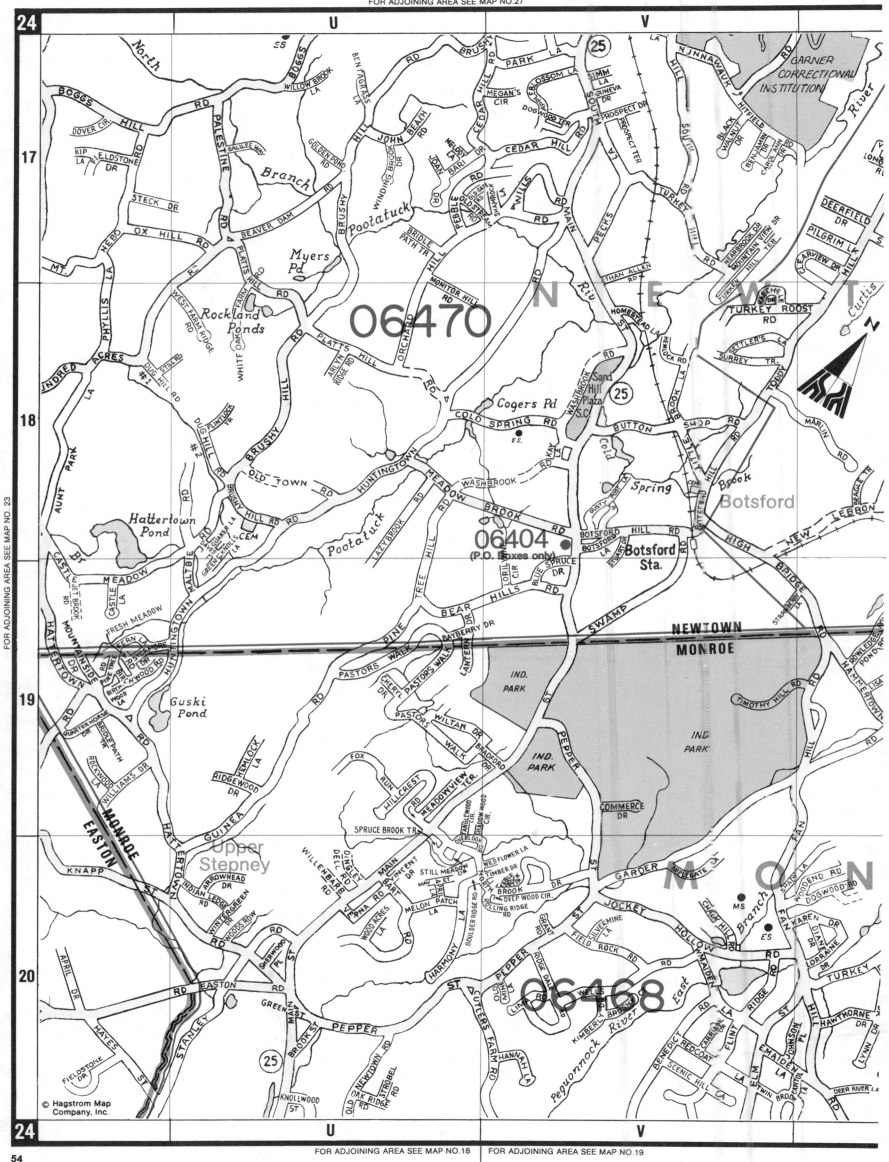

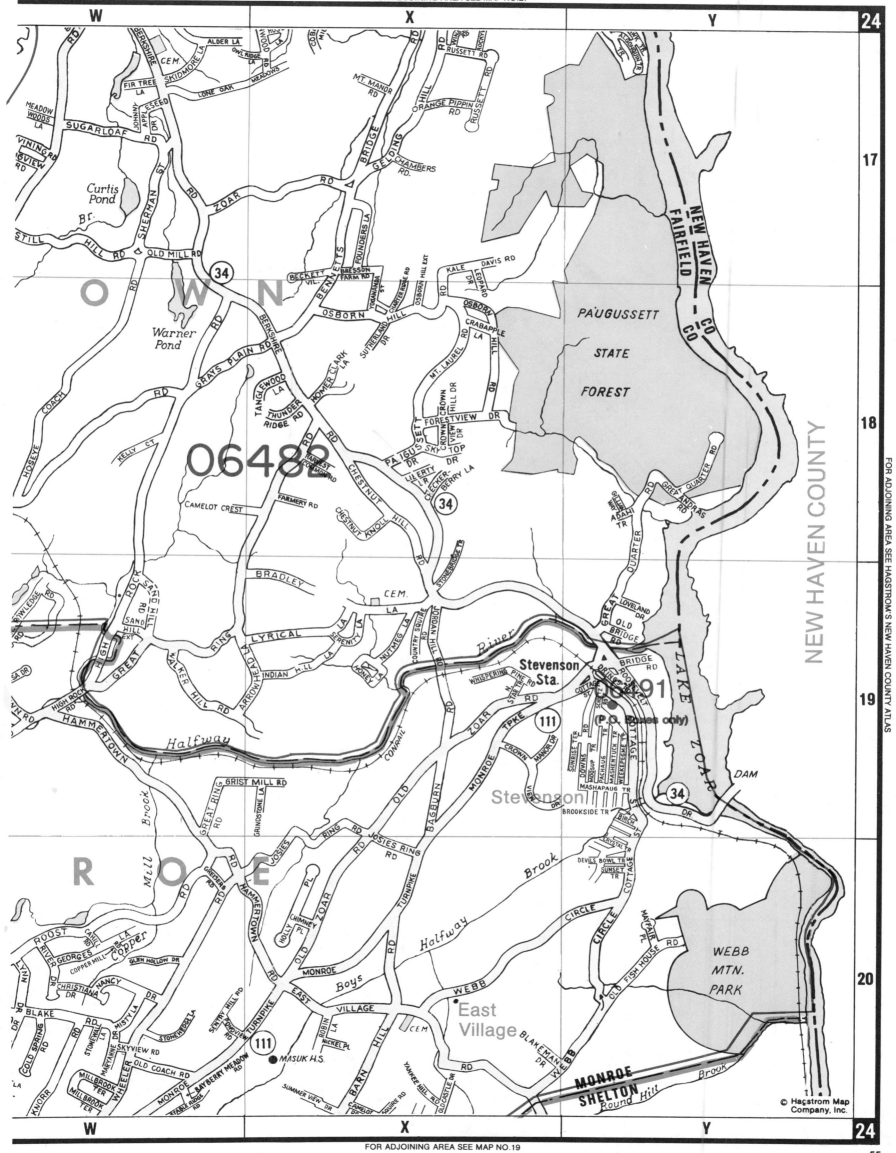

FOR ADJOINING AREA SEE HAGSTROM'S WESTCHESTER COUNTY ATLAS

FOR ADJOINING AREA SEE HAGSTROM'S WESTCHESTER COUNTY ATLAS

25
L
M
N
14
15
16
17
WESTCHESTER
COUNTY
WESTCHESTER COUNTY
FAIRFIELD COUNTY
NY
CO
N
RIDGEFIELD
Ridgefield
Ridgebury
06877
Scott Ridge
Ridgebury Mtn
Ned Mountain
Round Mtn
MAMANASCO LAKE
Round Lake
Pierrepont Lake
Fox Hill Lake
Taylors Pond
SETH LOW PIERREPONT ST. PK.
Richardson Park
RIDGEFIELD HS
Sachem Hill Field
PUMPING STATION SWAMP
Titicus
Mopus Br.
(Hidden Lake) Turtle Pond
COPP'S HILL COMMON
S.C. TOWN HALL
WEST MOUNTAIN RD
OLD WEST MOUNTAIN RD
SPRING VALLEY RD
RIDGEBURY RD
NO. SALEM RD
MOPUS BRIDGE RD
OLD SIB RD
BARLOW MOUNTAIN RD
DANBURY RD
OSCALETA RD
PEACEABLE ST
MAIN ST
CATOONAH ST
PROSPECT ST
102
116
35
1 STEBBINS CLOSE
2 OLCOTT WAY
3 QUINCY CLOSE
4 CARPENTER CLOSE
5 LAWSON LA
6 COOK CLOSE
7 KEELER CLOSE
© Hagstrom Map Company, Inc.

FOR ADJOINING AREA SEE MAP NO. 22

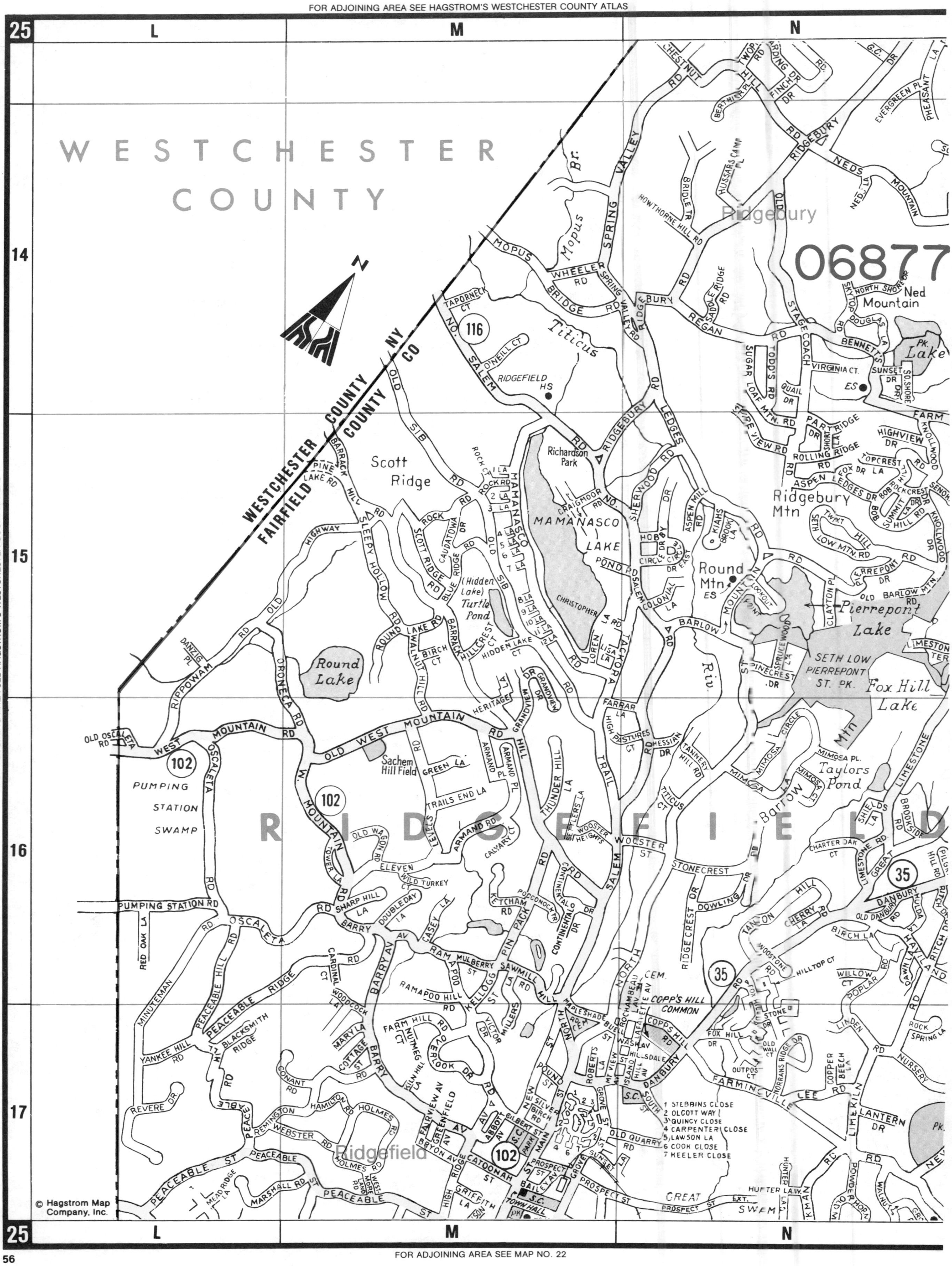

25
0 P Q

14

DANBURY

DANBURY MUNICIPAL AIRPORT

DANBURY FAIR MALL

Miry Brook

Spruce Mtn

Moses Mtn

MOUNTAIN

Thomas Mtn

Tarrywile Lake

Pine Mtn

Windwing

Wataba Lake (Rainbow Lake)

Bennett Ponds

WOOSTER STATE PARK

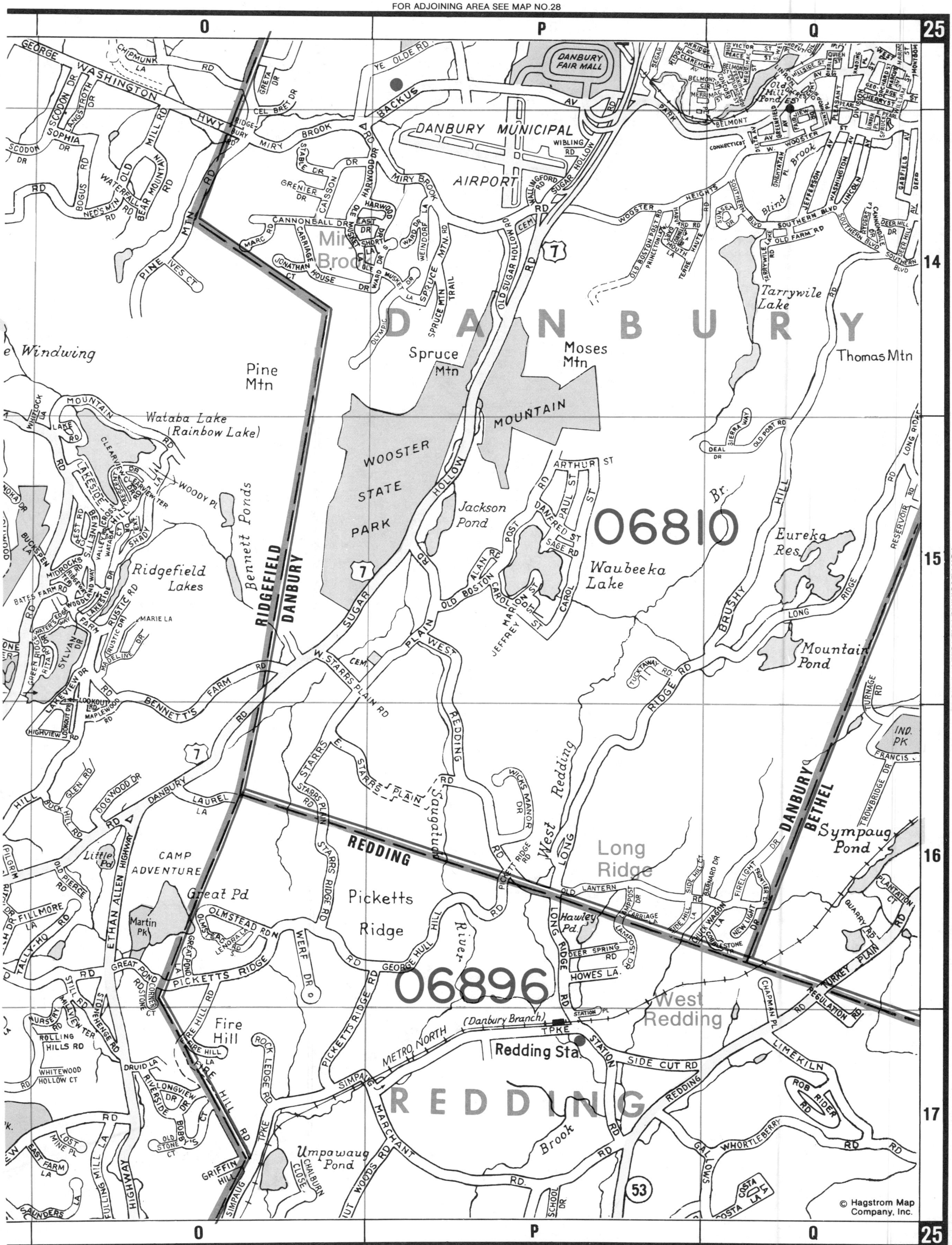

Ridgefield Lakes

Jackson Pond

06810

Waubeeka Lake

Eureka Res.

Mountain Pond

15

RIDGEFIELD
DANBURY

W. Starrs Plain Rd

Camp Adventure

Great Pd

Little Pd

Martin Pk

Picketts Ridge

06896

West Redding

REDDING

Long Ridge

Hawley Pd.

DANBURY
BETHEL

Sympaug Pond

IND. PK

16

Fire Hill

Umpawaug Pond

Redding Sta.

(Danbury Branch)

METRO NORTH

West Redding

R E D D I N G

53

17

25
0 P Q

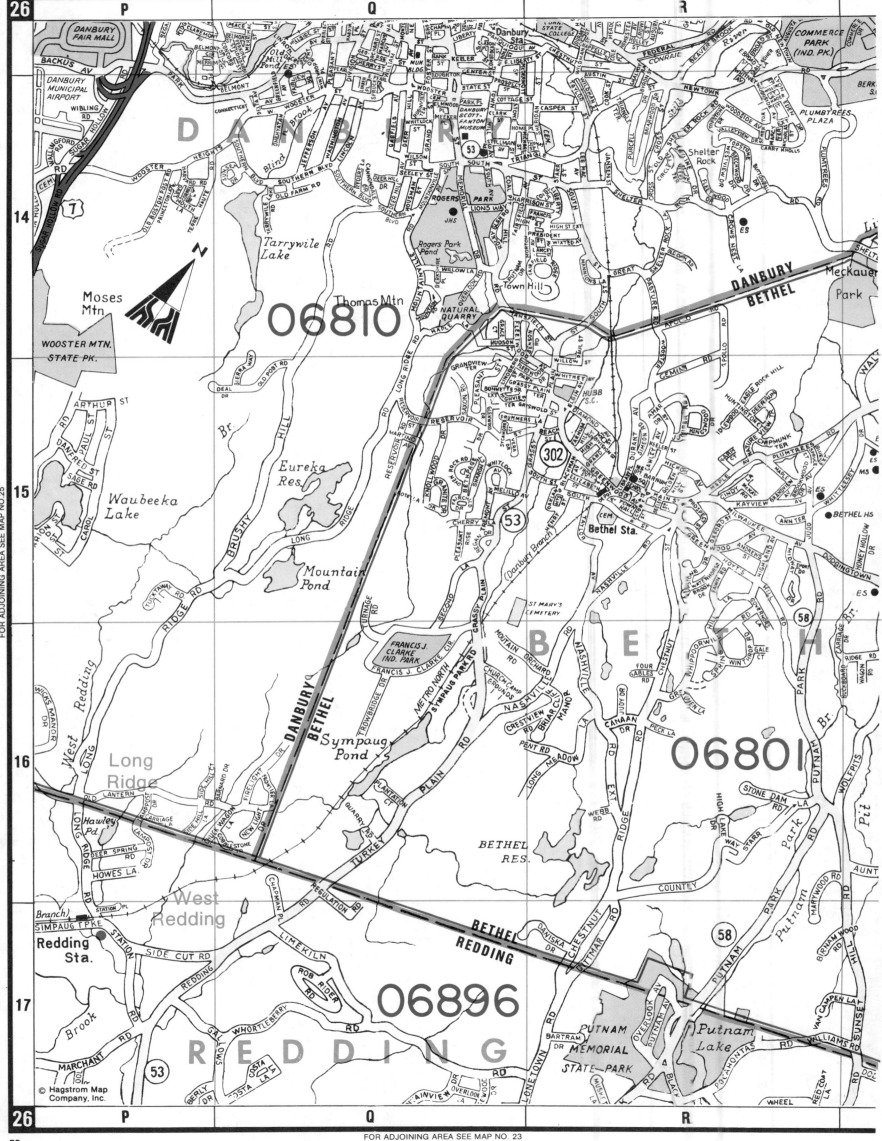

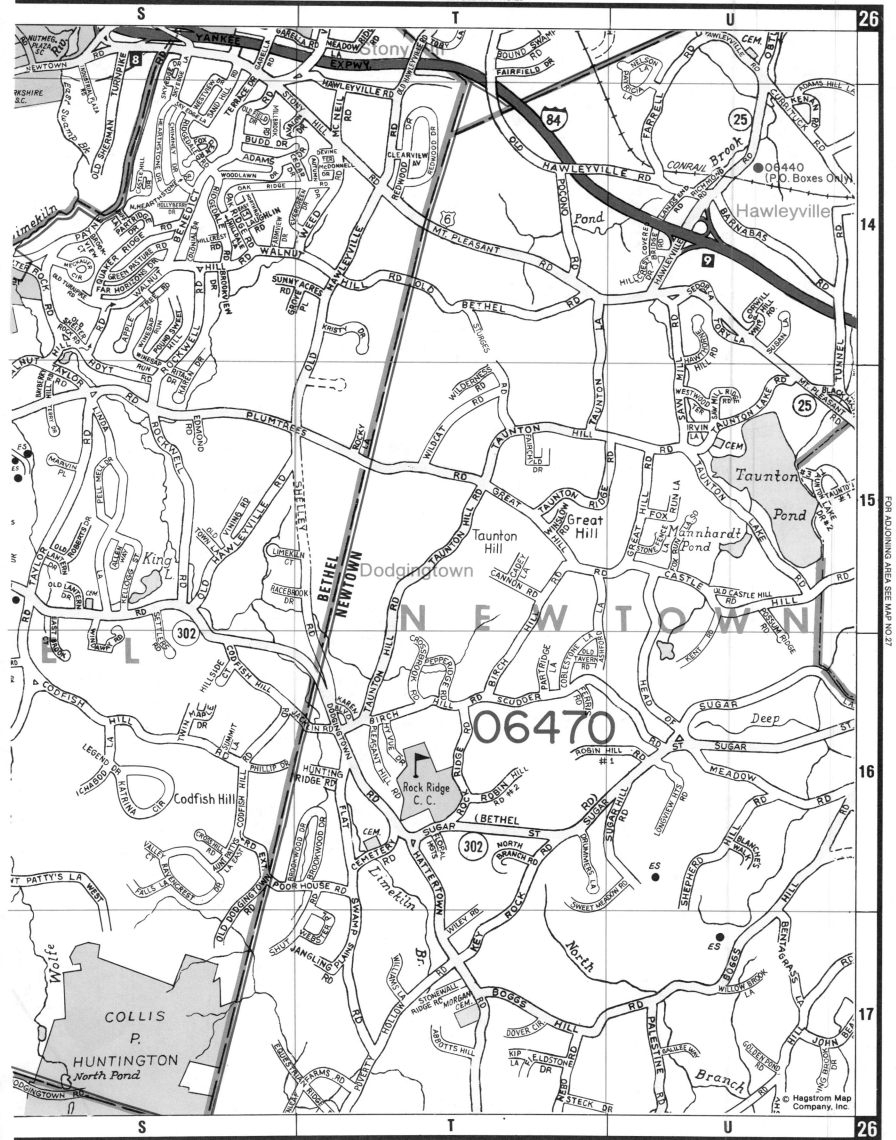

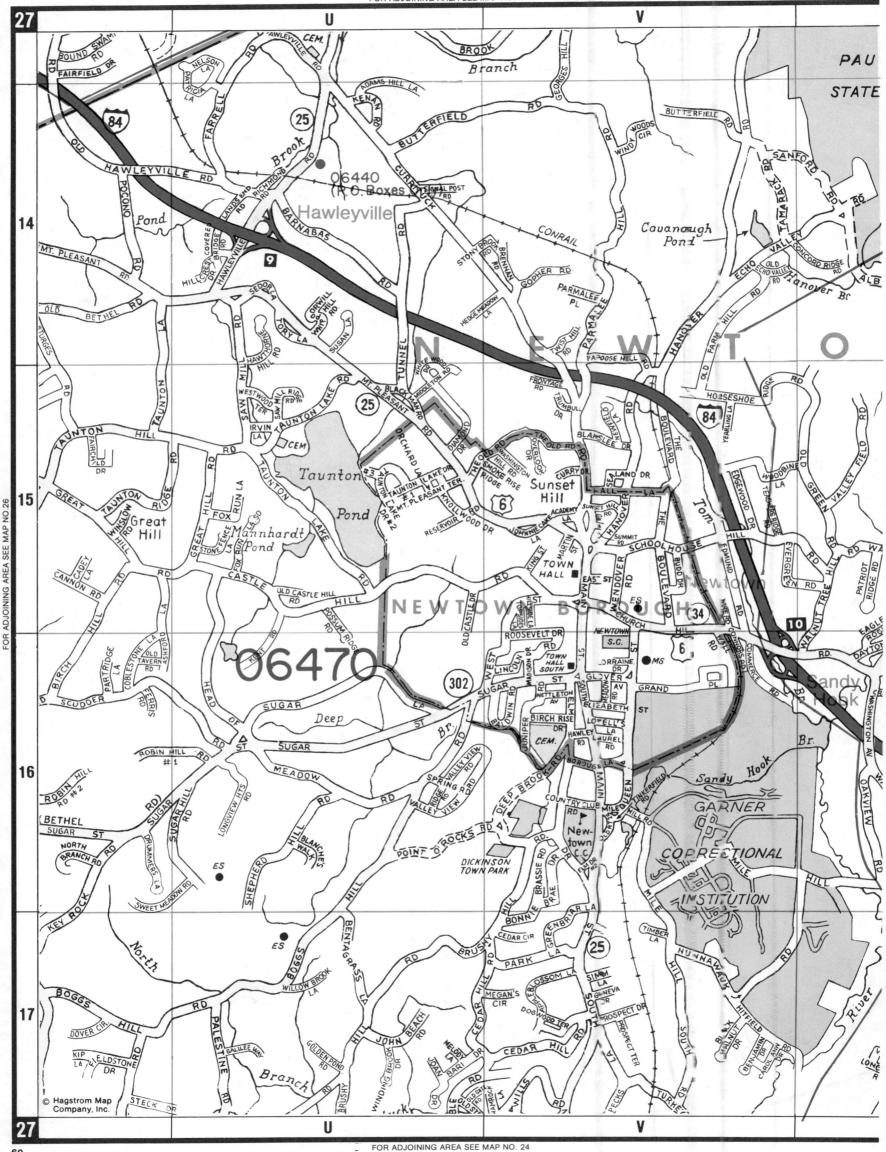

W X Y **27**

NEW HAVEN

COUNTY

14

IGUSSET

E FOREST

LAKE LILLINONAH

SHEPAUG DAM

Housatonic

Shady Rest

HOUSATONIC

PINE PERAUG

OVERLOOK KNOLL

DEER TR

SHEPAUG RD

SHADY REST RD

ANTRES AV

MAC CIRCLE

TENDIE CIRCLE

HILL RD

LESTER RD

CROWS NEST LA

THOMAS LA

FORD

ANTLER PINE

ACORN DR

HILL RD

ROLLING MEADOWS LA

BLACK BRIDGE RIDGE

FARM FIELD RIDGE

WALNUT TREE HILL

BRIDGE END FARM LA

RIVERS EDGE RD

WALNUT LA

HICKORY LA

15

WALNUT

GLEN ST PARK

GLEN RD

ROCKY GLEN RD

PINE S

ST

OAK DR

LINDEN DR

MAPLE DR

SPRUCE DR

BUTTON BALL DR

CEM

BEECH

FLEETWOOD

FAR VIEW

ROSE LAKE

BROOK DR

MAPLEWOOD

CALICO TR

N

SUNNY VIEW TER

JOHNSON DR

CHERRY HTS

CHERRY

BLACK CHERRY LA

GOODYEAR RD

NARRAGANSETT

TIMBER MILL RD

POOTATUCK

MOCCASIN

NURO

CRICKET TR

TOMAHAWK TR

QUAIL TR

CHIPMUNK TR

BRIDGE DR

Pootatuck Park

CENTER ST

RD

WATERVICH DR

FAIRFIELD CO NEW HAVEN CO

Riverside

Crestwood DR

Dickenson DR

ES

TREADWELL PARK

CHIMNEY SWIFT RD

JO MAR DR

PHILO CURTIS

RIVERSIDE RD

RD

BANCROFT RD

UNDERHILL RD

FOREST

BERKSHIRE

ENGLESIDE RD

EAGLE DR

CAPITOL

PARK RD

CLOVER RD

16

6

11

34

84

WASHINGTON AV

NEWTOWN HS

BRIDGE RD

06482

ELANA LA

BISHOP CIR

POLE RD

JEREMIAH

BRISTLE LA

BRANDYWINE LA

FOX HOLLOW LA

MORGAN DR

RD

SWEETBRIAR LA

THE CLEARING

LAKEVIEW TER

River

Cedarhurs

CEDARHURST

MOHAWK TR

ALGONQUIN TR

OLD MILE HILL RD

BERKSHIRE CEM

MISTY VALE RD

ALDER LA

SKIDMORE LA

ROSE

FANNYWOOD RD

COBBLERS

MILL RUN

OWL RIDGE LA

MEADOWS

RD

MT. MANOR RD

ORANGE PIPPIN RD

RUSSETT RD

RUSSETT RD

ROCKYWOOD DR

PAUGUSSETT STATE FOREST

17

FIR TREE LA

MEADOW WOODS LA

SUGARLOAF

HILL RD

APPLESEED DR

LONE OAK

VINING RD

GVIEW RD

TODDY

AN ST RD

Curtis Pond

ZOAR RD

BRIDGE

BENNETTS

GELDING RD

CHAMBERS RD

© Hagstrom Map Company, Inc.

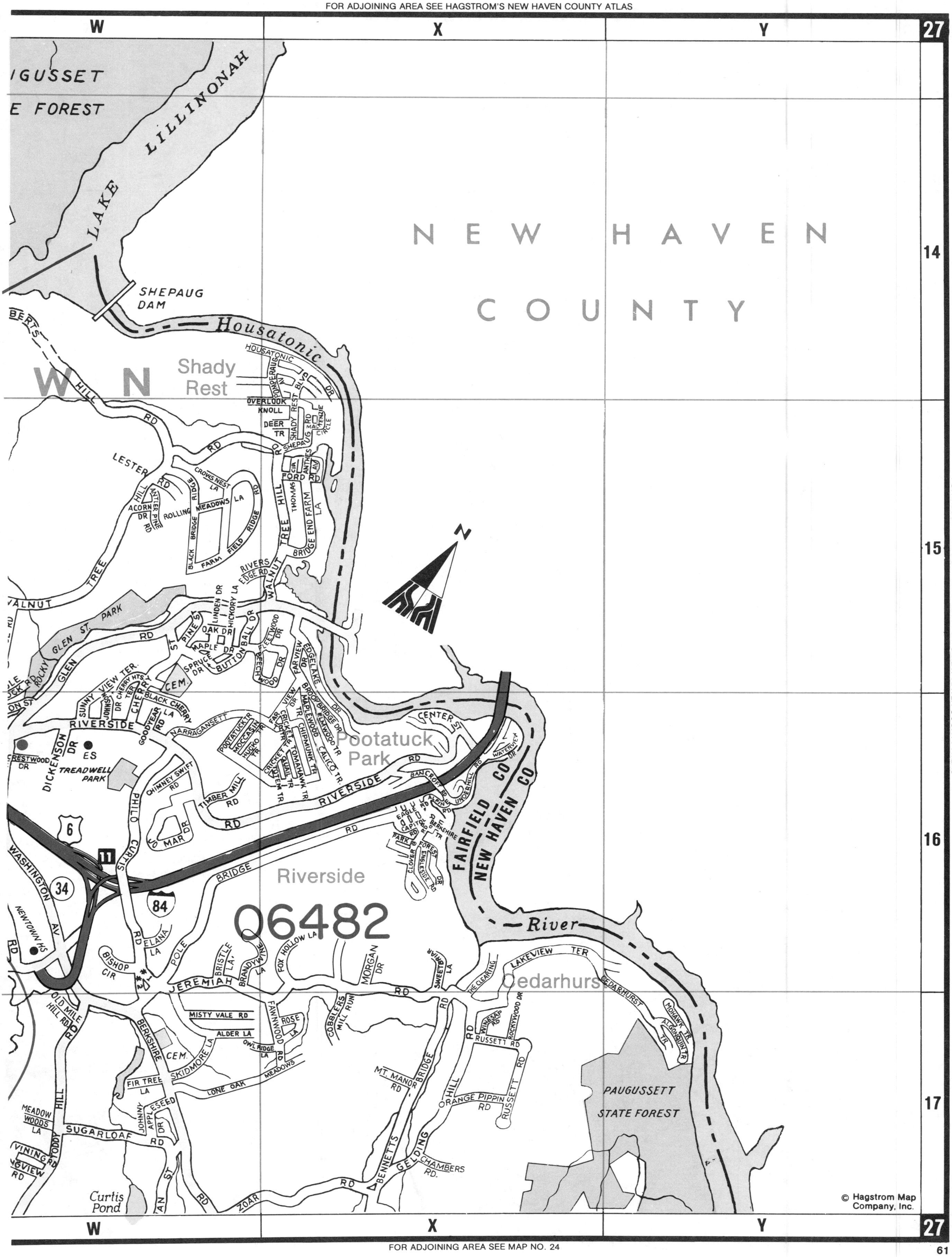

W X Y **27**

FOR ADJOINING AREA SEE HAGSTROM'S DUTCHESS/PUTNAM COUNTIES ATLAS

FOR ADJOINING AREA SEE HAGSTROM'S WESTCHESTER COUNTY ATLAS | FOR ADJOINING AREA SEE HAGSTROM'S DUTCHESS/PUTNAM COUNTIES ATLAS

28
N
O
P
11
12
13
PUTNAM COUNTY
PUTNAM COUNTY NY
FAIRFIELD COUNTY CT
WESTCHESTER COUNTY NY
DANBURY
RIDGEFIELD
RIDGEFIELD
06877
Ridgebury
Boggs Pond
Stanley Lasker Richter Memorial Park and Municipal Golf Course
Farrington's Pond
Sanfords Pond
WEST LAKE RESERVOIR
Sawmill Riv.
REST AREA
KENOSIA LAKE
Ridgefield Golf Course
CEM.
LAKE AV EXT. CEMETERY
ORCHARD IND. PK.
DANBURY FAIR MALL
DANBURY MUNICIPAL AIRPORT
IVES CENT. PERFORMI...
WESTERN CONNECTICUT STATE UNIVERS...
W. KING
DEER
PINE VIEW DR
MIDDLE
PARK
LARCH DR
ALLAN
LOUIS DR
BIRCH
ROCKWOOD LA
CUSHING DR
RIVER
KILIAN
TIMBER CREST
AUTUMN DR
VARIAN DR
JOHN PERRY DR
RICHTER
HERITAGE
JARROD DR
CENTENNIAL
JOES HILL RD
TIFFANY DR
RALTO CT
TANGLEWOOD DR
IRONWOOD DR
LAKE CREST DR
HACK
WINTERGREEN HILL
MAPLECREST
MAPLEWOOD DR
CEDAR
CANTERBURY CT
ELMCREST DR
LINDENCREST DR
DRIFTWAY POINT
WEST LAKE SHORE DR
WESTWOOD
SUNSET RIDGE
WOOD TER
FARVIEW TER
DEVONSHIRE DR
HALL PASSWAY
JANDEC
QUAIL RUN
HALL ST
DRIFTWAY
6
202
MILL PLAIN RD
84
1
2
MILL PLAIN RD CUT OFF
OLD MILL PLAIN
AUNT HACK RD
PINDLE LA
CONRAIL
SAW MILL RD
TURNER ST
BLUEBERRY LA
OLD RIDGEBURY RD
LARSON DR
LAKE RD
KENOSIA PARK
KENOSIA AV
BRIAR RIDGE RD
ADVOCATE
UNION CIR.
BENSON DR
FLIRTATION DR
NORTH RIDGEBURY RD
SCHOOLHOUSE PL
KEELER DR
KEELER PL
POWDERMAKER DR
SHADOW LAKE RD
AARON'S CT
BEAVER BROOK RD
OLD TROLLEY RD
CHIPMUNK LA
GEORGE WASHINGTON HWY
CANTERBURY LA
SARAH BISHOP RD
BENSON RD
CHESTNUT HILL RD
DILLMAN CT
TWOPENCE
PARLEY RD.
HARDING DR
FINCH DR
BERTHIER PL
EVERGREEN PL
PHEASANT LA
SCODON DR
LANGSTROTH
SOPHIA DR
NEDS MOUNTAIN RD
NEDS LA
HUSSARS CAMP PL
BOGUS RD
WATERFALL
NED'S MTN RD
BEAR MOUNTAIN RD
OLD MILL RD
RIDGEBURY RD
BRIAR RIDGE
NOTEWORTHY DR
ROLFS DR
GRETA DR
CEL BREY DR
MIRY BROOK RD
STABLE DR
GRENIER DR
CAISSON DR
HARWOOD DR
HARWOOD
CANNONBALL DR EAST
BACKUS AV
YE OLDE RD
PRECISION RD
STILL
KENMERE BLVD
BLUEBERRY LA
HUCKLEBERRY LA
KIMBERLY TR
WINDAWAY
KEN OAKS DR
BOULEVARD DR
ELMBROOK RD
WATSON DR
WOODLAND HILL RD
AMITY LA
COLLEGE PARK DR
CRESTDALE RD
CHURCHILL
SCHOOL
ES
MS
WIBLING RD
WALLINGFORD RD
SUGAR HOLLOW
© Hagstrom Map Company, Inc.

FOR ADJOINING AREA SEE MAP NO.25

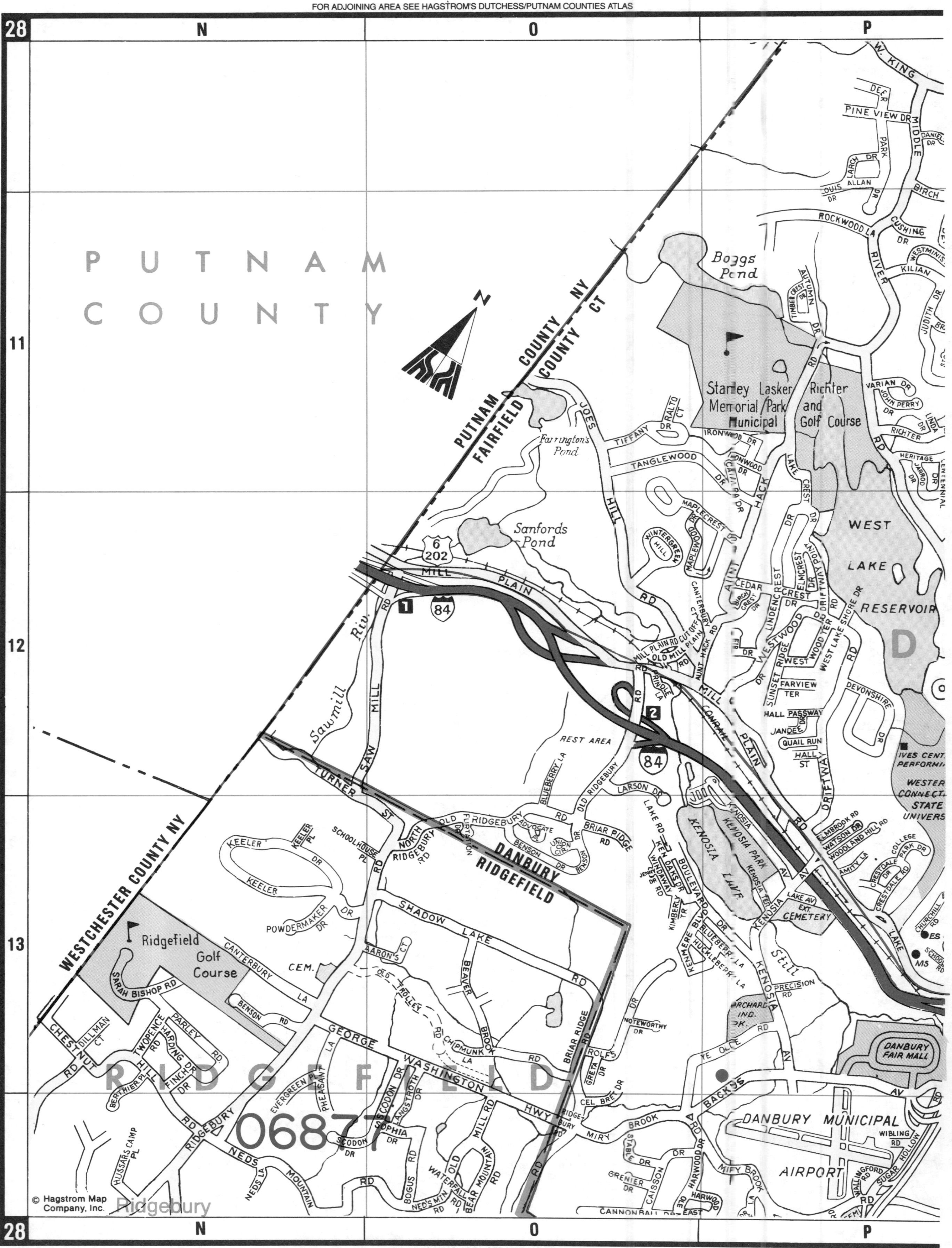

FOR ADJOINING AREA SEE MAP NO.30

28
Q
R
11
12
13
NEW FAIRFIELD
DANBURY
06812
06811
06810
MARGERIE RESERVOIR
EAST LAKE RES.
Padanaram Res.
UPPER KOHANZA RES.
LOWER KOHANZA RES.
Dickens Pond
Rogers Pond
Mercers Pond
Doyles Pond
Kellners Pond
Old Mill Pond
Lake Wackawana
Lake Candlewood
DANBURY BAY
BEAR MOUNTAIN RESERVATION
FEDERAL CORRECTIONAL INSTITUTION OF DANBURY
DANBURY TOWN PARK
Ridgewood Country Club
WOOSTER CEMETERY
DANBURY HOSPITAL
WESTERN CONN. STATE COLLEGE
COUNTY COURT HOUSE
DANBURY SCOTT-FANTON MUSEUM
COMMERCE PARK (IND. PK.)
BERKSHIRE S.C.
NUTMEG PLAZA S.C.
PLUMBTREES PLAZA
Shelter Rock
Still River
Beaver Brook
Kohanza Brook
Blind Brook
East Swamp Bk.
Hayestown
Margerie Manor
Hollywyle Park
Germantown
Cedar Heights
Pleasant Acres
Downtown Danbury
Danbury Sta.
DANBURY HS
HS
JHS
ES
39
37
84
6-7 202
53
4
5
6
7
3
© Hagstrom Map Company, Inc.
28
Q
R

FOR ADJOINING AREA SEE MAP NO.29

FOR ADJOINING AREA SEE MAP NO.26

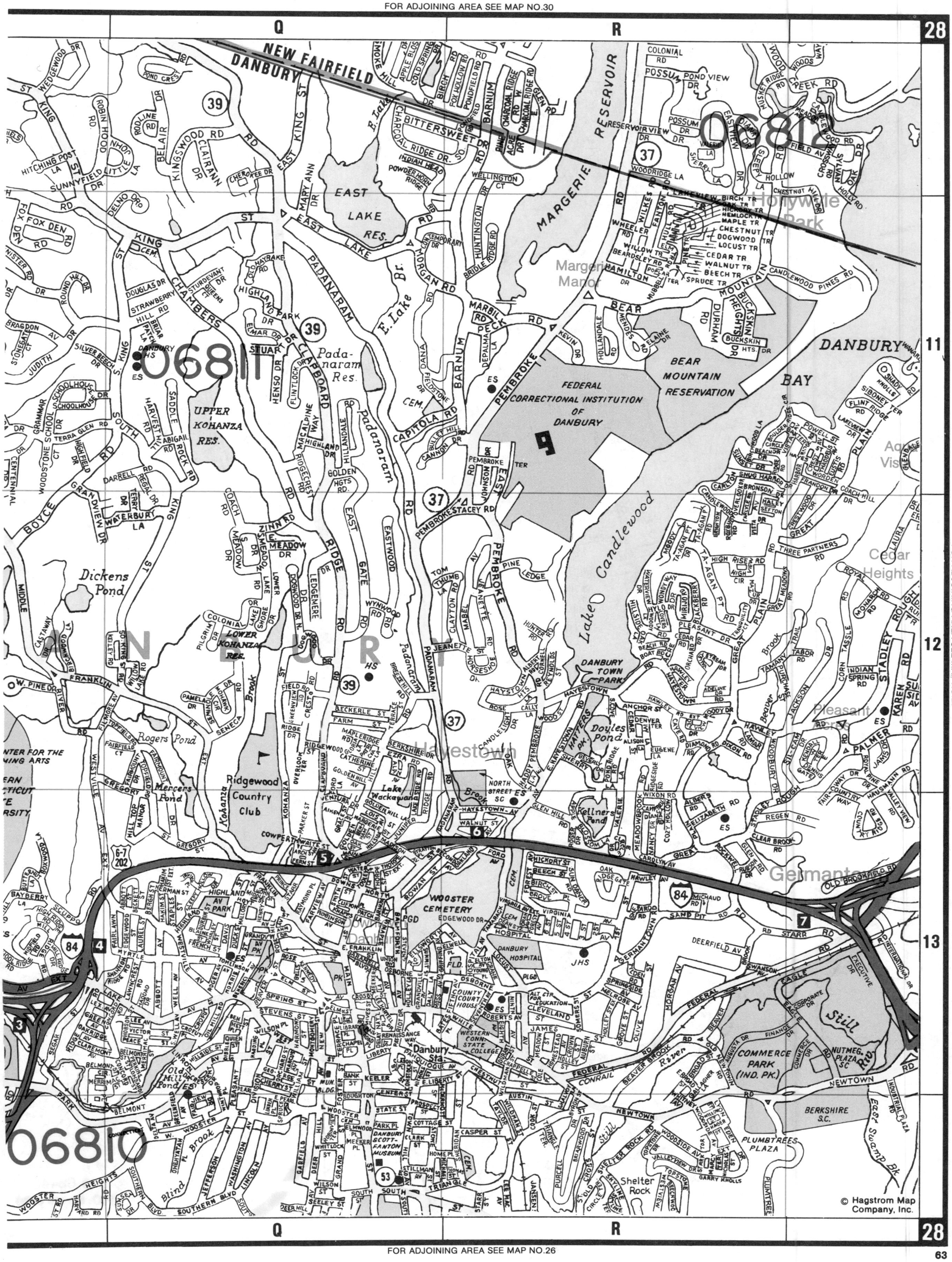

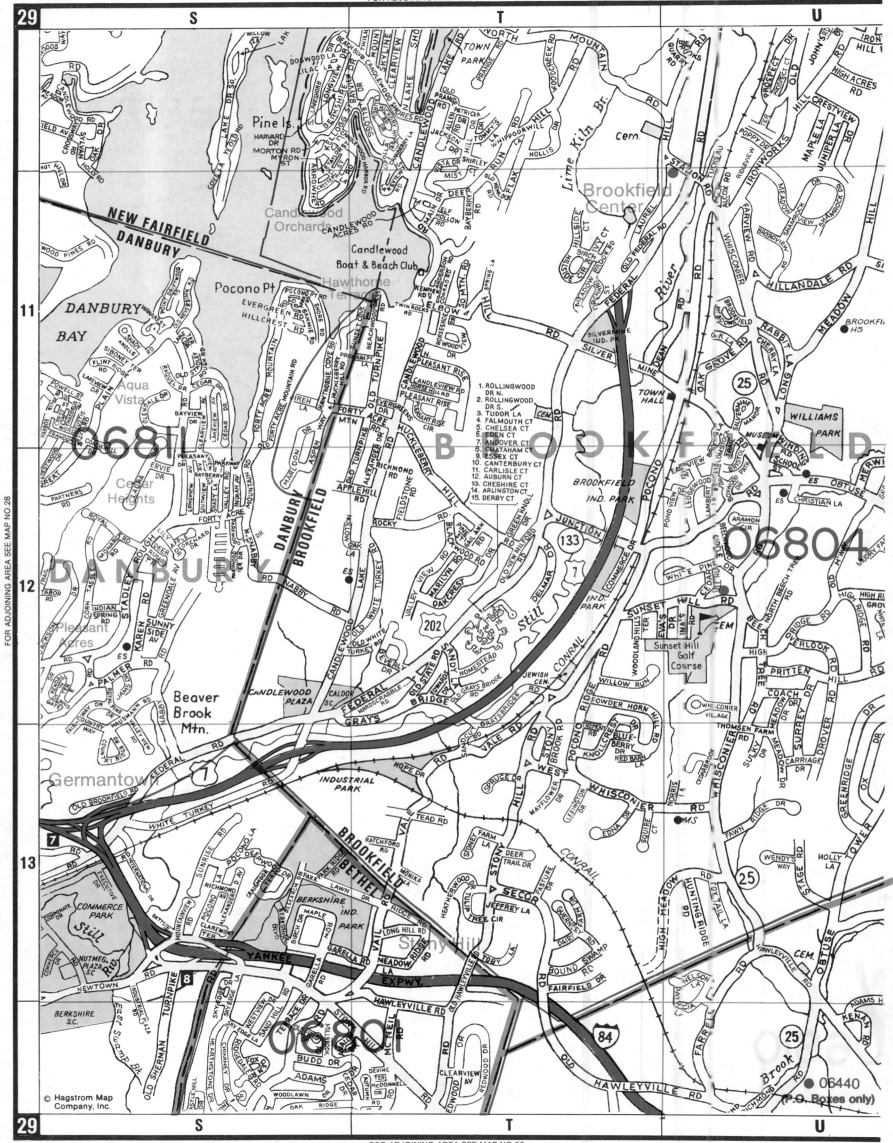

1. ROLLINGWOOD DR N.
2. ROLLINGWOOD DR S.
3. TUDOR LA
4. FALMOUTH CT
5. CHELSEA CT
6. EDEN CT
7. ANDOVER CT
8. CHATAHAM CT
9. ESSEX CT
10. CANTERBURY CT
11. CARLISLE CT
12. AUBURN CT
13. CHESHIRE CT
14. ARLINGTON CT
15. DERBY CT

© Hagstrom Map Company, Inc.

FOR ADJOINING AREA SEE HAGSTROM'S LITCHFIELD COUNTY POCKET MAP

29
V
W
U
V
10
10
11
12
13
FOR ADJOINING AREA SEE MAP NO.30
06776
LITCHFIELD CO
FAIRFIELD CO
BROOKFIELD
06804
PUMPKIN HILL RD
NEW BRIDGE RD
GREENVIEW RD
HEMLOCK RD
HEMLOCK RD EXT
ROCKY HILL RD
ALDRICH RD
DIANA DR
PHOEBE LA
FARM RD
PURITAN VALLEY RD
OLD MIDDLE
OLD BRIDGE RD
LONG MEADOW HILL RD
GRASSY
ROBIN LA
ROBINS LA
SOJO RD
TERRY LA
RICHARDS RD
BALDWIN HILL RD
JOHN'S RD
IRONWORKS HILL RD
WHISPERING WAY
LOGGING TRAIL LA
LITCHFIELD CO
FAIRFIELD CO
LAKE LILLINONAH
LITCHFIELD COUNTY
Southville
SOUTHVILLE
COOPER RD
RIDGE RD
SKYLINE
BERRY
River
Hitch
IRON ORE HILL RD EXT.
IRON ORE
RIVERFORD
LOGGING TRAIL LA
FALLS DR
DEERFIELD RD
KIMBERLY DR
HOP BROOK RD
COVE RD
BARKWOOD
SIGNAL HILL RD
HIDDEN BROOK DR
HEARTSTONE DR
OBTUSE RD
MURPHY'S LA
CHICKADEE LA
LYNDENWOOD DR
BROOK MANOR RD
BROOKDALE LA
JASON CT
DORSET LA
MUSIC HILL RD
NO.
ASHWOOD LA
CANNON RD
MAPLE TREE RD
FREDDY'S LA
WINDWOOD RD
BIG BUCK LA
133
HILL
YANKEE
FARM
GALLOWS RD
FERNBROOK DR
SO.
APACHE
ARAPAHOE
OBTUSE HILL
Obtuse Hill
RIDGE
HEATHER LA
TOWER
CROSS RD
CHEROKEE DR
NAVAHO DR
BRAE RD
ARAPAHOE RD
DUNSINANE RD
BANQUO
LAKE GEORGE DR
GALLOPING HILL RD
CAWDOR BURN RD
BONNY RD
PARK HILL RD
SOUTH RIDGE RD
OLD WOODS RD
Dingle
ROCKS RD
FLEETWOOD LA
SYCAMORE
LILLINONAH DR
RIDGE RD
WOODY
DRIFTWAY DR
SCENIC VIEW DR
DINGLE BROOK LA
HANOVER RD
LAKE
STATE BOAT LAUNCHING AREA
Br.
DINGLEBROOK RD
TRAILING RIDGE RD
BROOKFIELD
NEWTOWN
OBTUSE
NEWBURY RD
PHEASANT RIDGE RD
LAKE GEORGE RD
POND BROOK RD
SILVER CITY RD
Pond Brook
POND BROOK
Branch
GEORGES HILL RD
HILL LA
NEWTOWN
BUTTERFIELD RD
WOODS CIR
WINDY
SANFORD
06470
CURRIT
SIGNAL POST
PAUGUSSET STATE FOREST
LAKE LILLINONAH
LITCHFIELD CO
NEW HAVEN CO
Shepaug
NEW HAVEN COUNTY
N
© Hagstrom Map Company, Inc.

FOR ADJOINING AREA SEE HAGSTROM'S NEW HAVEN COUNTY ATLAS

FOR ADJOINING AREA SEE MAP NO.27

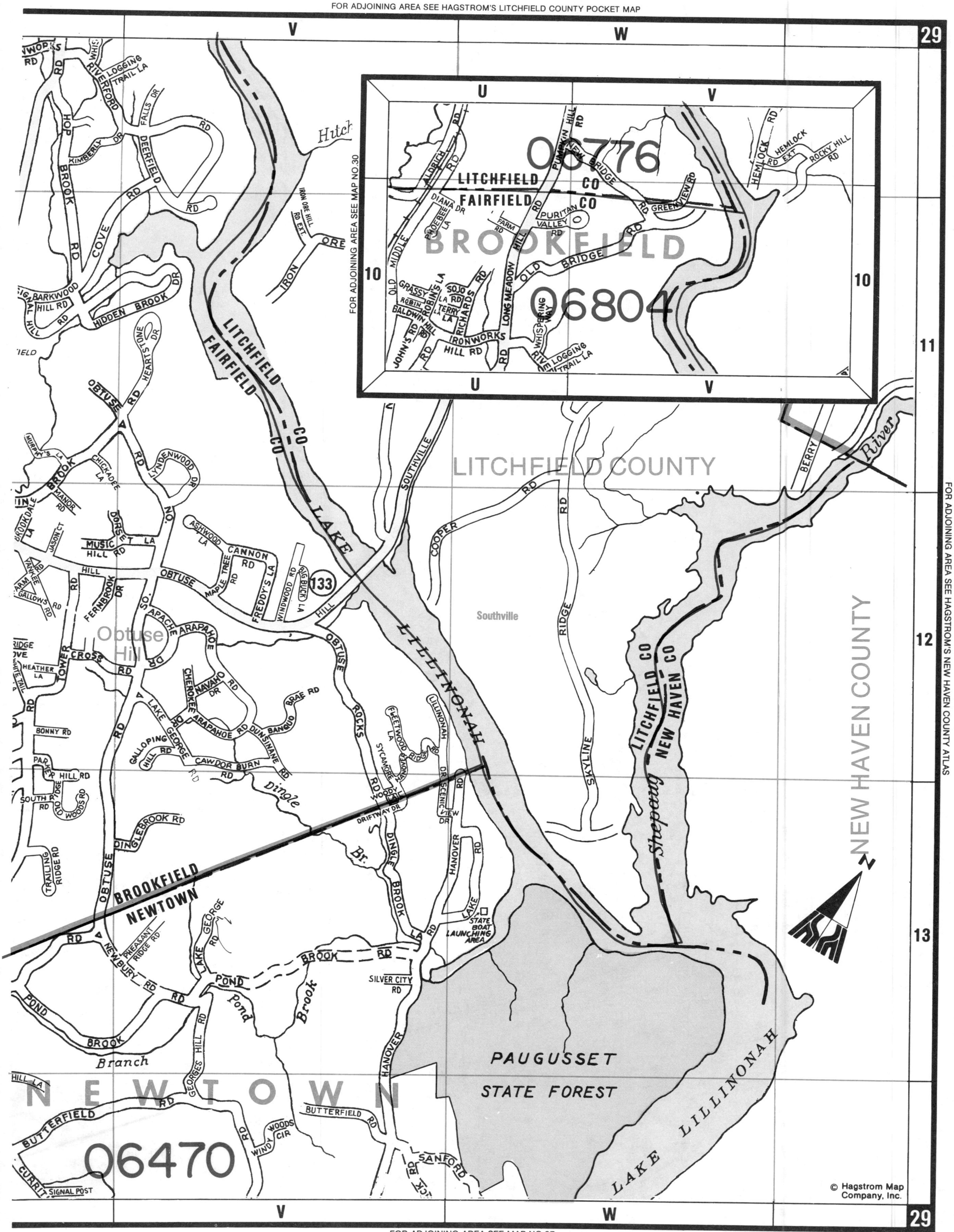

30   P   Q   R

7

DUTCHESS COUNTY

P U T N A M

C O U N T Y

POOTATUCK STATE FOREST

Brook

Quaker

BANK ST

37

HAVILAND HOLLOW RD

CEM.

Beaver Bog Mtn

8

PUTNAM COUNTY NY

Quaker Rd

Gerows Mill Pd.

Gerow

TWIN PONDS CT

ELWELL RD

HANDOL LA

N E W F A

Brook

PINE HILL RD

PINEWOOD DR

FARMERS LA

OAK TREE LA

NORTH FORTY DR

Columbia Dr

Cornell Rd

MAPLE LA

CLOVERLEAF DR

CEM.

BEAVER BOG

HIGH VIEW TER

WARWICK

PRINCETON LA

JEWEL LA

SUNNYSIDE LA

DOUGLAS LA

JOEL'S DR

LEONARD DR

GARNET DR

Woods

HILLSIDE RD

WALNUT RIDGE RD

9

FAWN CREST

Bigelow Corners

39

JENNIFER

BIGELOW RD

Studder Brook

Fairwood

CEM.

06

TOWN PARK

BALL POND

Mertens Mill Pd.

WHITE BIRCH RD

MEADOWBROOK RD

Ball POND RD

Ball POND

TWIN PONDS

OLD BRIDGE RD

Short Woods

HICKORY LA

SHORT

WELDON

WOODS

HUNTINGTON LA

BROOK WOOD RD

RITA DR

KAREN DR

OAKWOOD RD

MIDGE ROW

OVERBROOK DR

BRIDGEVIEW DR

Pond

Br.

FAIRWOOD S.C.

SUNSWEPT

GILLOTTI

CEM.

JHS

NEW FAIRFIELD HS

New Fairfield

SPRING DR

RITA ES

GILLOTTI RD

BUTTERNUT

ES

MEM. FIELD

TH

BRUSH HILL

Westview Trails

STATE LINE

FIELDSTONE DR

DONNA DR

MILLTOWN

SADLERIDGE RD

HOOVER PL

COOLIDGE

BALL POND RD

BAYBERRY LA

TIMBER LA

AUTUMN RIDGE RD

HARVEST

Taylor Corners

ERIN DR

CARRIAGE LA

MacBean Hts.

WHIPSTICK RD

RITA RD

WILLIAMS

INDIAN HILL RD

MIDDLETON DR

DONNELLY DR

MEETING HOUSE RD

MAC BEAN

MARGENE DR

BRUSH HILL RD

OLD RT. 39

COTTONTAIL LA

HILLTOP DR

SAW MILL RD

10

MILLTOWN RD

WEST KING ST

Corner Pd.

BERNLOU DR

WEDGEWOOD DR

COOPER RD

Titicus Mtn.

Titicus Mtn.

POND CREST

EAST LAKE RD

OLD FARM RD

OLD ORCHARD RD

BLACK THORN

APPLE BLOSSOM

COLD SPRINGS RD

PONDFIELD RD

BARNIM

CHARCOAL RIDGE

COLONIAL DR

POSSUM DR

POND VIEW DR

RESERVOIRVIEW DR

EASTVIEW

DIANA DR

NEW FAIRFIELD

DANBURY

WEST KING ST

MIDDLE PARK DR

DEF. R

PINE VIEW DR

DANIELS DR

ROBIN HOOD RD

ROD LINE RD

BELAIR DR

39

KINGSWOOD RD

CLAIRANN DR

KING ST

EAST KING ST

BITTERSWEET DR

CHARCOAL RIDGE DR

INDIAN HEAD

POWDER HORN RIDGE

WELLINGTON CT

Reservoir

MARGERIE

37

WOODRIDGE LA

POSSUM DR

VALERIE

LAKEVIEW

BIRCH TR

06811

LARCH DR

LOUIS ALLAN DR

BIRCH RD

ROCKWOOD LA

CUSHING DR

FOX DEN RD

FOX DEN DR

KING ST

HITCHING POST LA

SUNNYFIELD DR

DELNO DR

CHEROKEE DR

MARY ANN DR

EAST LAKE RES.

TEMPORARY RD

D A N B U R Y

Margerie Manor

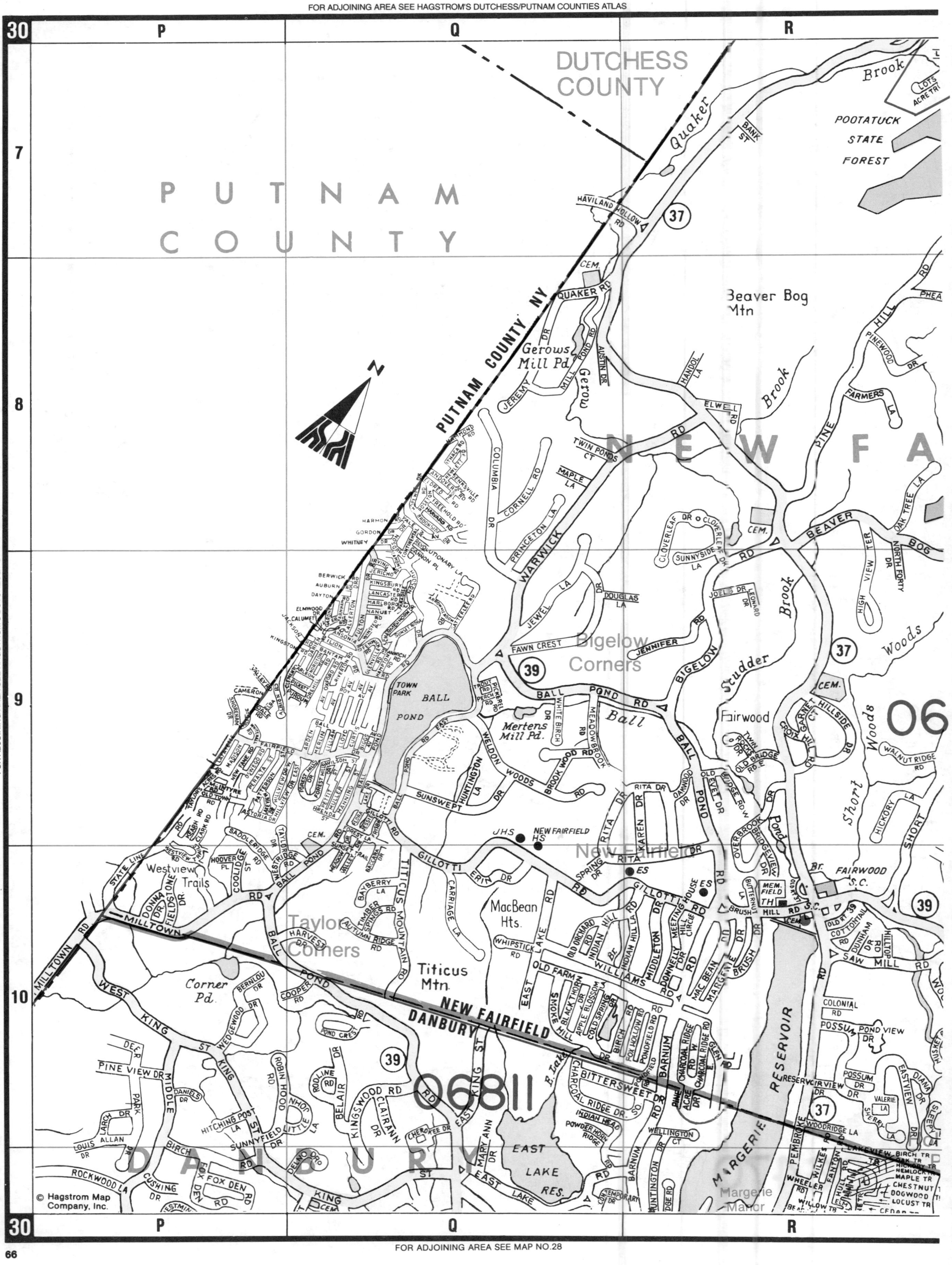

© Hagstrom Map Company, Inc.

30   P   Q   R

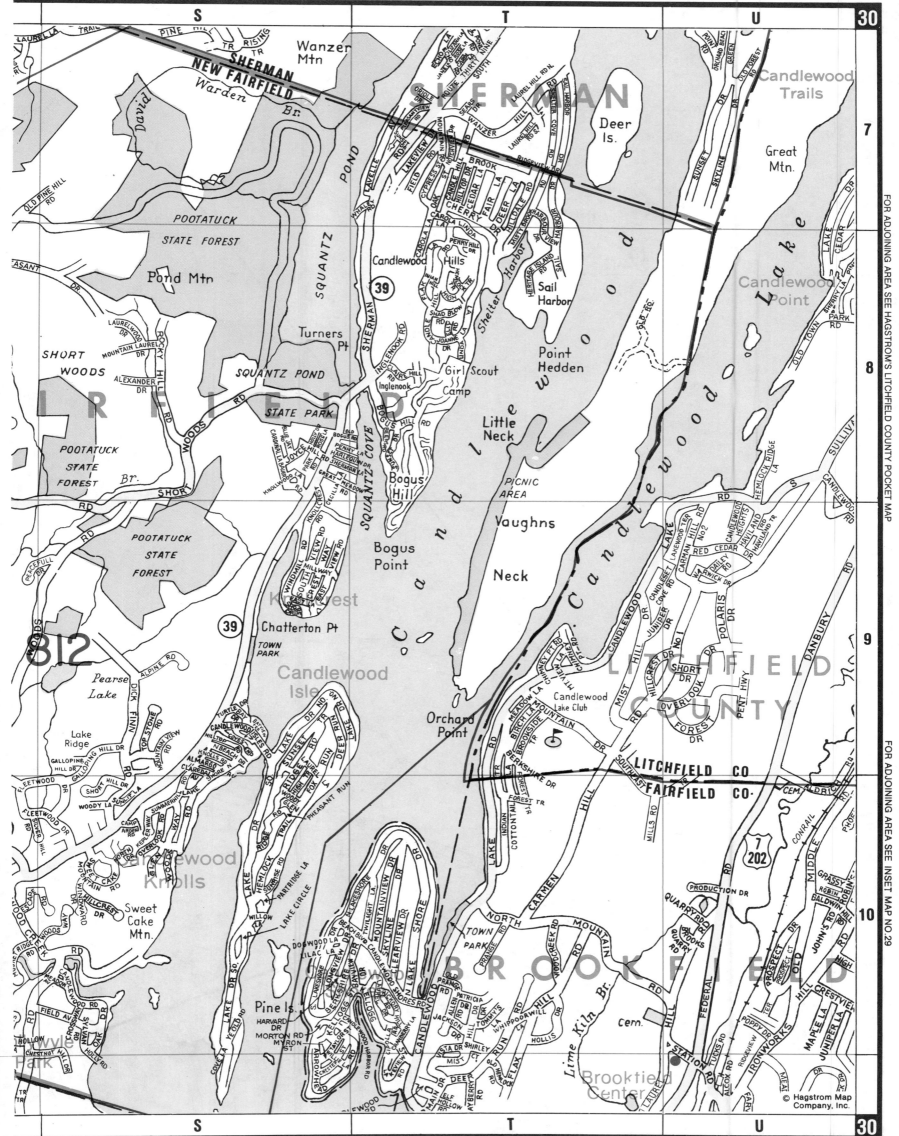

FOR ADJOINING AREA SEE HAGSTROM'S DUTCHESS/PUTNAM COUNTIES ATLAS

FOR ADJOINING AREA SEE HAGSTROM'S DUTCHESS/PUTNAM COUNTIES ATLAS

31
R
S
T
4
5
6
7
DUTCHESS COUNTY
DUTCHESS COUNTY NY
FAIRFIELD COUNTY CT
N
Turner Mtn
Great
Tollgate
BRIGGS
HILL RD
CHIMNEY HILL RD
THIRTY SEVEN
Greenwoods Br
OLD GREENWOODS RD EXT
SOUTH
BRIDGEWORTH LA
MEADOW LA
TANDEM LA
WAKEMAN HILL RD
06784
SHERMA
ORANGE PEPPER RD
AUTUMN DR
Glen RD
COZIER HILL RD
WOODS RD
THIRTY NINE
Quaker Br
HOLLOW BROOK RD
CHAPEL HILL
COBURN RD W.
NUTMEG LA
37
COBURN CEM.
COBURN RD E.
LEACH HOLLOW RD
HIGHLANDS RD
Glen Br.
GLEN VIEW DR
WAGON WHEEL RD
BARLOW FARM RD
Timber Lake
TIMBER LAKE RD
TIMBER LAKE RD N.
MEMORY LA
Lake Mauweha
PEACE PIPE LA
MAUWEEHOO HILL
SQUAW VALLEY LA
COOTE HILL
Pepper Pond
PEPPER POND TR
HARDSCRABBLE RD
PARKER RD
SOUTH ROUTE THIRTY SEVEN
DURGY LA
Valley Pond
LONG MEADOW TR
39
NORTH COVE RD
DEER HILL RD
PINEWOOD SHORES
Deer Pd
BIG TR
PINE HILL TR
RISING SUN TR
LAUREL LA
BIG TRAIL
LOTS ACRE TR
Brook
Wanzer Mtn
SHERMAN
NEW FAIRFIELD
Warden Br.
LAUREL HILL RD
WANZER HILL
RIDGEVIEW
Quaker
BANK ST
POOTATUCK STATE FOREST
06812
David
SQUANTZ POND
LAKEVIEW
BROOK
HOLLOW RD
37
NEW FAIRFIELD
OLD PINE HILL RD
PINE HILL RD
POOTATUCK STATE FOREST
© Hagstrom Map Company, Inc.
31
R
S
T

FOR ADJOINING AREA SEE MAP NO.30

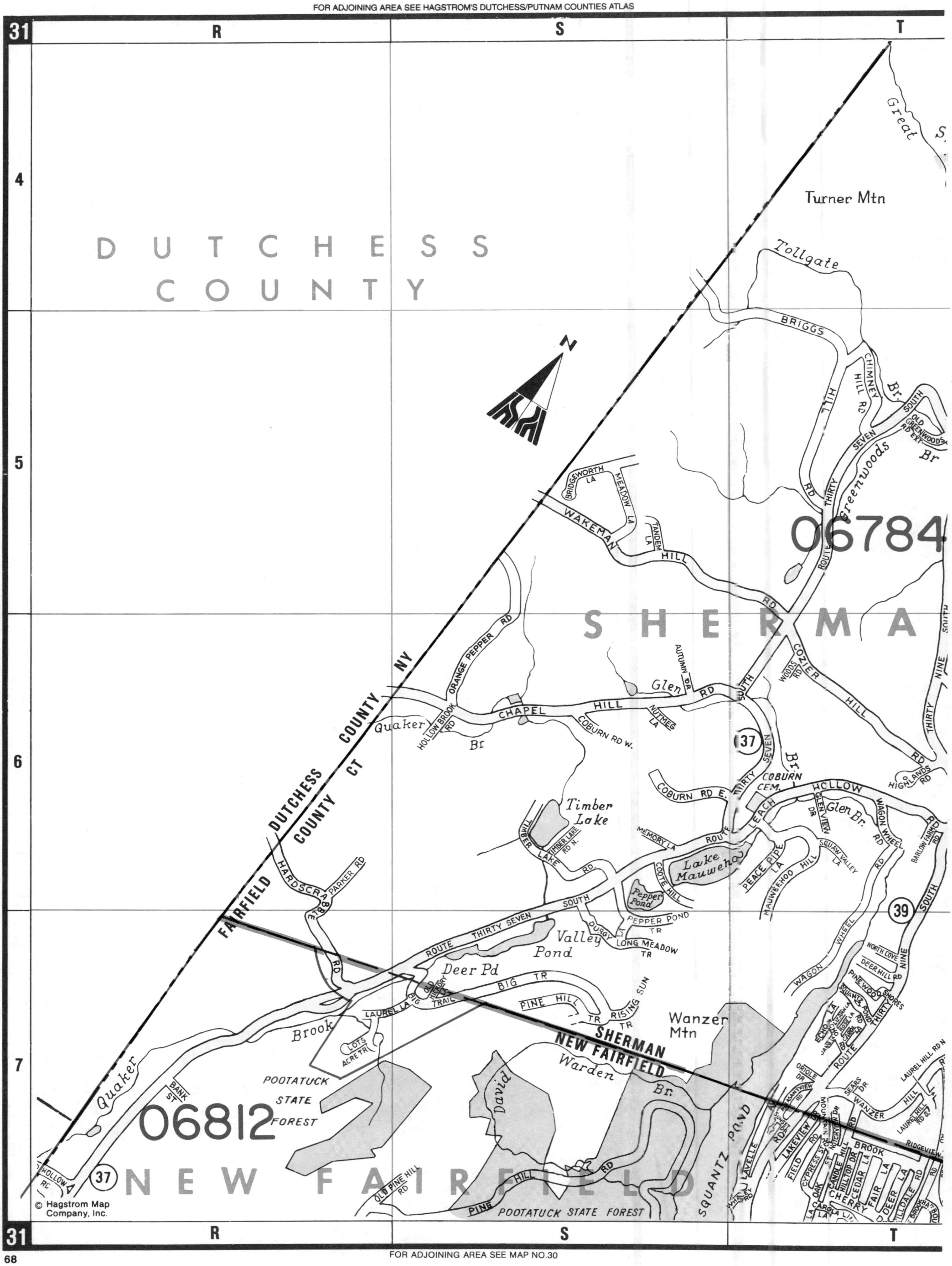

U   V

4

SHERMAN MEADOWS

Spring Lake

Sherman

Morrissey Br.

NORTH RD
CHURCH RD
BABBLING BROOK DR
CROOKED FURROWS LA
CEM.
BRIARWOOD DR
GELSTON RD
NINE
DODGE DR N
JERICHO RD N

Naromiyocknowhusunkata

Barnes Hill

SUNSET DR
OSBORN RD

HOLTON RD
STILSON HILL RD
SQUASH RD
Housatonic

39

SUNNY LA
ROUTE RIDGE RD
JERICHO RD S
BRIMSMADE RD
LA ANDREA PL

EAST

7 Kent

SHOPPING CENTER
TOWN HALL
CENTER MAW
CEM.
ES
BENCHMARK RD
COLONIAL PARK
GREENWOODS
ROUTE 37
ATHLETIC FIELD
Route Thirty Seven **37**
OLD STILSON HILL RD
BOARDMAN MANOR
7

Towner Hill

37

5

Br.

TOWN BEACH
MILL RD
HILLSIDE DR
SUNRISE PASS
SPRING LA
HUBBELL MTN RD
SHORE DR
POINT
CEDAR POINT
BROOKSIDE DR
PARTRIDGE TR
HUBBELL MTN RD

06776

JOTHAM RD
MT RD
CANDLEWOOD RD

Boardman Bridge

CEDAR LA
LOCUST PT LA
HEMLOCK LA
CIRCLE DR
CREST
SPUR LA
OAK
CEDAR LA EXT
SPRINGSIDE LA
ATCHISON COVE RD
FOX RUN
HOLIDAY
Atchison Cove
HUBBELL MTN
BULLYMUCK RD

River

Boardman

N E W   M I L F O R D

Allens Cove

N

MARY BEE LA
LEDGEWOOD DR
DEER RUN
ISLAND VIEW
CANDL

Holiday Point

Hubbell Hill

BLUEBERRY LA

L I T C H F I E L D

C O U N T Y

6

ROUTE
LAKE SHORE WOODS RD
CHESTNUT HILL RD
ORCHARD REST RD

Candlewood Lake

Thistle Is.

MILL POND RD

Haviland Mill Pd

SHERMAN
NEW MILFORD
MT RD

CANDLELIGHT FARMS AIRPORT

LAKE DR
CANDLEWOOD LAKE RD N
RIVERVIEW
SCHAGHTICOKE TRAIL RD

KENT RD

EAGLES NEST DR
CANDLEWOOD LAKE DR
POND

BIRCH HILL RD
LINDEN DR
WILLOW DR
TAMARACK DR
Millstone Ridge

CEM.

FORT HILL RD No.1

FORT HILL RD No.2

OLD BALL PK RD

SHORE DR
TERRACE RD
GREEN
ANDREW
Emerald Lake
Green Is.
Green Pond

New Milford Bay

CANDLEWOOD SPRINGS

FORT HILL
CALDWELL DR
MALLORY DR
SPRING
NICHOLAS ST
BRIDGE

SHELTER COVE RD
RAIL HARBOR RD
SKYLINE DR
SUNSET DR
WOODEN SHOE RD
ORCHARD BEACH RD
OLD FOREST

Deer Is.

Great Mtn.

JUNIPER LA
APPLE
ECHO DR
POPLAR LA
HICKORY LA
CHESTNUT LA
OAK LA
STELLA
MAPLE LA

FERRISS EST RD
LEDGE LA
EDGEWOOD
JERUSALEM RD
SUNNY VALLEY LA
SUNNY VALLEY

BIRCH HILL RD

ROAD TO SCHOOL RD
CEM.
HOWE RD
DARTMOUTH RD
SHERWOOD RD

STIRLING DR
WEST
FORDYCE RD

7 202

NEW MILFORD PLAZA

ANDERSON AV

7

DANBURY
DODD
TOWER HILL RD

© Hagstrom Map Company, Inc.

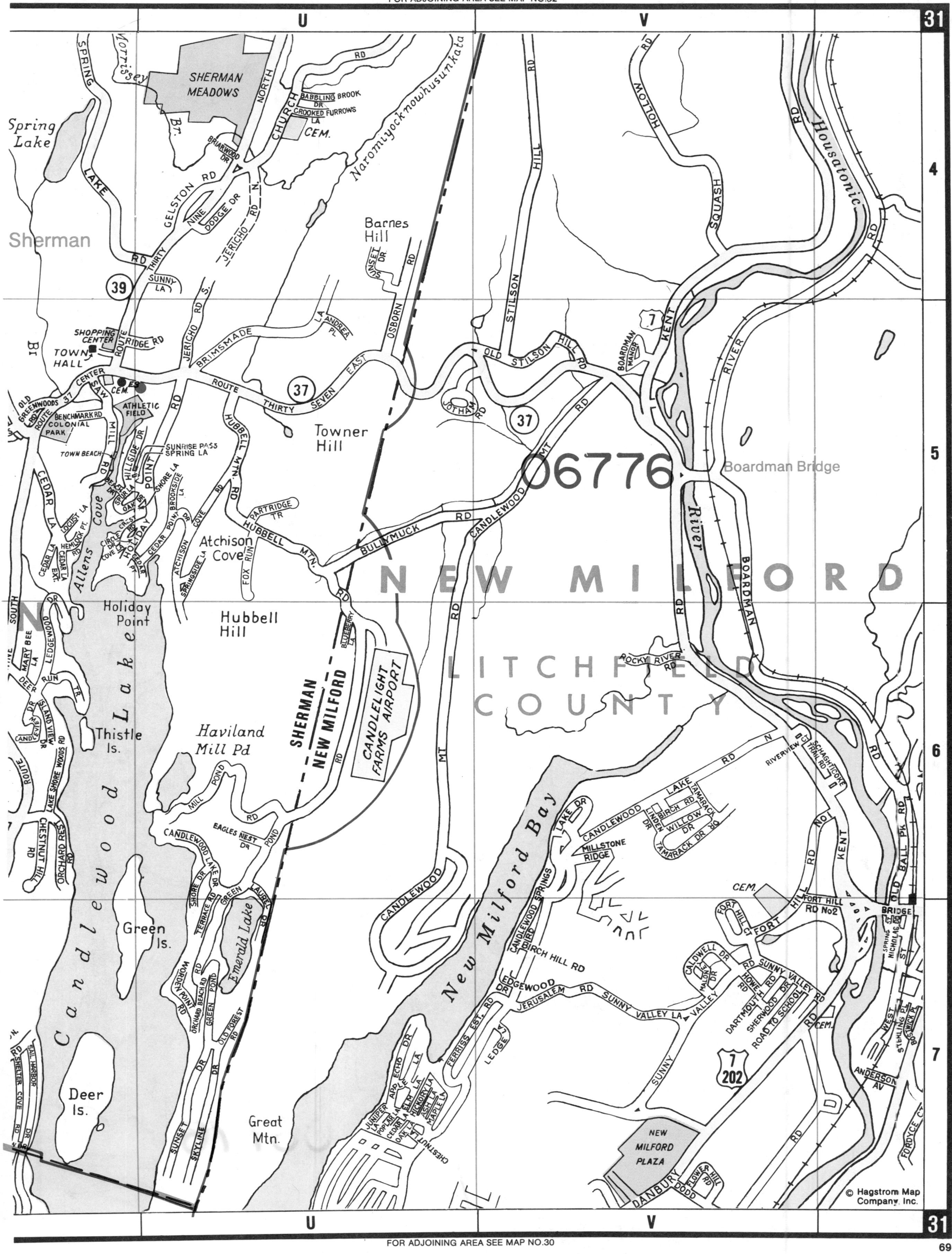

FOR ADJOINING AREA SEE HAGSTROM'S LITCHFIELD COUNTY POCKET MAP

32   T   U   V   **32**

1

DUTCHESS

COUNTY

Ten Mile River

KENT

NEW MILFORD

Housatonic

7

Tenmile Trail Hill

Appalachian

Route FIFTY FIVE

55

N

Evergreen DR

Hoyt RD

Anderson RD E.

Anderson RD W.

Anderson RD

Smoke Ridge DR

Southview DR

2

Cloverleaf Farm N.

Cloverleaf Farm S.

Wimsink RD

Anderson RD EXT.

Anderson RD EXT.

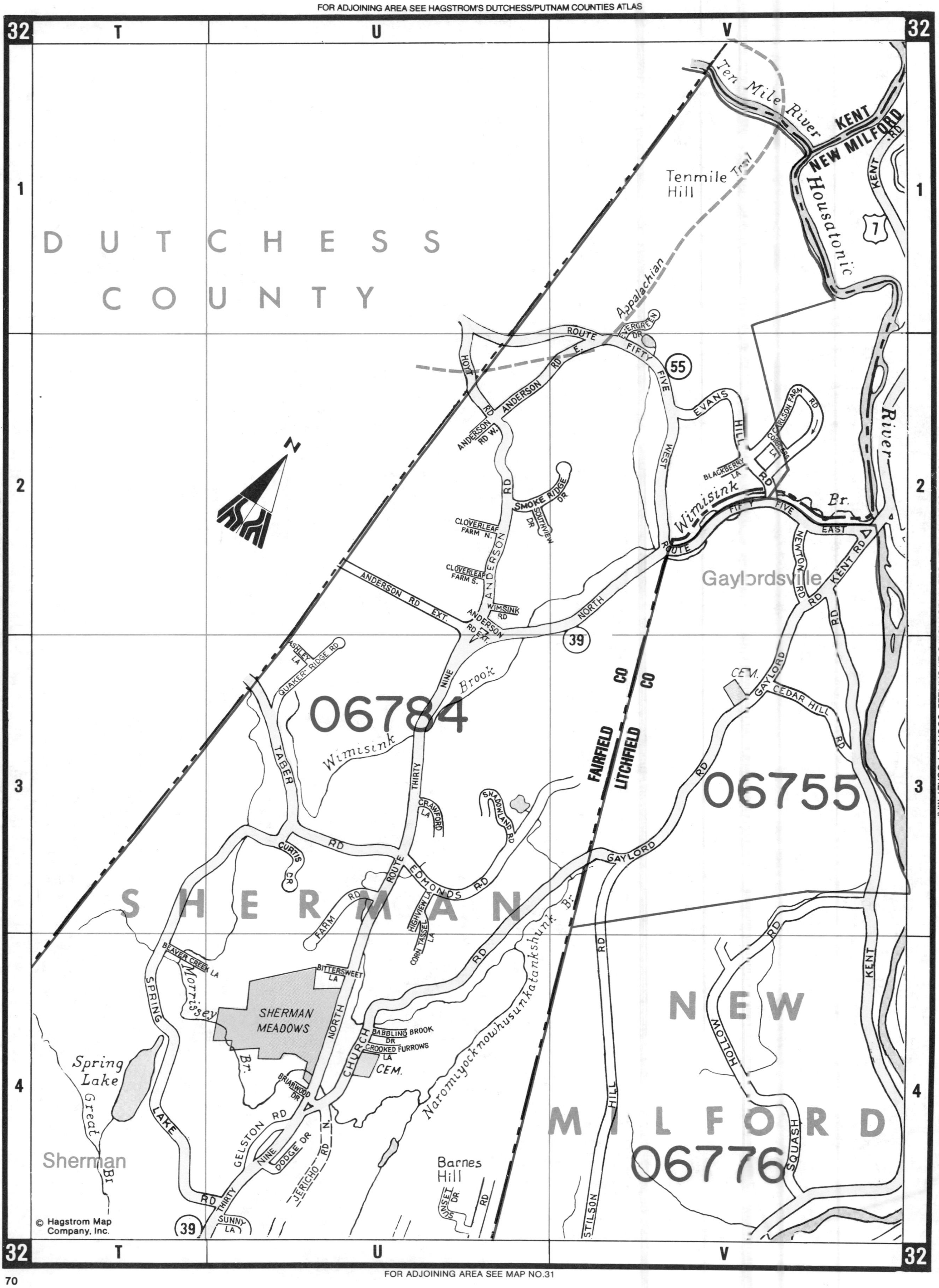

ANDERSON RD EXT

Blackberry LA

Carlson Farm RD

Coburg LA

Wimisink

Evans Hill RD

West Route FIFTY FIVE East

North Route

Gaylordsville

Newtown RD

Kent RD

River

Br.

Ashley LA

Quaker Ridge RD

Nine Brook

06784

Wimisink

39

CEM.

Gaylord RD

Cedar Hill RD

06755

3

Taber RD

Curtis CR

Crawford LA

Thirty RD

Shadowland RD

FAIRFIELD CO

LITCHFIELD CO

Gaylord RD

S H E R M A N

Farm RD

Edmonds RD

Route RD

Highview LA

Corn Tassel LA

Gaylord RD

Beaver Creek LA

Morrissey

Naromiyocknowhusunkatankshunk Br.

NEW

Spring Lake RD

Bittersweet LA

North Church RD

SHERMAN MEADOWS

Babbling Brook DR

Crooked Furrows LA

CEM.

Stilson Hill RD

Squash Hollow RD

Kent RD

MILFORD

4

Spring Lake

Great Br.

Gelston RD

Nine RD

Briarwood DR

Dodge DR

Jericho RD N.

Barnes Hill

Sunset DR

06776

Sherman

Thirty RD

Sunny LA

39

32   T   U   V   **32**

Fairfield County

Index to Streets and Roads

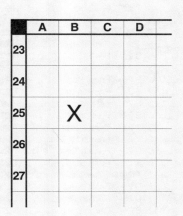

USING THE "BLUE LINE" GRID SQUARE LOCATION SYSTEM

Blue lines are drawn horizontally and vertically on the map, forming grid squares. These squares can be identified by letters and numbers appearing in the map margins. Streets and roads are listed alphabetically in the index by political divisions within the county. The letters and numbers after the name give the grid square and map number on which the street appears.

For example, to locate Valley Dr. in Greenwich, find the heading for Greenwich in the index. The B25 1 after the street name shows that Valley Dr. can be located within grid square B25 on map 1, as shown to the right.

NOTES:
Numbered streets are indexed after the alphabetical listing.
"*" indicates that street name is not shown on map due to lack of space.

ABBREVIATIONS USED ON HAGSTROM MAPS

Av	Avenue	MS	Middle School
BH	Borough Hall	Mun Bldg	Municipal Building
Blvd	Boulevard	N	North
Boro	Borough	Pk	Park
Br	Brook	Pkwy	Parkway
CC	Country Club	Pl	Place
Cem	Cemetery	Plz	Plaza
CH	City Hall	PO	Post Office
Cir	Circle	PS	Public School
CO	County	Pt	Point
Cor	Corner	Rd	Road
Cr	Creek	Res	Reservoir
Cres	Crescent	Riv	River
Ct	Court	RR	Railroad
Dr	Drive	Rte	Route
E	East	S	South
ES	Elementary School	Sq	Square
Expwy	Expressway	St	Street
Ext	Extension	Sta	Station
GC	Golf Club	Ter	Terrace
Hgts	Heights	TH	Town Hall
HS	High School	Tpke	Turnpike
Hwy	Highway	Tr	Trail
IS	Intermediate School	Twp	Township
Isl	Island	W	West
JHS	Junior High School	Wk	Walk
La	Lane		

STREET	MAP	GRID

BETHEL

STREET	MAP	GRID
Adams Dr	26	S 15
Allen Way	26	S 15
Amar Dr	26	R 15
Andrews St	26	R 15
Ann Ter	26	R 15
Apollo Rd	26	R 14
Apple Tree Rd	26	S 14
Aunt Patty's La E	26	S 16
Aunt Patty's La W	26	S 16
Autumn Dr	26	T 14
Avalon Dr	26	S 14
Barnum, P T Sq	26	R 15
Bayberry Hill Rd	26	R 15
Beach St	26	R 15
Benedict Rd	26	S 14
Benson Rd	26	R 14
Berkshire Blvd	29	S 13
Bethpage Dr	26	Q 15
Birch Dr	29	S 13
Birnam Wood Rd	26	R 17
Blackman Av	26	R 15
Blue Spruce Ct	26	R 15
Bonnette Dr	26	Q 15
Bonnette Dr Ext	26	Q 15
Briarcliff Manor	26	R 16
Brookview Ct	26	S 14
Brookview Dr	26	S 14
Brookwood Dr	26	R 15
Buckboard Ridge Rd	26	S 16

STREET	MAP	GRID
Budd Dr	26	S 14
Buff La	26	S 14
Canaan Dr	26	R 16
Carriage Dr	26	R 16
Castle Hill Dr	26	S 14
Cawley Av	26	R 15
Cedar Dr	26	S 14
Cherry La	26	Q 15
Chestnut Ridge Rd	26	R 17
Chestnut St	26	R 16
Chimney Dr	26	S 16
Chipmunk Ter	26	R 15
Church Camp Grounds	26	Q 16
Cindy La	26	R 15
Clearview Av	26	T 14
Codfish Hill Rd	26	S 16
Codfish Hill Rd Ext	26	S 16
Colonial Dr	26	S 16
Country Way	26	R 16
Crestview Rd	26	Q 16
Cross Hill Rd	26	S 16
Daniska Av	26	R 17
Deepwood Dr	29	S 13
Deer Run	26	R 15
Depot Pl	26	R 15
Devine Ter	26	T 14
Diamond Av	26	R 15
Dittmar Rd	26	R 17
Division St	26	R 15
Dodgingtown Rd	26	S 14
Drummers La	26	Q 15

STREET	MAP	GRID
Durant Av	26	R 15
Eagle Rock Hill	26	R 15
East Brook Ct	26	S 15
East La	26	S 14
Edmond Rd	26	S 15
Elgin Av	26	R 15
Elizabeth St	26	R 16
Evergreen Dr	26	S 14
Fairchild Dr	26	Q 15
Falls La	26	S 16
Far Horizons Dr	26	S 14
Farm Ct	26	R 15
Farmview Dr	26	S 15
Farnum Hill St	26	R 15
Fawn Rd	26	R 15
Fleetwood Av	26	Q 14
Fleetwood Park Dr	26	Q 15
Four Gables Rd	26	R 16
Fox Den Rd	26	S 14
Francis J Clarke Cir	26	Q 16
Front St	26	R 15
Gale Ct	26	R 16
Garella Rd	29	S 13
Gemini Rd	26	R 15
Glenwood Dr	26	Q 15
Golden Hill St	26	R 15
Governors La	26	R 15
Grace Ct	26	Q 14
Grand St	26	R 15
Grandview Av	26	R 15
Grandview Ter	26	Q 15
Granite Dr	26	Q 15
Grassy Plain St	26	R 15

STREET	MAP	GRID
Grassy Plain Ter	26	Q 15
Green Pasture Rd	26	S 14
Greenwood Av	26	R 15
Gretchen La	26	R 16
Griswold St	26	R 15
Grove Pl	26	S 14
Hawleyville Rd	26	T 14
Hearthstone Dr	26	S 14
Henry St	26	S 15
Hickok Av	26	R 15
High Lake Dr	26	R 16
High St	26	R 15
Highland Av	26	R 15
Highview Ter	26	Q 15
Hillcrest Rd	26	S 14
Hilldale La	26	S 14
Hillside Ct	26	S 16
Hollyberry Dr	26	S 14
Honey Hollow Dr	26	S 15
Hoyt Rd	26	S 15
Hoyt's Hill Rd	26	S 15
Hudson St	26	Q 14
Huntington Ct	26	R 15
Ichabod La	26	S 16
Idlewood	26	R 15
Interstate Hwy 84	26	T 14
Jacklin Rd	26	T 16
Judd Av	26	R 15
Judy Dr	26	R 16
Juniper Rd	26	R 15

STREET	MAP	GRID
Karen Dr	26	S 15
Katrina Cir	26	S 16
Kayview Av	26	R 15
Keeler St	26	R 15
Kellogg St	26	S 15
Kingswood Dr	26	R 15
Knollwood Dr	26	Q 15
Kristy Dr	26	T 14
Laughlin Rd	26	S 14
Legend Dr	26	S 16
Library Pl	26	R 15
Limekiln Ct	26	S 15
Linda La	26	S 15
Lindberg St	26	Q 15
Long Hill Rd	29	T 13
Long Meadow La	26	R 16
Main St	26	R 15
Mansfield St	26	Q 14
Maple Av	26	R 15
Maple Av Ext	26	R 15
Maple La	26	Q 14
Maple Row	29	S 13
Martino Av	26	Q 15
Marvin Pl	26	S 15
Marywood Rd	26	R 17
McDonnell Dr	26	T 14
McKay Rd	26	R 15
McNeil Rd	26	T 14
Meadow La	29	T 13
Meckauer Cir	26	S 14
Melillo Av	26	Q 15
Midway Dr	26	R 15
Millbrook Rd	26	S 14
Milwaukee Av	26	R 15

STREET	MAP	GRID
Mountain Orchard Rd	26	Q 16
Nashville Rd	26	R 15
Nashville Rd Ext	26	R 16
Natureview Tr	26	R 15
North Hearthstone Dr	26	S 14
North Rd	26	S 14
Oak Ridge Rd	26	S 14
Oakland Hgts	26	R 15
Old Dodgingtown Rd	26	S 17
Old Field Dr	26	S 14
Old Hawleyville Rd	26	S 14
Old Lantern Dr	26	S 15
Old Lantern Rd	26	S 15
Old Shelter Rock Rd	26	S 14
Old Town La	26	S 14
Old Turnpike Rd	26	S 14
Oven Rock Rd	26	Q 15
Overlook Av	26	R 17
Oxford St	26	R 15
Park Lawn Dr	29	S 13
Park Ridge Rd	29	S 13
Partridge Dr	26	S 15
Paul St	26	R 14
Payne Rd	26	S 14
Peck La	26	R 16
Pell Mell Dr	26	S 15
Pent Rd	26	R 16
Phillip Dr	26	S 16

STREET	MAP	GRID
Plantation Ct	26	Q 16
Pleasant Rise	26	Q 15
Pleasant St	26	Q 15
Pleasantview Ter	26	Q 14
Plumtrees Rd	26	S 15
Pound Sweet Hill	26	S 14
Prospect St	26	R 15
Putnam Park Rd	26	R 17
Quaker Ridge Rd	26	S 14
Quarry Rd	26	Q 16
Racebrook Dr	26	S 15
Raven Crest Dr	26	S 16
Rector St	26	R 15
Redwood Dr	26	T 14
Regan Dr	26	Q 15
Research Dr	29	S 13
Reservoir St	26	Q 15
Ridge Rd	29	T 13
Ridgedale Rd	26	S 14
Rita Dr	26	S 15
Roberts Dr	26	S 15
Rockwell Rd	26	S 15
Rocky La	26	T 15
Rotella Dr	26	Q 15
Sand Hill Rd	26	S 14
Saxon St	26	Q 15
School St	26	R 15
Second La	26	Q 15
Seeley St	26	R 15
Settlers Rd	26	S 15
Sharon Ct	26	Q 15

STREET	MAP	GRID
Shelley Rd	26	T 15
Shelter Rock Rd	26	S 14
Short Dr	26	R 15
Simeon Rd	26	R 15
Sky Edge Dr	26	S 14
Sky Edge La	26	S 14
South St	26	Q 15
Spring Hill La	26	R 16
Starr La	26	R 16
State Route 53	26	Q 15
State Route 58	26	R 15
State Route 302	26	R 15
Stone Dam Rd	26	R 16
Stony Hill Rd	26	S 14
Summit La	26	S 16
Sunny Acres Rd	26	S 14
Sunset Hill Rd	26	S 17
Sycamore Ct	26	Q 15
Sympaug Park Rd	26	Q 16
Taylor Av	26	R 15
Taylor Rd	26	S 15
Terrace Dr	26	S 14
Terry Dr	26	S 15
Topstone Dr	26	R 15
Tremont Av	26	Q 15
Trowbridge Dr	26	Q 16
Turkey Plain Rd	26	Q 16
Turnage La	26	Q 16
Twin Maple Dr	26	S 16
US Hwy 6	26	T 14
Vail Rd	29	T 13
Valley Ct	26	S 16
Van Campen La	26	R 17
Vera Dr	26	Q 15
Vining Rd	26	S 15
Wagon Rd	26	S 16
Walnut Hill Rd	26	S 14
Waterhorse Brook Dr	26	R 15
Webb Rd	26	R 16
Weed Rd	26	T 14
Westview Dr	26	S 14
Whippoorwill Rd	26	R 16
Whitlock Av	26	Q 15
Whitney Av	26	R 15
Whittlesey Dr	26	R 15
Williams Rd	26	R 17
Willow St	26	R 15
Windaway Rd	26	S 16
Wine Sap Run	26	S 14
Winthrop Rd	26	R 16
Wolfpits Rd	26	S 16
Woodlawn Dr	26	S 14
Wooster St	26	R 14
Yankee Expwy	29	S 13

BRIDGEPORT

STREET	MAP	GRID
Abner Ct	12	T 25
Acorn Av	12	T 25
Acton Rd	12	T 24
Adams St	5	T 27
Admiral St	5	S 27
Adolf Pl	5	S 26
Agnes St	12	T 25
Alameda Pl	5	U 26
Alanson Rd	5	U 27
Alba Av	5	T 25
Albemarle St	12	S 25
Albert Sq	5	S 27
Albion St	5	S 27
Aldine Av	5	S 26
Aldo St	5	S 25
Alex St	5	U 27
Alexander Av	5	T 26
Alexander Dr	5	S 26
Alfred St	5	R 27
Alice Rd	12	T 25
Alice St	5	T 26
Allen St	5	T 27
Alpine St	5	U 26
Alsace St	5	S 27
Amaryk Pl	5	S 26
Ameridge Dr	12	T 25
Amos St	5	T 26
Amsterdam Av	5	T 25
Anchorage Dr	5	R 27
Anchorage Dr	5	R 28
Andover St	5	S 27
Ann St	5	T 27
Anson St	5	T 26
Anthony St	5	S 27
Anton Dr	12	T 25
Anton St	12	T 24
Arcade	5	T 27
Arcadia Av	5	S 26
Arch St	5	T 27
Arctic St	5	T 26
Ardmore St	12	S 25
Arlington St	5	T 26
Armitage Dr	5	R 28
Armstrong Pl	5	T 26
Arthur St	5	R 27
Ash St	5	S 27
Ashley St	5	T 26
Ashton St	12	S 25
Astor St	5	S 27
Astoria Av	5	S 26
Asylum St	5	U 26
Atlantic St	5	S 27
Atwater St	5	S 26
Austin St	5	S 27
Autumn St	5	S 27
Baker St	5	T 25
Baldwin St	5	T 27
Balmforth St	5	R 27
Balsam Av	5	U 25
Bancroft Av	5	S 26
Bank	5	T 27
Bankside St	12	S 25
Barbieri Cir	5	S 25
Barclay St	5	U 26
Barnum Av	5	T 27
Barnum Blvd	5	S 27
Barnum Dyke	5	S 27
Bartlett St	5	T 25
Bartram Av	5	R 27
Bassick Av	5	S 27
Batel La	12	U 25
Battery Park Dr	5	R 28
Bay St	5	T 28
Beach Pl	5	S 26
Beach St	5	T 27
Beachview Av	5	R 27
Beacon Ct	5	R 27
Beacon St	5	R 27
Bear Paw Rd	12	T 24
Beardsley Dr	5	U 26
Beardsley St	5	U 26
Beardsley Ter	5	U 26
Beatrice St	5	U 27
Beauvue Ter	12	T 25
Bedford Av	5	S 27
Beecher St	5	T 26
Beechmont Av	5	T 25
Beechwood Av	5	S 26
Beers St	5	T 26
Bell St	5	U 27
Belmont Av	5	S 27
Benham Av	5	S 27
Bennett St	5	R 27
Benson St	5	S 26
Benson Ter	5	S 26
Berkeley Pl	5	U 26
Berkshire Av	5	T 26
Bertha St	5	T 25
Beverly Dr	5	U 25
Beverly Pl	5	U 25
Bick Ter	5	S 26
Bird St	5	S 27
Birdsey St	5	U 27
Birdseye St	5	S 26
Birmingham St	5	S 25
Bishop Av	5	U 27
Black Rock Av	5	S 27
Blackman Pl	5	S 26
Blackstone St	5	T 28
Blueberry Rd	5	U 25
Bluff St	5	T 25
Bond St	5	U 27
Booth St	5	T 27
Boston Av	5	T 26
Boston Ter	5	U 27
Bostwick Av	5	S 27
Bowker Pl	5	T 25
Bradley St	5	U 26
Bretton St	5	T 25
Brewster St	5	R 27
Breyer Av	5	T 25
Briarwood Av	5	S 26
Britton Av	5	R 27
Broad Bridge Rd	5	U 25
Broad St	5	T 27
Broadway	5	T 25
Bronx Av	5	T 26
Brookfield Av	5	U 27
Brooklawn Av	5	S 26
Brooklawn Pl	5	S 26
Brooks St	5	T 27
Brookside Av	12	U 25
Brothwell St	5	S 26
Bruce Blvd	5	U 27
Brush St	12	T 25
Bryant Pl	5	S 27
Buckingham	5	S 27
Buena Way	5	S 27
Bunnell St	5	T 27
Burnham St	5	S 27
Burnsford Av	5	T 25
Burr Ct	5	S 27
Burr Rd	5	S 27
Burroughs St	5	T 27
Butler Av	5	S 27
Bywater La	5	R 27
Cairnbrook Dr	12	S 25
Calderwood Ct	5	R 27
Calhoun Av	5	T 27
Calhoun Pl	5	T 27
California St	5	T 27
Calvert Pl	5	U 25
Calvin Av	5	S 26
Cambridge St	12	T 25
Camp Pl	12	U 25
Campbell Rd	12	S 24
Canaan Ct	5	U 27
Canaan Rd	5	U 27
Canfield Av	5	R 27
Cannon St	5	T 27
Capitol Av	5	S 26
Carleton Av	5	S 26
Carlson St	5	U 25
Carnegie St	5	U 27
Caroline St	5	T 27
Carrie St	5	U 27
Carroll Av	5	T 28
Carroll Ct	5	T 27
Carter Ct	5	T 26
Cartright St	5	S 26
Carver St	5	U 26
Catherine St	5	T 26
Cedar Creek Dr	5	S 27
Cedar St	5	T 27
Center St	5	T 26
Center St Ext	5	T 26
Central Av	5	T 28
Chalmers Av	5	S 26
Chamberlain Av	5	T 26
Chamberlain Pl	5	T 26
Chapel St	5	T 27
Charles St	5	T 26
Charlotte St	5	T 27
Charron St	12	T 25
Chase St	5	T 26
Chatham Ter	12	T 25
Cherry Hill Dr	12	T 25
Cherry St	5	S 27
Chestnut St	5	T 26
Chopsey Hill Rd	5	T 26
Church St	5	T 27
Circular Av	5	R 27
City View Av	12	U 25
Clair St	5	U 25
Clarence St	5	T 27
Clarke St	5	S 25
Clarkson St	5	R 27
Clearview Cir	12	T 25
Clearview Dr	12	T 25
Clermont Av	5	U 27
Cleveland Av	5	S 26
Clifford St	5	T 27
Clifton Pl	5	U 25
Clinton Av	5	S 26
Clover Hill Av	12	U 25
Coggswell St	5	U 26
Cole	5	S 27
Coleman St	5	U 27
Colonial Av	5	T 26
Colony St	5	U 26
Colorado Av	5	S 26
Columbia Ct	5	S 27
Columbia St	5	S 27
Columbus Pl	5	T 26
Commercial St	5	T 26
Concord St	5	T 26
Congress St	5	T 27
Connecticut Av	5	T 27
Connecticut Tpke	5	S 27
Conner St	12	T 25
Corn Tassel Rd	12	T 24
Cornell St	5	T 25
Cornhill St	12	S 25
Cornwall St	5	S 27
Cottage Pl	5	T 27
Cottage St	5	S 27
Cotter Dr	12	S 24
Court A	5	U 27
Court D	5	U 27
Courtland	5	T 27
Courtland Av	5	R 27
Couse St	5	S 27
Cowles St	5	U 27
Crescent Av	5	T 27
Crescent Pl	5	T 27
Crestview Dr	12	S 25
Cross St	5	U 27
Crown St	5	U 26
Crowther Av	5	R 27
Cumberland Dr	12	T 24
Currier St	5	T 27
Daisy Ct	5	T 26
Dale St	5	U 25
Dande St	5	S 26
Daniel Dr	12	T 24
Daniels St	12	U 25
Davenport St	5	U 28
Davidson St	5	R 27
Davis Av	5	R 27
Dayton Rd	5	U 25
Deacon St	5	T 27
Dean Pl	5	T 26
De Forest Av	5	T 28
De Kalb Av	5	T 28
Denver Av	5	S 27
Denver Ct	5	S 27
D'Eramo Pl	12	S 25
Derman Cir	12	T 24
Dewey La	5	S 26
Dewey St	5	S 27
Dewhirst St	5	T 25
Dexter Dr	12	T 24
Division St	5	U 25
Dixon St	5	S 26
Dobson St	12	T 24
Dodd St	5	U 25
Dogwood Dr	12	U 25
Donald Ct	12	S 24
Dora Cir	5	S 26
Doreen Dr	12	S 24
Douglas St	5	T 25
Dover St	5	U 27
Down St	5	T 25
Downmoor Av	5	T 25
Duane Pl	5	U 25
Dupont Pl	5	U 26
Durando Pl	5	R 27
Eagle St	5	T 27
Earl Av	5	T 25
East Av	5	U 27
East Eaton St	5	S 26
East Kensington Pl	5	U 26
East Main St	5	T 27
East Pasadena Pl	5	U 26
East St	5	U 27
East Thorne St	5	T 25
East Washington Av	5	T 27
Eastway Rd	12	T 25
Eastwood Rd	12	U 25
Eaton St	5	S 26
Eckart St	12	S 24
Edgemoor Rd	12	T 25
Edgewood St	5	S 27
Edna Av	5	U 26
Edwards St	5	U 25
Edwin St	5	U 27
Elias	5	T 27
Elizabeth St	5	U 27
Ellis La	5	T 26
Ellsworth St	5	R 27
Elm Ct	5	T 26
Elm St	5	T 27
Elmsford Rd	12	T 24
Elmwood Av	5	S 27
Elmwood Pl	5	S 27
Emerald St	5	U 26
Emra St	12	T 25
Englewood Av	12	T 25
Enid St	12	T 25
Eric St	5	U 25
Essex St	5	U 26
Evans St	5	U 25
Everett St	5	T 26
Evergreen St	5	T 26
Evers Ct	5	U 26
Evers Pl	5	U 26
Evers St	5	U 26
Evitts La	5	T 27
Exeter St	5	T 25
Ezra St	5	T 27
Fairbanks St	5	U 27
Fairfax Rd	5	U 26
Fairfield Av	5	R 27
Fairlawn Av	5	R 27
Fairmount St	5	T 26
Fairview Av	5	T 25
Fairview Av Ext	5	T 26
Fayerweather St	5	R 27
Federal St	5	T 26
Fern St	12	T 25
Ferris St	5	R 27
Fiske Av	12	U 25
Flanders St	5	T 26
Fleet St	12	T 25
Fleetwood Pl	5	U 26
Flint St	5	T 25
Florence Av	5	U 27
Flower St	5	R 27
Folino Dr	12	S 24
Ford Pl	5	U 27
Forest Ct	5	S 27
Forest St	5	S 27
Forestview Rd	12	T 25
Foster Sq	5	U 26
Fox St	5	R 27
Frances St	5	T 26
Frank St	5	T 26
Franklin St	5	T 27
Freeman St	5	U 27
Fremont St	5	S 27
French Pl	5	T 26
French St	5	T 26
French Town Rd	12	T 25
Front St	5	T 26
Fulton St	5	T 27
Funston Av	5	U 25
Garden Dr	5	T 26
Garden St	5	S 27
Garden Ter	5	R 27
Garfield Av	5	S 26
Garland Av	5	T 26
Gary St	5	U 27
Gaspee Rd	12	T 24
Geduldig St	12	S 25
Gem Av	5	T 26
George St	5	T 26
Gilbert St	5	T 27
Gilman St	5	R 27
Gilmore St	5	T 27
Glen Cir	5	U 25
Glen Ct	5	U 25
Glen Pl	5	U 25
Glen St	5	U 25
Glenbrook Rd	5	U 25
Glendale Av	12	T 25
Glenvale Cir	7	V 25
Glenvale Tr	7	V 25
Glenwood Av	5	T 26
Goddard Av	5	U 26
Gold St	5	T 27
Golden Hill St	5	T 27
Golden Rod Av	12	T 25
Goodman St	5	S 26
Goodsell St	5	T 26
Goodwin St	5	T 27
Grace St	5	U 27
Grand St	5	T 26
Grandview Av	12	U 25
Granfield Av	5	U 27
Grant St	5	U 27
Grasso Ter	5	S 26
Green St	5	T 27
Greenfield Dr	5	S 26
Greenhouse Rd	12	S 25
Greenwood St	5	T 26
Gregory St	5	S 27
Grenelle St	12	T 25
Grey Rock Rd	12	U 25
Greystone Rd	5	U 26
Griffen Av	12	T 25
Grove St	5	S 27
Groves Av	5	R 27
Guilford Dr	12	T 24
Gurdon St	5	T 26
Gustav St	5	T 25
Hackley St	5	R 27
Haddon St	5	R 27
Hadley St	5	U 26
Hale Ter	5	U 27
Hallett St	5	T 27
Hallock St	12	T 25
Hamilton St	5	T 27
Hancock Av	5	S 27
Hanford Av	5	R 27
Hanover St	5	S 27
Hansen Av	5	R 27
Harbor	5	R 27
Harborview Av	5	R 27
Harborview Pl	5	R 27
Harlem Av	5	T 26
Harmony St	5	T 25
Harral Av	5	T 27
Harriet St	5	T 27
Harrison	5	T 27
Hart St	5	T 25
Hart St	5	T 26
Harvard St	5	T 26
Harvey St	5	U 27
Hastings St	5	U 26
Hawley Av	5	T 26
Hawthorne St	5	T 26
Hayes St	5	T 26
Hazel Av	5	T 27
Hazelwood Av	5	S 27
Helen St	5	T 27
Hemlock St	5	R 27
Henderson St	5	U 25
Henry St	5	T 27
Heppinstall Dr	12	S 24
Herald Av	12	T 25
Herbert St	5	T 26
Heritage Pl	12	U 24
Herkimer St	5	S 26
Hewitt Ct	5	U 27
Hewitt St	5	U 27
Hickory St	5	U 26
Hicks St	5	T 26
Higgins Av	5	T 25
Highland Av	5	T 27
Highridge Dr	5	S 26
Hill	5	T 26
Hillcrest Rd	5	U 25
Hillhouse Av	5	T 25
Hillside Av	5	S 26
Hilltop Rd	5	R 27
Hillview St	12	T 24
Holland Av	5	S 27
Holland Hill Cir	7	V 25
Holland Rd	5	U 25
Hollister	6	U 28
Holly St	5	T 27
Hollywood Av	5	U 25
Holroyd St	5	T 26
Homestead Av	5	R 27
Hooker Rd	5	U 26
Hoover St	5	U 27
Hope St	5	R 27
Horace St	5	U 26
Hough Av	5	T 27
Housatonic Av	5	T 27
Houston Av	5	U 25
Houston St	5	T 27
Howard Av	5	S 27
Howard Ct	5	S 27
Howard Pl	5	S 27
Howe Dr	5	S 28
Howe St	5	T 27
Hubbell St	5	S 27
Hudson St	5	T 26
Hughes Av	5	S 26
Hunting St	5	T 26
Huntington Rd	5	T 26
Huntington Tpke	5	U 26
Hurd Av	5	T 26
Hurlock Rd	5	S 26
Huron St	5	U 27
Imperial St	5	T 26
Indian Av	5	T 26
Indian Field Rd	12	T 24
Infield St	5	T 26
Ingleside Pl	5	S 27
Interior St	5	T 25
Interstate Hwy 95	5	U 28
Intervale Rd	7	V 25
Iranistan Av	5	S 26
Iranistan Pl	5	S 27
Island Brook Av	5	T 26
Island Brook Av Ext	5	T 26
Ives Ct	5	T 26
Iwanicki Cir	7	V 25
Jackson Av	5	S 26
James St	5	S 26
Jane St	5	T 26
Janet Cir	12	S 25
Jefferson St	5	T 27
Jennifer Cir	7	V 25
Jennings Av	5	U 26
Jetland Pl	5	R 27
Jetland St	5	R 27
Jewett Av	12	T 25
Jilly Jam Rd	12	T 25
John St	5	S 27
Johnson St	5	S 27
Jones Av	5	T 26
Joseph St	5	T 26
Jourmire Rd	12	T 24
Judson Pl	5	U 27
Julian Dr	5	T 26
Kaechele Pl	12	T 25
Kaechele Rd	12	T 24
Karen Ct	12	U 25
Keeler Av	5	T 25
Kelsey St	5	U 27
Kennedy Dr	12	T 25
Kensington Pl	5	U 25
Kent Av	5	U 27
Kent St	5	U 26
Kevin Rd	12	T 24
Kiefer St	5	T 27
King St	5	R 27
Kingsbury Rd	5	U 26
Knoll Pl	5	U 26
Knowlton St	5	T 26
Kossuth St	5	T 27
Lafayette Blvd	5	T 27
Lafayette Cir	5	T 27
Lafayette St	5	T 27
Lake Av	5	R 27
Lake St	5	T 26
Lakeshore Ter	12	T 25
Lakeside Dr	12	T 25
Lakeview Av	5	U 25
Lance Cir	12	T 24
Landsdowne St	12	T 25
Lansing Pl	5	T 25
Laurel Av	5	S 26
Laurel Ct	5	S 27
Laurel Pl	5	S 26
Lawn St	5	S 26
Lawrence St	5	S 26
Lealand St	12	T 24
Lee Av	5	S 27
Leighton Rd	12	T 24
Lenox Av	5	S 27
Leonard Dr	12	T 24
Lesbia St	5	S 27
Leslie Rd	12	T 25
Lewis Pl	5	U 27
Lewis St	5	S 27
Lexington Av	5	T 26
Lincoln Av	5	S 26
Lincoln Blvd	5	T 26
Linda Dr	12	T 24
Linden Av	5	S 27
Lindley St	5	T 26
Linen Av	5	T 26
Linwood Av	5	S 26
Little Deer Rd	12	T 24
Little St	5	S 27
Livingston Pl	5	U 26
Livingston St	5	R 27
Locust St	5	T 26
Loft St	12	U 25
Loftus Cir	12	T 24
Logan St	5	U 27
Loretta Pl	12	T 25
Lorraine St	5	S 26
Lorraine Ter	5	S 26
Louisiana Av	5	U 26
Lourmel St	12	T 25
Lumber St	5	T 27
Luther St	12	T 25
Lycett St	12	T 24

73

STREET	MAP	GRID
High Ridge Grove	29	U 12
High Ridge Rd	29	U 12
Hillandale Rd	29	U 11
Hillside Cir	29	T 11
Hillside Ct	29	T 11
Hilltop Dr	29	V 13
Hollis Dr	29	T 10
Hollow Oak La	29	T 12
Holly La	29	U 13
Homestead La	29	T 12
Hop Brook Rd	29	U 10
Hope Dr	29	T 13
Horsehill Rd	29	T 11
Horseshoe Dr	29	T 11
Huckleberry Hill Rd	29	T 11
Hunting Ridge Rd	29	U 13
Ina's Rd	29	U 12
Indian Tr	30	T 10
Interstate Hwy 84	26	T 14
Ironworks Hill Rd	29	U 11
Ivy Ct	29	T 11
Jackson Dr	29	T 10
Jason Ct	29	U 12
Jeffrey La	29	T 13
John's Rd	29	U 10
Junction Rd	29	T 12
Juniper La	29	U 10
Kellogg St	30	S 10
Kennen Rd	29	T 11
Kimberly Dr	29	U 10
Knollcrest Dr	29	T 13
Lake George Rd	29	V 12
Lakeview Dr	30	T 10
Lakeview Rd	29	T 11
Lambert La	29	U 12
Laurel Dr	30	T 10
Laurel Hill Rd	29	T 11
Ledgewood Dr	29	U 12
Lexington Dr	29	T 13
Lilac La	30	S 10
Lillinonah Dr	29	V 12
Logging Trail La	29	U 10
Long Meadow Hill Rd	29	U 11
Longview Dr	30	S 10
Lyndenwood Dr	29	V 11
Main Dr	29	T 11
Manor Rd	29	U 12
Maple La	29	U 10
Maple Tree Rd	29	V 12
Marilyn Rd	29	T 12
Mayflower Dr	29	T 13
Meadow Brook Rd	29	T 11
Meadow Dr	29	U 12
Meadowview Dr	29	U 11
Merwin Brook Rd	29	U 12
Mills Rd	30	T 10
Mist Hill Dr	29	T 11
Monika La	29	T 13
Morton Rd	30	S 10
Mountainview Dr	30	T 10
Mudry Farm Rd	29	U 12
Murphy's La	29	U 11
Music Hill Rd	29	U 12
Myron St	30	S 10
Nabby Rd	29	S 12
Navaho Dr	29	V 12
New Bridge Rd	29	V 9
Norris La	29	T 13
North Beech Tree Rd	29	U 12
North Lake Shore Dr	30	T 10
North Mountain Rd	30	T 10
North Pleasant Rise	29	T 11
Oak Crest Dr	29	T 12
Oak Grove Rd	29	U 11
Oak La	29	U 11
Obtuse Hill	29	U 12
Obtuse Rd N	29	U 11
Obtuse Rd S	29	U 13
Obtuse Rocks Rd	29	V 12
Old Bridge Rd	29	U 10
Old Federal Rd	29	T 11
Old Grays Bridge Rd	29	T 12
Old Hawleyville Rd	26	T 14
Old Hemlock Rd	29	T 11
Old Hwy	29	U 12
Old Middle Rd	30	U 10
Old New Milford Rd	29	T 12
Old Prange Rd	30	T 10
Old Route 7	29	T 11
Old State Rd	29	T 12
Old Turnpike	29	T 11
Old White Turkey Rd	29	T 12
Old Woods Rd	29	U 13
Orchard St	29	T 11
Overlook Rd	29	U 12
Ox Dr	29	U 13
Parker Hill Rd	29	U 12
Pasture Dr	29	T 13
Patricia Dr	29	T 10
Phoebee La	29	U 10
Pine St	29	T 12
Pleasant Rise	29	T 11
Pleasant Rise Cir	29	T 11
Pocono Rd	29	T 12
Pocono Ridge Rd	29	T 13
Pond View Dr	29	U 12
Poppy Dr	30	U 10
Powder Horn Hill Rd	29	T 12
Prange Rd	29	T 10
Prange Rd #2	30	T 10
Premium Pt La	29	T 11
Pritten Hill Rd	29	U 12
Production Dr	30	U 10
Prospect Ct	30	U 10
Prospect Dr	30	U 10
Puritan Valley Rd	29	U 10
Quarry Rd	30	U 10
Rabbit La	29	U 11
Ratchford Rd	29	T 13
Red Barn La	29	T 13
Richards Rd	29	U 10
Richmond Rd	29	T 12
Ridge Rd	29	T 13
Ridgeview Ter	30	U 10
Riverford Rd	29	U 10
Robin's La	29	U 10
Rocky Rd	29	T 12
Rollingwood Dr N	29	T 12
Rollingwood Dr S	29	T 12
Sand Cut Rd	29	T 13
Sandy La	29	T 12
School St	29	U 12
Secor Rd	29	T 13
Shamrock Dr	29	U 10
Shirley Ct	29	T 10
Signal Hill Rd	29	U 11
Silvermine Manor	29	U 11
Silvermine Rd	29	T 11
Skyline Dr	30	T 10
Sojo Rd	29	U 10
South Lake Shore Dr	30	S 10
South Mountain Rd	29	T 11
South Ridge Rd	29	U 13
Southeast Tr	30	T 10
Spring La	29	T 13
Spruce Dr	29	T 13
Squire Ct	29	T 13
Stage Rd	29	U 13
State Route 25	29	U 10
State Route 133	29	T 12
Station Rd	29	U 10
Stoney Farm La	29	T 13
Stony Brook Rd	29	T 13
Stony Hill Rd	29	T 13
Sulky Dr	29	U 13
Sunset Hill Rd	29	T 12
Surrey Dr	29	U 13
Sycamore La	29	V 12
Taylor St	30	S 10
Tead Rd	29	T 13
Terry La	29	U 10
Thomsen Farm Rd	29	U 13
Toby La	29	T 13
Tommy's La	29	T 10
Tower Rd	29	U 12
Trailing Ridge Rd	29	U 13
Tremont Rd	29	T 13
Tucks Rd	29	U 11
Tudor La	29	T 12
Tulip Tree Cir	29	T 13
Twilight La	30	T 10
Twin Rocks Rd	29	T 11
US Hwy 7	29	T 11
US Hwy 202	29	T 12
Vale Rd	29	T 13
Valley View Rd	29	T 13
Vista Dr	29	T 10
Wendy's Way	29	U 13
West Whisconier Rd	29	T 13
Whippoorwill La	29	T 10
Whisconier Rd	29	U 13
Whisconier Village	29	U 12
Whispering Way	29	U 10
White Pine Dr	29	U 12
White Tail Way	29	U 12
Willie La	29	S 11
Willow Run	29	T 12
Winding Rd	29	U 11
Windwood Rd	29	V 12
Woodcreek Rd	30	T 10
Woodland Hills Ter	29	T 12
Woodview Dr	29	T 11
Woody La	29	V 13
Yankee Rd	29	U 12

DANBURY

STREET	MAP	GRID
Abbott Av	28	Q 13
Abbott St	28	Q 13
Abigail Rd	28	Q 11
Acre Dr	28	R 12
Adeline Dr	28	R 12
Advocate Pl	28	O 13
Aiken Av	28	Q 13
Alan Av	28	Q 12
Alan Rd	25	P 15
Albers Rd	28	R 13
Albert Rd	28	R 12
Alexander D Av	29	S 13
Alison La	28	R 12
Amity La	28	P 13
Anchor St	28	R 12
Ann Dr	28	Q 13
Apollo Rd	26	R 14
Apple Blossom La	28	R 13
Apple Orchard Dr	29	S 12
Arch St	28	Q 13
Arthur St	25	P 15
Aspen Way	29	S 11
Auburn St	28	R 13
Augusta Dr	28	R 13
Aunt Hack Rd	28	P 12
Austin St	26	R 14
Autumn Dr	28	P 11
Backus Av	25	P 14
Ball Pond Rd	30	P 10
Balmforth Av	28	Q 13
Bank St	28	Q 13
Barnard Dr	26	Q 16
Barnum Ct	28	Q 13
Barnum Rd	28	R 11
Bates Pl	28	Q 13
Baxter St	28	S 11
Bayberry La	28	P 13
Bayberry St	29	S 12
Bayview Dr	29	S 11
Beach Dr	28	R 11
Beach Rd	28	R 12
Bear Mountain Rd	28	R 11
Beardsley Rd	28	R 11
Beaver Brook Rd	28	R 13
Beaver St	28	Q 13
Beckerle St	28	Q 12
Beckett St	28	Q 13
Beech St	28	R 13
Beech Tr	28	R 11
Beechwood Dr	26	R 14
Belair Dr	30	Q 10
Bells La	28	Q 13
Belmont Cir	28	P 13
Belmont Pl	28	P 13
Belmont St	28	Q 13
Benedict Av	28	Q 13
Benham St	28	Q 13
Bennett Pl	28	Q 13
Benson Dr	28	O 13
Bergh St	28	Q 13
Berkshire Dr	28	Q 12
Berkshire Pl	26	Q 14
Bernlou Dr	30	P 10
Betts Rd	29	S 13
Beverly Dr	28	R 12
Birch Crest Dr	28	P 12
Birch Rd	28	P 11
Birch St	28	R 13
Birch Tr	28	R 11
Birchwood La	28	P 12
Birchwood La	28	R 11
Bittersweet Dr	30	Q 10
Blackberry Rd	28	R 12
Blaine St	28	Q 13
Blueberry La	28	O 13
Blueberry La	28	P 13
Boat Rd	28	R 12
Boughton St	26	Q 14
Boulder Ridge Cir	28	R 11
Boulevard Dr	28	O 13
Boxwood La	28	P 13
Boyce Rd	28	P 12
Bragdon Av	28	P 11
Breeze Hill Rd	28	Q 12
Briar Patch La	28	Q 11
Briar Ridge Rd	28	O 13
Briarwood Dr	26	R 14
Bridle Ridge Rd	28	R 11
Brighton St	28	R 12
Broad St	28	R 13
Bronson Dr	28	R 12
Brushy Hill Rd	26	Q 15
Buckskin Hgts Dr	28	R 11
Bullet Hill Rd	28	Q 11
Butternut La	28	P 13
Buttonball Dr	26	R 14
Byron St	26	R 14
Caisson Dr	25	O 14
Cally La	28	R 12
Campbell La	28	R 13
Candlelight Dr	28	R 12
Candlewood Dr	28	R 12
Candlewood Pines Rd	28	R 11
Cannon Dr	28	Q 11
Cannonball Dr	25	O 14
Cannondale Dr	26	Q 14
Canterbury Ct	28	O 12
Capitola Rd	28	Q 11
Carlton St	28	R 11
Carlyle Rd	28	R 12
Carol St	25	P 15
Carolyn Av	28	R 13
Carriage House Dr	25	O 14
Carriage La	25	P 16
Casper St	26	R 14
Castaway Dr	28	P 12
Catalpa Dr	28	P 11
Catherine St	28	Q 12
Caye Rd	28	R 12
Cedar Crest Dr	28	P 12
Cedar Dr	29	S 11
Cedar Rd	28	R 12
Cedar St	28	R 12
Cedar Tr	28	R 11
Cel Bret Dr	25	O 14
Centennial Dr	28	P 11
Center St	28	Q 13
Chambers Rd	28	Q 11
Chapel Pl	28	Q 13
Chappelle St	28	R 13
Charcoal Ridge Dr S	30	Q 10
Cherokee Dr	30	Q 10
Cherry St	28	Q 13
Chestnut St	28	R 13
Chestnut Tr	28	R 11
Chuck Wagon La	25	P 16
Churchill Rd	28	P 13
Circle Dr	28	R 11
Circle Dr E	28	R 13
Circle Dr W	28	R 13
Circle Ter	26	R 14
Clairann Dr	30	Q 10
Clapboard Ridge Rd	28	Q 11
Claremont Av	28	P 13
Claremont Ter	29	S 13
Clark St	26	Q 14
Clason Pl	28	Q 13
Clayton Rd	28	R 12
Clear Brook Rd	28	R 13
Clearview Av	29	S 11
Cleveland St	28	R 13
Clifton Pl	28	Q 13
Coach Hill Dr	28	S 11
Coach Rd	28	Q 12
Coal Pit Hill Rd	26	Q 14
Cobblestone Tr	26	Q 16
Colby La	26	R 14
Cole Pl	28	Q 13
College Park Dr	28	P 13
Colonial Dr	28	Q 12
Commerce Dr	28	S 13
Comstock St	28	Q 13
Concord Rd	28	Q 13
Concord St	28	Q 13
Connecticut Av	26	Q 14
Contemporary Dr	28	Q 11
Cook St	26	R 14
Cooper Rd	30	Q 10
Corn Tassle Rd	29	S 12
Cornell La	25	P 14
Cornell Rd	25	P 14
Cornell Rd	28	R 12
Corporate Dr	28	S 13
Cottage St	26	Q 14
Country Ridge Rd	29	S 13
Country Way	29	S 12
Cowperthwaite St	28	Q 13
Cozy Hollow Rd	28	R 13
Craigmoor Ter	29	S 13
Crane St	28	R 13
Crescent Dr	28	Q 13
Crest Av	28	S 11
Crest Rd	28	Q 12
Crestdale Dr	28	P 13
Crestdale Rd	28	P 13
Crestwood Dr	28	S 12
Crofut Pl	28	Q 13
Crofut St	28	Q 13
Crosby St	28	Q 13
Cross St	26	R 14
Crown St	28	R 13
Crow's Nest La	26	R 14
Cushing Dr	28	P 11
Daly La	28	Q 13
Dana Rd	28	Q 11
Danfred St	25	P 15
Daniels Dr	30	P 10
Darrell Rd	28	Q 11
Dartmouth La	25	P 14
Davis St	28	Q 13
Deal Dr	26	Q 15
Dean St	28	R 13
Deepwood Dr	29	S 13
Deer Hill Av	26	Q 14
Deer Hill Dr	26	Q 14
Deer Park Dr	30	P 10
Deer Run Tr	29	S 12
Deerfield Av	28	R 13
De Klyn's La	28	Q 13
Delay St	28	Q 13
Delno Dr	28	Q 11
Delta Av	26	Q 14
Delview Dr	28	R 12
Dennis Gate	28	S 12
Denver Ter	28	R 12
De Palma La	28	R 11
Devonshire Dr	28	P 12
Diamond Rd	28	R 12
Diana Rd	28	R 13
Dibble St	28	Q 13
Division St	28	Q 13
Dixon Rd	28	R 12
Dogwood Dr	28	Q 12
Dogwood Dr N	28	Q 12
Dogwood Tr	28	R 11
Douglas Dr	28	Q 11
Downs St	28	Q 13
Driftway Point Rd	28	P 12
Driftway Rd	28	P 13
Duck St	28	Q 13
Durant St	28	R 13
Durbin St	28	Q 13
Durham Rd	28	R 11
Eagle Rd	28	S 13
East Broad St	28	R 13
East Dr	25	O 14
East Franklin St	28	Q 13
East Gate Rd	28	Q 12
East Hayestown Rd	28	R 12
East King St	30	Q 10
East Lake Rd	28	Q 11
East Liberty St	28	Q 13
East Meadow Dr	28	Q 12
East Pearl St	26	Q 14
East Pembroke Rd	28	R 12
East Starrs Plain Rd	25	O 16
Eastwood Rd	28	Q 12
Eden Dr	26	R 14
Edgewood Dr	28	R 13
Edgewood St	28	Q 13
Elaine Dr	28	R 11
Elizabeth Rd	28	R 13
Ellsworth Av	28	Q 13
Elm St	28	Q 13
Elm Tr	28	R 11
Elmar Dr	28	Q 11
Elmbrook Rd	28	P 13
Elmcrest Dr	28	P 12
Elmwood Pl	26	Q 14
Elton Av	28	R 13
Elwell Pl	28	R 13
Ervie Dr	29	S 12
Eugene La	28	R 12
Eustis Rd	28	S 11
Evergreen Rd	29	S 11
Executive Dr	28	S 13
Ezra Rd	28	Q 12
Fairfield Av	26	Q 14
Fairfield Ct	28	Q 12
Fairfield Ridge	26	R 14
Fairlawn Av	28	Q 13
Fairmont Dr	28	Q 12
Fairview Dr	26	Q 14
Fairview Ter	28	P 12
Fairway Dr	29	S 13
Fanton Rd	28	R 11
Farm St	28	Q 12
Farview Av	28	Q 13
Farview Ter	28	P 12
Federal Rd	28	R 13
Federal Rd	29	S 13
Fern St	28	Q 13
Field Rd	28	Q 12
Fieldstone Dr	28	Q 11
Filmore Av	28	P 12
Finance Dr	28	R 13
Fir Dr	28	P 12
Firelight Dr	26	Q 16
Fleetwood Dr	26	R 14
Flint Ridge Rd	29	S 11
Flintlock Dr	28	Q 11
Flirtation Dr	28	O 13
Ford Av	28	R 13
Ford La	28	Q 12
Forest Av	28	R 13
Forty Acre Mountain Rd	29	S 11
Foster St	26	Q 14
Fox Den Rd	28	P 11
Francis Rd	26	R 14
Frandon Dr	28	S 11
Franklin St	28	Q 13
Franklin St Ext	28	P 12
French St	28	Q 13
Frontier La	26	Q 16
Gallagher La	28	R 13
Gammie Rd	29	S 11
Garamella Blvd	28	Q 13
Garfield Av	26	Q 14
Garry Knolls	26	R 14
George St	28	Q 13
Germantown Rd	28	R 13
Glen Hill Rd	28	R 13
Glen Rd	28	R 13
Glendale Dr	29	S 11
Gloria La	28	Q 12
Golden Hgts Rd	28	Q 11
Golden Hill Av	28	Q 12
Golden Hill La	28	Q 13
Golden Hill Rd	28	Q 13
Grace St	28	Q 13
Grammar School Dr	28	P 11
Grand St	26	Q 14
Grandview Av	28	Q 13
Grandview Dr	28	P 12
Grandville Av	28	Q 13
Great Meadows Rd	28	R 12
Great Pasture Rd	26	R 14
Great Plain Rd	28	R 12
Green Av	28	P 13
Greendale Av	29	S 12
Greenfield Av	26	Q 14
Greenview Rd	28	Q 12
Gregory St	28	Q 12
Grenier Dr	25	O 14
Greta Dr	28	O 13
Griffing Av	28	Q 13
Grove Pl	28	R 13
Grove St	28	R 13
Haddad Dr	28	Q 13
Haddy La	28	R 12
Hager St	26	R 14
Hakim St	28	Q 13
Hakim St Ext	28	Q 13
Haley St	28	R 12
Hall Passway	28	P 12
Hall St	28	P 12
Hamilton Dr	28	R 11
Harbor Ridge Rd	30	S 11
Harding Pl	28	Q 13
Harmony St	28	Q 13
Harrison St	26	Q 14
Harvard Rd	25	P 14
Harvest Hill Rd	28	Q 11
Harwood Dr	25	O 14
Hausmann Rd	29	S 12
Hawley Av	28	R 13
Hawley Rd	28	R 12
Hawley Rd Ext	28	R 12
Hawley Ter	28	R 12
Hawthorne Cove Rd	29	S 11
Hayes St	28	S 11
Hayestown Av	28	R 13
Hayestown Hgts	28	R 12
Hayestown Rd	28	R 12
Hemlock Tr	28	R 11
Henry St	28	Q 13
Henso Dr	28	Q 11
Heritage Dr	28	P 11
Herman St	28	Q 13
Hickory St	28	R 13
Hickory Tr	28	R 11
High Cir	28	R 12
High Ridge Rd	28	P 13
High Rise Rd	28	R 12
High St	26	R 14
High St Ext	26	R 14
High View Cir	28	R 12
Highfield Dr	28	P 11
Highland Av	28	Q 13
Highland Dr	28	Q 11
Highland Pk Dr	28	Q 11
Hill Top Manor	28	Q 13
Hillandale Rd	28	Q 11
Hillcrest Rd	29	S 11
Hillside Av	28	Q 13
Hillside Rd	28	R 12
Hillside St	28	Q 13
Hitching Post La	30	P 10
Hobson St	28	Q 13
Hollandale Rd	28	R 11
Holley La	28	Q 13
Holley St	28	R 13
Holley St Ext	28	R 13
Home Pl	26	Q 14

DARIEN

STREET	MAP	GRID
Barlow Plain Dr	4	Q 27
Barlow Rd	4	Q 27
Barnhill Ct	12	R 25
Barnhill Rd	12	R 25
Baros St	5	R 26
Barry Scott Dr	5	R 26
Barton Rd	5	R 27
Bay Edge Ct	5	R 27
Bayberry Rd	12	S 25
Beach Rd	4	Q 27
Beacon Sq	5	R 26
Beacon View Dr	5	R 26
Beagling Hill Cir	11	P 24
Beaumont Pl	4	Q 27
Beaumont St	4	Q 27
Beaver Brook La	12	S 25
Beaver St	5	S 26
Beechwood La	11	Q 25
Beechwood La	12	S 25
Beers Rd	12	R 23
Bel-Air La	5	R 26
Belmont St	4	Q 27
Benedict Av	5	S 25
Bennett St	12	S 25
Benson Pl	4	Q 27
Benton St	5	R 26
Berkeley Rd	5	S 26
Berrylane Ct	5	S 26
Berwick Av	5	R 26
Berwick Ct	5	R 27
Beth Dr	12	R 25
Beverly La	12	R 25
Bibbins Av	5	R 26
Birch Rd	4	Q 27
Birchwood Cir	5	R 26
Birchwood Dr	5	R 26
Biro St	5	R 26
Bittersweet Rd	11	Q 25
Black Rock Av	5	R 26
Black Rock Tpke	5	R 26
Black Rock Tpke	12	R 23
Blackmount Close	12	S 25
Blackmount La	12	S 25
Blaine St	4	Q 27
Blake Dr	4	Q 27
Bloomfield Dr	5	R 26
Blue Bell La	12	R 23
Blue Ridge Rd	5	S 26
Blueberry La	5	S 25
Bond St	12	S 25
Bonney Ter	4	P 27
Boroskey Dr	5	R 26
Boston Post Rd	4	Q 27
Bowman Way	4	P 28
Bradford St	5	R 26
Bradley St	4	Q 27
Brambley Hedge Cir	11	P 24
Brentwood Av	5	R 26
Brett La	11	Q 24
Brett Rd	11	Q 24
Bridget La	4	Q 27
Bridle Tr	12	R 25
Brighton View Rd	12	R 25
Brion Dr	12	S 25
Broad River La	4	Q 27
Bronson Av	4	Q 26
Bronson Rd	4	P 27
Brookbend Rd	4	Q 27
Brookdale Rd	5	R 26
Brookfield Av	5	S 26
Brooklawn Av	5	S 26
Brooklawn Pkwy	5	S 25
Brooklawn Ter	5	S 26
Brookmere Dr	5	R 26
Brookridge Av	5	S 25
Brookside Dr	5	R 25
Brookview Av	5	S 25
Brothwell St	4	Q 26
Browns La	4	Q 27
Buckboard La	12	R 25
Buena Vista Rd	5	S 25
Bulkley Dr	12	R 25
Bullard St	5	S 26
Bungalow Av	4	Q 27
Bunnell Cir	12	R 25
Burr St	11	Q 24
Burroughs Rd	5	R 26
Butternut La	4	P 26
Calf Pond La	11	Q 24
Calico La	11	Q 25
Cambridge St	5	R 27
Camden St	5	S 27
Camp Field Rd	5	R 26
Campbell Rd	11	Q 25
Candlewood Rd	5	R 26
Canterbury La	12	R 25
Cardinal Hill	4	P 27
Cardinal St	5	S 26
Carlton St	4	Q 27
Carlynn Dr	4	Q 28
Carriage Dr	4	Q 26
Carroll Rd	4	Q 26
Carter Henry Dr	4	Q 27
Carthage St	5	R 26
Cascade Dr	12	R 24
Casmir Dr	12	S 25
Castle Av	5	R 26
Catamount Rd	11	P 24
Catherine St	4	Q 27
Catherine Ter	4	Q 27
Cedar Rd	4	P 26
Cedarhurst La	5	R 26
Cedarwood La	12	S 25
Cemetery Rd	4	Q 26
Center St	4	P 27
Centerbrook Pl	5	R 26
Centerbrook Rd	5	R 26
Chambers St	5	R 27
Chapel Hill Dr	12	S 25
Chapman Av	5	R 26
Charles St	4	Q 28
Charter Oak Rd	4	Q 26
Chatham Rd	12	S 25
Chelsea St	4	Q 27
Cherry Hill Rd	12	S 24
Cherry La	11	Q 25
Chester Pl	4	P 27
Chestnut St	5	R 27
Christmas Tree La	4	P 27
Church Hill Rd	12	S 25
Church St	4	P 27
Churchill St	5	R 27
Cidermill La	4	Q 26
Circle La	5	S 26
Clare Dr	11	Q 24
Clarke St	5	S 25
Clinton St	4	Q 27
Club Dr	12	S 24
Coach La	12	R 25
Cobblers Hill Rd	4	Q 26
Coburn St	5	R 26
Coleman Rd	5	R 25
College Park Dr	4	Q 26
College Pl	4	Q 28
Collingwood Av	5	S 26
Colonese Rd	12	S 25
Colonial Dr	4	Q 27
Colony St	5	R 27
Commerce Dr	5	R 27
Commondage Way	4	Q 26
Concord St	5	R 27
Congress Pl	12	R 24
Congress St	11	Q 24
Congress St	12	R 24
Connecticut Tpke	4	Q 27
Coolidge	5	R 27
Coolidge Ct	5	S 27
Coral Dr	5	R 26
Cornell Rd	5	S 26
Country Rd	5	R 26
Coventry La	11	Q 24
Craig Ct	5	R 27
Craig Pl	4	Q 27
Crane St	5	S 26
Cranston St	4	Q 27
Creconoof Rd	12	R 25
Crescent Rd	4	Q 27
Crest Ter N	12	S 25
Crestwood Rd	5	R 27
Crimson La	5	R 26
Cross Hwy	11	P 24
Crystal La	4	Q 26
Cummings Av	4	Q 28
Curtis Ter	12	S 25
Curtis Ter N	12	S 25
Cynthia Dr	4	Q 26
Dalewood Av	5	R 27
Daley Dr	4	Q 28
Darrell Dr	4	Q 27
Darrow Dr	4	P 27
Dave's La	4	P 26
Davis Rd	12	S 25
Dawn St	5	R 26
Daybreak Rd	4	P 26
Deep Wood Rd	12	R 25
Deer Park Rd	5	R 26
Deer Run	4	Q 26
Deerfield St	5	R 26
Dell Dale Rd	5	R 25
Denise Ter	5	R 26
Dill Rd	5	R 26
Division Av	5	R 26
Dogwood La	5	R 26
Donna Dr	12	S 24
Doreen Dr	4	Q 26
Dorking Dr	4	Q 27
Dorothy St	5	S 25
Drake La	4	Q 26
Dresden St	5	R 26
Drumm Rd	4	Q 26
Duck Farm Rd	4	Q 26
Dudley Dr	4	Q 26
Duka Av	5	R 27
Dunham Rd	11	Q 25
Dunhill Dr	4	P 28
Dunnlea Rd	4	Q 26
Dwight St	4	Q 27
Eagle Dr	5	S 26
East Paulding St	4	Q 27
Eastbourne Rd	5	R 27
Eastfield Cir	12	S 24
Eastfield Dr	12	S 24
Eastfield Dr Ext	12	S 24
Eastfield Ter	12	S 24
Eastlawn St	4	Q 28
Eastlea Rd	11	Q 24
Easton Tpke	12	S 24
Eastwood Rd	5	S 25
Echo La	12	S 25
Edge Hill Pl	4	Q 27
Edge Hill Rd	4	Q 27
Edgewood Pl	5	S 25
Edgewood Rd	5	S 25
Edison Av	5	R 26
Edward St	4	Q 28
Elderberry La	5	R 26
Eleanor Ter	4	Q 27
Eleven O'Clock Rd	11	Q 24
Eliot Pl	4	Q 27
Eliot St	4	Q 27
Elizabeth St	5	R 26
Elm St	4	Q 27
Elvira La	11	Q 24
Emmy La	4	Q 26
Ermine St	4	Q 27
Essex St	5	S 26
Euclid Av	5	S 26
Eunice Av	4	Q 28
Evelyn Dr	4	P 26
Evergreen Hill Rd	11	Q 24
Exchange Pl	5	S 26
Fair Oak Dr	11	P 25
Fairchild Av	5	R 26
Fairfield Beach Rd	4	P 28
Fairfield Pl	4	P 27
Fairfield Woods Rd	5	R 25
Fairland Dr	5	R 25
Fairmont Dr	12	R 25
Fairmount Ter	5	S 26
Fairview Av	5	R 27
Fairway Green	5	S 26
Fallow Field La	11	Q 24
Fallow Field Rd	11	Q 23
Falmouth Rd	12	S 25
Farist Rd	5	R 25
Farmington Av	5	S 25
Farmstead Hill	11	Q 25
Fencerow Dr	11	P 24
Ferguson Dr	4	Q 26
Fern St	4	Q 27
Ferncliff Rd	5	S 25
Fieldcrest Dr	5	R 26
Fields Rock Rd	4	Q 26
Figlar Av	5	R 26
Finn St	5	R 26
Fiske St	5	R 27
Flax Rd	4	P 27
Fleming La	11	P 25
Flintlock Rd	4	P 26
Flora Blvd	4	P 27
Florence La	12	R 25
Flower House Dr	4	Q 26
Flushing Av	12	S 25
Fogg Wood Cir	17	Q 23
Fogg Wood Rd	17	Q 23
Forest Av	4	Q 28
Fortuna Dr	4	P 27
Four Seasons Rd	12	S 25
Fox Run Rd	4	Q 26
Fox St	4	Q 28
Francis St	4	Q 27
Frank St	5	R 27
French St	4	P 28
Frog Pond La	11	Q 25
Fulling Mill La	4	Q 26
Galloping Hill Rd	12	R 25
Garden Ct	5	S 25
Garden Dr	5	S 25
Garden Sq	5	S 25
Gate Ridge Dr	12	S 25
Gate Stone La	12	R 23
Gay Bowers Rd	11	Q 25
Gaynos Dr	12	S 24
Geneva Ter	4	Q 27
Georgia St	5	R 27
Gilbert Hwy	11	P 23
Ginger Cir	12	S 25
Glenarden Dr	5	R 26
Glenarden Dr S	5	R 26
Glenridge Rd	12	R 25
Glover St	4	Q 26
Godfrey Rd	12	S 25
Golden Pond La	11	Q 25
Golf View Ter	12	S 25
Gorham Rd	4	P 27
Gould Av	4	Q 27
Governors La	4	Q 26
Grace St	5	R 26
Grandview Rd	12	S 25
Granville St	4	Q 27
Grasmere Av	5	R 27
Gray Rock Rd	4	P 26
Green Acre La	5	R 27
Green Knolls La	5	R 26
Greenbrier Cir	5	R 26
Greenbrier Rd	5	R 26
Greenfield Hill Rd	11	Q 25
Greenfield Pl	5	S 25
Greenfield St	5	S 26
Greenlawn Dr	5	S 25
Greenleigh Rd	12	S 25
Gristmill La	4	P 26
Gunston Rd	4	P 27
Half Mile La	4	P 26
Half Mile Rd	4	P 26
Halley Av	5	R 26
Halley Ct	5	R 27
Hanford Dr	4	Q 26
Harbor La	4	P 27
Harbor Rd	4	P 27
Harris St	5	R 27
Harvester Rd	12	S 25
Harwich Rd	12	S 25
Hawthorne Dr	12	S 24
Hazel St	5	R 26
Heather La	4	Q 26
Helen St	4	Q 27
Hemlock Hills Rd N	12	R 24
Hemlock Hills Rd S	12	R 24
Hemlock Rd	11	Q 24
Henderson Rd	4	Q 27
Henry St	4	Q 26
Hersh Rd	5	R 26
Hibiscus	5	R 27
Hickory La	11	Q 25
High Circle La	12	R 25
High Ct	5	R 27
High Meadow Rd	4	Q 26
High Point La	11	Q 25
High Ridge Rd	5	R 25
High St	5	R 25
Highland La	12	S 25
Highlawn Rd	5	R 26
Hill Brook La	11	Q 25
Hill Farm Rd	4	Q 26
Hillandale Rd	5	S 25
Hillcrest Rd	4	Q 27
Hillside Rd	4	Q 26
Hillside Rd	11	Q 25
Hillside Ter	11	Q 25
Hilltop Dr	4	P 27
Hitching Post La	5	R 26
Holiday Rd	12	S 24
Holland Hill Rd	5	R 27
Hollis St	4	Q 27
Hollow Tree Cir	11	P 25
Holly Dale Rd	12	R 25
Home Fair Dr	5	R 25
Home St	5	R 27
Homeland St	5	S 25
Homestead La	11	Q 23
Honeysuckle La	4	Q 27
Horace Ct	4	Q 27
Hornbeam Rd	12	R 24
Horseshoe La	11	P 25
Howard St	4	Q 27
Hoydens Hill Rd	12	R 23
Hoydens La	12	R 24
Hubbell La	11	Q 25
Hulls Farm Rd	4	P 26
Hulls Hwy	4	P 26
Hunter La	4	Q 26
Hunter Rd	4	Q 26
Hunter St	5	S 27
Hurd St	4	Q 27
Huyadi Av	5	R 26
Indian Point Rd	12	R 25
Ingleside Rd	11	P 25
Interstate Hwy 95	5	R 27
Inverary Close	12	S 25
Inwood Rd	5	S 25
Ironside Rd	11	P 25
Ivy La	4	P 26
Jackman Av	5	S 25
James St	4	Q 28
Jarvis Ct	4	Q 28
Jay Cir	5	R 25
Jefferson St	12	S 24
Jelliff La	4	P 27
Jeniford Rd	5	R 26
Jennie La	11	P 25
Jennings Rd	5	R 26
Jessica La	4	P 26
Joan Dr	12	R 25
John St	4	P 27
Johnson Dr	5	R 27
Judd St	5	R 26
Judges Hollow Rd	11	Q 23
Judson Rd	4	Q 27
Juniper La	4	P 26
Kalan Cir	5	R 26
Karen St	5	R 26
Katona Dr	5	R 26
Kenard St	5	R 27
Kenwood Av	5	R 27
King St	5	S 26
Kings Dr	4	P 27
Kings Hwy Cutoff	5	R 27
Kings Hwy E	5	R 26
Kings Hwy W	4	P 27
Kings La	4	P 27
Kinnie Dr	4	Q 27
Knapps Hwy	5	R 26
Knapps Park Dr	5	S 26
Knoll, The	4	P 26
Knollwood Dr	5	R 26
Labbance La	11	P 25
Lacey Pl	4	P 27
Lagana La	5	R 26
Lakeside Ct	5	R 26
Lakeside Dr	4	Q 26
Lakeview Ct	12	R 25
Lakeview Dr	12	R 25
Lakeview Pl	12	R 25
Lakewood Dr	12	R 24
Lalley Blvd	4	Q 27
Lamplighter La	12	R 24
Lampwick La	12	R 23
Lancelot Dr	11	Q 25
Lantern Rd	4	Q 26
Larbert Rd	4	P 27
Larkspur Rd	5	R 26
Laslo Ter	5	R 25
Laurel St	5	R 26
Laurelbrook La	11	Q 25
Lawrence Rd	4	Q 26
Lee Dr	4	P 27
Lenox Rd	5	R 26
Leslie La	11	Q 23
Lewis Dr	5	S 26
Lilac La	12	R 25
Lilalyn Dr	12	S 25
Limerick Rd	4	Q 26
Lind St	4	Q 28
Lindamir La	12	R 25
Lindbergh Ct	4	Q 27
Lindbergh St	4	Q 27
Linley Dr	5	S 25
Linwood Av	4	Q 27
Lisbon Dr	12	S 25
Little Brook Rd	5	S 25
Livingston St	5	S 25
Lloyd Dr	12	S 25
Lloyd Pl	12	S 25
Lockwood Cir	12	S 25
Lockwood Rd	12	S 25
Lola St	12	S 25
London Ter	12	S 25
Long Meadow Rd	11	Q 24
Longdean Rd	4	Q 28
Longfellow Av	5	R 26
Longview Av	5	R 27
Lookout Dr N	5	S 26
Lookout Dr S	5	S 26
Lota Dr	5	R 26
Lounsbury Rd	12	S 24
Louvain St	12	S 25
Lovers La	5	R 26
Lu Manior	11	Q 25
Lu Manor Dr	12	S 25
Lucille St	5	R 25
Lucille St N	12	R 25
Ludlowe Ct	4	Q 27
Ludlowe Rd	4	Q 27
Lyman Rd	12	R 25
Lynnbrook Rd	5	S 26
Main St	4	P 27
Maple Dr	4	Q 26
Margemere Dr	5	R 26
Marian Rd	5	S 25
Mariners Way	4	Q 27
Marlborough Ter	5	S 26
Marne Av	5	S 26
Marsh Dr	5	R 26
Martingale La	11	Q 25
Maryland Av	5	R 27
Mason St	5	S 26
Massachusetts Av	5	R 27
May St	5	R 26
Mayfair Rd	5	R 26
Mayflower Cir	5	R 26
Mayweed Rd	5	R 26
Meadow Ct	4	P 27
Meadow St	5	R 27
Meadowbrook Rd	5	R 27
Meadowcrest Dr	12	S 25
Meadowcroft Rd	5	R 26
Meeting House La	11	Q 25
Melin Dr	11	Q 25
Mellow St	4	Q 27
Melody Ct	5	R 26
Melody La	5	R 26
Melville Av	5	S 25
Melville Dr	5	S 25
Memory La	5	R 26
Merritt Pkwy	12	S 24
Merritt St	5	S 25
Merry Meet Cir	11	P 24
Merton St	4	Q 27
Merwins La	11	P 25
Middlebrook Dr N	4	Q 26
Middlebrook Dr S	4	Q 26
Middlebrook Pl	4	Q 26
Midlock Rd	11	Q 24
Milandale Rd	5	R 26
Milbank Rd	11	Q 25
Mile Common	11	Q 23
Mill Hill La	4	P 27
Mill Hill Rd	4	P 26
Mill Hill Ter	4	P 26
Mill Plain Green	4	Q 27
Mill Plain Rd	4	Q 26
Mill River Rd	4	Q 26
Millard St	4	Q 27
Miller	4	Q 27
Millspaugh Dr	4	Q 26
Milton St	5	R 27
Mine Hill Rd	11	Q 25
Miro St	5	R 26
Misty Wood La	11	Q 23
Mohican Hill Rd	12	R 24
Mona Ter	4	Q 28
Montauk St	5	S 25
Moody Av	5	S 26
Morehouse Dr	12	R 24
Morehouse Hwy	5	R 25
Morehouse Hwy	12	R 23
Morehouse La	4	P 26
Moritz Pl	5	R 26
Morning Dew Cir	11	P 24
Mountain Laurel Rd	5	R 25
Mulberry Hill Rd	11	P 24
Myren St	4	Q 28
Narrow St	4	Q 27
Nathan Hale St	5	R 26
Nelson Pl	5	S 25
Nepas Rd	12	R 25
New England Av	5	R 27
New Hampshire Av	5	R 27
New St	12	S 25
Newell Pl	5	R 27
Newman Pl	5	S 25
Newport Pl	12	R 25
Newton	5	R 27
Nichols Av	5	S 26
Nichols St	4	Q 27
Nonopoge Rd	12	R 25
Norcliff La	4	Q 28
Nordstrand Av	5	S 26
North Benson Rd	4	Q 27
North Cedar Rd	4	Q 26
North Hill La	12	R 23
North Pine Creek Rd	4	Q 27
North Renwick Dr	5	S 26
North St	11	Q 23
Northfield Rd	4	Q 27
Northwick Dr	12	S 25
Northwood Rd	5	S 25
Noyes Rd	4	Q 27
Nutmeg La	5	R 26
Oak Bluff Rd	12	S 25
Oakwood Dr	5	R 26
Old Academy Rd	11	Q 25
Old Barn Rd	4	Q 27
Old Black Rock Tpke	12	R 25
Old Coach Rd	12	R 25
Old Dam Rd	4	P 28
Old Dam Rd E	4	Q 28
Old Elm Rd	12	S 25
Old Farm La	5	S 26
Old Farm Rd	5	S 26
Old Field Rd	4	P 27
Old Hickory Rd	11	P 25
Old Mill Rd	4	Q 26
Old Oaks Rd	5	S 26
Old Orchard Pk	4	Q 27
Old Post Rd	4	P 27
Old Post Rd	4	Q 27
Old South Rd	4	P 27
Old Spring Rd	5	R 27
Old Stratfield Rd	5	R 26
Oldfield Dr	4	Q 28
One Rod Hwy	4	Q 28
Open Gate La	4	Q 27
Orange St	4	Q 27
Orchard Hill Dr	4	Q 26
Orchard Hill La	4	Q 26

STREET	MAP	GRID
Creamer Hill Rd	14	C 20
Crescent Rd	1	D 25
Crocker	1	D 25
Cross	1	A 25
Cross La	1	C 25
Cross Ridge Dr	2	E 25
Crown La	15	E 22
Curt Ter	8	A 24
Cutler Rd	14	B 20
Daffodil La	9	E 24
Dairy Rd	8	C 23
Dale Dr	1	A 25
Dandy Dr	1	D 25
Dartmouth Rd	8	D 24
Davenport Av	1	B 25
Davis Av	1	A 25
Dawn Harbor La	1	D 26
Day	14	C 20
Dayton Av	1	B 25
Dearfield Dr	1	B 25
Dearfield La	1	B 25
Decatur	1	D 25
Deep Gorge Rd	8	B 24
Deepwoods Rd	1	D 26
Deer La	8	C 24
Deer Park Ct	8	C 24
Deer Park Meadow Rd	8	C 24
DeKraft Rd	14	C 22
Delavan Av	1	A 25
De Luca Dr	9	E 24
Delwood La	8	C 24
Dempsey La	8	D 23
Den La	1	A 25
Desiree Dr	9	E 23
Dewart Rd	14	D 22
Dialstone La	1	D 25
Diary Rd	8	C 23
Dingletown Rd	8	D 23
Division	1	A 25
Division	8	C 24
Dogwood La	8	C 23
Doolittle	2	E 25
Dorchester La	1	D 25
Doubling Rd	8	C 24
Douglas Dr	8	A 24
Doverton Dr	14	B 22
Dovey La	1	D 26
Driftway	1	A 26
Drinkwater Pl	1	D 26
Druid La	1	D 25
Dublin Hill Dr	8	D 24
Duncan Dr	8	B 23
Dunwoodie Pl	8	D 23
Durkin Pl	1	D 25
Dwight La	14	B 21
East Byway	8	A 24
East Elm	1	C 25
East Lawn La	8	A 23
East Lyon Farm Dr	8	B 24
East Point La	1	D 27
East Putnam Av	1	C 25
East Weaver	1	B 25
Ebert Rd	9	E 23
Echo La	8	C 24
Edgar Rd	14	D 20
Edgewater Dr	1	D 26
Edgewood Av	1	B 25
Edgewood Dr	1	B 25
Edgewood Pl	1	B 25
Edson La	8	C 23
Edward Pl	2	E 25
Eggleston La	1	D 26
Elizabeth La	1	D 25
Ellin Dr	8	A 24
Elm	9	E 24
Elm Pl	1	C 25
Elskip La	8	B 23
Ernel Dr	1	D 25
Essex Dr	8	A 24
Esther Pl	1	D 26
Ettl La	8	A 24
Ettl La Ext	8	A 24
Eugene	1	A 25
Evergreen Rd	8	C 24
Fado La	8	D 24
Fairchild La	14	B 21
Fairfield Av	1	D 26
Fairfield Rd	8	C 24
Fairgreen La	1	D 26
Fairview Ter	8	A 24
Fairway La	8	D 24
Farley	8	B 24
Farms Rd	15	E 21
Farwell La	14	C 20
Fawcett Pl	1	B 25
Ferncliff Rd	8	D 23
Ferraro Ct	1	D 25
Ferris Dr	1	D 25
Field	9	E 24
Field Point Cir	1	B 26
Field Point Dr	1	B 26
Field Point Rd	1	B 25
Field Rd	1	D 26
Field Ridge Rd	1	C 25
Fitch La	1	D 25
Flagler Dr	8	D 23
Fletcher Av	8	A 24
Flintlock Rd	8	B 24
Florence Rd	2	E 25
Flower La	1	B 25
Ford La	1	D 26
Forest Av	1	D 26
Fort Hills La	8	C 23
Fox Run La	8	B 24
Fox's La	1	B 25
Francine Dr	8	C 24
Francis La	8	A 24
French Rd	8	C 23
Frontage Rd	1	A 25
Frontier Rd	8	D 23
Frost Rd	8	C 23
Gabriel La	1	B 25
Game Cock Rd	1	A 26
Gard Ct	8	A 24
Garden Pl	1	A 25
Gaston Farms Rd	14	D 20
Gate Field Dr	14	C 22
Gateway La	14	A 21
George	1	D 26
Gerald Ct	1	D 25
Gerry	1	B 25
Gilliam La	1	D 26
Ginkgo La	8	C 24
Gisbourne Pl	2	E 26
Glen	1	B 25
Glen Avon Dr	1	C 26
Glen Ct	1	B 25
Glen Rd	8	C 24
Glen Ridge Rd	8	A 24
Glendale	1	D 25
Glenville	8	A 24
Glenville Rd	8	B 24
Glenwood Dr	1	B 26
Gold	1	A 25
Golf Club Rd	8	C 24
Gordon La	8	C 23
Grace	1	D 26
Grace Pl	1	D 26
Grahamton La	8	C 23
Grand	1	B 25
Grange	1	B 25
Grant Av	1	D 26
Grass Isl Rd	1	B 25
Gray Oaks La	14	D 22
Green La	1	B 25
Greenbriar La	14	C 22
Greenway Dr	8	B 24
Greenwich Av	1	B 25
Greenwich Cove Dr	1	D 26
Greenwich Hills Dr	8	A 24
Gregory Rd	9	E 24
Grey Rock Dr	8	B 24
Griffith Rd	1	D 25
Grigg	1	B 25
Grimes Rd	1	D 26
Grossett Rd	1	D 26
Grove	1	D 25
Grove La	1	B 25
Guards Rd	15	E 20
Guilford La	8	A 24
Guinea Rd	9	E 23
Halock Dr	8	A 24
Halsey Dr	2	E 25
Halstead Av	1	A 25
Hamilton Av	1	B 25
Harbor Dr	1	B 26
Hard Scrabble Rd	14	B 21
Harding Rd	1	D 26
Harkim Rd	8	B 23
Harold	1	D 25
Harold Av	1	B 25
Hartford Av	1	A 25
Hassake Rd	2	E 25
Havemeyer La	2	E 25
Havemeyer Pl	1	B 25
Hawkwood La	8	D 24
Hawthorne	1	B 25
Hawthorne N	8	B 24
Hearthstone Dr	1	D 25
Heather La	8	B 23
Hedgerow La	14	C 22
Hekma Rd	15	E 21
Hemlock Dr	1	B 25
Hendrie Av	1	D 25
Hendrie Dr	1	D 26
Hendrie Dr Ext	1	D 26
Hendrie La	1	D 25
Henry	1	A 25
Heronvue	14	B 21
Hervey	1	A 25
Hettiefred Rd	8	A 23
Heusted Dr	1	D 26
Hickory Dr	1	A 25
Hidden Brook Rd	1	D 26
High	1	A 25
Highgate Rd	1	C 26
Highland Farm Rd	14	C 21
Highland Pl	1	B 25
Highland Rd	1	A 25
Highmeadow Rd	2	E 25
Highview Av	1	D 26
Highview Rd	8	B 24
Hill La Av	1	D 26
Hill Rd	8	D 24
Hill Top Rd	1	A 25
Hillcrest La	2	E 25
Hillcrest Park Rd	9	E 24
Hillside Av	1	A 25
Hillside Dr	8	B 24
Hillside Rd	1	C 25
Hilton Heath	8	D 24
Hines La	1	D 25
Hobart Av	1	A 25
Hobart Dr	8	B 24
Hollis	8	C 24
Hollow Wood La	1	A 25
Holly Hill La	1	B 25
Holly Way	8	D 24
Holm Rd	14	B 22
Holman La	1	D 26
Home Pl	1	C 25
Homestead La	1	A 25
Homestead Rd	8	B 24
Hooker La	9	E 23
Hoover Rd	1	D 25
Hope Farm La	14	C 22
Horse Isl Rd	1	C 26
Horseneck La	1	B 25
Horseshoe Rd	9	E 23
Howard Rd	15	E 21
Huckleberry La	14	C 22
Hunt Ter	8	A 24
Hunter	2	E 25
Hunter Pl	1	C 25
Hunting Ridge Rd	14	D 22
Huntzinger Dr	8	B 24
Hurlingham Dr	14	D 20
Husted La	8	C 24
Hycliff Rd	14	B 22
Idar Ct	1	B 25
Idlewild Manor	1	B 25
Indian Chase Dr	1	C 26
Indian Dr	1	D 27
Indian Field Rd	1	C 26
Indian Harbor Dr	1	B 25
Indian Head Rd	1	C 26
Indian Knoll Pl	14	B 22
Indian Mill Rd	9	E 24
Indian Pass	1	C 25
Indian Pt La	1	C 26
Indian Rock La	8	D 24
Indian Spring Rd	8	B 24
Innis La	1	D 26
Interlaken Rd	14	D 22
Interstate Hwy 95	1	B 25
Interstate Hwy 95	2	E 25
Interstate Hwy 684	14	B 20
Intervale Pl	1	B 25
Intrieri La	1	C 25
Iron Horse La	1	D 26
Irvine Rd	1	D 26
Island La	1	B 25
Ivanhoe La	8	D 23
Ivy	1	A 25
Jackson	1	D 25
Jada La	8	D 24
James E	1	A 26
James W	1	A 25
Janet Ct	1	D 25
Jeffrey Rd	8	D 24
Jenifer La	1	D 25
Jo Fran La	8	C 24
John	14	B 21
Jones Park Dr	1	D 26
Jos Evaristo Av	1	B 25
Joshua La	8	D 23
Juniper Hill Rd	9	E 23
Juniper La	1	D 25
Kandahar Rd	8	B 24
Kemondo Rd	8	D 24
Kenilworth Ter	8	C 24
Kensington Ct	1	D 26
Kent Pl	1	D 25
Keofferam Rd	1	D 26
Kernan Pl	2	E 26
Khakum Dr	8	C 23
Khakum Wood Rd	8	C 23
King	8	A 23
King	14	A 22
Kinsman La	1	C 25
Kirby	1	A 25
Kitchawan La	8	B 24
Knoll	1	D 26
Knollwood Dr	8	C 24
Knollwood Dr E	8	C 24
Konitterock Rd	8	C 23
Laddins Rock Rd	1	D 25
Lafayette Ct	1	C 25
Lafayette Pl	1	C 25
Lake Av	1	B 25
Lake Av	8	C 24
Lake Dr	1	D 26
Lake Dr S	1	D 26
Lake View Dr	1	D 25
Lakewood Cir N	1	B 25
Lakewood Cir S	1	B 25
Lancer Rd	1	D 25
Langhorne La	14	C 21
Lantern La	8	A 24
Lapham La	14	B 21
Lark's Dr	8	B 24
Larkspur La	14	C 22
Laub Pond Rd	14	B 21
Lauder La	8	B 24
Lauder Way	8	B 24
Laurel La	8	C 23
Laurel La Spur	8	C 23
Lawrence	1	C 25
Ledge Rd	1	D 27
Leeward La	1	D 26
Lefrentz Rd	14	C 20
LeGrande Av	1	C 25
Le June Ct	2	E 25
Lenox Dr	1	C 25
Leonard Av	1	D 25
Leslie Av	8	B 23
Lewis	1	C 25
Lewis Ct	1	C 25
Lexington Av	1	C 25
Lia Fail Way	1	D 25
Liberty Way	1	C 25
Licata Ter	9	E 24
Lighthouse La	1	D 27
Lillian Pl	1	D 26
Limerick Pl	9	E 23
Lincoln Av	1	C 25
Linden Pl	8	B 24
Lindsay Pl	8	B 24
Lindsey Dr	8	D 23
Linwood Av	1	D 25
Lismore La	8	B 23
Lisso Av	2	E 25
Lita Dr	8	C 24
Little Cove Pl	1	D 26
Livingston Pl	1	B 25
Loading Rock Rd	1	D 25
Loch La	14	D 22
Lockwood Av	1	D 26
Lockwood Dr	1	D 26
Lockwood La	1	D 25
Lockwood Rd	1	D 25
Locust	1	C 25
Locust Rd	14	A 21
Londonderry Dr	8	D 23
Long Meadow Ct	1	D 25
Long Meadow Rd	1	D 25
Long View Av	1	D 26
Louden	1	A 25
Loughlin Av	1	C 25
Lower Cross Rd	14	D 21
Lucy	1	A 25
Lyon Av	1	B 25
MacArthur Dr	2	E 25
MacKenzie Glen	8	D 23
MacPherson Dr	8	C 24
Magill Dr	8	C 24
Maher Av	1	C 25
Maher Ct	1	C 25
Mahon La	1	D 25
Maiden La	8	B 23
Mallard Dr	1	C 25
Manetti La	8	D 24
Manor Rd	1	D 25
Mansion Pl	8	A 23
Maple	9	E 24
Maple Av	1	C 25
Maple Dr	2	E 25
Maple La	1	C 26
Maplewood Dr	1	C 25
Mark Tr	14	B 20
Marks Rd	1	D 26
Marlow Ct	1	C 26
Marsh La	1	D 26
Marshall	2	E 25
Martin Dale	8	C 24
Martin Dale N	8	C 24
Mary La	1	D 25
Mason	1	B 25
Mavis La	14	D 22
Mayfair La	8	B 23
Mayo Av	1	B 25
Mead Av	1	A 26
Mead Av	1	D 25
Mead La	8	B 23
Mead Point Dr	1	C 26
Meadow Dr	1	D 25
Meadow Dr	8	B 24
Meadow La	8	B 23
Meadow Marsh La	1	D 26
Meadow Pl	1	D 26
Meadow Rd	1	D 26
Meadow Rd	8	C 24
Meadow Wood Dr	1	B 26
Meadowbank Rd	1	D 27
Meadowcroft La	8	C 23
Meeting House Rd	15	E 22
Melrose Av	1	B 25
Memory La	8	B 23
Menendez Ct	8	C 24
Mercia La	1	B 25
Mere Av	1	D 26
Merritt Pkwy	8	A 23
Merry La	14	D 21
Meyer Pl	1	D 25
Miami Ct	1	D 25
Mianus View Ter	8	D 24
Midbrook La	1	D 25
Middle Way	1	D 27
Midwood Dr	8	B 24
Midwood La	2	E 25
Midwood Rd	8	C 24
Mill	1	A 25
Mill Pond Ct	1	D 25
Millbank Av	1	C 25
Miller La	1	D 25
Mills Rd	14	D 21
Miltiades Av	1	D 25
Mimosa Dr	9	E 24
Minerva Pl	1	D 26
Mitchell Pl	8	A 24
Mohawk La	15	E 22
Monica Rd	1	A 25
Montgomery La	8	D 24
Mooreland Rd	14	C 21
Morgan Av	8	A 24
Morningside Dr	1	C 25
Mortimer Dr	1	D 26
Moshier	1	B 25
Mount Airy Rd	8	B 24
Mount Laurel Dr	14	D 20
Mountain Wood Dr	14	C 22
Mulberry La	1	D 25
Muriel Pl	8	A 24
Museum Dr	1	B 25
Muskrat Pond Dr	1	B 25
Nassau Pl	1	D 25
Nawthorne Rd	1	D 26
Nearwater La	1	D 25
Nedley La	8	A 24
Neighborly Way	1	D 25
Neil La	1	D 25
New	1	A 25
New Lebanon Av	1	A 25
Newman	1	D 25
Newton	1	C 25
Nicholas Av	8	A 24
Nichols Rd	14	B 20
Nickel	1	A 25
Nimitz	2	E 25
Nipowin La	1	C 26
Norias	1	A 26
Normandy La	1	D 26
North	8	C 24
North	14	D 22
North Av	1	D 26
North Crossway	1	D 27
North Maple Av	8	C 24
North Old Stone Bridge Rd	8	D 24
North Porchuck Rd	14	B 21
North Stanwich Rd	15	E 21
North Tulip	1	D 25
North Water	1	A 25
North Way	1	D 26
Northfield	8	C 24
Northridge Rd	2	E 25
Norton La	2	E 25
Nutmeg Dr	8	B 23
Oak	1	A 25
Oak Dr	1	D 26
Oakley La	14	D 22
Oakridge	1	B 25
Oakwood La	8	C 23
Ocean View Av	1	A 25
Old Camp La	8	D 24
Old Church Rd	1	C 25
Old Club House Rd	1	D 26
Old Farm La	9	E 24
Old Field Point Rd	1	B 25
Old Forge Rd	8	D 23
Old Greenwich La	1	D 25
Old Kings Hwy	2	E 25
Old Mill Rd	14	B 21
Old Mill Rd N	14	C 22
Old Orchard Rd	1	D 25
Old Post Rd #1	1	C 25
Old Post Rd #2	1	B 25
Old Post Rd #3	1	B 25
Old Post Rd #6	1	C 25
Old Stone Bridge Rd	8	D 24
Old Track Rd	1	B 25
Old Wagon Rd	2	E 25
Oneida Ct	1	C 25
Oneida Dr	1	B 25
Orchard	1	D 25
Orchard Ct	1	D 25
Orchard Dr	1	C 25
Orchard Hill La	8	B 23
Orchard Pl	1	C 25
Osceola Dr	1	C 25
Osee Pl	1	D 25
Otter Rock Rd	1	B 26
Oval Av	1	D 26
Overlook Dr	1	C 25
Owenoke Way	1	D 26
Oxer Pl	1	A 25
Paddock Dr	14	D 21
Palmer	1	D 25
Palmer Hill Rd	9	E 24
Palmer Island Rd	1	D 26
Palmer La	1	D 26
Palmer Ter	1	D 26
Park	9	E 24
Park Av	1	C 25
Park Pl	1	C 25
Parsonage La	8	C 24
Parsonage Rd	8	C 23
Partridge Hill La	14	D 20
Partridge Hollow Rd	14	C 20
Patricia La	8	D 24
Patterson Av	8	C 24
Pear La	1	B 26
Peck Av	1	A 26
Pecksland Rd	8	B 23
Peepers Hollow	14	B 22
Pell Pl	1	D 26
Pemberwick Rd	1	A 25
Pemberwick Rd	8	B 24
Pepper Hill La	8	B 24
Perkeley La	1	D 26
Perkins Rd	8	D 23
Perna La	1	D 25
Perry Pl	1	D 25
Perryridge Rd	1	C 25
Peters Rd	1	D 25
Pheasant La	8	C 24
Pierce Rd	1	D 25
Pierson Rd	14	B 20
Pilgrim Dr	8	A 24
Pilgrim Dr Ext	8	A 24
Pilot Rock La	1	C 26
Pin Oak La	9	E 23
Pine	1	A 25
Pine Ridge La	8	D 24
Pine Ridge Rd	8	D 24
Pinecrest Rd	1	D 26
Pinecroft Rd	8	C 23
Pinetum La	8	D 24
Pintail La	1	C 25
Pleasant	1	D 25
Pleasant View Pl	2	E 25
Plow La	8	C 24
Pond Pl	1	D 25
Ponderosa Dr	8	D 24
Porchuck Rd	14	B 22
Potter Dr	1	D 26
Powell	8	A 24
Prescott	8	B 24
Primrose Dr	14	B 22
Prospect	1	A 25
Prospect	1	B 25
Prospect Dr	8	B 24
Put Rd	8	B 24
Putnam Ct	1	C 25
Quail Rd	14	B 22
Quaker La	14	B 21
Quaker Ridge Rd	14	B 22
Quarry Knoll	1	C 25
Quintard Av	1	D 26
Railroad Av	1	B 25
Rainbow Dr	1	D 25
Randolph Pl	1	D 25
Random Rd	1	D 26
Raphael Pl	1	D 25
Rapids La	8	C 24
Raymond	1	D 26
Red Coat La	14	D 22
Red Top Rd	1	D 26
Reed La	1	D 25
Reginald	1	D 26
Relay Ct	1	D 25
Relay Pl	1	D 25
Revere Rd	2	E 25
Rex	1	A 25
Reynolds Pl	1	B 25
Reynwood Manor	14	D 21
Richard	1	A 25
Richland Rd	1	A 25
Richmond Dr	1	D 25
Richmond Hill Rd	14	B 21
Ricki-Beth La	9	E 24
Ridge	8	D 24
Ridge Pl	1	B 25
Ridge Rd	8	D 24
Ridgebrook Rd	8	C 24
Ridgeview Av	8	C 24
Ridgeway	8	B 24

STREET	MAP	GRID
Rincard Ter	8	A 23
Rippowam Rd	1	D 25
Ritch Av	1	A 25
Ritch Av	1	B 25
River	1	A 25
River Av	1	A 26
River La	1	D 25
River Rd	1	D 25
River Rd	9	E 24
River Rd Ext	1	D 25
River Run	8	B 24
River View Ct	8	A 24
River West	8	B 24
Riverdale Av	1	A 25
Riverside Av	1	D 25
Riverside La	1	D 25
Riversville Rd	8	B 24
Riversville Rd	14	B 21
Roberta La	8	C 24
Robertson La	1	D 25
Robin Pl	2	E 25
Rock Maple Rd	9	E 23
Rock Ridge Av	8	B 24
Rockland Pl	1	B 25
Rockmere Av	1	D 25
Rockview Dr	1	B 25
Rockwood La	8	C 23
Rockwood La Spur	8	C 23
Rocky Point Rd	1	D 27
Rodwell Av	1	B 25
Roger Dr	14	C 22
Ronald La	9	E 24
Roosevelt Av	1	D 26
Round Hill Club Rd	8	B 23
Round Hill Rd	8	C 24
Round Hill Rd	14	C 21
Rustic View Rd	8	D 24
Rye Lake Av	14	A 21
Sabine Farm Rd	14	C 22
Sachem La	1	C 25
Sachem Rd	1	C 25
Saddle Ridge Rd	8	B 23
Saint Claire Av	1	D 26
Saint Roch's Pl	1	B 25
Salem	1	C 25
Sandy La	14	B 22
Sawmill La	8	D 24
Sawmill Ter	8	D 23
Sayles	1	D 25
Schofield	1	D 25
School	1	D 25
Scott La	15	E 20
Scott Rd	15	E 20
Seagate Rd	1	C 26
Seitz La	1	D 25
Seldon La	14	B 21
Seneca Pl	1	B 25
Serenity La	9	E 24
Seton La	8	A 24
Shady Brook La	2	E 26
Shady La	8	A 24
Shannon La	9	E 23
Shaw Pl	1	D 26
Sheephill Rd	1	D 25
Sheffield Way	8	B 23
Sheldrake Rd	8	C 24
Shelter Dr	9	E 24
Sherman Av	1	A 25
Sherwood Av	8	A 23
Sherwood Pl	1	C 25
Shoal Point La	1	D 26
Shore Acre Dr	1	D 26
Shore Dr	1	B 25
Shore Rd	1	B 25
Shore Rd	1	D 26
Shorehame Club Dr	1	D 27
Shoreland Ct	1	D 26
Shorelands Pl	1	D 26
Shubert La	1	D 25
Sickle Bar La	1	D 25
Sidney Lanier La	8	B 24
Silo Cir	1	D 25
Silver	1	A 25
Silver Beech Rd	1	D 25
Simmons La	14	C 22
Sinoway Rd	1	D 25
Sioux Pl	8	B 24
Sky Ridge Rd	14	D 22
Skylark Rd	8	C 24
Smith N	1	A 25
Smith Rd	1	B 26
Smith S	1	A 25
Somerset La	1	D 25
Sound Beach Av	1	D 25
Sound Beach Av Ext	1	D 25
Sound Shore Dr	1	C 25
Sound View Ct	1	B 25
Soundview Dr	1	B 25
South	9	E 24
South Crossway	1	D 27
South End Ct	1	D 26
South New	1	A 25
South Stanwich Rd	14	D 22
South Water	1	A 25
Sparrow La	8	C 24
Spezzano Dr	1	D 25
Split Timber Pl	2	E 25
Spring	1	B 25
Spring	1	D 26
Spring House Rd	14	C 22
Spring Rd	1	C 25
Spruce	1	A 25
Spur Rd	8	C 24
Stag La	14	D 22
Stallion Tr	14	D 22
Stanwich La	1	C 25
Stanwich Rd	1	C 25
Stanwich Rd	8	D 24
State Route 15	14	B 22
Station St	1	C 25
Steamboat Rd	1	B 26
Steel Hollow La	8	D 24
Steeple Chase	14	B 20
Stepping Stone La	8	D 24
Sterling Rd	14	C 20
Stiles La	14	B 20
Stillview Dr	8	B 24
Stirrup La	1	D 25
Stone Av	1	B 25
Stonehedge Dr N	8	A 23
Stonehedge Dr S	8	A 23
Stoney Ridge La	1	D 26
Stoney Wilde La	8	C 23
Stormy Circle Dr	1	A 26
Strawbridge La	8	B 24
Strickland Rd	1	C 25
Stuart Dr	2	E 25
Suburban Av	1	D 25
Summit Rd	1	D 26
Summit Ridge Rd	9	E 24
Sumner Rd	14	C 20
Sundance Rd	9	E 24
Sunset Rd	1	D 26
Sunshine Av	1	D 25
Surrey Dr	2	E 25
Susan La	1	D 25
Sutro Pl	8	A 24
Swan Ter	1	C 25
Sweet Briar La	9	E 24
Sylvan La	1	D 26
Taconic Rd	8	D 23
Taconic Rd	14	D 22
Tait Rd	1	D 26
Talbot La	1	A 25
Tamarack Pl	8	A 24
Taylor Dr	1	C 25
Terrace Av	1	D 26
Thistle La	8	B 24
Thomas	1	D 25
Thornhill Rd	1	D 25
Thrushwood Dr	1	D 26
Thunder Mountain Rd	8	B 23
Tingue	1	A 25
Tinker La	14	C 22
Tod La	15	E 22
Tods Drift Way	1	D 27
Tomac Av	1	D 26
Tomac Ct	2	E 26
Tomac La	2	E 26
Tomahawk La	8	D 24
Tomney Rd	1	C 25
Topping Rd	14	C 21
Tory Rd	1	D 25
Tower La	1	D 26
Tower Rd	1	D 26
Tracy Ter	14	B 21
Tree Top Ter	8	B 24
Tremont	1	D 25
Tulip	1	D 25
Turner Dr	8	B 24
Twin Lakes La	1	D 26
Tyler La	1	D 25
Upland Dr	1	B 25
Upland E	8	A 24
Upland Rd	1	B 25
Upland W	8	A 24
Upper Cross Rd	14	D 20
US Hwy 1	1	A 25
US Hwy 1	2	E 25
Ute Pl	1	B 25
Valley	1	D 25
Valley Dr	1	B 25
Valley Rd	9	E 24
Valleywood Rd	1	C 25
Van Loon La	1	D 27
Vernon	1	C 25
Verona Dr	1	D 25
View	1	A 25
View	1	B 25
Vinci Dr	1	A 25
Vineyard La	8	B 24
Vista Av	1	D 26
Vista Dr	1	B 26
Volunteer La	1	C 25
Wahneta Rd	1	D 26
Walker Ct	8	A 24
Wallasy Way	1	D 25
Walnut	9	E 24
Walsh La	1	B 25
Wampus Rd	1	D 25
Washington Av	1	C 25
Watch Hill Dr	8	A 24
Watch Tower La	2	E 25
Waterfall La	8	D 24
Weather Vane La	1	D 25
Weaver	1	B 25
Weaver Pl	1	A 25
Webb Av	1	D 26
Wellington	1	A 25
Wellington Ct	1	A 25
Welwyn Rd	1	D 26
Wendle Pl	2	E 25
Wescott	1	D 25
Wescott Ct	1	D 25
Wessels Pl	1	A 25
Wesskum Wood Rd	1	D 26
West Brother Dr	1	C 25
West Crossway	1	D 27
West Elm	1	B 25
West End Av	1	D 26
West La	14	B 20
West Lyon Dr	8	B 24
West Putnam Av	1	A 25
West Way	1	D 27
Western Junior Hwy	1	A 25
Weston Hill Rd	1	D 26
Westview Pl	1	D 25
Wheeler Rd	14	D 22
Whiffle Tree Way	1	D 25
White Birch La	8	D 24
Whitney Dr	14	B 21
Widgeon Way	1	C 25
Wigmore	1	D 25
Wilbur Peck Ct	1	C 25
Wild Flower Tr	8	B 23
Wildwood Dr	1	C 25
Will-Merry La	14	C 22
William	1	A 25
Willow La	1	D 26
Willow Rd	1	D 26
Willow Run Rd	8	A 23
Willowmere Av	1	D 26
Willowmere Cir	1	D 26
Willowmere Point	1	D 26
Wilmot La	1	D 25
Wilshire Rd	14	D 20
Windabout Dr	8	B 24
Winding La	8	B 24
Windrose Way	1	C 26
Windsor La	9	E 24
Windy Knolls	1	A 25
Winterset Rd	8	D 23
Winthrop Dr	1	D 25
Witherall Dr	8	B 24
Wood Rd	1	C 25
Wooddale Rd	8	C 23
Woodland Dr	1	B 25
Woods Av	8	A 24
Woodside Dr	1	C 25
Woodside Rd	8	C 24
Wyckham Hill La	14	D 22
Wyndover La	9	E 24
Wyngate Rd	8	D 24
Wynn La	8	D 23
Wynwood Rd	8	C 23
Zaccheus Mead La	8	B 23
Zygmont La	15	E 20

MONROE

STREET	MAP	GRID
Academy La	19	V 21
Alpine Rd	19	V 20
Applegate La	24	V 20
April La	24	U 20
Arbor Rd	19	V 21
Arrowhead Dr	24	U 20
Arrowhead La	24	X 19
Autumn Dr	18	U 21
Bagburn Rd	24	X 19
Bardugone La	19	V 21
Barn Hill Rd	19	X 20
Bart Rd	24	U 20
Barton Rd	19	V 21
Bayberry Meadow Rd	19	W20
Beardsley Dr	19	V 21
Beaver Cir	19	W20
Bellevale	18	U 20
Benedict Rd	24	V 20
Birch Tr	24	Y 19
Birchwood La	23	T 19
Birchwood Rd	23	T 19
Blake Rd	24	W20
Blakeman Dr	24	X 20
Blue Hills Rd	19	X 20
Blueberry Hill Rd	19	V 21
Blueberry La	19	V 21
Bob White Ter	19	V 21
Boot Shop La	19	V 21
Booth Hill Rd	19	W21
Boulder Ridge Rd	24	U 20
Bradford Dr	24	V 19
Bradley Dr	19	X 20
Bridge Rd	24	Y 19
Bridle Path Tr	23	T 19
Brinsmaid Rd	19	X 20
Brook	24	U 20
Brookside Dr	19	V 21
Brookside Tr	24	Y 19
Brushy Ct	24	V 20
Bugg Hill Dr	19	V 20
Cahill Rd	24	W20
Camelot Dr	19	X 20
Canterbury La	19	X 20
Capitol La	19	W20
Captains Hill Rd	19	X 20
Carcass Rd	19	W20
Cardinal La	19	W21
Carmen La	18	T 20
Carriage Dr	24	V 20
Cedar La	19	V 21
Cedar Ter	19	V 21
Chalk Hill Rd	24	V 20
Cheryl Dr	24	U 19
Chimney Pl	24	X 20
Christiana Dr	24	W20
Church	19	V 20
Cold Spring Rd	24	W20
Colonial Dr	19	W20
Commerce Dr	24	V 19
Copper Mill Rd	24	W20
Cottage	24	Y 19
Cotton Tail La	19	W21
Country Ridge Rd	18	U 21
Countryside Dr	19	V 20
Craig Dr	19	W21
Crescent Pl	18	U 21
Crestwood Rd	19	V 20
Cross Hill Rd	19	V 20
Crossbow La	19	V 20
Crown View Dr	24	X 19
Crystal Tr	24	Y 20
Curtis La	19	V 20
Cutlers Farm Rd	18	U 21
Cutlers Farm Rd	24	V 20
Deep River La	19	W20
Deep Wood Cir	24	V 20
Deerfield La	19	W20
Devils Bowl Tr	24	Y 20
Diane Dr	24	W20
Dingley Dell Rd	24	U 20
Dogwood Rd	24	W20
Doris Dr	19	V 20
Downs Rd	24	Y 19
Driftwood Rd	19	V 20
Drings Rd	24	Y 19
Eagle Rock Cir	24	V 20
East Dale Dr	18	U 21
East Maiden La	24	V 20
East Village Rd	24	X 20
Easton Rd	24	U 20
Edgewood Rd	19	V 20
Elaine Dr	19	W21
Elm	19	V 21
Elm	24	V 20
Evergreen La	19	V 20
Fairlea Dr	19	X 20
Fan Hill Rd	19	W20
Fan Hill Rd	24	W19
Far Horizon Dr	19	V 20
Far Mill Rd	19	V 21
Farm View Rd	18	U 21
Fernwood Rd	19	V 20
Field Rock Rd	24	V 20
Flint Ridge Rd	24	V 20
Forest Rd	19	V 21
Founders Way	19	W20
Fox Run	24	U 19
Fresh Meadow Rd	23	T 19
Gardner Rd	24	V 20
Gay Bower Rd	19	V 21
Georges La	24	W20
Gerardo Dr	19	W20
Glen Hollow Dr	24	W20
Glenbrook Rd	19	V 21
Goodhill La	19	W21
Grant Rd	24	V 20
Gray	19	W21
Great Hollow Rd	18	U 20
Great Ring Rd	24	W19
Green	24	U 20
Greenfield Hill Rd	19	X 20
Greenlawn Rd	19	V 21
Greenwood Dr	18	T 20
Greenwood La	19	V 21
Greisers Rd	24	W20
Grindstone La	24	X 19
Grist Mill	24	W19
Guinea Rd	24	U 19
Hamlet La	19	X 20
Hammertown Rd	24	W19
Hannah La	24	U 20
Harmony La	24	V 20
Harvester Rd	19	V 20
Hattertown Rd	23	T 19
Hattertown Rd	24	U 20
Hawley La	19	V 20
Hawthorne Dr	24	W20
Hayes	18	T 20
Hearthstone Rd	19	W20
Heather Rd	19	V 20
Hedges La	19	X 20
Hemlock La	24	U 19
Heritage Dr	19	W21
Hickory La	18	U 21
Hidden Knolls Cir	19	V 20
High Meadow Rd	19	V 20
High Ridge Dr	19	V 21
High Rock Rd	24	W19
Highfield Dr	19	X 20
Hillcrest Rd	24	U 19
Hillside La	19	X 20
Hiram Hill Rd	18	T 20
Historic Dr	19	W20
Holly Pl	24	X 20
Hunter Ridge Rd	19	W21
Huntingtown Rd	23	T 19
Hurd Av	19	W20
Indian Ledge Rd	24	U 20
Israel Hill Rd	19	X 21
Jackson Dr	19	V 21
Jay La	19	V 20
Jays Rd	19	V 21
Jeanette	19	W20
Joan Dr	19	V 21
Jockey Hollow Rd	24	V 20
Johnson Pl	24	V 20
Jones Hill Rd	19	W21
Jordan Hill Rd	24	X 19
Josie's Ring Rd	24	X 20
Judd Rd	18	U 20
Karen Dr	24	W20
Kettle Creek La	19	W20
Kimberly Dr	24	V 20
Knapp	23	T 20
Knollwood	18	U 20
Knorr Rd	19	W20
Lantern Dr	24	U 19
Lanthorne Rd	19	V 20
Laurel Dr	18	U 21
Lazy Brook Rd	19	W20
Lima Rd	24	V 20
Lisa Dr	24	W19
Little Fox La	18	U 21
Lois Cir	19	V 21
Longview Rd	19	V 20
Lorraine Dr	24	W20
Lovers La	19	V 20
Lyndon	19	V 21
Lynn Dr	24	W20
Main	18	U 20
Manor Dr	24	X 19
Maple Cir	18	U 20
Maple Dr	18	U 20
Maple Ter	18	U 20
Maplewood Dr	19	V 20
Maryanne Dr	24	W20
Mashapaug Tr	24	Y 19
Mashentuck Tr	24	Y 19
May Ct	24	U 20
Mayfair Ct	19	V 21
Mayfair Pl	24	Y 20
Meadow Brook Dr	19	V 20
Meadow's End Rd	19	V 20
Meadowview Ter	24	U 19
Melon Patch La	24	U 20
Mill	18	U 21
Millbrook Ter	19	W20
Millo Dr	19	V 20
Misty La	24	W20
Monroe Tpke	19	V 21
Monroe Tpke	24	X 19
Montar Dr	19	V 21
Moose Hill Rd	19	V 21
Moss Rd	19	V 20
Mossup Tr	24	Y 19
Mountainside Dr	23	T 19
Nancy Dr	24	W20
Nelson Brook Rd	19	X 20
Newtown Tpke	18	U 20
Newtown Tpke	24	U 20
Nickel Pl	24	X 20
North Hillside La	19	X 20
North Star Tr	24	X 19
Northbrook Dr	24	V 20
Northwood Rd	19	V 21
Oak Ridge	18	U 20
Oakwood Dr	19	V 21
Old Castle Dr	19	X 20
Old Coach Rd	19	W20
Old Fish House Rd	24	Y 20
Old Mine La	24	V 20
Old Newtown Rd	18	U 20
Old Tannery Rd	19	W20
Old Zoar Rd	24	X 19
Osborn La	19	W21
Overlook Dr	24	U 20
Pachaug Tr	24	Y 19
Pamela Dr	19	W21
Partridge Dr	18	U 21
Pastors Wk	24	U 19
Patmar Cir	18	U 20
Patmar Dr	18	U 20
Patmar La	18	U 20
Patmar Ter	18	U 20
Pebble Rd	18	U 20
Pepper	24	U 20
Pepperidge Rd	19	V 21
Pequonnock Ridge Rd	19	V 20
Perry Dr	19	W20
Pheasant La	18	U 21
Pilgrim La	18	U 20
Pine Tree Rd	23	T 19
Plumer La	19	W20
Pocatopaug Tr	24	Y 19
Pond View Rd	24	W20
Porters Hill Rd	19	V 21
Purdy Hill Rd	18	U 20
Quarry Ridge Rd	19	X 20
Quarter Horse Dr	23	T 19
Redcoat La	24	V 20
Richards Dr	19	V 21
Richmond Dr	19	W20
Ridge Dale Rd	24	V 20
Ridgewood Dr	24	U 19
Ripton Ridge Rd	19	W21
River Dr	24	W20
Robin La	24	X 20
Rockwood La	23	T 19
Rolling Ridge Rd	24	V 20
Roosevelt Dr	24	Y 19
Round Hill Rd	19	X 20
Rowledge Pond Rd	24	W19
Ruth	19	W20
Ryegate Ter	19	V 21
Saddle Hill Rd	19	W20
Saxony Dr	19	V 20
Scenic Hill La	19	V 20
Scholtz Rd	24	Y 19
School	19	V 21
Sentry Hill Rd	24	W20
Settler's Farm Rd	19	W20
Shadow Wood Cir	24	V 20
Shady La	24	V 20
Shawnee La	19	V 21
Sheep Meadow Dr	18	U 21
Shelton Rd	19	W20
Sherman Cir	18	U 21
Sherwood Pl	24	U 20
Silvermine La	24	V 20
Skyview Rd	24	W20
Sleepy Hollow Dr	18	U 21
Spinning Wheel Rd	19	W20
Spring Hill Rd	18	U 21
Spruce Brook Tr	24	U 20
Squire Rd	19	X 20
Stable Ridge Rd	19	W20
Stag La	19	V 21
Stanley Rd	18	T 20
Stanley Rd	24	U 20
Still Meadow Cir	24	U 20
Stone Hedge La	24	W20
Stonewall La	24	W20
Stoney Brook Dr	19	W20
Strobel Rd	18	U 20
Sturbridge La	18	T 20
Summer View Dr	19	X 20
Sunrise Cir	19	W21
Sunrise Ter	24	Y 19
Sunset Hill Dr	19	X 20
Sunset Tr	24	Y 20

STREET	MAP	GRID
Surrey La	19	V 20
Swendsen Dr	19	X 20
Sycamore Dr	23	T 19
Tanglewood Cir	24	U 19
Timber Dr	24	V 20
Timothy Hill Rd	24	V 19
Todd Dr	19	W21
Toll Gate Rd	19	V 20
Tulip Dr	19	W21
Turkey Roost Rd	24	W20
Twin Brook Ter	19	V 20
Valley View Rd	19	X 20
Velvet	18	T 20
Verna Rd	24	U 20
Vincent Dr	24	U 20
Walnut	19	W21
Watch Hill Rd	18	U 20
Wayne Rd	19	W21
Weather Vane Hill	19	X 20
Webb Cir	24	Y 20
Weekepegme Tr	24	Y 19
Wells Rd	24	V 20
West Maiden La	24	V 20
Westview Dr	18	U 21
Wheeler Rd	19	W21
Wheeler Rd	24	W20
Whispering Pine Rd	24	X 19
Whitewood Dr	19	W21
Wild Flower La	24	V 20
Willenbarb Rd	24	U 20
William Henry Dr	19	W20
Williams Dr	23	T 19
Williamsburg Dr	19	W21
Wiltan Dr	24	U 19
Windsor Rd	19	V 20
Winslow Ter	19	V 21
Wintergreen Dr	24	U 20
Winthrop Pl	19	W21
Wood Acres La	24	U 20
Wood Creek Dr	19	V 21
Wood End Rd	24	W20
Woodend Rd	24	W20
Woodlawn Rd	19	V 21
Woods Row	24	U 20
Woodycrest Rd	18	T 20
Yankee Hill Rd	19	X 20

NEW CANAAN

STREET	MAP	GRID
Adams La	9	H 23
Alan La	15	H 20
Alpine Ter	16	J 21
Amy's La	16	K 22
Anthony La	16	K 23
Apple Tree La	16	J 21
Arrowhead Tr	15	H 22
Ash Tree La	16	J 23
Autumn La	10	J 23
Bald Hill Rd	20	L 20
Bank	16	J 23
Barnegat Rd	20	J 20
Bartling Dr	15	H 22
Bayberry Rd	16	J 22
Beacon Hill La	16	K 22
Beech Rd	16	K 23
Benedict Hill Rd	20	K 21
Bennington Pl	15	H 22
Betsy's La	16	K 23
Bickford La	9	H 23
Birchwood Av	16	K 23
Bittersweet La	16	K 22
Bob Hill La	20	L 21
Bowery Rd	20	J 20
Braeburn Dr	16	K 23
Bridle Path La	15	H 22
Brinckerhoff Av	16	J 23
Briscoe Rd	20	K 20
Brook	16	J 22
Brooks Rd	16	J 23
Brookside Rd	10	J 24
Brookwood La	16	J 21
Brushy Ridge Rd	16	J 22
Burtis Av	16	J 22
Butler La	10	J 24
Buttery Rd	16	K 23
Canaan La	16	J 22
Canoe Hill Rd	16	K 22
Carriage La	15	H 22
Carter	16	K 23
Cascade Rd	15	H 22
Cecil Pl	16	K 23
Cedar La	16	K 23
Charles Pl	16	J 22
Charter Oak Dr	10	J 24
Charter Oak La	10	J 24
Cheese Spring Rd	16	L 21
Cherry	16	J 22
Chichester Rd	15	H 22
Church	16	J 23
Clapboard Hill Rd	16	K 23
Clearview La	15	H 21
Colonial Ct	16	J 23
Colonial Rd	20	K 21
Comstock Hill Rd	16	K 23
Conrad Rd	10	J 24
Country Club Rd	16	J 21
Cross	16	J 22
Cross Ridge Rd	20	K 20
Crystal	16	J 23
Dabney Rd	16	K 23
Danforth Dr	20	L 20
Dans Hwy	15	H 20
Danvers La	16	J 23
Davenport Ridge Rd	9	H 23
Deacon's Way	16	K 22
Deep Valley Rd	16	K 21
Deer Park Rd	16	K 21
Dew La	10	J 24
Dogwood La	15	H 22
Douglas Rd	16	J 23
Down River Rd	16	J 23
Driftway La	9	H 23
Drummond La	16	J 22
Dunning Rd	16	J 22
East Av	16	J 22
East Cross Rd	9	H 23
East Hills Dr	16	J 23
East Maple	16	J 23
Echo Hill Rd	16	K 23
Elm	16	J 22
Elm Pl	16	J 23
Evergreen Rd	16	L 21
Fable Farm Rd	16	K 22
Fairty Dr	16	J 23
Farm Rd	16	J 23
Father Peters La	16	K 21
Fawn La	16	L 22
Ferris Hill Rd	16	K 22
Field Crest Rd	16	J 23
Fitch La	16	K 23
Forest	16	J 22
Four Winds La	15	H 22
Fox Run Rd	16	L 21
Frogtown Rd	9	H 23
Garibaldi La	16	J 22
Gerdes Rd	10	J 24
Gerrish La	16	J 22
Glen Dr	16	J 22
Gower Rd	16	J 23
Grace	16	J 23
Gravel Isl Rd	16	K 21
Gray Squirrel Dr	10	J 24
Green Av	16	J 23
Green Meadow La	16	J 23
Greenley Rd	15	H 21
Grove	16	J 22
Hampton La	16	J 22
Hanford La	15	H 22
Harrison Av	16	J 23
Hawks Hill Rd	9	H 23
Hawthorne Rd	16	J 23
Heather Dr	16	K 23
Hemlock Hill Rd	16	J 21
Heritage Hill Rd	16	J 22
Hickock Rd	16	K 21
Hickory Dr	16	K 23
Hidden Meadow La	16	K 21
High View Ter	16	J 23
Hill	16	J 22
Hill Crest Rd	9	H 23
Hillside Av	16	J 22
Hillsley Rd	10	J 24
Holly Rd	16	J 23
Hollywood Av	16	J 23
Holmewood La	16	J 22
Hope Av	16	J 23
Horton La	10	J 24
Hoyt	16	J 23
Hoyt Farm Dr	16	K 23
Hoyt Farm Rd	16	K 23
Huckleberry Hill Rd	16	K 22
Hunter's Creek La	20	J 20
Husted La	16	J 22
Indian Rock Rd	16	J 21
Indian Waters Dr	9	H 23
Inwood Rd	16	K 23
Jelliff Mill Rd	9	H 23
Jennifer La	20	K 20
John Marshall Pl	16	J 21
Jonathan Rd	20	J 20
Journey's End Rd	20	L 20
Juniper Rd	16	K 23
Kelley Green	16	J 23
Kimberly Pl	16	J 22
Knapp La	9	H 23
Knollwood La	16	L 21
Lakeview Av	16	J 23
Lakewind Rd	15	H 21
Lambert Rd	16	J 22
Lantern Ridge Rd	20	L 20
Lapham Rd	9	H 24
Laurel Rd	15	H 21
Laurel Rd	16	K 22
Ledge Av	16	J 22
Leslie La	16	J 23
Lincoln Dr	16	J 23
Little Brook Rd	16	K 23
Llewellyn Dr	15	H 22
Lockwood Av	16	J 23
Locust Av	16	J 22
Logan Rd	20	J 20
Lone Tree Farm Rd	16	K 22
Long Lots Rd	16	K 23
Lost District Dr	15	H 20
Lost District Dr	20	J 20
Louises La	20	J 20
Ludlowe Rd	16	K 22
Lukes Wood Rd	20	J 20
Main St	16	J 22
Maple	16	J 23
Mariomi Rd	16	K 22
Marshall Ridge Rd	16	J 23
Marvin Ridge Rd	10	J 24
Mead	16	J 23
Meadow La	16	J 23
Merritt Pkwy	10	J 24
Michigan Rd	16	K 21
Michigan Rd	20	J 20
Middle Ridge	16	K 23
Mill Ct	16	J 23
Mill Rd	16	L 23
Millport Av	16	J 23
Morse Ct	16	J 22
Mortimer	16	J 23
Myanos Rd	15	H 22
New Canaan Rd	16	K 22
New La	16	J 22
New Norwalk Rd	10	K 23
New Norwalk Rd	16	J 22
Norholt Dr	16	K 22
North Wilton Rd	20	K 20
Nubel La	16	K 23
Nursery Rd	10	J 24
Nutmeg La	16	J 22
Oak	16	J 23
Oak Grove Pl	16	J 23
Oenoke La	16	J 22
Oenoke Ridge	16	J 22
Ogden Rd	20	J 20
Old Norwalk Rd	16	J 23
Old Rock La	10	J 24
Old Stamford Rd	9	H 23
Old Studio Rd	16	J 23
Olmstead Ct	16	J 23
Orchard Dr	16	J 23
Orchard La	16	J 23
Osborn La	16	K 21
Overlook Dr	16	J 23
Parade Hill La	16	J 22
Parade Hill Rd	16	J 22
Parish La	16	J 23
Parish Rd	16	J 22
Parish Rd N	16	J 22
Park	16	J 23
Park Pl	16	J 23
Parry Rd	9	H 23
Parting Brook Rd	16	L 21
Partridge Rd	16	K 21
Pepper La	16	K 22
Pequot La	15	H 20
Pheasant Dr	16	K 22
Pine	16	J 22
Pinney Rd	20	J 20
Pocconock Tr	16	K 23
Pond View La	16	K 21
Ponus Ridge	9	H 23
Ponus Ridge	15	H 20
Proprietors Crossing	20	J 20
Prospect Pl	16	J 22
Putnam Rd	16	J 23
Ramhorne Rd	15	H 21
Raymond	16	J 23
Reeder La	16	J 21
Reservoir La	15	H 21
Rian's Pl	16	J 22
Richards La	16	J 23
Richmond Hill Rd	16	J 23
Rilling Ridge Rd	16	K 23
Rippowam Rd	15	H 21
River	16	J 22
River Wind Rd	15	H 21
Riverbank Ct	16	J 22
Rocky Brook Rd	20	L 21
Rocky Nook Rd	20	J 20
Rosebrook Rd	16	K 22
Running Brook La	9	H 23
Rural Dr	16	J 22
Sagamore Tr	9	H 23
Saint George La	20	J 20
Saint John Pl	16	J 22
Salem Rd	16	K 22
Scofield La	16	J 22
Selleck Pl	16	J 23
Seminary	16	J 22
Shadow La	16	K 23
Shady Knoll La	9	H 23
Shady La	16	J 23
Shagbark Dr	10	J 24
Shaker Rd	16	K 23
Sheridan Dr	20	K 20
Sherwood La	15	H 21
Silver Ridge Rd	16	K 23
Silvermine Rd	16	K 22
Siwanoy La	16	J 22
Skyview La	9	H 23
Sleepy Hollow Rd	16	K 21
Smith Ridge La	16	K 21
Smith Ridge Rd	16	J 22
Snowberry La	16	K 23
Sound View La	16	K 21
South Av	10	J 24
South Bald Hill Rd	20	L 21
Southwood Dr	16	J 23
Spring Water La	9	H 23
Squire's La	15	H 20
State Route 15	9	H 23
State Route 15	10	J 24
State Route 106	16	J 22
State Route 123	16	K 21
State Route 124	16	J 22
State Route 124	20	J 20
Stonehenge Dr	15	H 21
Stoneleigh Rd	16	K 23
Strawberry Hill Rd	16	J 22
Sturbridge Hill Rd	16	K 22
Summer	16	J 23
Summit Ridge Rd	16	J 23
Sunrise Av	16	J 23
Sunset Hill Rd	16	J 22
Surrey Rd	16	J 23
Talmadge Hill Rd	9	H 24
Thayer Dr	16	K 22
Thayer Pond Rd	16	K 22
Thrush La	16	K 21
Thurton Dr	9	H 23
Toby's La	15	H 21
Tommy's La	16	J 23
Toquam Rd	15	H 22
Trinity Pass Rd	15	H 20
Turner Hill Rd	16	K 21
Turning Mill La	16	K 22
Turtle Back La E	20	J 21
Turtle Back La W	20	J 21
Turtle Back Rd	16	J 21
Turtle Back Rd S	16	J 21
Twin Pond La	16	K 22
Urban	16	J 22
Valley La	16	K 21
Valley Rd	16	K 22
Village Dr	16	J 23
Vitti	16	J 22
Wahackme La	16	J 22
Wahackme Rd	15	H 22
Wakeman Rd	20	J 20
Ward La	9	H 23
Wardwell Dr	16	K 22
Wascussue Ct	15	H 22
Weeburn Dr	16	K 23
Weed	9	H 23
Welles La	9	H 23
Wellesley Dr	15	H 21
West Cross Rd	9	H 23
West Hills Rd	16	J 21
West Rd	16	J 22
West Rd	20	J 20
Whiffle Tree La	10	J 24
White Birch Rd	10	J 24
White Fall La	15	H 20
White Oak Shade La	10	J 24
White Oak Shade Rd	10	J 24
Whitney Av	16	J 23
Willowbrook La	16	J 23
Windrow La	16	J 22
Winfield La	15	H 22
Wing Rd	15	H 22
Woodland Rd	16	J 23
Woodridge Cir	15	H 21
Woodridge Dr	16	J 21
Woods End Rd	16	J 22
Woodway Ridge La	9	H 23
Wydendown Rd	16	K 21

NEW FAIRFIELD

STREET	MAP	GRID
Albion Rd	30	P 9
Alexander Dr	30	S 8
Almargo Av	30	S 9
Alpine Rd	30	S 9
Andover Rd	30	Q 8
Angleside	30	P 9
Ansonia Rd	30	Q 9
Apple Blossom La	30	Q 10
Arden Av	30	Q 9
Arrow Meadow Rd	30	Q 9
Astoria Dr	30	P 9
Auburn Rd	30	Q 9
Austin Dr	30	Q 8
Autumn Ridge Rd	30	Q 10
Baccara Dr	30	Q 10
Ball Av	30	Q 9
Ball Pond Rd	30	P 10
Ball Pond Rd E	30	Q 9
Bank	30	R 7
Bantam Rd	30	Q 9
Barnum Rd	30	R 10
Bauer Rd	30	S 8
Bay Dr	30	S 9
Bayberry La	30	Q 10
Bayview Ter	30	S 9
Bear Mountain Rd	30	R 10
Beaver Bog Rd	30	R 8
Beers Rd	30	T 8
Berwick Rd	30	Q 9
Big Trail, The	31	S 7
Bigelow Rd	30	R 9
Biggs Av	30	Q 9
Black Thorn Dr	30	Q 10
Blue Jay Rd	30	S 8
Bogus Hill Rd	30	T 8
Brenda	30	Q 9
Bridgeview Dr	30	R 9
Brook Dr	31	T 7
Brook Wood Rd	30	Q 9
Brookside Dr	30	Q 8
Brush Dr	30	R 10
Brush Hill Rd	30	R 10
Butternut La	30	R 10
Calumet Rd	30	Q 9
Calverton Dr	30	Q 9
Cameron Rd	30	P 9
Camp Arden Rd	30	S 10
Candle Hill Rd	30	T 8
Candlewood Dr	30	S 10
Candlewood Isles Rd	30	S 9
Candlewood Rd	30	S 10
Cannon Pl	30	Q 9
Cardinal La	30	S 8
Carleon Rd	30	Q 9
Carola La	31	T 7
Carriage La	30	Q 10
Cecilia La	30	S 8
Cedar La	31	T 7
Charcoal Ridge Rd E	30	R 10
Charcoal Ridge Rd W	30	R 10
Cherry Dr	31	T 7
Chestnut Hill Dr	30	R 10
Claire Hill Rd	30	T 8
Claredal Av	30	S 9
Clark Rd	30	P 9
Clement Rd	30	Q 9
Cloverleaf Dr	30	R 8
Cold Spring Dr	30	Q 10
Colonial Rd	30	R 10
Columbia Dr	30	Q 8
Continental Av	30	Q 8
Coolidge	30	P 10
Cornell Rd	30	Q 8
Cottontail Rd	30	R 10
Cove La	30	S 10
Coves End	30	S 9
Croix Hill Rd	30	R 9
Crossway	30	S 10
Curtis Av	30	Q 9
Cypress	31	T 7
Dale Rd	30	P 9
Darien Rd	30	Q 9
Dayton Rd	30	Q 9
Deer La	31	T 7
Deer Run	30	S 9
Diana Dr	30	R 10
Dick Finn Rd	30	S 9
Donna Dr	30	P 10
Donnelly Dr	30	R 10
Douglas La	30	Q 9
Dunham Dr	30	R 10
East La	30	S 9
East Lake Rd	30	Q 10
East View Dr	30	R 10
East View Rd	30	S 9
Elba	30	P 9
Eldred Rd	30	Q 8
Elly Rd	30	T 8
Elmwood Dr	30	Q 9
Elwell Rd	30	R 8
Erie Rd	30	Q 9
Erin Dr	30	Q 10
Escape Rd	30	R 10
Evet Dr	30	R 9
Fair La	31	T 7
Fairfield Dr	30	P 9
Farmers La	30	R 8
Fawn Crest Dr	30	Q 9
Fenwick Rd	30	Q 9
Field Av	30	S 10
Field Rd	31	T 7
Fieldstone Dr	30	P 10
Flak La	30	T 8
Fleetwood Dr	30	S 10
Flora	30	Q 9
Forest Hills Dr	30	Q 9
Forest La	30	Q 9
Fox Hollow Rd	30	R 10
Fox Run	30	S 9
Freehold Rd	30	Q 8
Frisbie	30	Q 9
Fulton Dr	30	Q 9
Galloping Hill Dr	30	S 9
Gardner	30	Q 9
Garnet Ct	30	R 9
Gillotti Rd	30	Q 10
Glen Rd	30	R 10
Glen Way	30	S 10
Glenville Rd	30	Q 9
Gordon Dr	30	Q 8
Great Meadow Rd	30	S 8
Hammond Rd	30	Q 8
Hampton Rd	30	Q 9
Handol La	30	R 8
Harbour View Dr	30	T 7
Hardscrabble Rd	31	R 7
Harlequin Dr	30	S 8
Harmon Dr	30	Q 8
Harvard Rd	30	Q 8
Harvest Dr	30	Q 10
Haviland Hollow Rd	30	Q 7
Hemlock Tr	30	S 10
Heritage Isl Rd	30	T 8
Hewletts Rd	30	Q 8
Hickory La	30	R 9
High Tr	30	S 10
High View Ter	30	R 9
Hillcrest Dr	30	S 10
Hilldale Rd	31	T 7
Hillside Dr	30	R 9
Hilltop Dr	31	T 7
Hilltop Rd	30	R 10
Hillview Dr E	30	P 9
Hillview Dr W	30	P 9
Holly Dr	30	S 8
Holly Rd	30	S 10
Hoover Pl	30	P 10
Hopewell Dr	30	Q 8
Hudson Dr	30	Q 8
Huntington La	30	Q 9
Ilion Rd	30	Q 9
Indian Hill	30	T 8
Indian Hill La	30	R 10
Indian Hill Rd	30	Q 10
Inglenook Rd	30	T 8
Irving Rd	30	Q 9
Ithaca Rd	30	Q 8
Jackson Rd	30	Q 9
Jenksville Rd	30	Q 8
Jennifer Rd	30	R 9
Jeremy Dr	30	Q 8
Jericho Rd	30	Q 9
Jessie	30	Q 9
Jewel La	30	Q 9
Joanne Dr	30	T 8
Joel's Dr	30	R 9
Joyce Hill Rd	30	S 8
Karen Dr	30	R 9
Kearn Rd	30	P 9
Kepler Way	30	S 10
Kingsbury Rd	30	Q 9
Kingston Rd	30	Q 9
Knollcrest Rd	30	S 9
Knolls Rd	30	S 9
Knollwood La	30	S 8
Lafayette Rd	30	P 9
Lake Cir	30	S 10
Lake Dr	30	Q 9
Lake Dr N	30	S 9
Lake Dr S	30	S 10
Lake Shore N	30	S 10
Lakeview Dr	30	P 9
Lakeview Dr	31	T 7
Lamont Rd	30	Q 9
Lancaster Rd	30	Q 9
Laurel La	31	R 7
Laurelwood Dr	30	S 8
Lavelle Av	31	T 7
Leonard Dr	30	R 9

STREET	MAP	GRID
Lillian Av	30	Q 9
Linda La	30	T 8
Lloyd Av	30	Q 9
Lots Acre Tr	31	R 7
Mac Bean Dr	30	R 10
Madison Rd	30	P 9
Manning	30	Q 9
Maple La	30	Q 8
Margerie Dr	30	R 10
Marlboro Rd	30	Q 9
McIntyre Rd	30	P 9
Meadow Av	30	S 10
Meadow Dr	30	Q 10
Meadowbrook Rd	30	Q 9
Meeting House Hill Cir	30	R 10
Merlin Av	30	Q 9
Middleton Dr	30	R 10
Mill Pond Rd	30	Q 8
Milltown Rd	30	P 10
Millway	30	S 9
Misty Brook Rd	30	T 7
Mountain Laurel Dr	30	S 8
Mountain Rd	30	R 10
Mountain Rd	31	T 7
Mountain View Av	30	S 9
Muller	30	Q 9
Musket Ridge Rd	30	R 10
Nanuet Rd	30	Q 9
Newfane Rd	30	P 9
North Beach Dr	30	S 9
North Dr	30	S 10
North Forty Dr	30	R 9
Norton Rd	30	Q 9
Notchview Dr	31	T 7
Oak	31	T 7
Oak Dr	30	S 10
Oak Tree La	30	R 8
Oakwood Dr	30	R 9
Old Bogus Rd	30	S 8
Old Bridge Rd E	30	R 9
Old Bridge Rd W	30	R 9
Old Farm Rd	30	Q 10
Old Orchard Rd	30	Q 10
Old Pine Hill Rd	31	R 7
Old Rd	30	T 8
Old Rte 37	30	R 10
Old Rte 39	30	R 10
Old Town Rd	30	P 9
Orehill Rd	30	Q 9
Oswego Rd	30	P 9
Overbrook Dr	30	R 9
Overlook Rd	30	S 10
Oxford Rd	30	Q 9
Paradise Ct	30	Q 9
Park Rd	30	S 8
Partridge La	30	S 10
Patterson	30	P 9
Peaceful Dr	30	R 9
Penny La	30	S 8
Peralta	30	P 9
Perch Rd	30	Q 9
Perry Hill Dr	30	T 8
Pettit	30	Q 9
Pheasant Dr	30	R 8
Pheasant Run	30	S 10
Pickerel Rd	30	Q 9
Pickett Rd	30	Q 9
Pine Hill Rd	30	R 8
Pinewood Dr	30	R 8
Pleasant View Rd	31	T 7
Pond View Dr	30	R 10
Pondfield Rd	30	R 10
Possum Dr	30	R 10
Princeton La	30	Q 9
Purdum Rd	30	Q 9
Quaker Rd	30	Q 8
Reservoir View Dr	30	R 10
Revolutionary La	30	Q 8
Ridge Rd	30	S 10
Rita Dr	30	Q 9
Riverton Rd	30	Q 9
Rocky Hill Rd	30	S 8
Rose La	30	S 8

STREET	MAP	GRID
Roseton Rd	30	Q 8
Roy Av	30	Q 9
Saddleridge Rd	30	P 9
Sail Harbour Dr	30	T 8
Satterlee Rd	30	Q 9
Saw Mill Rd	30	R 10
Schermerhorn Dr	30	Q 9
Shad Blow Rd	30	T 8
Sherman La	30	S 8
Sherry La	30	R 10
Shore Dr	30	S 9
Shoreham Dr	30	P 9
Short Hill Dr	30	S 9
Shortwoods Rd	30	R 9
Silver Hill Dr	30	S 10
Sleepy Hollow Rd	30	R 10
Smoke Hill Dr	30	Q 10
South View Rd	30	S 9
Spring Dr	30	Q 10
Stanwich Rd	30	Q 9
State Line Rd	30	P 9
State Route 37	30	R 10
State Route 37	31	R 7
State Route 39	30	Q 9
Stoney Way	30	R 10
Summerhill Rd	30	S 10
Sunlit La	30	S 10
Sunnyside La	30	R 9
Sunrise Rd	30	S 10
Sunset Dr	30	T 8
Sunset Dr	31	T 7
Sunset Ridge	30	Q 9
Sunset Tr	30	Q 9
Sunswept Dr	30	Q 9
Sweet Cake Mtn Rd	30	S 10
Sylvan Rd	30	S 10
Taylor Dr	30	P 9
Taylor's Acres Rd	30	P 9
Throop Pl	30	Q 8
Timber Springs Rd	30	Q 10
Titicus Mountain Rd	30	Q 10
Top Stone Rd	30	S 9
Trout Rd	30	Q 9
Turtle Dr	30	S 9
Twin Ponds Ct	30	Q 8
Twin Rocks Dr	30	R 9
Valerie La	30	R 10
Valley Dr	30	Q 9
Valley Rd	30	P 9
Walnut Ridge Rd	30	R 9
Warwick Rd	30	Q 9
Weldon Woods Rd	30	Q 9
West Ridge Rd	30	P 10
Westview Trails Rd	30	P 9
Whaley Rd	31	T 7
Whipstick Rd	30	Q 10
White Birch Dr	30	Q 9
Whitehall Rd	30	P 9
Whitney Dr	30	Q 8
Williams Rd	30	Q 10
Willow La	30	S 10
Wilson	30	Q 9
Windmill Rd	30	S 9
Windward Dr	30	S 10
Winsted Pl	30	Q 9
Wood Creek Rd	30	R 10
Woodridge La	30	R 10
Woods Rd	30	S 10
Woods Way	30	S 10
Woody Glen	30	S 10
Woody La	30	S 10
Yale Av	30	Q 8
Ye Old Rd	30	S 10

NEWTOWN

STREET	MAP	GRID
Abbotts Hill	23	T 17
Academy La	27	V 15
Acorn Dr	27	W15
Adahi Tr	24	Y 18
Adams Hill La	27	U 14
Alberts Hill Rd	27	W14
Alder La	27	W17
Algonquin Tr	27	Y 17
Alpine Rd	27	X 16
Andras Rd	24	Y 18
Anthers Av	27	X 15
Antler Pine Rd	27	W15
Apple Blossom La	24	V 17
Arlyn Ridge Rd	24	U 18
Arrowhead La	24	X 19
Ashford La	26	T 15
Aunt Park La	23	T 18
Baldwin Rd	27	V 16
Bancroft Rd	27	X 16
Bari Dr	24	U 17
Barnabas Rd	27	U 14
Bayberry Rd	24	U 19
Beagle Tr	24	W19
Bear Hills Rd	24	U 19
Beaver Dam Rd	27	U 17
Beckett Village	24	X 17
Beechwood Dr	27	X 15
Benjamin Dr	24	V 17
Bennetts Bridge Rd	24	X 17
Bentagrass La	27	U 17
Berkshire Rd	24	X 18
Berkshire Rd	27	W17
Berkshire Tr	27	X 16
Birch Hill Rd	26	T 16
Birch Rise Dr	27	V 16
Bishop Cir	27	W16
Black Bridge Ridge	27	W15
Black Walnut Dr	24	V 17
Blackman Rd	27	U 15
Blakeslee Dr	27	V 15
Blanche's Wk	27	U 16
Blue Spruce Dr	24	V 19
Boggs Hill Rd	23	T 17
Boggs Hill Rd	27	U 16
Bonnie Brae Dr	27	V 16
Borough La	27	V 16
Botsford Hill Rd	24	V 18
Botsford La	24	V 18
Boulevard, The	27	V 15
Bradley La	24	X 19
Brandywine La	27	W16
Brassie Rd	27	V 16
Brennan Rd	27	V 14
Bresson Farm Rd	24	X 17
Bridge End Farm La	27	X 15
Bridle Path Tr	24	U 17
Bristle La	27	W16
Brookridge Dr	27	X 15
Brookwood Dr	26	T 16
Brushy Hill Rd	24	U 17
Budd Dr	27	V 15
Butterfield Rd	27	U 14
Button Shop Rd	24	V 18
Buttonball Dr	27	W15
Cadey La	26	T 15
Calico Tr	27	X 16
Camelot Crest	24	W18
Cannon Rd	26	T 15
Capitol Rd	27	X 16
Carol Ann Dr	24	V 17
Castle Hill Rd	27	U 15
Castle La	23	T 19
Castle Meadow Rd	23	T 19
Cedar Cir	27	V 17
Cedar Hill Rd	24	V 17
Cedarhurst Tr	27	Y 17
Cemetery Rd	26	T 16
Center	27	X 16
Chambers Rd	24	X 17
Charter Ridge Rd	24	X 18
Checkerberry La	24	X 18
Cherry	27	W15
Cherry Hgts Ter	27	W15
Chestnut Hill Rd	24	X 18
Chestnut Knoll	24	X 18
Chimney Swift Rd	27	W16
Chipmunk Tr	27	V 16
Church Hill Rd	27	V 15
Clearing, The	27	X 16

STREET	MAP	GRID
Clearview Dr	24	W17
Cobblers Mill Run	27	X 17
Cobblestone La	26	T 16
Cold Spring Rd	24	V 16
Concord Ridge Rd	27	W14
Connors Rd	27	V 16
Country Club Rd	27	V 16
Country Squire Rd	24	X 19
Covered Bridge Rd	27	U 14
Crabapple La	24	X 18
Crestwood Dr	27	W16
Cricket Tr	27	X 16
Cross Brook Rd	26	T 16
Crown Hill Dr	24	X 18
Crown View Dr	24	X 18
Crows Nest La	27	W15
Currituck Rd	27	U 14
Curry Dr	27	U 15
Danbury-Newton Rd	26	T 14
Daves La	24	U 18
Dayton	27	W16
Deep Brook Rd	27	V 16
Deer Tr	27	X 15
Deerfield Dr	24	W17
Diamond Dr	27	U 15
Dickenson Dr	27	W16
Dingle Brook La	29	V 13
Dodgingtown Rd	26	T 16
Dogwood Ter	24	V 17
Dover Cir	23	T 17
Driftway Dr	29	V 13
Drummers La	26	T 16
Dug Hill Rd #1	23	T 18
Dug Hill Rd #2	24	U 18
Dusty La	24	V 18
Eagle Rd	27	X 16
Eagle Rock Rd	27	W15
East	27	V 15
Echo Valley Rd	27	V 14
Eden Hill Rd	23	T 18
Edge Lake Dr	27	X 15
Edgewood Dr	27	V 15
Edmund Rd	27	V 15
Elana La	27	W16
Elizabeth	27	V 16
Elm Dr	27	V 16
Elmwood Tr	27	X 16
Engleside Rd	27	X 16
Equestrian Ridge Rd	23	S 17
Ethan Allen Rd	24	V 17
Evergreen Rd	27	V 15
Fairchild Dr	26	T 15
Far View Dr	27	X 15
Farm Dr	27	V 15
Farm Field Ridge Rd	27	W15
Farm Meadow Rd	23	S 18
Farmery Rd	24	X 18
Farrell Rd	27	U 14
Fawnwood Rd	27	X 17
Fern La	23	T 19
Ferris Rd	26	T 16
Fieldstone Dr	23	T 17
Fir Tree La	24	W17
Flat Swamp Rd	26	T 16
Fleetwood Dr	27	X 15
Flintlock Tr	24	U 18
Floral Hgts	26	T 16
Ford Rd	27	X 15
Forest Dr	27	X 16
Forestview Dr	24	X 18
Founders La	24	X 17
Fox Hollow La	27	X 16
Fox Run La	27	U 15
Fox Run La S	27	U 15
Frontage Rd	27	V 15
Galilee Way	24	U 17
Gelding Hill Rd	27	X 17
Georges Hill Rd	29	V 13
Gillian Way	24	Y 18
Glen Rd	27	W15
Glover Av	27	V 16

STREET	MAP	GRID
Golden Pond Rd	24	U 17
Goodyear Rd	27	W16
Gopher Rd	27	V 14
Grand Pl	27	V 16
Grays Plain Rd	24	W18
Great Hill Rd	26	T 15
Great Quarter Rd	27	Y 16
Great Ring Rd	24	W19
Green Knolls La	24	U 18
Greenbriar La	27	V 17
Greenleaf Farms Rd	23	S 17
Guneva Dr	24	V 17
Hall La	27	V 15
Hanover Rd	27	V 15
Harvest Common Rd	24	X 18
Hattertown Rd	23	T 17
Hawley Rd	27	V 16
Hawleyville Rd	27	U 13
Hawthorne Hill Rd	27	U 16
Head of Meadow Rd	27	U 16
Hedge Meadow La	27	U 14
Hemlock Rd	24	V 18
Hickory La	27	W15
Hidden Valley Rd	27	X 16
High Bridge Rd	24	V 18
High Rock Rd	24	W18
Hillcrest Dr	27	U 14
Hillside La	27	V 15
Hitfield Rd	24	X 18
Homer Clark La	24	X 18
Homestead La	24	V 18
Honey La	24	X 19
Hopewell Rd	23	S 18
Horseshoe Ridge Rd	27	V 15
Hoseye Coach Rd	24	W18
Housatonic Dr	27	X 14
Hucko Tr	27	W16
Hundred Acres Rd	23	T 18
Hunting Ridge Rd	26	T 16
Huntingtown Rd	24	U 18
Hy Vue Dr	26	T 16
Indian Hill La	24	X 19
Interstate Hwy 84	26	T 14
Interstate Hwy 84	27	W16
Irvin La	27	U 15
Jacklin Rd	26	T 16
Jangling Plains Rd	26	T 17
Jeremiah Rd	27	W16
Jet Brook Rd	23	T 17
Jo Mar Dr	27	W16
Joan Dr	24	U 17
John Beach Rd	24	U 17
Johnnie Cake La	27	V 15
Johnny Appleseed Dr	24	W17
Johnson Dr	27	W16
Jordan Hill Dr	24	X 19
Juniper Rd	27	V 16
Kaechele Dr	24	V 18
Kale Davis Rd	24	X 17
Karen Blvd	26	T 16
Kay La	24	V 18
Kelly Ct	24	W18
Kenan Rd	27	U 14
Kent Rd	27	U 16
Key Rock Rd	26	T 17
King	27	V 15
Kip La	23	T 17
Knollwood Dr	27	U 15
Lake George Rd	29	V 13
Lake Rd	29	W13
Lakeview Ter	27	X 16
Land's End Rd	27	U 14
Lantern Dr	24	U 19
Laurel Rd	27	V 16

STREET	MAP	GRID
Lazybrook Rd	24	U 18
Leopard Dr	24	X 17
Lester Rd	27	W15
Liberty Dr	24	X 18
Lincoln Rd	27	V 16
Linden Dr	27	W15
Little Brook La	24	V 18
Lone Oak Meadows	27	W17
Longview Hgts Rd	27	U 16
Longview Rd	24	W17
Lorilynne Cir	24	V 19
Lorraine Dr	27	V 16
Loveland Dr	24	Y 19
Lovell's La	27	V 16
Lyrical La	24	X 19
Mackenzie Cr	27	X 15
Madison Dr	27	V 16
Main	27	V 15
Maltbie Rd	24	U 19
Maple Dr	27	W15
Maplewood Tr	27	X 16
Marlin Rd	24	V 18
Marlin	27	V 15
Meadow Brook Rd	24	U 18
Meadow Rd	27	V 16
Meadow Woods La	24	W17
Megan's Cir	24	V 17
Melody La	24	U 17
Middleton Rd	27	U 15
Mile Hill Rd S	27	V 17
Misty Vale Rd	27	W17
Moccasin Tr	27	W16
Mohawk Tr	27	Y 17
Monitor Hill Rd	24	U 18
Morgan Dr	27	X 16
Morris Rd	23	S 18
Mount Laurel Rd	24	X 18
Mount Nebo Rd	23	T 17
Mount Pleasant Rd	26	T 14
Mount Pleasant Rd	27	U 15
Mount Pleasant Ter	27	U 15
Mountain Manor Rd	24	X 17
Mountain View Dr	24	V 17
Narragansett Tr	27	W16
Nearbrook Dr	24	V 17
Nelson La	29	U 13
Nettleton Av	27	V 16
New Lebbon Rd	24	W18
Newbury Rd	29	V 13
Newfield La	27	V 15
North Branch Rd	26	T 16
Nunnawauk Rd	27	V 17
Nutmeg La	24	X 19
Oak Dr	27	W15
Oak Ridge Rd	23	T 18
Oakview Rd	27	W16
Obtuse Rd	29	U 13
Old Bethel Rd	26	T 14
Old Bridge Rd	24	Y 19
Old Castle Dr	27	U 15
Old Castle Hill Rd	27	U 15
Old Farm Hill Rd	27	V 14
Old Gate La	24	V 17
Old Green Rd	29	U 13
Old Hawleyville Rd	26	T 14
Old Mile Hill Rd	27	W17
Old Mill Rd	24	W17
Old Purdy Station Rd	23	T 18
Old Rd, The	27	V 15
Old Rte 25	27	V 16
Old Stream Rd	24	U 17
Old Tavern Rd	26	T 16
Old Town Rd	24	U 18
Orange Pippin Rd	24	X 17
Orchard Hill Rd	24	U 18
Orchard La	27	U 15
Osborn Hill Ext	24	X 18

STREET	MAP	GRID
Osborn Hill Rd	24	X 18
Overlook Dr	27	V 15
Overlook Knoll	27	W15
Owl Ridge La	27	W17
Ox Hill Rd	23	T 17
Palestine Rd	24	U 17
Papoose Hill Rd	27	V 15
Park La	27	V 17
Park Rd	27	X 16
Parmalee Hill Rd	27	V 14
Parmalee Pl	27	V 14
Partridge La	26	T 16
Pastor's Wk	24	U 19
Patricia La	29	U 13
Patriot Ridge Rd	27	W15
Paugusett Rd	24	X 18
Pebble Rd	24	U 17
Pecks La	24	V 17
Pepperidge Rd	26	T 16
Pheasant Ridge Rd	29	V 13
Philo Curtis Rd #1	27	W16
Philo Curtis Rd #2	27	W16
Phyllis La	23	T 18
Pilgrim La	24	W17
Pine	27	W15
Pine Tree Hill Rd	24	U 19
Pine Tree Rd	23	T 19
Platts Hill Rd	24	U 18
Pleasant Hill Rd	26	T 16
Plum Trees Rd	26	T 15
Pocono Rd	26	T 14
Point O'Rocks Rd	27	U 16
Pole Bridge Rd	27	W16
Pomperaug Av	27	X 14
Pond Brook Rd	29	U 13
Poor House Rd	26	T 16
Pootatuck Tr	27	W16
Possum Ridge Rd	27	U 15
Post La	24	W18
Poverty Hollow Rd	24	V 18
Prospect Dr	24	V 17
Prospect Ter	27	V 17
Purdy Station Rd	23	T 17
Putnam Dr	23	T 19
Quail Tr	27	X 16
Quaker La	24	U 18
Queen	27	V 16
Reservoir Rd	27	U 15
Richmond Rd	27	U 14
Ridge Rd	27	U 16
Rivers Edge Rd	27	W15
Riverside Rd	27	W16
Robin Hill Rd #1	26	T 16
Robin Hill Rd #2	27	U 16
Rock Ridge Rd	26	T 16
Rockywood Dr	27	X 17
Rolling Meadows La	27	W15
Roosevelt Dr	27	V 16
Rose La	27	X 17
Rowledge Rd	24	W19
Russett Rd	27	X 17
Saddle Ridge Rd	23	T 18
Sand Hill Ext	24	W19
Sand Hill Rd	24	W19
Sanford Rd	27	W14
Saw Mill Rd	27	U 15
Saw Mill Ridge Rd	27	U 15
Scenic View Dr	29	V 13
Schoolhouse Hill Rd	27	V 15
Scudder Rd	26	T 16
Sealand Dr	27	V 15
Sedor La	27	U 14
Serenity La	24	X 19
Settler's La	24	V 18
Shady Rest Blvd	27	X 15
Shamrock La	24	V 17
Shelley Rd	26	T 15
Shepaug Rd	27	X 15

STREET	MAP	GRID
Shepherd Hill Rd	27	U 16
Sherman	24	W17
Shut Rd	26	S 17
Signal Post Rd	27	U 14
Silver City Rd	29	V 13
Simm La	24	V 17
Skidmore La	27	W17
Sky Top Dr	24	X 18
Smoke Rise Ridge	27	V 15
South Main	24	V 17
South Main	27	V 16
Split Rock Rd	23	T 18
Spring Rd	27	U 16
Spruce Dr	27	W15
State Route 25	24	V 17
State Route 25	27	U 15
State Route 34	24	X 18
State Route 34	27	V 15
Steck Dr	23	T 17
Still Hill Rd	24	W17
Still Rd	24	U 18
Stone Fence La	27	U 15
Stone Wall Ridge Rd	23	T 17
Stonebridge Tr	24	X 19
Stonybrook Rd	27	U 14
Storm Ridge Rd	23	S 18
Strawberry La	24	V 19
Stuart Dr	24	V 19
Sturges Rd	26	T 15
Sugar	26	T 16
Sugar	27	U 16
Sugar Hill Rd	27	U 16
Sugar La	27	U 16
Sugarloaf Rd	24	W17
Summit Rd	27	V 15
Sunny View Ter	27	W15
Sunset Hill Rd	27	V 15
Surrey Tr	24	V 18
Susan La	27	U 14
Sutherland Dr	24	X 18
Swamp Rd	24	V 19
Sweet Briar La	27	X 16
Sweet Meadow Rd	26	T 16
Sycamore Dr	23	T 19
Tamarack Rd	27	V 14
Tanglewood La	24	X 18
Taunton Hill Rd	26	T 15
Taunton La	26	T 15
Taunton Lake Dr #1	27	U 15
Taunton Lake Dr #2	27	U 15
Taunton Lake Dr #3	27	U 15
Taunton Lake Rd	27	U 15
Taunton Ridge Rd	26	T 15
Teachers Ridge Rd	27	V 15
Thomas Circle	27	X 15
Thunder Ridge Rd	24	X 18
Timber La	27	V 17
Tinkerfield Rd	27	V 16
Toddy Hill Rd	24	V 18
Tomahawk Tr	27	X 16
Topsides La	27	V 15
Tory La	27	U 14
Totem Tr	27	X 16
Town's End Rd #1	23	S 19
Town's End Rd #2	23	S 19
Trumbull Dr	27	V 15
Tunnel Rd	27	U 14
Turkey Hill Rd	24	V 17
Turkey Hill Ter	24	V 17
Turkey Roost Rd	24	V 18
Underhill	27	X 16
US Hwy 6	27	V 15
US Hwy 202	26	T 16
US Hwy 202	27	W16
US Hwy 302	27	U 16
Valley Field Rd	27	W15
Valley View Rd	27	U 16
Vining Rd	24	W17
Walker Hill Rd	24	W19
Wall Rd	27	V 16
Walnut Tree Hill Rd	27	W15
Washbrook Rd	24	V 18
Washington Av	27	W16
Washington Hill Rd	27	V 15
Waterview Dr	27	X 16
Webster Pl	26	T 17
Wendover Rd	27	V 15
West	27	V 16
West Farm Ridge Rd	24	U 18
Westwood Ter	27	U 15
Whippoorwill Hill Rd	27	U 14
White Farm Rd	24	U 18
White Oak Farm Rd	24	U 18
Whitewood Rd	27	U 15
Wildcat Rd	26	T 15
Wilderness Rd	26	T 15
Wiley Rd	26	T 17
Williams La	26	T 17
Willow Brook La	24	U 17
Wills Rd	24	V 17
Winding Brook Dr	24	U 17
Windy Woods Cir	27	V 14
Winesap Rd	27	X 17
Winslow Rd	26	T 15
Wire Rd	27	V 15
Woodbine La	27	V 15
Yearling La	27	V 15
Yogananda	24	X 18
Zoar Rd	24	X 17

NORWALK

STREET	MAP	GRID
Academy	10	L 25
Acorn La	3	J 26
Adams Av	10	L 25
Adams La	16	L 23
Adamson Av	3	K 27
Admiral La	11	N 23
Aiken	10	L 25
Albrecht Ct	3	L 26
Alden Av	3	L 26
Alewives Rd	10	J 24
Algonquin Rd	10	M24
Allen Ct	10	M25
Allen Rd	10	M24
Allview Av	3	K 26
Alrowood Dr	10	M25
Alvin Dr	16	L 23
Ambler Dr	10	L 25
Amundsen	3	L 26
Anchor Rd	3	J 27
Anderson Rd	10	M24
Ann	3	K 26
Anson Rd	10	K 24
Apple	10	L 25
Apple Tree La	10	K 24
April Ct	10	L 24
April La	10	L 24
Arbor Ct	3	K 26
Arbor Dr	3	K 26
Arch	10	L 25
Argentine Way	16	L 23
Arlington	10	K 24
Armstrong Ct	3	L 26
Arnold La	3	J 26
Arrowhead Ct	10	M24
Assisi Way	10	M25
Auburn	3	K 26
Austin	3	K 26
Autumn	10	K 25
Avenue A	3	K 26
Avenue B	3	K 26
Avenue C	3	K 26
Avenue D	3	K 26
Avenue E	3	K 26
Aviation Ct	3	K 26
Avon	10	L 25
Baker La	10	M25
Baldwin Rd	10	M25
Barbara Dr	10	L 25
Barclay Ct	3	J 27
Barjune Rd	10	L 24
Barnfield Rd	3	J 27
Barnum Av	10	L 25
Bartlett Av	10	K 24
Bartlett Manor	10	K 24
Bates Ct	3	K 26
Baxter Dr	3	K 26
Bayberry La	10	L 24
Bayne	16	M23
Bayne Ct	16	M23
Bayview Av	3	K 26
Beacon	3	L 26
Beau	10	K 25
Beauford Rd	3	K 26
Bedford Av	10	L 25
Beechwood Rd	10	J 25
Belair Rd	10	K 24
Belden Av	10	L 25
Belfor Rd	10	K 24
Belle Av	3	K 26
Benedict	10	K 25
Benedict Ct	10	K 25
Berkeley	10	L 25
Bethel	3	L 26
Betmarlea Rd	10	J 25
Betts Pl	3	L 26
Bettswood Rd	10	L 25
Beverly Pl	10	K 25
Birch	10	L 25
Birchside Dr	10	K 24
Bishop	10	M25
Bissell Rd	10	K 24
Bittersweet Tr	3	J 27
Blackberry La	10	K 24
Blackstone Dr	3	L 27
Blake	10	L 25
Blue Mountain Rd	10	L 25
Bluff Av	3	J 27
Bobwhite Dr	10	L 25
Bond	3	L 26
Bonnybrook Rd	10	J 25
Bonnybrook Tr	10	J 25
Boulder Cir	10	J 25
Boulder Ct	10	J 25
Boulder Rd	10	J 25
Bouton	3	K 26
Bow End Rd	10	M24
Boxwood Rd	10	L 24
Bramble La	10	J 24
Branford	3	L 26
Braybourne Dr	3	L 26
Breezy La	10	M25
Brenner La	11	N23
Brenner Rd	11	N23
Briar	3	J 26
Bridge	3	L 26
Brierwood Rd	10	L 24
Broad	10	L 24
Broad Ct	10	L 24
Broadview Ter	10	L 25
Brook	10	L 25
Brookfield	10	M25
Brookhill La	10	L 24
Brooklawn Av	3	K 26
Brookside Av	10	J 24
Brookside Ct	3	J 26
Browne Pl	3	J 27
Brush	10	K 25
Bryan Rd	3	J 27
Bucciarelli La	10	K 25
Buckingham Pl	10	L 25
Buckthorn Rd	10	M24
Buda	3	K 26
Bumblebee La	10	M24
Burchard La	3	J 27
Burlington Ct	10	L 25
Burlington Dr	10	L 25
Burnell Blvd	10	L 25
Burr Pl	3	L 26
Burritt Av	3	K 26
Burwell	3	K 27
Butler	10	L 25
Butternut La	10	L 24
Buttery Rd	16	K 23
Buttonball Tr	10	L 25
Byington La	10	L 25
Byrd Rd	10	K 25
Byselle Rd	10	L 25
Caddy Dr	10	L 24
Caesar	10	L 25
Calf Pasture Beach Rd	3	L 27
Camelot Dr	10	K 25
Camp	10	L 25
Cana Ct	10	K 24
Candlewood La	10	J 25
Canfield Av	3	L 27
Cannon	10	L 25
Canterbury Rd	10	M25
Captain's Walk Rd	3	J 27
Cardinal	3	K 26
Carlin	10	L 25
Carlisle	10	K 25
Carlson Ct	3	L 26
Carol Dr	3	L 26
Carolyn Ct	3	J 26
Carothers La	10	M25
Carriage Dr	10	K 24
Carter Rd	16	K 23
Catalina Dr	3	K 28
Catalpa	3	L 26
Catherine	10	L 25
Cavanaugh	10	K 24
Cavray Rd E	3	L 26
Cavray Rd W	3	L 26
Cedar	3	K 26
Cedar	10	K 25
Cedar Crest Pl	10	K 25
Cemetery	3	L 26
Center Av	10	L 25
Center Av Ext	10	L 25
Channel Av	3	K 27
Chapel	10	L 25
Charcoal Rd	3	J 26
Charles	3	L 26
Chatham Dr	3	K 26
Chelene Rd	3	L 26
Chester	10	K 25
Chestnut	3	K 26
Chestnut Hill Rd	10	M24
Chestnut Hill Rd	17	N 23
Chimmons Isl Rd	3	K 28
Chipmunk La	10	J 24
Chipping La	10	K 25
Cholwell Pl	10	M24
Christopher Ct	10	M25
Christopher La	10	M25
Christy	10	K 25
Church	10	K 25
Cider La	10	M25
Cindy La	10	M24
Clara Dr	10	M25
Clarke Ct	3	J 27
Clarmore Dr	10	K 25
Clay	3	K 26
Clearview Av	10	L 25
Cleveland Ter	3	K 26
Cliff	3	L 26
Cliff Pl	3	J 27
Clifford	3	J 26
Cliffview Dr	10	L 24
Clinton Av	10	K 25
Cloverly Cir	3	L 26
Coachman's Ct	10	K 24
Cobblers Ct	10	L 24
Cobblers La	10	L 24
Coldspring	10	K 25
College	10	L 25
Colonial Pl	10	L 25
Colony Pl	3	L 26
Columbine La	10	M24
Comber Dr	3	L 27
Commerce	10	L 25
Compass Rd	3	J 27
Comstock Hill Av	10	K 24
Comstock Hill Rd	10	K 24
Concord	3	K 26
Connecticut Av	10	J 25
Connecticut Tpke	3	J 26
Cook	3	J 27
Coolidge	10	L 25
Cornwall Ct	10	K 24
Cornwall Dr	10	K 24
Cornwall Rd	10	K 24
Cory La	10	L 25
Cossitt Rd	10	K 25
Cottage	3	L 26
Cottontail Rd	3	J 26
Couch	3	K 26
Country Club Ct	10	M25
Country Club Rd	10	M25
Country La	10	M25
County	10	M25
Cove Av	3	L 26
Coventry Pl	10	K 25
Covewood Dr	3	J 27
Covlee Dr	3	L 26
Cox Pl	3	J 27
Cranbury Rd	10	M24
Cranbury Woods Rd	10	M24
Craw Av	3	J 27
Creeping Hemlock Dr	10	L 24
Crescent	3	K 26
Crescent Beach Rd	3	J 27
Crest Rd	3	J 27
Crestline	3	K 26
Cricket La	10	J 25
Crinklewood La	10	M24
Crockett	3	J 27
Crocus La	10	L 24
Crooked La	3	J 27
Crooked Tr	3	J 26
Cross	10	L 25
Cross Pl	3	J 27
Crossland Pl	3	M26
Crown Av	3	K 26
Cudlipp	3	J 26
Cutrone Rd	10	K 25
Dairy Farm Ct	3	L 26
Dairy Farm Rd	3	L 26
Dancing Bear Rd	3	J 27
Daphne Dr	10	M25
Daskams La	10	L 25
Davenport	10	L 25
Davis	10	L 24
Dawn Rd	10	M24
Day	3	K 26
Deane	3	J 26
Deane Ct	3	J 26
Decker	3	L 27
Deepwood La	3	J 26
Deerfield	3	K 26
Deerwood Ct	10	M25
Deerwood Manor	10	M25
Delaware Av	10	L 25
Dellwood Rd	10	J 25
Depot Pl	3	L 26
Derby Rd	10	J 25
Devils Garden Rd	3	J 26
Devon Av	10	K 25
Devonshire Rd	10	K 24
Dewal Ct	16	M23
Dewal Dr	16	M23
Diane	10	K 24
Dibble	3	J 26
DiSesa Ct	10	L 25
Dixie La	10	K 25
Dock Rd	3	K 27
Dogwood La	10	L 24
Dolphin Rd	3	L 27
Donna Dr	10	K 25
Donohue Dr	10	L 24
Dorlon	3	K 27
Dorset Ct	10	M24
Dorset Rd	10	M25
Douglas Dr	10	K 24
Dover	10	K 25
Dragon La	10	K 24
Driftwood La	10	L 24
Drum Rd	3	J 27
Dry Hill Ct	10	L 25
Dry Hill Rd	10	M25
Duck Pond Rd	3	L 26
Duke Pl	3	J 27
Eagle Rd	10	K 25
Earl	3	K 26
East Av	3	L 26
East Av	10	L 25
East Beach Dr	3	J 27
East Meadow La	10	L 25
East Rocks Rd	10	L 25
East Wall	10	L 25
Eastwood Rd	10	L 24
Echo La	10	L 24
Eclipse Av	10	L 25
Edgewater Pl	3	L 26
Edgewood	3	K 26
Edith La	10	L 24
Edlie Av	3	L 26
Elaine	10	K 25
Eleanor La	10	K 24
Elizabeth	3	K 26
Ellen	10	M24
Elliott	3	L 27
Ells	10	K 24
Elm	10	L 25
Elmcrest Ter	10	K 25
Elmwood Av	3	K 26
Elton Ct	3	L 26
Ely Av	3	K 26
Emerald	10	L 24
Emerson	3	L 26
Englewood Rd	3	J 27
Ensign Rd	3	J 27
Eric Ct	10	M25
Erin Ct	3	J 26
Esquire Rd	10	L 25
Eugene Dr	3	J 26
Evergreen Ter	3	J 26
Eversley Av	3	L 26
Fair	10	L 25
Fairfield Av	3	K 26
Fairfield Ter	10	L 24
Fairview	10	K 25
Fairview Av	10	K 25
Fairweather Dr	10	L 25
Farm Creek Rd	3	J 27
Father Colon Pl	10	L 25
Fawn Ridge La	10	M23
Felix La	10	K 24
Fenwick Pl	3	L 26
Fern	3	K 26
Ferris Av	10	K 25
Field	10	M24
Fifth	3	L 26
Filbert Rd	10	L 25
Fillow	10	J 24
Fillow Ct	3	J 27
Finch Ct	3	J 26
Finley	10	K 25
Fireside Ct	10	K 25
First	3	L 26
Fishman Dr	10	K 25
Fitch	3	L 26
Flax Hill Rd	3	K 26
Flicker La	3	J 27
Flintlock Rd	10	J 25
Flower La	10	K 24
Folwell Rd	10	L 25
Forbell Dr	10	K 24
Fordham Dr	3	L 26
Forest Hill Rd	10	J 24
Fort Point	3	L 26
Foster La	3	J 27
Foursons Ct	10	L 25
Fourth	3	L 26
Fox Run Rd	10	K 24
Foxboro Dr	10	M23
France	10	L 25
Frances Av	3	K 26
Frank	10	M24
Franklin	3	K 26
Freedman Dr	10	K 25
Fremont Pl	10	L 25
French Farm Rd	10	L 23
Friendly Rd	10	M25
Frost	10	K 25
Fullin Ct	10	M25
Fullin Rd	10	M25
Fullmar La	10	K 24
Garden Pl	3	L 26
Garfield	3	K 26
Garner	3	K 26
Geneva Rd	10	J 25
Genoa	10	L 25
George Av	10	L 25
Gibson Ct	3	K 26
Gilbert	3	L 26
Gilbert Hill Rd	3	J 26
Gillys La	10	K 25
Girard	10	K 25
Glasser	3	K 26
Glen Av	10	K 24
Glendenning	10	L 25
Glenwood Av	10	K 25
Glover Av	10	L 24
Godfrey	10	L 25
Gold	10	L 24
Golden Ct	3	J 27
Golden Hill	3	K 26
Goldstein Pl	3	K 26
Goodrow	3	L 26
Gordon	10	K 24
Gould's La	10	M25
Grand	10	L 25
Grandview Av	10	K 25
Granite Dr	10	M24
Gray Rock Rd	3	K 26
Gray Squirrel Dr	10	J 24
Great Marsh Rd	3	L 26
Green Beach Dr	3	J 27
Green La	10	K 24
Greenfield Rd	3	L 26
Greenhill Rd	16	K 23
Greenwood Pl	3	K 27
Gregory Blvd	3	L 26
Gregory Ct	3	L 27
Grescham Av	10	L 25
Grey Hollow Rd	16	L 23
Grist Mill Rd	10	L 23
Grove	3	K 26
Grumman Av	10	M23
Grumman Ct	10	M24
Guild Dr	16	K 23
Gull Rd	3	J 27
Gwendolyn	3	L 26
Hadik Pkwy	3	K 26
Half Mile Rd	10	M24
Hamilton Av	3	K 26
Hanford Pl	3	K 26
Harbor Av	10	L 25
Harbor Pl	3	J 27
Harbor View Av	3	K 27
Harding	3	K 26
Harriet	10	L 25
Harris	10	K 24
Harrison Av	10	L 25
Harstrom Pl	3	J 27
Harvann Rd	10	K 24
Harvard	10	L 25
Harvey	3	L 26
Haviland	3	K 26
Hawkins Av	3	L 26
Hawthorne Dr	10	L 25
Hayes Av	3	L 26
Hazel	10	L 25
Heathcote Rd	16	M23
Heather La	3	L 26
Hedge Dr	10	L 25
Hemlock Pl	3	K 26
Hendricks Av	3	L 26
Henry	3	K 26
Henry Ext	3	K 26
Heritage Hill Rd	10	M24
Hermanny Ct	3	L 26
Heron Lake La	11	N24
Heron Rd	3	L 26
Hiawatha La	3	M26
Hickory Rd	10	L 25
Hideaway La	10	M24
High	10	L 25
Highbrook Rd	10	L 25
Highland Av	3	J 27
Highland Ct	3	J 26
Highview Av	10	L 25
Highwood Av	10	K 25
Hill	10	L 25
Hill Ct	10	L 25
Hillandale Manor	3	M26
Hillcrest Pl	16	L 23
Hills Ct	10	M25
Hillside	3	K 26
Hilltop Rd	3	J 27
Hillwood Pl	10	K 24
Holiday Dr	10	M25
Hollow Spring Rd	3	J 26
Hollow Tree Ct	3	K 26
Hollow Tree Rd	3	K 26
Holly	10	L 25
Holmes	10	L 25
Homer	10	L 25
Honey Hill Rd	10	L 24
Honeysuckle Dr	10	M25
Horton	10	L 25
Howard Av	3	L 26

STREET	MAP	GRID
Upland Ct	3	K 26
US Hwy 1	10	J 25
US Hwy 7	10	L 24
Vail	10	K 24
Valley Rd	3	J 27
Valley View Ct	10	L 24
Valley View Rd	10	L 24
Van Buren Av	10	L 25
Van Ness	10	K 25
Van Tassel Ct	10	L 25
Van Zant	3	L 26
Vanderbilt Av	3	J 26
Vespucci Rd	10	L 23
Victory Ct	3	L 26
Villaway Rd	3	L 26
Vincent Pl	3	J 27
Visconti	10	L 25
Vollmer Av	10	L 25
Wake Robin Rd	10	M24
Wall	10	L 25
Wallace Av	3	L 27
Walnut Av	10	L 25
Walter Av	10	L 25
Ward	10	L 25
Warren	10	K 25
Washington	3	K 26
Washington Av	10	L 24
Water	3	K 26
Waterbury Rd	3	M26
Watering La	10	J 25
Watson Ct	3	J 26
Wayfaring Rd	10	M24
Weather Bell Dr	11	N 24
Weatherly La	10	K 25
Weed Av	10	J 24
Well Av	3	J 27
Wenbos Gate	10	L 24
West Av	3	K 26
West Av	10	L 25
West Cedar	10	J 25
West Couch	3	K 26
West Dover	10	K 25
West End Rd	10	K 25
West Lake Ct	10	J 24
West Main	10	L 25
West Meadow Pl	3	K 26
West Norwalk Rd	10	J 25
West Rocks Rd	10	L 24
West Washington	3	K 26
Westmere Av	3	J 27
Westport Av	10	L 25
Westview La	3	K 26
Whitebirch Ct	3	M26
Wilbur	3	K 26
Wild Rose La	10	K 25
Wildmere La	10	L 25
Wildwood La	16	L 23
Willard Rd	10	M25
William	3	L 26
Willow	3	L 26
Willruss	10	K 24
Willruss Ct	10	K 24
Wilson Av	3	J 27
Wilton Av	10	L 25
Winding La	10	L 24
Windsor Pl	3	K 26
Windward Rd	10	K 25
Winfield	3	L 26
Winfield Ct	3	L 26
Winnipauk Dr	10	L 24
Winter	3	J 26
Winterset Dr	10	M24
Winthrop Av	10	L 25
Witch La	3	J 27
Wolfpit Av	10	M25
Wood	3	K 26
Woodacre Rd	10	K 24
Woodbine	3	J 26
Woodbury Av	10	K 25
Woodchuck Ct	3	J 26
Woodchuck Ct W	3	J 26
Woodchuck La	3	J 26
Woodcrest Rd	10	L 25
Woodland Ct	3	L 26
Woodland Rd	3	J 27
Woodlawn Av	3	K 26
Woodley La	10	M24
Woods End Rd	10	K 24
Woodside Av	3	L 26
Woodward Av	3	K 27
Wynne Rd	10	K 25
Yale	10	L 25
Yankee Doodle Ct	3	L 26
Yarmouth Rd	3	J 27
Yew	16	L 23
Yorkshire Rd	10	K 25
Yost	3	K 27

REDDING

STREET	MAP	GRID
Alexander Rd	23	Q 18
Apple La	22	P 19
Archers La	22	P 18
Barlow Dr	23	R 20
Barrett La	22	P 18
Bartram Dr	23	R 17
Bayberry La	22	O 17
Beauiles Rd	23	Q 18
Beck Rd	23	S 18
Beech La	23	R 19
Beeholm Rd	22	O 19
Black Rock Tpke	23	R 17
Blueberry Hill Rd	22	O 19
Brick School Dr	22	P 17
Bridle Rd	23	S 20
Broad	22	O 19
Brookside Av	22	O 19
Chalburn Close	22	O 17
Chalburn Rd	22	O 17
Chapman Pl	26	Q 16
Charles Sanford Rd	23	S 20
Chestnut Woods Rd	22	O 17
Church	22	O 19
Church Hill La	23	R 19
Church Hill Rd	23	R 19
Church St S	22	O 20
Circlewood Rd	23	R 20
Connary La	22	O 19
Costa La	23	Q 17
Coverly Rd	22	P 19
Cross Hwy	23	Q 19
Dahlia La	23	R 18
Dan Beard La	23	Q 18
Dayton Rd	22	P 19
Deacon Abbott Rd	23	Q 18
Deacon Abbott Rd S	23	Q 18
Deer Hill Rd	23	Q 19
Deer Spring Rd	25	P 16
Diamond Hill Rd	22	P 18
Dodgingtown Rd	23	S 17
Dorethy Rd	22	P 19
Drummer La	23	Q 18
Dry River Ct	23	Q 19
Duck Run Rd	23	Q 18
Edgewood Rd	23	R 20
Ethan Allen Hwy (Route 7)	22	O 18
Farview Farm Rd	22	O 19
Fire Hill La	25	O 17
Fire Hill Rd	25	O 17
Fire Tower Rd	22	O 18
Foundry Rd	23	S 19
Fox Run Rd	22	P 18
Gallows Hill Rd	22	P 17
Gallows Hill Rd	23	Q 17
George Hull Hill Rd	25	P 16
Georgetown By-Pass	22	O 20
Giles Hill Rd	23	R 19
Glen Hill Rd	22	P 19
Glen Rd	22	P 19
Goodridge Rd	23	S 19
Goodsell Hill Rd	22	O 19
Granite Ridge Rd	22	P 18
Great Meadow Rd	23	S 19
Great Oak La	23	Q 18
Great Pasture Rd	23	Q 18
Great Pond La	25	O 16
Greenbush Rd	23	Q 19
Guardhouse Dr	22	P 17
Hattertown Rd	23	S 19
Hemlock Tr	23	Q 19
High Ridge Rd	23	R 18
Highland Av	22	O 20
Hillside La	22	O 19
Hopewell Wood Rd	23	R 18
Howes La	25	P 16
Huckleberry Rd	23	Q 19
Indian Hill Rd	22	O 19
Iris La	23	R 19
Jeremiah Sanford Rd	22	P 17
John Applegate Rd	22	O 20
John Read Rd	23	R 18
Kimberly Dr	22	P 17
Lampost Dr	25	P 16
Ledgeway Rd	23	R 20
Ledgewood Rd	22	P 19
Lee La	22	P 19
Lenora La	25	O 16
Limekiln Rd	26	Q 17
Little Boston La	22	O 19
Little Egypt Rd	23	Q 20
Little River La	23	R 18
Lockwood Rd	22	P 19
Lonetown Rd	23	Q 19
Long Meadow La	23	R 19
Long Ridge Rd	25	P 16
Mail Coach Rd	23	Q 19
Main	22	O 20
Mallory La	22	P 19
Maple	22	O 20
Marchant Rd	22	P 17
Mark Twain La	22	P 18
Marli La	23	Q 18
Mattatuck Tr	23	R 19
Meadows Edge	23	R 19
Meeker Hill Rd	23	R 19
Middlebrook Pond Rd	23	R 18
Mine Hill Rd	22	O 18
Mohawk Tr	23	Q 18
Morrill Rd	22	P 19
Mountain Laurel La	22	O 18
Mountain Rd	22	O 19
Mountainview Dr	23	Q 17
Musket La	23	R 17
Newell Rd	23	Q 18
Newtown Tpke	21	Q 20
Newtown Tpke	23	Q 19
North Park Av	23	S 20
North Park Av Ext	23	S 19
Old Dimon Rd	22	P 20
Old Field La	23	R 18
Old Hattertown Rd	23	S 19
Old Mill Rd	22	O 20
Old Redding Rd	22	O 18
Old Stagecoach Rd	23	Q 18
Old Weston Rd	22	O 20
Olmstead Rd N	25	O 16
Olmstead Rd S	25	O 16
Orchard Dr	22	P 19
Overlook Av	23	R 17
Overlook La	23	Q 17
Packer Brook Rd	23	R 18
Park Av S	23	S 20
Parsons La	22	O 19
Peaceable	22	O 19
Pheasant Ridge Rd	23	R 18
Picketts Ridge Rd	22	O 18
Picketts Ridge Rd	25	O 17
Pine Av	22	O 20
Pine Mountain Rd	22	O 19
Pinetree Rd	23	R 20
Pocohantas Rd	23	R 17
Portland Av	22	O 19
Portland Hill Rd	22	O 19
Poverty Hollow Rd	23	R 20
Putnam Av	23	R 17
Putnam Hill Dr	23	R 17
Putnam Park Rd	23	R 17
Red Coat La	23	R 17
Redding Rd	22	O 19
Redding Rd	25	P 17
Regulation Rd	26	Q 16
Ridgewood Dr	23	Q 17
Rob Rider Rd	23	Q 17
Rock House Rd	23	S 20
Rock Ledge Rd	25	O 17
Sandfordtown Rd	23	Q 19
Sergeant's La	22	O 18
Seventy Acre Rd	22	O 18
Shady La	23	Q 19
Sherman Tpke	23	Q 19
Side Cut Rd	25	P 17
Silversmith La	23	R 19
Simpaug Tpke	22	O 17
Smith	22	O 19
South La	23	R 19
Sport Hill Rd	23	S 20
Spur Rd	23	S 20
Starrs Ridge Rd	25	O 16
State Route 53	22	P 17
State Route 53	25	P 17
State Route 58	18	R 20
State Route 58	23	R 18
State Route 107	23	Q 18
Station Pl	25	P 16
Station Rd	22	P 17
Stepney Rd	23	S 19
Sullivan Dr	23	R 19
Sullivan Rd	23	R 18
Sunny View Dr	23	R 18
Sunset Hill Rd	23	R 18
Thankful Bradley Rd	22	O 20
Top Ledge Rd	22	O 18
Topstone Rd	22	O 17
Tudor Rd	22	P 20
Tunxis Tr	23	R 19
Turney Rd	23	R 19
Umpawaug Rd	22	O 19
Umpawaug Rd	23	S 18
Uncle John's Rd	23	S 19
US Hwy 7	22	O 18
Wagon Wheel Rd	23	R 17
Wayside La	22	P 19
Werf Dr	25	O 16
West Woodland Dr	23	S 20
West Woodland Dr Spur	23	S 20
White Birch Rd	22	P 18
Whortleberry Rd	23	Q 17
Winding Brook Ct	23	Q 18
Winding Brook La	23	Q 18
Wood Rd	23	R 17
Woodland Ter	23	S 20

RIDGEFIELD

STREET	MAP	GRID
Aaron's Ct	28	O 13
Acorn Pl	22	L 19
Acre La	22	M 18
Adams Rd	22	N 18
Armand Pl	25	M 16
Armand Rd	25	M 16
Ascot Way	22	M 18
Ashbee La	22	O 18
Aspen Ledges Dr	25	N 15
Aspen Mill Rd	25	N 15
Bailey Av	22	M 17
Banks Hill Pl	22	N 17
Barlow Mountain Rd	25	N 15
Barrack Hill Rd	25	M 15
Barry Av	25	M 16
Bates Farm Rd	25	O 15
Bayberry Hill Rd	22	N 18
Bear Mountain Rd	25	O 14
Beaver Brook Rd	28	O 13
Beechwood La	22	N 19
Bennett's Farm Rd	25	N 14
Benson Rd	28	N 13
Berthier Pl	28	N 13
Birch Ct	25	M 15
Birch La	25	N 16
Blackman Rd	22	N 17
Blacksmith Rd	25	L 17
Blacksmith Ridge	25	L 17
Bloomer Rd	22	N 18
Blue Ridge Rd	25	M 15
Bob Hill Rd	25	N 15
Bobby's Ct	22	O 17
Bogus Rd	25	O 14
Boulder Hill La	22	M 18
Boulder Hill Rd	22	M 18
Branchville Rd	22	M 17
Briar Ridge Rd	28	O 13
Bridle Tr	25	N 14
Brook La	22	N 19
Brookside Rd	25	N 16
Bruschi La	22	N 19
Buck Hill Rd	25	O 16
Buckspen La	25	O 15
Buell	25	M 17
Bypass Rd	22	L 17
Byron Av	22	M 17
Cains Hill Rd	22	O 17
Calvary Ct	25	M 16
Canterbury La	28	N 13
Cardinal Ct	25	M 16
Carpenter Close	22	M 17
Casa Torch Rd	22	M 18
Casey La	25	M 16
Catoonah	22	M 17
Cattle Pen la	22	M 19
Caudatowa Dr	25	M 15
Cedar La	22	L 18
Charter Oak Ct	25	N 16
Cherry La	25	N 16
Chestnut Hill Rd	28	N 13
Chipmunk La	28	O 13
Christopher Rd	25	M 15
Circle Dr	25	N 15
Circle Dr E	25	N 15
Clayton Pl	25	N 15
Clearview Dr	25	O 15
Clearview Ter	25	O 15
Cobblers La	22	L 17
Coconut Rd	25	M 17
Colonial La	25	N 15
Comstock Ct	22	M 19
Conant Rd	22	M 17
Continental Dr	25	M 16
Cook Close	22	M 17
Cooper Hill Rd	22	N 18
Cooper Rd	22	N 18
Copper Beech La	25	N 17
Copps Hill Rd	25	N 17
Corbin Dr	25	O 15
Corner Stone Ct	25	O 16
Cottage	25	M 17
Country Club Rd	22	L 18
Craigmoor Rd	25	M 15
Craigmoor Rd Ext	25	M 15
Cranberry La	22	M 18
Creamery La	22	M 18
Crescent Dr	25	O 15
Crest Rd	25	O 15
Cross Hill Rd	25	O 15
Danbury Rd	22	N 17
Danbury Rd	25	O 16
Danbury-Ridgefield Rd	25	N 17
Danzig Pl	25	N 16
Davis La	22	M 19
Dawn La	25	N 16
Deer Hill Dr	22	L 18
Deer Track Hill Rd	22	O 17
Depot Rd	22	N 19
Dillman Ct	28	N 13
Dogberry La	22	N 17
Dogwood Dr	25	O 16
Donnelly Dr	22	M 19
Doubleday La	25	M 16
Douglas La	25	N 14
Dowling Dr	25	N 16
Downesbury Ct	22	N 18
Druid La	25	O 17
East Farm La	22	O 17
East Ridge	22	M 17
Eleven Levels Rd	25	M 16
Ethan Allen Hwy	22	O 17
Ethan Allen Hwy	25	O 16
Evergreen Pl	28	N 13
Fairfield Ct	22	M 18
Fairview Av	22	M 17
Farm Hill Rd	25	M 17
Farmingville Rd	22	N 17
Farrar La	25	N 16
Fieldcrest Dr	22	M 19
Fillmore La	25	N 16
Finch Dr	28	N 13
Fire Hill Rd	25	O 17
Flat Rock Dr	22	L 18
Florida Hill Rd	22	N 18
Florida Rd	22	N 18
Forest Dr	22	M 19
Fox Dr	25	N 15
Fox Hill Dr	25	N 17
Fulling Mill La	22	O 17
Gay Rd	22	M 19
George Washington Hwy	25	N 15
Gilbert	22	M 17
Glen Rd	25	O 16
Glenbrook Ct	22	N 18
Golf La	22	M 17
Governor	22	M 17
Grand View Dr	25	M 15
Great Hill Rd	25	N 16
Great Pond Rd	25	O 16
Great Rocks Pl	22	M 19
Green La	25	M 16
Greenfield	22	M 17
Greenridge Dr	25	O 15
Griffin Hill Rd	22	O 17
Griffith La	22	M 17
Grove	22	M 17
Halpin La	22	M 17
Hamilton Rd	22	M 17
Harding Dr	28	N 13
Harvey Rd	22	N 18
Hauley Pl	22	N 17
Haviland Rd	25	N 16
Hawthorne Hill Rd	25	N 14
Hayes La	22	M 18
Heritage La	25	M 15
Hermit La	22	N 18
Hessian Dr	25	N 16
Hickory La	22	O 18
Hidden Lake Ct	25	M 15
High Pastures Ct	25	N 16
High Ridge Av	22	M 17
High Valley Rd	22	N 18
Highcliff Ter	25	O 15
Highview Dr	25	N 15
Highview Rd	25	O 16
Hillcrest Ct	25	M 15
Hillsdale	25	N 17
Hilltop Ct	25	N 16
Hobby Dr	25	N 15
Holmes Rd	22	M 17
Huckleberry La	22	M 18
Hulda La	25	N 16
Hull Pl	22	N 17
Hunter La	22	N 17
Hunter La W	22	N 17
Hussars Camp Pl	25	N 14
Indian Cave Rd	22	N 18
Island Hill Av	25	N 17
Ives Ct	25	O 14
Ivy Hill Rd	22	M 18
Ivy Hill Rd	25	N 17
Jackson Ct	22	M 17
Jefferson Rd	22	N 18
Jeffro Dr	22	N 18
Keeler Close	22	M 17
Keeler Dr	28	N 13
Keeler Pl	28	N 13
Kellogg	25	M 16
Ketcham Rd	25	M 16
Kiahs Brook La	25	N 15
Kiln Hill La	22	M 17
King La	22	M 17
Kingswood Pl	22	O 17
Knollwood Dr	25	N 15
Lafayette Av	25	N 17
Lake Rd	25	O 15
Lakeside Dr	25	O 15
Lakeside Dr Ext	25	O 15
Lakeview Dr	25	O 15
Langstroth Dr	25	O 14
Lantern Dr	22	N 17
Laurel Hill Rd	22	N 18
Laurel La	25	O 16
Lawson La	22	M 17
Ledges Rd	25	N 15
Lee Rd	22	N 17
Lewis Dr	22	M 17
Limekiln Rd	25	N 17
Limestone Rd	25	N 16
Limestone Ter	25	N 15
Lincoln La	22	M 18
Linden Rd	25	N 17
Lisa La	25	M 15
Little Ridge Rd	22	N 18
Longview Dr	22	O 17
Lookout Dr	25	O 16
Lookout Pt	25	N 15
Lookout Rd	25	O 16
Loren La	25	M 15
Lost Mine Pl	22	O 17
Lounsbury La	22	N 18
Lounsbury Rd	22	N 17
Madeline Dr	25	O 15
Main	22	M 17
Mallory Hill Rd	22	N 19
Mamanasco Rd	25	M 15
Manor Rd	22	M 17
Maple Shade Rd	25	M 17
Maplewood Rd	25	O 16
Marcadon Av	22	M 18
Marie La	25	O 15
Market	22	M 17
Marshall Rd	22	M 17
Mary La	25	M 17
Mead Ridge Dr	22	L 17
Mead Ridge La	22	L 17
Mead Ridge Rd	22	L 17
Memory La	22	L 18
Middlebrook La	22	N 19
Midrocks Rd	25	O 15
Mill View Ter	25	O 17
Millers La	25	M 16
Mimosa Cir	25	N 16
Mimosa Ct	25	N 16
Mimosa La	25	N 16
Mimosa Pl	25	N 16
Minuteman Rd	25	L 16
Mopus Bridge Rd	25	M 14
Morganti Ct	22	M 19
Mount View Av	25	M 17
Mountain Rd	25	M 17
Mulberry	25	M 16
Neds La	25	N 14
Neds Mount Rd	25	N 14
New	25	M 17
New Rd	22	O 17
Nod Hill Rd	22	M 20
Nod Rd	22	M 19
Nod West Dr	22	M 19
Norrans Ridge Dr	25	N 17
North	25	N 16
North Ridgebury Rd	28	O 13
North Salem Rd	25	M 14
North Shore Dr	25	N 14
North Valley Rd	22	N 18
Nursery Rd	25	O 17
Nutmeg Ct	25	M 17

STREET	MAP	GRID
Nutmeg Ridge	22	N 18
Oak Tree La	22	N 19
Olcott Way	22	M 17
Old Barlow Mountain Rd	25	N 15
Old Branchville Rd	22	N 18
Old Danbury Rd	25	N 16
Old Hwy	22	O 17
Old Hwy	25	L 15
Old Main Hwy	22	O 19
Old Mill Rd	25	O 14
Old Musket La	22	N 17
Old Oscaleta Rd	25	L 16
Old Pierce Rd	25	O 16
Old Quarry Rd	22	N 17
Old Redding Rd	22	O 18
Old Sib Rd	25	M 15
Old South Salem Rd	22	L 17
Old Stagecoach Rd	25	N 14
Old Stone Ct	22	O 17
Old Town Rd	22	N 19
Old Trolley Rd	28	O 13
Old Wagon Rd	25	M 16
Old Wall Ct	25	N 17
Old Washington Rd	22	N 18
Old West La	28	N 13
Old West Mountain Rd	25	M 16
Olmstead La	22	M 18
O'Neill Ct	25	M 14
Orchard La	22	M 18
Oroneca Rd	25	L 15
Oscaleta Rd	25	L 16
Outpost Ct	25	N 17
Overlook Dr	25	M 17
Overlook Rd	25	O 16
Park La	22	N 19
Parley La	22	M 17
Parley Rd	28	N 13
Partridge Dr	25	N 15
Peaceable	22	L 17
Peaceable Hill Rd	25	L 17
Peaceable Ridge	25	L 16
Pellham La	22	N 19
Perry La	22	M 18
Pheasant La	28	N 13
Pierrepont Dr	25	N 15
Pilgrim Hill Rd	25	N 16
Pin Pack Rd	25	M 16
Pine Lake Rd	25	M 15
Pine Mtn Rd	25	O 14
Pinecrest Dr	25	N 15
Playground Rd	22	N 19
Pocconock Tr	25	M 16
Pond Rd	25	M 15
Poplar Rd	25	N 16
Portland Av	22	O 19
Portland Hill Rd	22	O 19
Pound	22	M 17
Powder Horn Dr	22	N 17
Powdermaker Rd	28	N 13
Prospect	22	M 17
Prospect Ridge	22	M 17
Pump La	22	L 18
Pumping Station Rd	25	L 16
Quail Dr	25	N 14
Quincy Close	22	M 17
Ramapoo Hill Rd	25	M 16
Ramapoo Rd	25	M 16
Red Oak La	25	L 16
Regan Rd	25	N 14
Remington Rd	22	M 17
Revere Dr	25	L 17
Revere Pl	22	N 18
Richardson Dr	22	O 17
Ridgebury Rd	25	M 15
Ridgecrest Dr	25	N 16
Ridgeway Ter	25	O 15
Ridgewood Rd	22	N 18
Rippowam Rd	25	L 15
Rising Ridge Rd	22	N 19
Rita Rd	25	O 15
Ritch Dr	25	N 16
Riverside Dr	22	O 17
Roberts La	25	M 17
Rochambeau Av	25	N 17
Rock Ct	25	M 15
Rock Rd	25	M 15
Rock Spring La	25	N 17
Rockcrest Dr	25	N 15
Rockwell Rd	22	M 18
Rolling Hill Rd	25	O 17
Rolling Ridge Rd	25	N 15
Round Lake Rd	25	M 15
Rowland La	22	M 17
Rustic Dr	25	O 15
Rustic Rd	25	O 15
Saddle Ridge Rd	25	N 14
Saint John's Rd	22	M 18
Sanford Station Rd	22	O 18
Sarah Bishop Rd	28	N 13
Saunders La	22	O 17
Sawmill Hill Rd	25	M 16
Sawmill Rd	28	O 13
Schoolhouse Pl	28	N 13
Scodon Dr	25	O 14
Scott Ridge Rd	25	M 15
Senoka Dr	25	N 15
Serfillipi La	22	M 18
Seth Low Mountain Rd	25	N 15
Settlers La	25	M 16
Seventy Acre Rd	22	O 18
Seymour La	22	M 18
Shadblow Hill Rd	22	N 18
Shadow La	22	M 17
Shadow Lake Rd	28	O 13
Shady La	25	O 15
Sharp Hill La	25	M 16
Sherwood Rd	25	N 15
Shields La	25	N 16
Short La	25	N 15
Silver Birch La	22	M 17
Silver Brook Rd	22	L 19
Silver Hill Rd	22	M 19
Silver Spring La	22	L 19
Silver Spring Park Rd	22	L 19
Silver Spring Rd	22	L 18
Skytop Rd	25	N 14
Sleepy Hollow Rd	25	M 15
Sophia Dr	25	O 14
Soundview Rd	22	M 18
South	22	N 17
South Olmstead La	22	M 18
South Salem Rd	22	L 17
South Shore Dr	25	N 14
Southridge Ct	22	L 19
Spectacle La	22	M 19
Spire View Rd	25	N 15
Split Level Rd	22	M 18
Spring Rd	22	L 19
Spring Valley Rd	25	M 14
Sprucewood La	25	N 15
Stagecoach Rd	25	N 14
Standish Dr	22	N 18
State Route 33	22	M 18
State Route 35	22	M 17
State Route 35	25	N 16
State Route 102	22	N 18
State Route 102	25	M 16
State Route 116	25	M 14
State Route 116	28	N 13
Stebbins Close	22	M 17
Still Rd	25	O 16
Stone Dr	25	N 17
Stonecrest Rd	25	N 16
Stonehenge Rd	25	O 17
Stony Hill Rd	22	N 18
Stony Hill Ter	22	N 18
Strawberry Ridge Rd	22	N 19
Sugar Loaf Mtn Rd	25	N 14
Summit La	25	N 15
Sunset Dr	25	N 14
Sunset La	22	M 17
Sycamore La	22	L 18
Sylvan Dr	25	O 15
Tackora Tr	25	M 15
Tally-Ho Rd	25	O 16
Tanglewood Ct	22	M 18
Tannery Hill Rd	25	N 16
Tanton Hill Rd	25	N 16
Taporneck Ct	25	M 14
Thunder Hill La	25	M 16
Titicus Ct	25	N 16
Todd's Rd	25	N 14
Topcrest La	25	N 15
Topstone Rd	22	O 17
Tower Rd	25	M 16
Trails End La	25	M 16
Turner	28	N 12
Twin Ridge Rd	22	M 18
Twixt Hill Rd	25	N 15
Twopence Rd	28	N 13
US Hwy 7	22	O 18
US Hwy 7	25	O 16
Victor Dr	25	M 17
Virginia Ct	25	N 14
Walnut Grove Rd	22	N 17
Walnut Hill Rd	25	M 15
Washington Av	25	N 17
Wataba Ct	25	O 15
Waterfall Rd	25	O 14
Water's Edge Way	25	O 15
Webster Rd	22	M 17
West Branchville Rd	22	O 19
West La	22	L 18
West Mountain Rd	25	M 16
Westmoreland Rd	22	M 17
Wheeler Rd	25	M 14
Whipstick Rd	22	M 18
White Birch Rd	22	L 19
White Birches Rd	22	N 19
Whitewood Hollow Ct	25	O 17
Whitlock La	25	N 14
Wier Farm La	22	N 19
Wild Turkey Ct	25	M 16
Willow Ct	25	N 16
Wilridge Rd	22	N 19
Wilton Rd E	22	M 18
Wilton Rd W	22	M 18
Windy Ridge	22	M 18
Woodchuck La	22	M 18
Woodcock La	25	M 16
Woodland Way	25	O 15
Woodlawn Dr	22	M 18
Woodstone Rd	25	N 16
Woody Pl	25	O 15
Wooster	25	N 16
Wooster Hgts	25	M 16
Yankee Hill Rd	25	L 17
1st La	25	M 15
2nd La	25	M 15
3rd La	25	M 15
4th La	25	M 15
5th La	25	M 15
6th La	25	M 15
7th La	25	M 15
8th La	25	M 15
9th La	25	M 15
10th La	25	M 15
11th La	25	M 15
12th La	25	M 15

SHELTON

STREET	MAP	GRID
Abbey La	19	X 22
Access Rd	13	Y 23
Adams Dr	13	W23
Agawam Tr	13	X 25
Algonkin Rd	13	X 25
Alice Ct	19	X 21
Allyndale Ct	13	X 25
Andrew Dr	13	X 24
Angell Av	7	Z 24
Ann Av	7	Z 24
Anna	7	Z 24
Ansonia Av	13	Y 23
Applewood Dr	19	X 21
April La	13	V 23
Armstrong Rd	13	X 24
Arrowhead La	19	X 22
Arthur's Ct	13	X 24
Asbury Ridge	13	Y 24
Aspetuck Tr	13	X 23
Astor Dr	19	Y 21
Astoria La	19	X 22
Autumn Ridge Rd	13	W23
Ballaro Dr	19	W21
Barbara Dr	13	Y 24
Barney Park Rd	19	W22
Barry Rd	19	X 22
Basking Brook La	13	Y 23
Basking Ridge Rd	13	Y 23
Bayberry La	13	W23
Beacon Hill Ter	13	X 23
Bear Path Dr	19	Y 22
Beard	7	Z 23
Beard Sawmill Rd	13	X 24
Beardsley	13	Y 23
Beardsley Rd	19	X 21
Beech	13	Y 23
Beech Tree Hill Rd	19	X 20
Beecher Av	7	Z 23
Bella La	13	W23
Belmont Av	7	Z 24
Beverly Hill Dr	19	W22
Beverly La	19	W22
Big Horn Rd	19	X 20
Biltmore Rd	19	Y 22
Birch	13	Y 23
Birchbank Rd	19	Y 20
Birchwood La	19	X 22
Birdseye Rd	19	X 22
Birdseye Rd Ext	19	X 22
Black Birch Ct	13	Y 23
Blackberry La	13	W23
Black's Hill Rd	13	Y 23
Blaho Dr	13	Y 25
Blueberry La	13	W23
Bodyk Pl	7	Z 23
Boehm Cir	19	W22
Bona Vista Ter	19	Y 21
Bonita Dr	19	W21
Bonnie Brook Dr	13	V 23
Booth Hill Rd	19	W21
Boulder Path	19	Y 20
Boysenberry La	13	W23
Braeloch Way	13	X 22
Brentley Dr	19	W22
Brewster La	7	Z 23
Briarcliff Rd	13	W23
Bridge	7	Z 23
Bridgeport Av	7	Z 23
Bridgeport Expwy	13	W24
Bristol Dr	13	Y 23
Broc Ter	13	Y 24
Brook	7	Z 23
Brookfield Dr	13	X 23
Brookpine Dr	19	Y 22
Brookwood La	19	X 21
Brownson Dr	19	X 22
Bruce Dr	7	Z 24
Bryant La	19	Y 20
Buck Hill Rd	13	X 23
Budd Cir	13	Y 23
Buddington Rd	13	X 24
Buttercup La	13	W23
Button Rd	19	X 22
Byron Pl	19	Y 20
Cali Dr	13	W23
Cameo Dr	19	W21
Canal E	7	Z 23
Canal W	7	Z 23
Canfield Dr	13	W23
Canoe Brook	13	X 23
Capitol Dr	13	V 23
Captains Watch	19	X 22
Cardinal Dr	13	W23
Carley	7	Z 23
Carriage Dr	13	X 23
Cathy Dr	13	X 23
Catlin Pl	7	Z 24
Cayer Cir	19	W22
Cedarhill Rd	19	X 22
Cedarwood La	19	X 22
Center	7	Z 23
Centerview Dr	13	X 23
Chamberlain Dr	19	X 22
Charles	7	Z 23
Chaucer Dr	19	Y 20
Chestnut	7	Z 23
Christine Dr	19	W22
Christmas Tree Hill Rd	19	X 21
Church	13	X 23
Cliff	7	Z 23
Cliff St Ext	7	Z 23
Clinton Dr	19	V 21
Cloverdale Av	13	W23
Coachman's La	19	W22
Cobblestone Dr	19	X 22
Cold Spring Cir	13	X 24
Colony	7	Z 24
Columbia Dr	19	W22
Commerce Dr	13	X 24
Commodore Av	19	Y 22
Congress Av	7	Z 23
Connecticut Av	7	Z 23
Constitution Blvd N	19	Y 22
Constitution Blvd S	13	Y 24
Controls Dr	13	Y 24
Coppel La	13	X 24
Copper Penny La	19	W22
Coppermine Rd	19	Y 21
Coral Dr	13	V 23
Coram Av	7	Z 23
Coram Rd	7	Z 24
Corn Hill Rd	19	W22
Cornell	7	Z 23
Corporate Dr	13	X 24
Cots	13	Y 23
Country Ridge Dr	13	W23
Country Walk	13	X 23
Courtland Dr	13	X 23
Cranberry La	13	W23
Cranston Av	7	Z 24
Cree Tr	13	Y 25
Crescent	7	Z 23
Crescent Dr	13	W24
Crestwood Pl	19	X 22
Cribbins Av	19	Y 22
Cross	7	Z 23
Curran La	19	W22
Cynthia La	19	Y 21
Daisy Dr	13	W23
Dana Av	7	Z 24
Danube Dr	19	V 22
Darrin Dr	13	W23
Dartmouth Dr	19	W22
David Dr	13	Y 24
Daybreak La	13	X 24
Deborah Dr	13	W23
Deer Run	13	X 23
Deer Run La	19	Y 22
Deerfield Dr	19	W22
Dexter Dr	19	X 22
Dickinson Dr	19	Y 20
Dimon Rd	19	Y 20
Division Av	7	Z 23
Dodge Dr	19	Y 21
Doe Pl	13	X 23
Dogwood Dr	19	X 22
Dogwood La	7	Z 24
Dome Dr	13	X 24
Donovan La	13	Y 23
Douglas Ct	19	X 21
Driftwood La	19	Y 22
Eagle Dr	19	W21
Eagles Landing	13	X 23
Earl	13	X 23
East Av	7	Z 23
East Village Rd	19	Y 20
Edgewood Av	7	Z 24
Edward	19	Y 22
Elaine Av	19	V 21
Elderberry	13	W23
Elizabeth	13	W23
Elliot Dr	19	X 20
Elm	7	Z 23
Emerson Dr	19	Y 20
Enterprise	7	Z 24
Enterprise Dr	13	X 24
Evelyn Dr	19	W21
Evergreen Ct	19	V 22
Fair Oaks Dr	19	V 22
Fairfield Av	7	Z 23
Fairlane Dr	19	W21
Fairlea Dr	19	Y 22
Fairmont Pl	7	Z 23
Fairview Av	7	Z 24
Falcon La	13	Y 25
Falmouth Dr	13	Y 23
Fanny	7	Z 24
Far Horizons Dr	19	Y 20
Far Mill	19	Y 21
Far Mill Crossing	13	X 24
Farm House La	13	W23
Fawn Hill Rd	19	V 22
Federal Rd	19	V 22
Fern Dr	13	V 23
Fieldstone Dr	13	X 22
Fisher Ct	13	X 23
Florence Dr	19	W22
Foley Av	19	Y 22
Forest Av	13	Y 23
Forest Pkwy	13	Y 24
Fort Hill Av	7	Z 22
Fox Hunt Rd	19	Y 20
Fox Run	13	X 23
Frank Dr	19	W21
Galen Rd	19	Y 20
Garden Ter	13	Y 24
Geissler Dr	7	Z 22
Gene Dr	13	W23
George	7	Z 22
Gilbert	7	Z 23
Glendale Ter	7	Z 24
Golden Hill La	19	Y 20
Golden Av	7	Z 23
Gordon Av	7	Z 24
Grandison Pl	19	Y 21
Gray	19	W21
Great Oak Rd	13	X 23
Greenacre Dr	19	W21
Greenbrier Rd	13	V 23
Greenfield Dr	13	V 23
Greenwich Pl	13	W24
Greenwood La	19	V 21
Gristmill La	13	X 24
Grove	7	Z 23
Hamburg	7	Z 24
Hamilton Dr	19	W22
Harvard Av	7	Z 23
Haven La	19	X 21
Havemill Dr	19	W22
Hawley Rd	13	X 23
Hawthorne Av	7	Z 24
Hazel Ct	13	W23
Heartstone Dr	19	W22
Heather Hill Rd	19	W21
Hemlock Dr	19	X 22
Henry Dr	19	Y 21
Hiawatha Tr	19	Y 20
Hickory Hill	13	Y 23
Hickory La	19	Y 21
Hidden Pond La	13	W23
High	7	Z 23
High Hill	13	X 23
High Plains Rd	13	Y 23
High Ridge Rd	19	W22
Highland Av	7	Z 23
Highmeadow Rd	19	V 22
Hill	7	Z 23
Hill Ext	7	Z 23
Hillside Av	7	Z 23
Hilltop Dr	19	Y 22
Holly La	13	W23
Honeybee La	13	V 23
Horse Stable Cir	19	W22
Howard Av	7	Z 23
Howe Av	7	Z 23
Hull	7	Z 23
Hunters Creek	13	X 23
Hunters Ridge Rd	13	W23
Huntington	13	X 23
Huntington Av	7	Z 23
Huntington Cir	13	W23
Hurd	19	V 22
Indian Well Rd	19	Y 20
Inwood Ct	19	W22
Isinglass Rd	13	W24
Israel Hill Rd	19	X 20
Ivy Brook Dr	13	Y 24
Ivy La	13	Y 24
James Farm Rd	13	X 24
Jane	7	Z 23
Jardin Cir	13	Y 23
Jean Ct	13	Y 23
Jefferson	7	Z 23
Jenyfer Ct	7	Z 24
Jodie La	19	Y 20
Joel La	13	Y 24
John	7	Z 23
John Dominick Dr	13	X 23
Jonathan La	19	X 20
Jordon Av	7	Z 24
Joseph Ct	7	Z 24
Judson	13	X 24
Judson Cir	13	X 24
Julie	19	V 21
Kanungum Tr	13	X 25
Katherine Ct	7	Z 24
Kathleen Rd	19	W22
Kazo Dr	13	W24
Kent Ct	19	W22
Keron Dr	13	Y 24
King	7	Z 23
Kings Hwy	13	X 24
Kneen	7	Z 23
Kneen Ct	7	Z 23
Knollbrook	13	Y 23
Knollwood Ter	7	Z 24
Kohlers Farm Rd	19	X 22
Ladas Pl	7	Z 24
Ladyslipper Dr	13	V 23
Laguna La	19	Y 21
Lake Rd	13	Y 23
Lake Rd	19	Y 22
Lakeview Av	7	Z 22
Lakeview Av Ext	7	Z 22
Lane	13	X 23
Lark La	19	X 22
Laurel	7	Z 23
Laurel Glen Dr	13	W23
Laurel Hgts Rd	7	Z 24
Laurel La	7	Z 23
Laurel Wood Dr	13	Y 24
Lazy Brook Rd	19	W22
Leavenworth Rd	19	X 21
Ledgewood Rd #1	19	Y 22
Ledgewood Rd #2	19	Y 22
Lenore Dr	19	Y 21
L'Hermitage Dr	13	Y 23
Liberty	7	Z 23
Lily La	13	W23
Linda La	13	W23
Lisa Dr	19	W21
Little Fawn Dr	19	Y 22
Little Fox Run	19	Y 20
Long Hill Av	13	X 25
Long Hill Av	13	Y 24
Long Hill Cross Rd	13	X 24
Longfellow Rd	19	Y 20
Longmeadow Rd	13	X 23
Longview Rd	13	Y 24
Lucille Dr	19	X 22
Lynne Ter	13	Y 25
Lynnwood Ct	19	Y 20
Lynnwood Dr	19	Y 20
Lynx Run	13	X 23
Madison Av	7	Z 23
Maler Av	13	X 23
Maler Av	19	X 22
Maltby	7	Z 23
Manhassett Tr	13	X 25
Manton	7	Z 24
Maple	7	Z 23

87

STREET	MAP	GRID
Bayberrie Dr	2	E 25
Beach View Dr	2	F 27
Beal	2	E 26
Beckley Av	2	F 26
Bedford	2	F 25
Beechwood Rd	9	F 23
Beehler	2	E 26
Bel Aire Dr	9	F 24
Belden	2	E 26
Bell	2	F 25
Bellmere Av	2	F 25
Belltown Rd	9	G 24
Bend of River La	9	E 24
Benedict	2	F 26
Benedict Cir	2	F 26
Bennett	9	G 24
Bennington Ct	15	G 21
Benstone Rd	9	F 24
Bentwood Dr	15	F 21
Berges Av	9	F 24
Berkeley	2	E 26
Berrian Rd	9	F 24
Bertmoor Dr	9	G 24
Betts Av	2	E 26
Big Oak Cir	15	G 22
Big Oak La	9	G 23
Big Oak Rd	9	F 23
Birch	2	G 26
Birchwood Rd	9	G 24
Bird Song La	15	G 22
Bishop La	2	E 26
Bittersweet La	15	H 21
Blachley Rd	2	F 26
Black Rock Rd	15	H 20
Black Twig Pl	15	G 20
Black Wood La	9	G 23
Blackberry Dr	15	G 20
Blackberry Dr E	15	G 20
Blue Ridge Dr	9	G 23
Blue Rock Dr	15	H 22
Blue Spruce La	15	E 20
Blueberry Dr	9	E 24
Bon Air Av	9	G 24
Bond	2	F 26
Bonner	2	E 26
Bonny Glen Rd	15	H 20
Borglum	9	F 24
Boulder Brook Dr	15	F 22
Boulderol Rd	15	G 20
Bouton	9	G 24
Bouton Cir	9	G 24
Bouton W	9	G 24
Bowen	2	G 25
Boxwood Dr	2	F 25
Bracchi Dr	15	H 21
Bracewood La	2	F 25
Bradley Pl	9	F 23
Branch La	15	F 22
Brandt Rd	9	F 23
Brandywine Rd	9	G 23
Brantwood La	9	G 23
Breezy Hill Rd	15	G 20
Briar Brae Rd	15	G 21
Briar Brae Rd Connection	15	G 21
Briar Woods Tr	15	G 21
Briarwood La	9	F 23
Bridge	2	E 25
Bridle Path	9	F 24
Brighton Pl	2	F 25
Brightside Dr	2	F 27
Brinkerhoff Av	9	F 24
Broad	2	E 25
Broad Brook La	9	H 23
Brodwood Dr	9	E 24
Brook Run La	9	F 24
Brookdale Dr	15	G 22
Brookdale Rd	15	G 22
Brookhollow La	9	E 23
Brooklawn Av	2	F 25
Brookside Dr	2	G 26
Brookvale Pl	9	F 24
Brown Av	2	E 26
Brownhouse Rd	2	F 26
Brownley Dr	9	F 24
Brundage	9	G 24
Brushwood Rd	15	H 21
Buckingham Ct	9	F 24
Buckingham Dr	9	F 24
Buena Vista	9	G 24
Bungalow Pk	2	G 26
Burdick	2	F 25
Burley Av	2	E 26
Burns Rd	2	F 27
Burr	2	E 25
Burwood Av	2	E 26
Butternut La	15	F 22
Butternut Pl	15	F 22
Buxton Farm Rd	9	G 23
Cady	9	G 24
Calass La	15	H 20
Caldwell Av	2	F 26
Cambridge Rd	2	G 26
Camelot Ct	9	H 24
Camore	9	F 24
Camp Av	9	G 24
Campbell Dr	15	G 22
Canal	2	F 26
Canfield Dr	9	E 23
Cantwell Av	9	F 24
Caprice Dr	9	E 24
Carlisle Pl	2	E 26
Carolina Rd	2	E 25
Carriage Dr	9	E 24
Carriage Dr S	9	E 24
Carrington Dr	15	E 22
Carroll	9	G 24
Carter Dr	2	F 26
Cascade Ct	15	H 22
Cascade Rd	15	H 21
Case Rd	9	G 24
Castle Ct	2	G 25
Catoona La	2	E 26
Cedar	2	F 26
Cedar Cir	9	F 23
Cedar Hgts Rd	9	F 23
Cedar Wood Rd	15	H 21
Center	2	F 25
Center Ter	2	F 25
Central	2	G 25
Cerretta	9	G 24
Chapin La	9	H 23
Charles	2	F 26
Charles-Mary La	2	E 25
Chatfield	2	G 25
Chatham Rd	15	G 21
Cherry	2	F 26
Cherry Hill Rd	15	E 20
Chester	2	F 25
Chesterfield Rd	2	F 27
Chestnut	2	E 25
Chestnut Hill La	15	F 22
Chestnut Hill Rd	15	F 22
Church	2	G 25
Cider Mill Rd	15	F 21
Claremont	2	E 26
Clark	2	F 25
Clarks Hill Av	2	F 26
Clay Hill Rd	9	F 23
Clearview Av	9	G 24
Cleveland	2	G 25
Clifford Av	2	F 25
Clinton Av	2	E 26
Clorinda Ct	9	F 24
Clovelly Rd	2	F 25
Clover Hill Dr	9	F 24
Club Cir	9	G 23
Club Rd	9	G 24
Coachlamp La	2	E 25
Cody Dr	9	F 24
Cogswell La	9	E 23
Colahan	2	E 25
Cold Spring Rd	2	E 25
Coleton Rd	15	F 22
Colonial Rd	2	F 25
Colony Ct	9	F 24
Columbus Pl	9	G 24
Comet	2	F 26
Commerce Rd	2	E 25
Congress	2	E 26
Connecticut Av	2	E 25
Connecticut Tpke	2	F 26
Constance La	9	F 23
Cook Rd	2	E 26
Coolidge Av	2	F 25
Cooper's Pond Rd	9	F 24
Corbo Ter	2	E 25
Corn Cake La	9	F 23
Cottage	2	F 26
Country Club Rd	15	G 20
Court	2	F 25
Courtland Av	2	G 26
Courtland Cir	2	F 26
Courtland Hill	2	G 25
Cousins Rd	15	G 22
Cove Rd	2	F 26
Cove View Dr	2	G 26
Coventry Dr	15	G 20
Coventry Rd	15	G 20
Cow Path Dr	9	E 23
Cowan Av	2	F 25
Cowing Ct	2	G 25
Cowing Pl	2	G 25
Cowing Ter	2	G 25
Crab Apple Pl	15	G 20
Craig Ct	15	H 20
Crandall	2	F 26
Crane Rd	2	F 25
Crane Rd N	2	F 25
Crescent	2	G 25
Cresthill Pl	2	E 27
Crestview Av	9	G 24
Crestwood Dr	9	F 24
Cricket La	15	H 21
Crofts La	15	G 21
Crosby	2	E 26
Cross Country Tr	15	G 21
Cross Rd	9	F 24
Crystal	2	F 26
Crystal Lake Rd	9	F 23
Culloden Rd	2	F 26
Cummings Av	2	F 26
Cummings Park Rd	2	F 26
Cummings Point Rd	2	E 26
Cushing	9	G 24
Custer	2	F 26
Cypress Dr	15	H 22
Dads La	15	G 21
Daffodil Rd	15	H 21
Dagmar Pl	9	G 24
Dagmar Rd	9	G 24
Dale	2	F 26
Dale Pl	2	G 25
Daly	2	F 26
Dancy Dr	9	F 24
Dann Dr	9	F 24
Dannell Dr	9	F 24
Dartley	9	F 24
Daskam Pl	2	F 25
Davenport	2	E 26
Davenport Dr	2	E 26
Davenport Farm La E	9	H 23
Davenport Farm La N	15	H 22
Davenport Farm La S	9	H 23
Davenport Farm La W	9	H 23
Davenport Ridge La	9	G 23
Davenport Ridge Rd	9	G 23
Daycroft Rd	2	F 26
Deacon Hill Rd	9	F 24
Dean	2	F 26
Debera La	2	G 26
Dee La	2	E 26
Deep Spring La	9	H 24
Deep Valley Rd	15	E 22
Deep Valley Tr	15	E 22
Deepwood Rd	15	G 22
Deer Hill La	9	F 23
Deer La	9	F 24
Deer Meadow La	15	F 21
Deerfield Dr	15	G 22
Delaware Av	2	E 25
De Leo Dr	2	G 25
Delwood Rd	15	G 20
Deming La	15	G 22
Den Rd	9	F 23
Den Rd	15	F 22
Denicola Pl	9	G 24
Denise Dr	9	F 24
Denise Pl	9	F 24
Depinedo Av	2	E 25
Derry	9	G 23
Derwen	2	G 25
Diamond Crest La	15	G 22
Diaz	2	E 25
Division	2	E 26
Dock	2	F 26
Dogwood Ct	15	F 22
Dogwood La	9	F 23
Dogwood La	15	F 22
Dolphin Cove Quay	2	E 27
Dolsen Pl	2	F 25
Don Bob Rd	15	H 22
Donald Rd	9	G 24
Donata La	9	G 23
Doolittle Rd	9	F 23
Dora	2	G 26
Doral Farms Rd	9	F 23
Doris La	15	G 21
Dorlen Rd	2	F 25
Dorset La	9	H 24
Douglas Av	2	G 25
Downs Av	2	E 26
Drum Hill La	9	F 23
Dryden	2	E 25
Dubois	9	F 24
Duffy	2	F 26
Duke Dr	9	F 23
Dulan Dr	15	G 21
Duncanson	9	F 24
Dundee Rd	15	F 22
Dunn Av	9	G 23
Dunn Ct	9	F 23
Durant	2	E 26
Dyke La	2	E 26
Dzamba Grove	9	G 23
Eagle Dr	15	G 22
East	2	F 26
East Av	2	F 26
East Cross Rd	9	H 23
East Hill Rd	15	F 21
East Hunting Ridge Rd	15	G 21
East La	2	F 25
East Main	2	F 26
East Middle Patent Rd	15	E 20
East Ridge Rd	9	F 23
East Walnut	2	E 26
Eastover Rd	9	G 23
Echo Hill Dr	15	F 20
Eden La	9	G 23
Eden Rd	9	G 23
Edgewood Av	2	G 25
Edice Rd	9	F 24
Edison Rd	2	E 25
Edward Pl	9	G 24
Eighth	2	F 25
Elaine Dr	9	F 24
Eliot La	15	G 21
Elizabeth Av	9	G 24
Eljay's La	9	E 23
Elm	2	F 26
Elm Ct	2	F 26
Elm Tree Pl	2	G 25
Elmbrook Dr	2	F 25
Elmcroft Rd	2	E 26
Elmer	9	G 24
Elmwood	2	F 26
Ely Pl	2	F 25
Emerald La	9	G 23
Emery Dr	2	E 25
Emery Dr E	2	E 25
Emma Rd	9	F 24
Erickson Dr	15	F 21
Erskine Rd	15	F 20
Estwick Pl	9	G 24
Ethan Allen La	15	G 22
Euclid Av	2	F 26
Eureka Ter	2	E 26
Evergreen Ct	9	F 24
Fahey	9	G 24
Fairfield Av	2	E 26
Fairland	2	F 25
Fairmont Av	2	G 25
Fairview Av	2	E 27
Fairview Ct	2	G 26
Fairway Dr	15	H 20
Falmouth Rd	15	G 21
Fara Dr	9	F 24
Farm Hill Rd	9	E 23
Farms Rd	15	E 21
Farr Ter	2	E 25
Faucett	2	F 25
Fawn Dr	9	F 24
Fawnfield Rd	15	F 22
Federal	2	F 26
Fenway	2	F 25
Fernwood Dr	15	H 21
Ferris Av	2	E 25
Ferro Dr	2	F 26
Field	2	G 25
Fieldstone Cir	2	F 25
Fieldstone La	2	F 25
Fieldstone Rd	2	F 25
Fieldstone Ter	2	F 25
Fifth	2	F 25
Finney La	2	E 25
First	2	F 25
First Stamford Pl	2	E 26
Fishing Tr	15	G 21
Flint Rock Rd	15	F 22
Flora Pl	15	H 20
Florence Ct	9	F 24
Flying Cloud Rd	2	E 26
Forest	2	F 25
Forest Lawn Av	2	F 25
Forestwood Dr	15	F 22
Four Brock Cir	9	F 23
Four Brooks Rd	9	F 23
Fourth	2	F 25
Fowler	2	F 25
Fox Glen Dr	15	F 21
Fox Hill Rd	15	G 21
Fox Ridge Rd	15	F 21
Foxwood Rd	15	F 21
Francis Av	2	F 25
Frank	2	F 26
Frankel Pl	2	F 25
Franklyn	2	F 25
Frederick	2	F 26
Friar Tuck La	9	H 24
Friars La	9	H 23
Frisbie	2	F 25
Frost Pond Rd	15	H 21
Garden	2	E 26
Garland Dr	9	G 24
Gary Rd	15	G 22
Gatehouse Rd	2	E 26
Gatewood Rd	15	G 21
Gaxton Rd	9	G 23
Gaymoor Cir	9	G 24
Gaymoor Dr	9	G 24
General Waterbury La	9	E 24
George	2	F 26
Georgian Ct	15	G 22
Gerik Rd	9	G 23
Gilford	9	G 24
Givens Av	2	F 26
Gleason Av	2	F 26
Glen Av	2	G 25
Glen Ter	2	G 25
Glenbrook Rd	2	F 25
Glendale Cir	2	F 25
Glendale Dr	2	G 25
Glendale Rd	2	G 25
Golf View Cir	2	E 25
Goodwin	2	F 25
Grandview Av	2	E 25
Grant Av	2	F 26
Gray Birch Rd	15	F 20
Gray Farms Rd	9	G 24
Green	2	F 25
Greenbriar La	15	H 22
Greenfield Rd	2	F 25
Greenleaf Dr	9	E 24
Green's Cir	15	H 20
Greentree La	9	F 24
Greenway	9	G 24
Greenwich Av	2	E 26
Greenwood Hill	2	E 25
Gregory	2	F 26
Grenhart Rd	2	E 25
Greyrock Pl	2	F 25
Grove	2	F 26
Guernsey Av	2	F 26
Guinea Rd	9	E 23
Gun Club Rd	15	F 20
Gurley Rd	2	F 27
Gutzon Borgium Rd	9	G 23
Gypsy Moth Landing	2	E 26
Hackett Cir N	2	F 25
Hackett Cir S	2	F 25
Hackett Cir W	2	F 25
Haig Av	9	G 24
Hale	2	F 26
Half Moon Way	2	E 26
Hall Pl	2	E 26
Halliwell Dr	2	E 25
Hallmark Pl	2	F 25
Halloween Blvd	2	F 26
Halpin Av	9	F 24
Hamilton Av	2	F 25
Hampshire La	9	F 23
Hampton La	9	G 23
Hannah's Rd	15	G 22
Hanover	2	F 26
Hanrahan	2	F 25
Happy Hill Rd	15	G 20
Harbor	2	E 26
Harbor Dr	2	F 26
Harbor Plaza Dr	2	E 26
Harborview Av	2	F 26
Hardesty Rd	9	F 23
Harding Av	2	F 26
Harpsichord Tpke	15	F 21
Hartcroft Rd	9	F 23
Hartford Av	9	G 24
Hartswood Rd	9	F 23
Harvard Av	2	E 26
Harvest Hill La	9	G 24
Hastings La	9	G 24
Havemeyer La	2	E 25
Haviland Ct	15	G 22
Haviland Dr	15	G 21
Haviland Rd	15	G 21
Hawthorne	2	F 25
Hazard La	15	F 22
Hazel	2	E 25
Hazelwood La	9	F 24
Headlands	2	E 26
Heartstone Ct	2	F 26
Heather Dr	15	F 21
Hedge Brook La	15	F 21
Helen Pl	2	F 26
Heming Way	15	F 20
Hemlock Dr	9	F 24
Hendrie Ct	2	E 26
Henry	2	E 26
Heritage La	15	G 21
Hickory Dr	2	E 26
Hickory Rd	15	H 21
Hickory Way	9	G 24
Hidden Brook Dr	9	H 24
High	2	E 25
High Clear Dr	9	F 24
High Line Tr	9	E 23
High Line Tr S	9	E 23
High Ridge Rd	9	F 24
High Ridge Rd	15	G 22
High Rock Rd	15	F 21
High Valley Way	15	E 22
Highland Rd	2	F 25
Highview Av	9	G 24
Hillandale Av	2	F 25
Hillcrest Av	2	F 25
Hillhurst	2	E 25
Hillsbury La	15	G 21
Hillside Av	2	F 25
Hilltop Av	9	G 24
Hillview La	9	F 24
Hinckley Av	2	E 25
Hirsch Rd	9	F 24
Hobbie	2	F 26
Hobson	2	F 27
Holbrook Dr	2	F 25
Holcomb Av	2	F 25
Hollow Oak La	9	F 24
Holly Pl	2	F 26
Hollywood Ct	2	F 25
Home Ct	2	G 26
Homestead Av	2	E 26
Honey Hill Rd	15	F 22
Hoover Av	2	F 25
Hope	2	F 25
Hope	9	G 24
Hormez	2	F 25
Horse Shoe La	9	H 23
Horton	2	F 26
Houston Ter	2	G 26
Howard Rd	15	E 21
Howes Av	2	F 25
Hoyclo Rd	15	G 21
Hoyt	2	F 25
Hubbard Av	2	E 25
Hubbard Ct	2	E 25
Huckleberry Hollow	15	F 22
Hundley Ct	2	F 26
Hunting La	9	F 23
Hunting Ridge Rd	15	F 22
Hycliff Ter	2	E 25
Hyde	9	G 24
Idlewood Dr	9	G 24
Idlewood Pl	9	G 24
Indian Hill Rd	9	E 24
Indian La	2	E 26
Indian Rock Rd	15	F 21
Ingall	2	F 26
Ingleside Dr	15	H 21
Interlaken Rd	15	G 22
Interstate Hwy 95	2	E 25
Intervale Rd	9	G 23
Intervale Rd E	9	G 23
Iron Gate Rd	15	F 22
Iroquois Rd	2	F 26
Irving Av	2	E 26
Island Hgts Cir	2	G 26
Island Hgts Dr	2	G 26
Ivy	2	F 25
Jackson	2	E 26
James	2	F 26
Jamroga La	9	F 24
Janes La	15	G 22
Janice Rd	9	F 24
Jay Rd	9	F 23
Jeanne Ct	9	H 23
Jefferson	2	F 26
Jeffrey La	15	F 22
Jessup	9	F 24
Joan Rd	9	G 23
Joffre Av	9	G 24
Joffre Ct	9	G 24
John	2	F 26
Jonathan Dr	15	F 20
Jordan La	15	G 22
Joshua Slocomb Dock	2	E 26
Judy La	2	G 26
Judy Rd	15	F 20
June Rd	15	E 22
Kane Av	9	G 23
Katydid La	15	G 22
Keith	2	E 26
Ken Ct	9	F 23
Kenilworth Dr E	2	F 27
Kenilworth Dr W	2	F 27
Kennedy La	2	F 25
Kensington Rd	9	F 24
Kent Pl	2	G 25
Kerr Rd	9	G 24
Kerry La	2	G 25
Kijek	9	F 24
King	2	G 26
Kirkham Pl	2	G 25
Klondike Av	9	G 24
Knapp	9	G 24
Knickerbocker Av	9	G 24
Knobloch La	9	E 24
Knollwood Av	9	F 24
Knox Rd	9	G 24
Kramers Dr	2	G 26
Laddins La	2	E 26
Lafayette	2	F 26
Lake View Dr	9	F 24
Lakeside Dr	9	G 23
Lakeside Dr	15	G 22
Lakewood Dr	15	F 22
Lamark Rd	2	F 27
Lancaster Pl	9	F 23
Lancer La	9	F 23
La Nell Dr	2	F 26
Lantern Cir	9	F 24
Largo Dr	9	G 24
Largo Dr E	9	G 24
Larkin	2	G 25
Larkspur Rd	15	G 22
Laurel Ledge Ct	15	F 21
Laurel Ledge Rd	15	F 21
Laurel Rd	15	H 20

STREET	MAP	GRID
Lawn Av	2	F 26
Lawrence Hill Rd	15	F 21
Lawton Av	9	G 24
Ledge Brook Rd	9	E 23
Ledge La	2	G 25
Ledge Ter	2	G 25
Lee	2	F 26
Leeds	2	F 26
Lenox Av	2	G 25
Leon Pl	2	E 25
Leona Dr	9	H 24
Leonard	2	G 25
Leroy Pl	2	G 25
Leslie	2	E 25
Lewelyn Rd	2	F 26
Lewis Rd	9	F 23
Liberty	2	E 25
Liberty Pl	2	E 26
Lighthouse Way	2	E 27
Lillian	2	F 26
Limerick	2	F 26
Lincoln Av	2	F 26
Lindale	2	F 26
Linden	2	F 25
Lindsey Av	9	F 24
Lindstrom Rd	2	F 26
Linwood La	9	F 23
Lipton Pl	2	E 26
Lisa La	15	F 20
Little Hill Dr	9	F 24
Little John La	9	H 24
Lockwood Av	2	F 26
Locust La	2	F 25
Lolly La	15	G 22
London La	9	F 24
Long Close Rd	9	E 24
Long Hill Dr	9	F 24
Long Ridge Rd	9	F 24
Long Ridge Rd	15	F 21
Longview Av	9	F 24
Loughran Av	9	F 23
Loveland La	9	F 24
Loveland Rd	9	F 24
Loveland Rd W	9	F 24
Ludlow	2	E 26
Ludlow Pl	2	F 26
Lumanor Dr	15	H 22
Lund Av	9	G 24
Luther	2	F 25
Lyman Ct	15	F 22
Lyman Rd	15	F 22
MacArthur La	9	F 23
MacGregor Dr	9	E 23
Madeline Ct	9	H 24
Madison Pl	2	E 26
Magee Av	2	F 26
Maher Rd	2	F 26
Main	2	F 25
Maitland Rd	2	G 26
Malibu Rd	15	F 22
Maltbie Av	9	F 23
Malvern Rd	9	G 24
Manhattan	2	F 26
Manor	2	E 26
Maple Av	2	F 26
Mapletree Av	2	G 25
Maplewood Pl	9	F 23
Marian	9	G 24
Marie Pl	2	F 25
Mariners La	2	F 26
Market	2	F 26
Marlou La	2	F 25
Marschall Pl	9	F 24
Martin	2	F 26
Marva La	9	G 23
Mary Joy La	15	G 22
Mary Violet Rd	9	H 24
Maryanne La	9	G 24
Mather Rd	15	H 21
Mathews	2	G 26
Mayapple Rd	15	G 20
Mayflower Av	2	F 25
McClean Av	9	F 24
McClurg Av	2	E 26
McDougall Way	2	G 25
McIntosh Ct	15	G 20
McIntosh Rd	15	G 20
McMullen Av	2	F 26
Mead	9	G 24
Meadow	2	F 26
Meadow Park Av E	9	F 24
Meadow Park Av N	9	F 24
Meadow Park Av S	9	F 24
Meadow Park Av W	9	F 24
Megan La	9	G 24
Melrose Av	2	E 26
Mercedes La	9	F 24
Meredith La	15	G 22
Merrell Av	2	E 25
Merriebrook La	9	E 23
Merriland Rd	15	G 20
Merriman Rd	9	G 23
Merritt Pkwy	9	F 23
Mianus Rd	9	E 24
Michael Rd	15	H 22
Middle Ridge Rd	15	G 22
Middlebury	2	G 26
Midland Av	2	G 25
Midrocks Dr	15	F 22
Mill Brook Rd	9	E 23
Mill Brook Rd W	9	E 23
Mill Rd	15	F 21
Mill River	2	E 25
Mill Stone Cir	15	F 21
Mill Valley La	15	G 20
Millspring La	15	G 20
Millstream Rd	15	F 22
Milton	2	E 26
Minivale Rd	9	G 24
Minor Pl	2	E 25
Miramar La	2	F 27
Mission	2	E 26
Mitchell	2	F 26
Mitzi Rd	9	G 24
Mohawk La	2	E 26
Mohawk Tr	15	H 21
Mohegan Av	2	F 26
Moore	2	E 25
Morgan	2	F 25
Morris	2	F 25
Mountain Tr	15	G 21
Mountain Wood Rd	15	F 21
Mulberry	9	G 24
Munko Dr	9	F 23
Muriel Dr	9	G 24
Myano Ct	2	E 25
Myano La	2	E 25
Myrtle Av	2	F 26
Nash Pl	2	F 25
Nathan Hale Dr	9	E 23
Nelson	2	F 26
Neponsit	2	G 26
New England Dr	15	H 22
Newfield Av	9	G 24
Newfield Ct	9	F 24
Newfield Dr	9	G 23
Nichols Av	9	F 23
Nob Hill La	15	F 22
Nobile	2	E 25
Noble	2	E 26
Norman Rd	2	F 25
North	2	E 25
North Briar Brae Rd	15	G 21
North Lake Dr	15	F 20
North Lakeside Dr	15	G 22
North Meadows La	9	G 23
North Stamford Rd	15	G 22
North State	2	E 26
North Wood Rd	9	G 24
Northerly Woods Rd	15	E 20
Northill	9	G 24
Northville	9	G 24
Northwind Dr	15	G 21
Northwood La	9	F 23
Northwoods Rd	9	F 24
Norton Hill Pl	2	F 26
Norvel La	9	G 23
Nottingham Dr	9	H 24
Nurney	2	E 25
Nutmeg La	9	G 24
Nyselius Pl	9	G 24
Oak	2	F 25
Oakdale Rd	2	G 25
Oakhill	2	E 25
Oaklawn Av	9	F 24
Ocean Dr E	2	F 27
Ocean Dr N	2	F 27
Ocean Dr W	2	E 27
Ocean View Dr	2	F 27
Oenoke Pl	9	G 24
Ogden Rd	9	F 24
Old Barn Rd N	9	F 24
Old Barn Rd S	9	F 24
Old Barn Rd W	9	F 24
Old Colony Ct	9	G 24
Old Colony Rd	9	G 24
Old Logging Rd	15	G 22
Old Long Ridge Rd	15	F 21
Old Mill La	9	E 23
Old North Stamford Rd	2	F 25
Old Orchard La	15	F 22
Old Wagon Rd	15	F 20
Old Well Rd	9	H 23
Olga Dr	9	G 23
Omega Dr	9	G 24
Opper Rd	9	G 23
Orange	2	F 26
Orchard	2	E 26
Orlando Av	2	E 26
Oscar	2	F 25
Outlook	2	E 26
Over Hill Rd	9	F 23
Overbrook Dr	2	G 25
Overlook Pl	9	G 24
Owen	2	F 26
Ox La	2	E 26
Oxford Ct	2	E 25
Pacific	2	E 26
Pakenmer La	9	F 23
Pakenmer Rd	9	F 23
Palmer	9	G 24
Palmer Av	2	F 26
Palmers Hill Rd	2	E 25
Pamlynn Rd	9	G 23
Paragon La	2	F 25
Park	2	F 26
Parker Av	2	G 25
Parry Ct	9	H 23
Parry Rd	9	G 23
Parsonage Rd	15	F 20
Partridge Rd	15	F 22
Patricia La	9	G 23
Paul Rd	9	E 24
Peak	9	G 23
Pell Pl	2	F 25
Pellon Pl	2	E 25
Pembroke Dr	15	H 22
Penzance Rd	2	F 25
Pepper Ridge Cir	9	G 24
Pepper Ridge Pl	9	F 24
Pepper Ridge Rd	9	F 24
Pequot La	2	E 26
Perna La	9	G 23
Perry	2	E 26
Pershing Av	9	G 24
Peveril Rd	2	F 26
Phaiban La	9	E 24
Pheasant La	9	F 23
Phillips Pl	2	G 25
Piave	2	E 25
Pierce Pl	2	F 25
Pilgrim Wk	2	F 25
Pin Oak Cir	15	G 21
Pine	2	E 25
Pine Hill Av	2	F 25
Pine Hill Ter	9	G 23
Pine Tree Dr	2	F 25
Pinewood Rd	15	H 21
Pinnacle Rock Rd	15	F 21
Pinner La	15	H 21
Pleasant	2	F 25
Pleasant	15	F 21
Plymouth Rd	2	F 25
Pond Rd	9	E 24
Pond View La	15	G 20
Ponus Av	2	F 26
Pony Trail Rd	15	E 21
Poplar	2	G 25
Poppy La	9	G 23
Powell Pl	2	F 25
Pressprich	2	E 26
Prince Pl	2	E 25
Progress Dr	2	E 25
Prospect	2	F 25
Provost Pl	2	E 25
Prudence Dr	9	G 24
Pulaski	2	E 26
Pumping Station Rd	2	F 26
Puritan La	2	F 25
Putnam La	2	E 26
Putter Dr	9	G 24
Quails Tr	15	H 21
Quaker Ridge Rd	15	G 21
Quarry Rd	15	H 22
Quasi	9	G 24
Quintard Ter	2	F 26
Rachelle Av	2	E 25
Radio Pl	2	G 25
Ralph	2	E 26
Ralsey Rd	2	E 27
Rambler La	9	H 23
Randall Av	2	F 25
Ranson	2	F 26
Rapids Rd	9	F 23
Raymond	2	F 26
Red Fox Rd	15	G 22
Redbird Rd	9	G 24
Redmont Rd	9	G 23
Reed Pl	9	F 24
Regent Ct	9	H 24
Relay Pl	2	E 25
Remington	2	E 26
Renwick	2	F 25
Research Dr	2	G 25
Reservoir La	15	H 21
Revere Dr	2	F 26
Revonah Av	2	F 25
Revonah Cir	2	F 25
Revonah Cir S	2	F 25
Reynolds Av	9	F 24
Richards Av	2	F 25
Richmond Hill Av	2	E 25
Richmond Pl	2	E 26
Ridge Brook La	15	G 20
Ridge Crest Rd	15	F 21
Ridge Park Av	9	F 24
Ridge Pl	2	F 25
Ridge Tree La	15	G 21
Ridgebrook Dr	15	G 20
Ridgeway	9	G 24
Ridgeway Plz	2	F 25
Ridgewood Av	2	G 25
Riding Stable Tr	15	H 20
Rippowam Pl	2	F 25
Rippowam Rd	2	F 26
Rising Rock Rd	15	F 22
River	2	F 25
River Hill Dr	9	F 24
River Pl	9	G 24
Riverbank Dr	15	E 22
Riverbank Rd	15	E 22
Riverside Av	2	F 25
Riverview Dr	2	G 26
Robert Ct	2	F 26
Robin	2	F 26
Robin Hood Rd	9	H 24
Robinson Dr	9	G 24
Rock Meadow La	15	G 20
Rock Rimmon Dr	15	G 21
Rock Rimmon La	15	G 21
Rock Rimmon Rd	15	G 21
Rock Spring Rd	2	F 25
Rockland Pl	2	E 26
Rockledge Dr	2	F 27
Rockridge La	9	F 23
Rocky Rapids Rd	15	F 21
Rogers Rd	2	E 27
Rolling Ridge Rd	15	G 20
Rolling Wood Dr	9	F 24
Rome Pl	9	F 24
Roosevelt Av	2	E 26
Rosano Rd	9	F 24
Rose	2	F 25
Rose Park Av	2	E 26
Round Hill Dr	15	F 21
Round Lake Rd	15	H 21
Roxbury Rd	9	F 23
Rugby	2	E 26
Rushmore Cir	9	G 23
Russet Rd	15	H 20
Rutz	2	G 25
Ryan	9	G 24
Sachem Pl	2	F 26
Saddle Hill La	15	G 21
Saddle Hill Rd	15	G 21
Saddle Rock Rd	2	E 27
Sagamore Rd	2	E 27
Saint Benedict Cir	2	F 26
Saint Charles Av	9	G 24
Saint George Av	2	E 25
Saint Mary	2	F 26
Salem Pl	9	G 24
Sally Ann La	15	H 20
Sandy La	9	G 24
Sanford La	9	G 24
Santina La	9	F 23
Sawmill Rd	15	F 22
Saxon Ct	9	G 23
Schuyler Av	2	E 25
Scofield Av	2	F 25
Scofieldtown Rd	15	G 21
Scott Pl	2	F 26
Sea Beach Dr	2	F 27
Sea View Av	2	F 26
Seaside Av	2	F 26
Seaton Rd	2	F 26
Second	2	F 25
Selby Pl	9	G 24
Selleck	2	E 26
Settler's Tr	15	G 21
Seventh	2	F 25
Severance Dr	2	E 25
Shadow La	9	G 23
Shadow Ridge Rd	9	F 23
Shady Knoll Dr	15	H 21
Shady La	15	G 21
Shagbark Rd	15	F 20
Shelburne Rd	2	E 25
Shelter Rock Rd	15	F 22
Sheridan	2	F 26
Sherman	2	F 26
Sherwood Rd	9	F 24
Shippan Av	2	E 27
Short Hill	9	G 24
Short Tr	15	G 21
Signal Rd	2	E 26
Silver	2	E 26
Silverhill La	9	F 24
Simsbury Rd	9	G 24
Sixth	2	F 25
Sky Meadow Dr	15	G 21
Skyline La	15	G 21
Skyview Ct	9	F 24
Skyview Dr	9	F 24
Sleepy Hollow La	9	G 24
Slice Dr	9	H 24
Smith	2	E 25
Smoke Hill Dr	15	F 22
Snow Crystal La	9	F 23
Somerset La	9	G 23
Sound Av	2	E 27
Soundview Av	2	F 26
Soundview Ct	2	F 26
Soundview Dr	2	F 27
South	2	E 26
South Atlantic	2	E 26
South Brook Dr	15	F 20
South Lake Dr	15	F 20
South Lindsey Av	2	F 25
South Sagamore La	2	E 27
South State	2	E 26
Southerly Woods Rd	15	E 20
Southfield Av	2	E 26
Southfield Village Ct	2	E 26
Southill	9	G 24
Southwest Dr	9	F 23
Spinning Wheel La	15	G 22
Spring	2	F 25
Spring Hill La E	15	H 21
Spring Hill La N	15	H 20
Spruce	2	E 25
Square Acre Dr	9	G 23
Stafford Rd	2	F 26
Stage	2	F 26
Stamford Av	2	E 27
Stamford Rd	15	G 22
Standish Rd	2	F 26
Stanley Ct	2	F 25
Stanton Dr	9	F 24
Stanton La	9	F 24
Stanwick Cir	9	F 24
Stanwick Pl	9	F 24
Starin Dr	2	E 25
Stark Pl	9	F 24
State Route 15	9	F 23
State Route 104	2	F 25
State Route 104	9	F 23
State Route 104	15	F 21
State Route 106	2	G 26
State Route 137	9	F 24
State Route 137	15	G 22
Station Pl	2	E 26
Stephen	2	E 25
Sterling Lake La	9	G 23
Sterling Pl	9	G 24
Stillview Rd	9	F 24
Stillwater Av	2	E 25
Stillwater Pl	2	E 25
Stillwater Rd	2	E 25
Stillwater Rd	9	F 24
Stone	2	E 26
Stone Fence La	15	F 20
Stone Hill Dr	15	F 22
Stone Wall Dr	9	F 24
Stony Brook Dr	9	E 24
Strawberry Hill Av	2	F 25
Strawberry Hill Ct	2	F 25
Strawberry Patch La	2	F 25
Strawberry Woods	2	F 25
Studio Ct	9	G 23
Studio Rd	9	G 23
Suburban Av	2	F 25
Summer	2	F 25
Summer Pl	2	F 25
Summit Pl	2	F 25
Summit Ridge Rd	9	E 24
Sun Dance Cir	9	F 23
Sun Dance Rd	9	F 23
Sunnyside Av	2	E 26
Sunset	9	G 24
Sunset Rd	15	G 21
Surrey Rd	15	F 21
Sussex Pl	9	G 24
Sutton Dr E	2	G 25
Sutton Dr W	2	G 25
Sutton Pl	2	G 25
Swampscott Rd	9	F 24
Swan La	9	G 24
Sweet Briar Ct	9	G 23
Sweet Briar La	9	G 23
Sweet Briar Rd	9	G 23
Sycamore Ter	2	E 25
Sylvan Knoll Rd	2	F 26
Sylvandale Av	2	E 25
Taconic Rd	15	E 21
Taff Av	2	E 26
Tall Oaks Ct	15	F 21
Tall Oaks Rd	15	F 21
Tally-Ho La	9	F 23
Talmadge La	9	G 23
Tanglewood La	15	G 20
Taylor	2	E 26
Taylor Reed Pl	2	G 25
Terrace Av	9	F 24
Terrace Pl	2	F 25
Theresa Ct	9	G 23
Third	2	F 25
Thornridge Dr	9	H 23
Thornwood Rd	15	H 21
Threadneedle La	2	E 26
Three Lakes Dr	9	F 24
Thunder Hill Dr	9	E 23
Timber La	9	F 23
Timber Mill Cir	15	F 22
Timber Mill Rd	15	F 22
Tioga Pl	2	F 25
Tod La	15	E 22
Todd La	9	G 24
Toilsome Brook Rd	2	F 25
Tommuck La	2	E 26
Toms Rd	2	F 25
Top Gallant Rd	2	E 26
Tower Av	9	G 24
Town Center Dr	2	F 26
Trailing Rock La	15	F 21
Travis Av	9	F 24
Treat Av	2	F 25
Tree La	9	G 24
Tree Top Ct	9	F 24
Treglia Ter	2	E 26
Tremont Av	2	G 25
Tresser Blvd	2	F 26
Trinity Pass Rd	15	H 20
Trumbull Gate	2	F 26
Tupper Dr	2	F 26
Turn of River Rd	9	G 23
Turner Rd	9	F 24
Tuttle	2	E 25
Twin Brook Dr	9	G 23
Twin Hills Rd	15	G 22
Tyler Dr	15	G 21
Uncas Rd	2	F 26
Underhill	2	F 25
Union	2	G 25
Unity Rd	9	F 24
Upland Rd	2	F 25
Upper Haig Av	9	G 24
Urban	2	F 25
Ursula Pl	2	F 26
US Hwy 1	2	E 25
Valley Rd	2	F 25
Valley View Dr	15	F 22
Van Buren Cir	2	F 25
Van Buskirk Av	2	F 26
Van Rensselear Av	2	E 27
Vanech Dr	9	F 24
Vassar Av	2	E 26
Vernon Pl	2	F 25
Verplanck Av	2	E 27
Very Merry Rd	15	G 22
Viaduct Rd	2	G 25
Victoria La	9	E 24
Victory	2	E 25
Vincent Av	2	F 25
Vincent Ct	2	F 25
Vine Pl	9	G 23
Vine Rd	9	G 23
Vineyard La	9	F 23
Virgil	2	E 25
Vista	2	E 25
Vuono Dr	2	E 25
Wake Robin La	9	F 23
Wallace	2	F 26
Wallacks Dr	2	F 27
Wallacks La	2	F 26
Wallenburg Dr	15	F 20
Walnut	2	E 26
Walter La	9	F 23
Walter Wheeler	2	E 26
Walton Pl	2	F 25
Wampanaw Av	2	F 26
Warchol La	9	F 23
Ward La	9	H 23
Wardwell	2	F 26
Warren	2	F 26
Warshaw Pl	2	E 26
Warwick La	9	F 24
Wascussee La	2	F 26
Wascussee La E	2	F 26
Washington Blvd	2	E 26
Washington Ct	2	F 25
Water	2	E 26
Waterbury Av	2	G 26
Waterford La	2	F 25
Waterside Pl	2	E 26
Waverly Pl	2	E 26
Webb Av	2	G 26
Webbs Hill Rd	9	F 23
Webster Rd	2	G 26
Wedgemere Rd	9	G 23
Weed Av	2	G 26
Weed Cir	2	G 26
Weed Hill Av	9	G 24
Weil	2	F 25
Wellington Dr	15	G 21
Wells Av	2	E 26
Wenzel Ter	2	F 25
West	2	E 26
West Av	2	E 26
West Bank La	9	E 24
West Broad	2	E 25
West Cross Rd	9	H 23

STREET	MAP	GRID
West Forestlawn Av	2	F 25
West Glen Dr	9	E 24
West Haviland La	15	G 22
West Hill Cir	9	E 24
West Hill La	9	F 23
West Hill Rd	9	E 24
West La	2	F 25
West Main	2	E 25
West North	2	E 25
West Park Pl	2	F 25
West Tr	15	G 21
West Washington Av	2	F 25
Westcott Rd	2	F 27
Westgate Dr	9	E 24
Westminster Rd	2	E 27
Westover Av	9	E 24
Westover La	9	E 24
Westover Rd	9	E 24
Westview La	9	E 24
Westwood Ct	9	F 24
Westwood Pl	9	F 24
Westwood Rd	9	F 24
Whistler Pl	9	G 24
White Birch La	9	F 24
White Birch Rd S	15	F 20
White Fox Rd	15	G 22
White Oak Ct	9	G 23
White Oak La	9	G 23
Whitewood La	9	F 23
Whitmore La	2	E 25
Whittaker	2	E 26
Whittaker Pl	2	F 25
Wild Duck Rd	15	F 22
Wild Horse Rd	9	F 23
Wilder Rd	9	F 23
Wildwood Rd	15	F 21
Willard Ter	9	G 23
William	2	F 26
Willoughby Rd	9	F 23
Willow	2	F 26
Willowbrook Av	2	F 26
Willowbrook Pl	2	F 26
Wilson	2	E 26
Wind Mill Cir	15	F 21
Windell Pl	2	G 25
Windermere La	9	E 23
Winding Brook La	9	E 23
Windsor Rd	2	E 25
Windward La	15	E 22
Winesap Rd	15	G 20
Winslow Dr	15	G 20
Winsted	2	E 26
Winter	9	G 23
Winthrop Pl	2	F 25
Winward La	15	E 22
Wire Mill Rd	9	F 23
Wishing Well La	9	F 24
Wood La	9	F 24
Wood Ridge Dr	9	F 24
Wood Ridge Dr S	9	F 24
Woodbine Rd	15	H 21
Woodbrook Dr	9	H 23
Woodbury Av	9	G 24
Woodchuck Rd	15	F 22
Woodcliff	2	F 25
Woodland Av	2	E 26
Woodland Pl	2	E 26
Woodledge Rd	9	G 24
Woodley Rd	15	G 22
Woodmere Rd	2	F 25
Woodrow	2	F 26
Woods End Rd	9	F 24
Woodside	2	F 25
Woodway Rd	9	H 24
Woody Tr	15	G 21
Woolsey Rd	2	F 27
Worth	2	F 26
Wright	2	E 25
Wyndover La	9	E 24
Wyndover La N	9	E 24
Wynnewood La	15	H 21
Yale Ct	9	F 24
Zora La	9	H 23

STRATFORD

STREET	MAP	GRID
Abram	7	V 26
Academy Hill	6	V 28
Academy Hill Ter	6	V 28
Access Rd	6	U 28
Acorn La	7	W25
Adams	6	U 28
Adolphson Av	7	V 26
Agawam Dr	7	X 25
Agresta Ter	5	U 27
Airway Dr	6	V 29
Albert Av	7	V 26
Albright Av	7	V 26
Alexandra Dr	7	W25
Alfred Ct	6	V 28
Algonquin La	7	X 25
Alice Ter	7	V 26
Allen	5	U 27
Allencrest Dr	7	V 26
Allyndale Dr	7	V 27
Alvord	7	V 26
Anderson	6	U 28
Andrew	7	V 26
Ann Ter	7	V 26
Anson	7	W26
Apache La	7	X 25
Arapaho La	7	X 25
Arbor	7	V 27
Arcadia Av	7	V 27
Argonne Dr	7	V 26
Armory Rd	7	V 25
Arrowhead Pl	7	W26
Arrowood Pl	7	W25
Arthur's Ct	13	X 24
Ash	6	U 29
Ashley Pl	5	U 27
Ashwood Ter	13	W25
Auburn	7	V 26
Audi La	7	V 26
Avery	7	W27
Avo	5	U 27
Avon	5	U 27
Baird Ct	5	U 26
Bannock La	7	X 25
Bannong La	7	X 25
Barbara La	7	V 26
Barnum Av	5	U 27
Barnum Av Cutoff	7	V 27
Barnum Ter	5	U 27
Barnum Ter Ext	5	U 27
Barrister Rd	7	W25
Barrows	7	W26
Barrows Ter	7	W26
Barton Dr	7	W26
Bates	6	U 28
Baton La	7	X 25
Baxter	6	V 29
Bayberry La	7	V 26
Bayfield La	7	X 25
Bayview Blvd	6	U 29
Beach	7	V 27
Beach Dr	6	U 29
Beacon	7	V 27
Beacon Point Rd	5	U 27
Beacon Point Rd	6	V 28
Bear Paw Rd	7	V 26
Beardsley Av	6	V 28
Beaver Dam Access Rd	13	W24
Beaver Dam Rd	7	W25
Beers Pl	7	V 27
Bell Aire Ter	7	V 26
Bell Ter	7	V 27
Belvidere Dr	5	U 27
Benjamin	5	U 27
Benton	6	U 28
Bern Dr	7	V 26
Beth Dr	7	V 25
Birch	6	U 29
Birch Dr	6	U 28
Birch Pl	7	V 26
Birchwood Sq	7	V 26
Birdseye	6	U 28
Biscayne Dr	7	V 26
Bison La	7	X 25
Bittersweet La	7	W27
Black Hawk La	7	X 25
Blakeman Pl	7	V 27
Blamey Cir	7	V 26
Blueberry La	7	V 25
Bodine Ct	5	U 27
Bolbone La	7	X 25
Booth	7	V 27
Boston Av	5	U 27
Boswell	6	U 28

STREET	MAP	GRID
Boulder Ridge Rd	7	V 25
Bowe Av	5	U 27
Boxelder La	7	X 25
Brandon Av	7	V 26
Brenair Ter	7	W26
Brewster	7	V 27
Briarfield Dr	7	V 26
Bridgeview Pl	7	W27
Brightwood Av	7	V 27
Brinsmayd Av	7	X 25
Broad	6	V 28
Broadbridge Av	7	V 27
Broadmere Rd	5	U 26
Bronson Rd	7	W26
Brookbend Dr	7	V 26
Brooklawn Rd	7	V 26
Brookside Dr	7	W27
Browning	6	U 28
Bruce Av	5	U 27
Bruce Blvd	6	U 28
Bryant Pl	7	V 27
Buckskin La	7	X 25
Bullard Ct	5	U 26
Bulldog Blvd	7	V 26
Bulmer Dr	7	W26
Bunnell Av	7	V 26
Bunny View Dr	7	W26
Burbank Av	7	V 25
Burbank Dr	7	V 26
Burr Pl	7	V 27
Burritt Av	5	U 27
Butternut La	7	W26
California	7	V 27
Cambridge	7	V 27
Cameo Ct	7	V 26
Cameo Rd	7	V 26
Canaan	5	U 27
Canaan Ct	5	U 27
Canal	7	V 27
Canary Pl	7	W26
Candlewood Rd	7	W25
Cannon Dr	7	V 26
Captains Wk	7	W27
Cardinal Pl	5	U 26
Carey	6	U 28
Carol Rd	5	U 27
Carriage Dr	7	V 26
Castle Dr	7	V 26
Catherine	7	V 27
Cayug La	7	X 25
Cayuga La	6	U 29
Cedar	6	U 29
Cedar Bark La	7	X 25
Cedarknoll Dr	7	W26
Cemetery Dr	7	V 27
Center	7	V 27
Century Dr	6	U 28
Champion Ter	7	V 26
Chanbrook Rd	7	W26
Chanda Dr	7	W26
Chapel	7	W26
Chapel Pl	7	W26
Chapokele La	7	X 25
Charles	6	U 28
Charlotte	7	X 26
Charlton	7	V 27
Chasta La	7	X 25
Chelsea	6	U 28
Cheraw La	7	X 25
Cherokee La	7	X 25
Cherry	6	U 29
Cherry Hill Rd	7	W26
Cheshire	7	W26
Chestnut	6	U 29
Chevvy	7	V 26
Cheyenne La	7	X 25
Chickadee La	7	W26
Chickasaw La	7	X 25
Church	7	V 27
Circle Dr	7	W25
Clarendon	7	V 27
Claudia Dr	5	U 26
Clements Dr	7	W27
Clifflawn Rd	7	V 26
Clinton Av	7	V 27
Clover	5	U 27
Cloverleaf Pl	6	V 28
Coach House Rd	7	W25
Coe Av	7	X 25
College	5	U 27
Collins	5	U 27
Colonial Dr	7	V 26

STREET	MAP	GRID
Colony	7	V 27
Columbus Av	6	U 28
Columbus Pl	6	U 28
Commanche La	7	X 25
Concord	7	V 27
Connecticut Tpke	6	U 28
Connors La	7	V 26
Coolidge	7	V 27
Copperkettle Dr	7	X 25
Corinthian Av	6	U 28
Cottage Pl	7	V 27
Country Club Cir	7	W26
Cove Pl	6	U 29
Craige Av	7	V 27
Creek La	7	X 25
Crested Ridge Ct	7	W25
Creston Rd	7	W27
Crestwood Rd	7	X 25
Crown	6	U 29
Cupheag Cres	5	U 26
Curtis Av	6	U 29
Curtis Pl	7	V 27
Cutspring Cir	7	W26
Cutspring Rd	7	W26
Dahl Av	7	V 26
Dakota La	7	X 25
Daniel Dr	7	V 26
David Pl	7	W26
Dawn Dr	13	X 25
Deepwood Rd	7	X 25
Deerfield Dr	7	V 26
Del Dr	7	V 26
Delaware Dr	7	V 26
Delwood Rd	7	V 26
Den Rd	7	V 26
Denise Dr	7	V 26
Dennis Dr	7	V 26
Denton Pl	7	V 26
Derby Pl	7	V 25
Dewey	6	U 28
Diane Ter	7	W27
Disbrow	7	V 27
Dodge Av	6	U 28
Dogwood Dr	7	V 26
Dorne Dr	6	V 29
Dorus	5	U 27
Douglas	7	V 26
Dover	6	U 28
Drake	7	V 26
Drome Av	6	U 28
Duke Dr	7	W27
Early Av	6	U 28
East	6	V 28
East Broadway	7	V 27
East Gate La	7	V 26
East Main	7	V 27
East Pkwy	7	V 27
Eaton	7	V 26
Edgewood Av	5	U 27
Edison	7	V 27
Edmund	7	V 27
Edwin	5	U 27
Elbert	6	U 28
Eleanor	5	U 26
Elfa	7	V 26
Elizabeth	7	V 27
Elizabeth Ter	7	V 27
Elk Ter	7	V 27
Elliott	7	V 27
Elm	6	V 28
Elm Ter	6	U 28
Elmhurst Av	7	W27
Embree	6	U 28
Emerald Pl	7	V 26
Emerson Dr	7	W27
Emery	7	V 27
Engine House Rd	7	X 25
Enterprise	6	U 28
Erie La	7	X 25
Essex Pl	7	V 27
Euclid Av	7	W25
Euerle	5	U 27
Eunice Pkwy	6	V 28
Eureka Av	7	W25
Evelyn	6	U 28
Everett	6	U 28
Evergreen Dr	7	W27
Evers	5	U 26
Evers La	5	U 26
Fairchild Rd	7	W26

STREET	MAP	GRID
Fairfax Dr	7	V 26
Fairlea Av	7	V 26
Fairview Av	7	V 27
Fallon Dr	6	V 28
Farmill Dr	7	X 25
Federal	7	V 26
Feeley	5	U 27
Fenelon Pl	7	V 27
Ferndale Av	7	V 26
Ferndale Pl	7	V 26
Fernwood Dr	7	V 26
Ferry Blvd	6	V 28
Fiddler Green Dr	13	X 25
Fifth Av	6	U 29
First Av	6	U 29
Fisher Ct	5	U 26
Fisk	6	U 28
Flagler Av	7	V 26
Flora Dr	7	W26
Floral Way	6	V 28
Florence	7	V 26
Forest Rd	7	W26
Fotch	6	U 28
Founders Way	7	X 26
Fourth Av	6	U 29
Fox Hill Pl	7	V 26
Fox Hill Rd	7	V 26
Frances Ter	7	W26
Franklin Av	5	U 27
Frash	6	U 28
Frederick	7	V 27
Freeman Av	7	V 26
Frog Pond La	7	V 27
Garden	7	V 27
Garden E	7	V 27
Garfield Av	6	U 28
Garibaldi Av	6	U 28
Garnet Pl	7	V 26
Gem	7	V 25
General	6	U 28
Gina Cir	7	W26
Glendale Rd	7	V 27
Glenfield Av	7	V 26
Glenn Dr	7	V 26
Glenovon	7	W26
Glenridge Rd	7	V 27
Glenridge Rd E	7	V 27
Glenwood Av	7	V 27
Goldbach Dr	7	V 25
Goodwin Pl	5	U 27
Graham	5	U 27
Grant	5	U 27
Granville	6	U 28
Green	6	U 28
Greenfield Av	7	V 26
Greenlawn Av	7	V 27
Greenvalley Rd	7	V 25
Gregory Cir	6	U 28
Griffin	6	U 28
Grissom Dr	7	V 26
Grove	6	U 29
Guzzi Dr	6	U 28
Hair	7	V 27
Hall Rd	7	W27
Hamilton Av	6	U 28
Hammerstone La	7	X 25
Hancock Av	5	U 27
Hanson	7	V 27
Happy Hollow Cir	7	X 25
Harding Av	6	U 28
Hartland	6	U 29
Harvard Av	7	V 27
Harvest Ridge Rd	7	W25
Harvey Pl	6	V 28
Hathaway Dr	6	U 28
Hawkins	7	W27
Hawley La	7	V 25
Hazelwood Ter	7	V 26
Helen Pl	7	V 27
Hemlock	6	U 29
Henry Av	5	U 27
Henry Av Ext	5	U 26
Henry Pl	5	U 27
Hickey	6	U 28
Hickory Woods La	7	W26
High Park Av	5	U 27
High View Dr	7	W26
Highland Av	7	V 26

STREET	MAP	GRID
Highland Ter	7	W26
Hillcrest Av	7	V 27
Hillside Av	7	V 27
Hillside Ter	7	W27
Hilltop Dr	7	W26
Hinman Av	7	X 25
Hitching Post La	7	V 26
Hollister	5	U 27
Hollydale Rd	7	V 26
Hollywood Av	7	V 26
Holmes	6	V 28
Homecrest Av	6	U 28
Homestead Av	7	V 27
Honeyspot Rd	6	U 28
Honeyspot Rd Ext	6	U 28
Horace	7	V 27
Hortense	7	V 27
Housatonic Av	6	V 28
Housatonic Av Ext	7	V 27
Howard	5	U 27
Hudson	7	W27
Hull Ct	7	V 26
Huntington Rd	7	V 27
Huntley Ter	7	W25
Hurd Av	7	V 27
Huron La	7	X 25
Hyde Ter	7	V 27
Interstate Hwy 95	6	U 28
Interstate Hwy 95	7	W27
Inwood Rd	5	U 27
Iroquois La	7	X 25
Islandview Rd	7	V 26
Ivy	6	U 29
Jackson Av	5	U 27
James	7	V 27
James Farm Rd	7	W25
Jane	6	V 28
Jefferson	6	U 29
Jessie Av	7	V 27
Job Av	6	U 28
Joel Av	6	U 28
John	7	V 26
Johnson Av	7	V 27
Johnson Ct	6	U 28
Johnson La	7	V 26
Judith Ter	7	W25
Judson Pl	7	V 27
Justice	6	U 28
Karen Av	7	V 26
Kasper Cir	5	U 26
Kasper Dr	5	U 26
Kathleen Dr	13	W25
Keane Pl	6	U 28
Keating Dr	7	W26
Kenwood Av	7	V 27
Kenyon	7	V 26
Ketcham Rd	6	U 28
King	7	V 27
Kings College Pl	6	V 28
Kings Row	7	W26
Klondike	7	V 27
Knollwood Dr	7	V 26
Knowlton	5	U 27
Kovach Dr	7	V 26
Lake	6	U 28
Lambert Dr	7	V 26
Landon	7	V 27
Lantern Rd	7	X 25
Larchmount Cir	7	X 25
Larkin Ct	6	U 28
Laughlin Rd	7	V 27
Laughlin Rd E	7	V 27
Laughlin Rd W	7	V 27
Laurel	6	U 28
Laurel Pl	6	U 28
Lawlor Ter	7	V 26
Leeward Dr	6	U 28
Legion Av	7	V 27
LeGrand Pl	7	W26
Leighton Dr	7	V 26
Lenox Av	5	U 27
Leonard	5	U 27
Leo's La	7	X 25
Leslie	7	X 26
Liberty	5	U 27
Light	5	U 27
Lighthouse Av	6	U 29
Lillibeth Dr	7	W26
Lincoln	7	V 26

STREET	MAP	GRID
Linden Av	7	V 27
Lindsley Pl	6	V 28
Lines Pl	5	U 26
Linksview Pl	7	W26
Linton	7	W25
Lobdell Dr	7	V 27
Lockwood Av	6	V 28
Lombard Dr	7	V 26
London Ter	7	V 27
Long Beach Blvd	6	U 28
Long Bow Rd	7	V 26
Longbranch Av	5	U 27
Longbrook Av	7	V 27
Lordship Blvd	6	U 28
Lordship Rd	6	U 29
Los Angeles Av	7	V 26
Lovell Pl	7	V 27
Luanne Rd	7	V 26
Lundy's La	7	V 27
Lupes Dr	5	U 27
Lyle Ter	7	W26
Lynnecrest Dr	5	U 27
MacArthur Dr	5	U 26
Main	6	U 28
Main	7	X 26
Main St Putney	7	W26
Manor Hill Rd	7	W26
Maple	6	U 29
Mapledale Av	5	U 26
Marchant Rd	7	W27
Marcroft	7	V 27
Marcus Dr	7	V 27
Margherita Lawn	6	U 29
Marie Dr	7	V 25
Marina Dr	7	V 26
Marr	6	U 28
Marsh Way	5	U 26
Martha	5	U 27
Martin Ter	7	V 26
Mary Av	5	U 27
Masarik Av	6	U 28
Masna Pl	7	V 25
Matthew Dr	7	W27
Maureen	6	U 29
Mayfair Pl	6	U 28
McGrath Ct	6	U 28
McKinley Av	6	U 28
McLean	6	U 28
McLeod Pl	7	V 26
McNair	5	U 26
McNeil Ter	7	V 27
McPadden Dr	6	U 28
McQuillan	5	U 27
Mead	6	U 28
Meadow	7	V 27
Meadow Wood Rd	7	W26
Meadowbrook Rd	7	W26
Meadowlark La	7	W26
Meadowlawn Rd	7	V 25
Meadowmere Rd	7	X 26
Meadowview Av	7	X 26
Meeting House Rd	7	X 25
Melville	7	V 27
Mercer	7	V 27
Meritine Av	7	V 26
Merritt Pkwy	7	W26
Middlebrook Rd	7	V 25
Midwood Tr	7	X 25
Milford Av	5	U 27
Mill Pond Cir	7	W26
Mill Pond Rd	7	W26
Mill River Dr	7	W26
Minor Av	7	V 27
Minor Cross	6	V 28
Moffitt	6	U 28
Mohawk	5	U 27
Monroe	7	V 26
Montauk La	7	X 25
Montero Dr	7	W27
Montrose Pl	7	V 27
Monument Pl	6	V 28
Morehouse Av	7	V 26
Morning Dew La	7	W26
Morning Glory Ter	7	W26
Morningside Dr	7	W26
Morningside Ter	7	W26
Motil Pl	7	W26
Mount Carmel Blvd	6	U 28

STREET	MAP	GRID
Mount Pleasant Av	7	V 26
Narraganset La	7	X 25
Nassau Rd	7	V 26
Nathan	5	U 27
Navajo La	7	X 25
Nelson	6	U 28
Nemergut Dr	7	W26
Newport Av	5	U 27
Newton	7	W27
Newtown Av	7	V 27
Niantic La	7	X 25
Nichols Av	7	V 26
Nichols Ter	7	V 27
Nightingale Dr	7	W26
Noble	5	U 27
Norman Cir	7	W27
North Abram	7	V 26
North Acre Pl	7	V 26
North Av	7	V 27
North Parade	7	V 27
North Pasture La	7	X 25
North Tr	7	X 25
Nutmeg La	7	W25
Oak Bluff Av	6	U 29
Oak Ridge Rd	7	W25
Oak Ter	7	V 27
Oakland	5	U 27
Oakland Pl	7	V 27
Oakview Dr	7	W25
Ocean Av	6	U 29
Oceanview Ter	7	V 26
Okenuck Tr	7	W26
Old Coach La	7	W26
Old Honeyspot Rd	6	U 28
Old South Av	6	U 28
Old Spring Rd	7	V 26
Old Town Dr	7	V 26
Olympia Av	7	V 27
Oneida La	7	X 25
Ontario	6	U 28
Opa La	7	X 25
Orange	6	U 28
Orchard	7	V 27
Orchard Hill Rd	7	V 26
Oronoque La	7	X 25
Oronoque Pl	7	X 26
Osborne	7	V 27
Otis	5	U 27
Ottawa La	7	X 25
Overland Dr	7	V 26
Oxbow La	7	W27
Pamela Dr	13	W25
Papp Ct	6	U 28
Paradise Ct	7	V 27
Paradise Green Pl	7	V 27
Park	7	V 27
Park Blvd	6	U 29
Park View La	7	V 26
Parkland Dr	7	V 25
Parkway Dr	7	V 27
Parkwood Rd	7	V 26
Pasadena Av	7	V 26
Patchen	5	U 27
Patricia Dr	13	X 25
Patterson Av	7	V 27
Paugasitt Dr	7	W26
Pauline	6	U 29
Pawnee La	7	X 25
Peace	5	U 27
Peace Acre La	7	X 25
Peacock Dr	7	V 26
Peard Ter	7	V 27
Pearl	7	V 27
Pearl Pl	7	V 26
Peat Pl	7	V 26
Peck	7	W27
Penny Meadow	7	X 25
Pentways 1 & 2	5	U 27
Pepperidge Cir	7	W25
Pequonnock Cir	7	W26
Pequot Av	7	W26
Peters La	7	W25
Phillips	7	V 27
Philo	6	U 28
Pilgrim La	7	X 25
Pine	6	U 29
Pine Needle Dr	7	X 25
Pine Tree Tr	7	X 25
Pinehurst Rd	7	V 26
Pitt	6	U 28
Piute La	7	X 25
Placid Av	6	U 28
Plainview Dr	7	V 27
Plane Tree Rd	7	V 25
Platt	7	W27
Pleasantview Av	7	V 27
Plymouth	7	V 27
Pond	7	V 27
Pootatuck Path	7	W26
Poplar	7	V 27
Porter	7	V 26
Post Oak Rd	7	V 25
Powder Mill Rd	7	X 25
Prayer Spring Rd	7	X 25
Preston Dr	7	W26
Prim	7	V 27
Priscilla La	6	U 28
Prospect Dr	6	U 29
Pumpkin Ground Rd	7	W25
Putnam	5	U 27
Putney	7	W26
Quail	7	V 26
Queens Av	7	V 27
Quenby Pl	7	V 25
Rachel Dr	5	U 27
Randolph	7	V 27
Raven Ter	7	W27
Ravencrest Dr	7	W27
Raymond	5	U 27
Red Bird Dr	7	V 26
Red Coach Dr	7	V 26
Red Fox Rd	7	V 26
Reed	7	V 27
Reed's La	7	V 26
Regency Ter	5	U 27
Reitter	7	V 26
Reitter W	5	U 26
Repko Cir	7	V 26
Research Dr	6	U 28
Reut Dr	7	V 25
Richard Cir	7	V 27
Richard Dr	7	V 25
Ridge Cl	7	V 26
Ridge Rd	7	V 26
Ridgefield Dr	7	V 26
Ripton Parish La	7	X 25
River Bend Rd	7	X 25
River Rd	7	W26
River Valley Rd	7	W26
Riverdale Dr	6	V 29
Riverton Ter	7	W26
Riverview Pl	7	V 27
Robin La	7	W26
Rockaway Av	5	U 27
Rockland Av	7	V 26
Rockwell Av	5	U 27
Roger Dr	7	V 26
Ronald Dr	7	V 26
Roosevelt Av	6	U 28
Roosevelt Forest Dr	7	W25
Rose	5	U 27
Rosebrook Dr	7	W26
Rosedale Ter	7	V 26
Rosemary Dr	6	V 28
Ross Dr	7	W26
Round Hill Rd	7	W26
Rowland	7	V 27
Ruby La	7	V 25
Running Brook La	7	X 25
Russell Rd	7	V 26
Rustown Dr	7	V 26
Ryan Av	6	U 28
Ryders La	7	X 26
Ryegate Ter	6	V 29
Sage	5	U 27
Saint Andrew	5	U 27
Saint Michael's Av	7	V 25
Salem Dr	7	V 25
Salmon Pl	7	V 26
Salvia	7	V 26
San Gabriel Av	7	V 27
San Pedro Av	7	V 26
Sands Av	6	U 28
Sanford Pl	7	V 26
Seabreeze Cir	7	V 26
Seabreeze Dr	7	V 26
Second Av	6	U 29
Second Hill La	7	V 26
Sedgewick Av	6	U 28
Sekelsky Dr	7	W25
Selleck Pl	7	V 27
Seminole La	7	X 25
September La	7	W26
Sequoia La	7	X 25
Seymour	5	U 27
Shady Hill Rd	7	X 25
Shanley	6	U 28
Sharon Rd	7	V 26
Shaw	6	U 28
Shea Ter	7	W26
Sheehan	6	U 28
Sheffeld Cir	7	V 26
Sheffield Dr	7	V 26
Sheppard	7	V 27
Sherbrook Rd	7	V 26
Sheridan	5	U 27
Sherman	5	U 27
Sherwood Pl	6	V 28
Shirley Dr	5	U 27
Shore Dr	6	U 28
Shore Rd	6	U 28
Shoreline Dr	6	U 29
Short Beach Rd	6	V 29
Shoshoni La	7	X 25
Sidney	7	V 27
Sikorsky Pl	5	U 26
Silver La	7	V 25
Singer Ct	5	U 26
Sioux La	7	X 25
Sixth Av	6	U 29
Smoke Valley	7	X 25
Sniffens La	6	V 28
Soho Sq	6	U 28
Sorghum Ter	7	V 25
Soundview Av	5	U 27
South Av	5	U 27
South La	7	X 25
South Tr	7	X 25
Southard Ct	7	V 27
Southfield Pl	7	V 26
Spada Blvd	6	U 28
Speer Dr	7	W26
Sperry Av	6	U 28
Spring	7	V 27
Springdale Av	7	V 26
Springdale Pl	7	V 26
Springview Av	7	V 26
Spruce	6	U 29
Spruce La	7	X 25
Stagg	6	U 28
State Route 8	13	W24
State Route 15	7	W26
State Route 108	7	V 26
State Route 110	7	V 27
State Route 113	6	V 28
State Route 113	7	V 26
State Route 130	6	U 27
Sterling Pl	7	V 26
Stiles	7	V 27
Stock	7	V 26
Stoneybrook Rd	5	U 26
Stratford Av	5	U 27
Stratford Av	6	U 28
Stratford Rd	6	U 29
Streckfus Dr	7	V 26
Streckfus Rd	6	U 29
Sturbridge Dr	7	V 26
Success Av	5	U 26
Sulik Ter	7	V 26
Sullivan La	7	V 26
Sultan	7	V 26
Summer	7	V 27
Summersweet Pl	7	W25
Summitt	5	U 27
Sun Ridge La	7	W25
Sunflower Av	7	V 26
Sunnybank Av	7	V 26
Sunnydale Pl	7	V 26
Sunnyside Ter	7	V 27
Sunrise Ter	7	V 26
Sunset Av	6	U 28
Surf Av	6	U 28
Surrey La	7	X 25
Sutton Av	7	V 27
Swanson Av	5	U 27
Sycamore Cir	5	U 26
Taft	6	U 28
Tanager Pl	7	W26
Tanglewood Rd	7	X 26
Tavern Rock Rd	7	W25
Teakwood Dr	7	V 26
Temple	7	V 27
Temple Ct	7	V 27
Terrill Rd	7	V 27
Terry Pl	7	V 27
Third Av	6	U 29
Thompson	5	U 27
Thornberg	7	W26
Timber Ridge Rd	7	V 25
Titterton Dr	7	W26
Tomlinson Pl	7	V 26
Topaz Pl	7	V 26
Torsey	7	W27
Tucci Dr	7	V 26
Turtle Run	7	X 25
Twin Oaks Ter	7	W25
Tyrone Pl	7	V 27
Ulrich Rd	7	V 27
Underwood Ct	5	U 26
Unity Dr	7	V 26
Val Dr	7	V 25
Valley Brook Ter	7	V 25
Valley Rd	6	U 29
Valley View Rd	7	W26
Van	7	V 27
Van Buskirk Av	7	V 27
Van Rensselaer Av	5	U 27
Vermont Av	6	U 29
Vernon	6	V 28
Victoria Lawn	6	U 29
Victory	5	U 27
Vielie	7	V 27
Villa	7	W27
Vine	7	V 27
Vought Pl	7	V 26
Wainwright Pl	7	V 26
Wakelee Av	7	V 27
Walker Dr	7	V 26
Walnut	6	U 29
Ward	7	W27
Wareham Pl	6	V 29
Warner Hill Rd	7	X 25
Warwick Av	7	V 27
Washburn Dr	7	V 26
Washington Pkwy	6	U 29
Watkins	6	U 28
Watson Blvd	6	U 28
Wayne	5	U 27
Weaver Dr	5	U 27
Weber Av	5	U 27
Wedge Wood Rd	7	X 25
Wellington	6	U 28
Wells Pl	6	V 28
West Av	5	U 27
West Beach Dr	6	U 29
West Broad	5	U 27
West Hillside Av	6	U 29
Westchester Dr	7	V 26
Westmore Pl	6	V 29
Wheeler Ter	7	V 27
Whippoorwill La	7	W26
White	6	V 28
Wiebe Av	7	V 27
Wigwam La	7	W26
Wiklund Av	5	U 27
Wilbar Dr	7	V 26
Wilbrook Rd	7	W26
Wilcoxson Av	7	V 27
Wild Wood Dr	7	W25
Willard	6	U 28
William	7	V 27
Willis	6	U 28
Willow Av	7	V 27
Windsor Av	7	V 27
Winfield Dr	5	U 27
Winter	7	V 27
Winton Pl	7	W26
Wood Av	7	V 27
Woodcrest Av	7	V 27
Woodend Rd	6	U 28
Woodland Av	7	W27
Woodlawn Av	7	V 27
Woodside Ter	7	V 27
Woodstock Av	7	V 27
Wooster Av	6	U 28
Wyoming	7	V 27
Yale	6	V 28
Yarwood	6	U 28
York	6	U 29
Yukon	5	U 27
Zenith Dr	7	V 25
Zoar	7	W27

TRUMBULL

STREET	MAP	GRID
Abric Dr	12	T 24
Academy Rd	18	U 22
Alden Av	12	U 23
Aldo Dr	12	U 24
Algonquin Tr	12	U 24
Alice Pl	12	U 24
Allan Dr	12	U 24
Alpine Rd	12	T 23
Anita Av	18	T 22
Ann	18	U 22
Anthony Pl	12	U 25
Apple Orchard La	7	V 25
Applegate La	13	W24
Aragon Dr	12	T 23
Arbutus La	19	V 22
Arden Rd	12	U 24
Argus La	18	U 22
Arliss Dr	18	U 21
Arrowhead Rd	12	U 24
Asbury Rd	18	T 22
Ascolese Rd	12	U 23
August La	19	V 21
Autumn Dr	18	U 21
Autumn Ridge Rd	18	T 21
Avalon Gate	12	U 25
Bailey	12	U 24
Baldwin Av	7	W25
Barbara	12	U 24
Barnswallow Dr	19	V 22
Barry Pl	12	U 24
Bassick Rd	12	T 23
Bayberry La	12	U 25
Beach Hill Dr	18	U 22
Beach Memorial Park Rd	13	V 24
Beachcroft La	12	T 23
Beacon Hill Rd	13	V 23
Bear Den Rd	13	V 23
Bear Paw Rd	19	V 21
Beardsley Pkwy	12	U 25
Beech	12	T 24
Beech Tree Cir	7	V 25
Beechwood Av	18	U 22
Beers	18	U 22
Berkshire Av	12	U 24
Berry La	12	U 25
Beverly Rd	13	V 24
Birch	12	T 24
Birdsall Av	12	U 23
Bittersweet La	12	U 23
Blackberry Rd	12	U 24
Blackhouse Rd	12	T 23
Blackstone Rd	12	U 24
Blue Jay Dr	18	T 22
Blue Ridge Dr	13	V 24
Blueberry Rd	5	U 25
Bob White La	7	V 25
Bolin Cir	12	U 24
Bonazzo Dr	12	U 25
Bonheur Rd	12	T 24
Bonita Av	12	U 23
Bonnie View Dr	12	T 24
Booth Hill Rd	7	V 25
Booth Hill Rd	13	V 23
Botsford Pl	12	T 24
Brandy La	12	T 23
Breton Woods Rd	18	T 21
Brewster Pl	12	T 23
Brian Dr	12	T 24
Briar Hill Dr	7	W25
Briarcroft Av	12	U 23
Briarwoods Ter	7	W25
Bridge Vista	12	U 25
Bridgeport Av	7	V 25
Brinsmade Crossing	12	U 24
Britanny Av	18	T 21
Broad Bridge Rd	12	U 25
Broadway	18	U 22
Brock	12	U 24
Brook Rd	12	T 23
Brookbend Rd	13	V 23
Brookhedge Rd	13	V 23
Brookside Dr	13	V 23
Brookview Dr	19	V 22
Buck Hill Rd	12	S 23
Bull Frog La	18	T 22
Bunker Hill Dr	18	U 22
Burton Av	12	U 24
Butternut La	13	V 24
Buttonwood Dr	12	T 24
Cal Dr	18	U 21
Caldron Dr	18	U 21
Calhoun Av	12	U 23
Camelot Dr	12	T 24
Campbell Rd	12	S 24
Candlewood Rd	12	T 24
Canoe Brook Rd	12	T 23
Canterbury La	12	U 23
Captain's Walk	18	T 22
Cardinal Cir	13	V 23
Carmel Ridge	18	U 22
Caroline	7	V 25
Carousel Dr	13	V 24
Carriage Dr	13	V 24
Catherine	12	U 23
Cedar	12	T 24
Cedar Crest Rd	12	U 24
Cedar Hill Dr	18	U 21
Ceil Rd	12	S 24
Cemetery Dr	7	V 25
Center Rd	7	V 25
Chalon Rd	13	V 23
Channing Rd	12	T 23
Chapel Hill Dr	18	T 21
Chatfield Dr	12	T 24
Chatham Dr	13	V 23
Cherry La	12	T 23
Cherrygate La	13	W24
Chestnut	12	T 24
Chestnut Hill Rd	12	T 24
Church Hill Rd	12	U 23
Civkin Dr	13	V 24
Claire Pl	12	T 23
Clarion Pl	13	V 23
Clark Rd	12	U 23
Classic Dr	19	V 22
Clearwater La	18	T 21
Clemens Av	18	U 22
Cliff View Dr	12	U 24
Clifford	12	U 23
Clinton	12	T 23
Clover Hill Rd	19	V 22
Cobbler's Hill Rd	13	V 23
Cold Spring Dr	18	T 21
Colonial Dr	18	T 22
Colony Av	12	T 24
Columbine Dr	12	U 24
Commerce Dr	13	V 25
Copper Kettle Rd	13	V 24
Coral Dr	13	V 23
Cornfield Rd	13	V 24
Cornwall La	12	T 23
Corporate Dr	18	U 21
Cottage	12	T 23
Cottage Pl	12	U 25
Cotton Tail Tr	18	T 22
Country Club Rd	13	V 23
Country La	12	U 24
Cove Pt	13	V 24
Coventry La	18	U 21
Crabapple Rd	18	T 22
Craig La	12	U 24
Cranbury Dr	19	V 22
Crescent La	18	U 21
Cricket La	13	V 23
Crocus La	18	U 22
Cromwell Rd	18	T 22
Crown	12	U 23
Cutler's Farm Rd	18	U 21
Cypress La	12	U 24
Dale Rd	12	T 23
Dalecot Dr	12	T 23
Daniels Farm Rd	12	U 24
Danube Dr	19	V 22
Dayton Cir	12	T 23
Dayton Rd	18	T 22
Deep Gorge Rd	19	V 21
Deepdene Rd	18	T 22
Deepwood Dr	18	T 22
Deer Run Dr	18	U 22
Deerfield Dr	12	T 24
Dell Cir	12	T 23
Devellis Dr	12	U 23
Doe Hollow Dr	13	V 23
Dogwood La	13	W24
Doris	18	U 22
Drew Cir	12	U 24
Driftwood La	12	T 23
Duane Pl	12	U 25
Dunellen Rd	18	U 22
Eastlake Rd	13	V 24
Eastwood Rd	12	U 24
Echo Hill Rd	18	U 22
Eddie Rd	12	U 25
Edgewood Av	12	U 23
Edinburg La	18	T 21
Edison Rd	12	T 24
Edith Av	13	V 24
Edmond	12	U 23
Elaine	12	U 24
Elaine Pl	12	T 24
Elberta Av	12	U 24
Eldor La	12	U 24
Eleven O'Clock La	12	T 23
Elizabeth	18	U 22
Elliott Cir	12	T 23
Elliott Rd	12	T 23
Ellsworth	12	U 23
Elmsted Rd	12	T 23
Elmwood Av	12	T 24
Endeavor	12	U 23
Erwin	7	V 25
Essex La	18	T 21
Ethel Rd	13	V 24
Evelyn	12	T 23
Evergreen La	12	U 24
Fairchild Av	12	T 24
Fairchild Cir	12	T 24
Fairlane Rd	19	V 22
Fairview Av	12	T 23
Fairway La	13	V 23
Farmstead La	18	T 21
Farmview Cir	19	V 22
Fawn Cir	13	V 23
Fawn Meadow Dr	18	T 22
Fern Cir	7	V 25
Fernwood Rd	12	T 23
Fieldcrest Rd	18	U 22
Fieldstone Ct	12	T 24
Finchwood Dr	13	W24
Firehouse Rd	19	V 22
Flint	12	U 23
Floral La	12	T 23
Forestview	12	U 25
Foster Av	12	U 25
Fox Ct	18	U 22
Fox Rd	18	U 22
Foxwood Rd	13	W24
Francis	12	T 24
Frank	12	T 23
Franklin	13	V 24
Frederick	12	T 23
Frelma Dr	12	T 23
Frenchtown Rd	12	T 24
Fresh Meadow Dr	18	T 21
Friar La	13	W24
Frost Hill Rd	12	T 23
Fuller Rd	18	T 21
Garden	12	T 24
Garland Cir	12	U 25
Garnet Pl	13	W25
Garnet Rd	13	W25
Garwood Rd	12	T 23
Gatehouse Rd	18	T 22
Gaylord Rd	12	T 24
George	18	U 22
Geraldine Cir	12	U 24
Geraldine Pl	12	U 24
Gibson Av	12	U 24
Gilbert Dr	12	T 23
Gingerbrook Dr	7	W25
Gisella Rd	18	U 22
Glen Spring Dr	12	T 23
Glenarden Rd	12	U 23
Glenbrook Rd	12	T 23

STREET	MAP	GRID
Glenwood Dr	12	U 24
Golden Hill	13	W24
Goldenrod Tr	18	T 22
Gorham Pl	12	T 24
Governor Trumbull Way	18	U 22
Grandview Dr	12	U 24
Granite Pl	12	U 23
Grayrock Rd	13	V 23
Great Brook Rd	12	U 23
Great Neck Rd	13	V 24
Green	12	T 24
Green Acres La	19	V 22
Green Ridge Rd	13	V 24
Greenbrier Rd	13	V 24
Greenfield Dr	12	T 24
Greenhaven Rd	13	V 23
Greenwood Dr	12	U 24
Gregory Pl	12	U 23
Griswold Av	12	U 23
Grove	12	T 24
Guilford Dr	12	T 24
Gwendolyn Dr	18	U 22
Hadley Dr	12	U 23
Hampton Rd	12	T 23
Hardy La	12	U 23
Harned Pl	18	U 22
Harvest Hill Dr	13	V 23
Harvester Rd	12	T 23
Harwood Ter	12	T 23
Haverhill Pl	18	T 22
Haverhill Rd	18	T 22
Haviland Dr	18	U 21
Hawley La	7	V 25
Haylot Rd	19	V 22
Hazelnut Dr	18	T 22
Heatherfield Dr	12	U 23
Heavenly La	12	U 23
Hedgehog Rd	12	U 23
Helen	12	U 24
Helena Rd	18	T 22
Hemlock Tr	13	V 23
Heritage Dr	18	T 22
Hickory	12	T 24
High Gate Rd	12	T 24
High Meadow Rd	13	V 23
High Ridge Rd	18	T 21
Highfield Dr	18	T 22
Highland Rd	12	T 24
Highwood Pl	19	V 22
Hill Cir	19	V 22
Hillandale Ter	13	V 24
Hillbrook Rd	13	V 23
Hillcrest Rd	12	U 25
Hillsboro Rd	19	V 22
Hillside Av	12	U 24
Hillspoint Rd	18	T 22
Hillston Rd	7	V 25
Hilltop Cir	7	V 25
Hilltop Dr	7	V 25
Histon Rd	12	T 23
Hitching Post La	12	T 24
Home	18	U 22
Horse Tavern Rd	18	T 22
Horseshoe Dr	12	T 24
Hunters La	18	T 21
Huntington Rd	7	W25
Huntington Tpke	7	V 25
Huntington Tpke	13	W24
Hurd Rd	19	V 22
Hyde Ter	18	U 22
Inca Dr	12	U 23
Indian Ledge Dr	19	V 22
Indian Ledge Park Rd	18	U 22
Indian Rd	12	T 24
Intervale Rd	7	V 25
Inverness Rd	18	T 22
Inwood Rd	12	T 24
Iron Gate Rd	19	V 22
Ironwood Rd	13	W24
Irving Rd	12	T 23
Isinglass Ter	13	V 24
Ivy La	13	V 24
Ivywood Pl	12	U 24
Jackson Dr	19	V 21
Jade Tree La	18	T 22
Jamestown Rd	18	U 22
Jefferson	12	T 23
Jeffrey Pl	12	U 24
Jerome Av	13	W24
Jerusalem Hill	7	V 25
Jog Hill Rd	13	V 23
John	18	U 22
Johnson	12	T 23
Judd Pl	12	T 24
Judson	12	T 24
Juniper Cir	12	U 25
Juniper Ridge Rd	7	V 25
Kachele	12	T 23
Kent La	18	T 21
Kenwood La	13	V 24
Killian Av	12	T 24
Kingsbury Dr	13	V 24
Kingston Rd	12	T 23
Kitcher Ct	18	T 21
Knecht Farm Rd	18	U 22
Knollcrest Ct	12	U 25
Knollcrest Dr	12	U 25
Koger Rd	12	T 24
Lafayette Dr	12	T 23
Lake Av	18	T 22
Lakeview Ter	18	T 22
Lakewood Dr	12	U 23
Lane Av	12	U 25
Lansing Av	12	U 25
Lantern Hill Rd	12	T 23
Larkspur Dr	12	U 24
Lauderdale Dr	12	T 23
Laurel	12	U 24
Laurie Rd	13	V 23
Lawn Cir	12	U 24
Lawrence Rd	12	U 24
Lealand	12	T 24
Leffert Rd	7	V 25
Leighton Rd	12	T 24
Leonard Pl	12	U 24
Lewis Rd	19	V 22
Lilac La	12	T 23
Lillian Dr	12	U 24
Lily Cir	18	U 22
Limerick Rd	18	T 22
Lincoln	13	V 24
Lindberg Dr	12	U 25
Lindeman Dr	12	U 24
Linden Av	12	T 24
Lindsay Pl	12	T 24
Lingale Rd	19	V 22
Linley Rd	12	U 24
Little Plain Rd	12	U 24
Lobsterback Rd	13	W24
Locust	12	U 23
Long Meadow Rd	12	U 23
Longview Rd	7	V 25
Lorma Av	12	T 24
Lorraine	12	T 24
Louis	18	U 22
Lounsbury Rd	12	U 24
Lullwater Rd	12	T 23
Lycett	12	T 24
Lynnbrook Rd	13	V 23
Lynwood Dr	18	U 22
MacArthur Rd	12	U 24
MacDonald Rd	13	V 24
Machalowski Rd	12	T 24
MacMath Dr	12	U 23
Madison Av	12	T 24
Madison Av	18	T 21
Maefair Ct	12	U 24
Magnolia Rd	18	U 22
Main	12	U 23
Mallett Dr	18	T 22
Manor Dr	12	U 24
Maple	12	T 24
Maple Ridge Rd	12	U 23
Marathon Rd	19	V 22
Marigold La	12	U 23
Marina Av	12	U 23
Mariner Cir	18	T 22
Marshall Av	12	U 25
May Cir	13	V 23
Mayfair Dr	18	T 21
Mayfair Pl	18	T 21
Mayfield Dr	12	U 23
Mayflower Dr	13	V 23
Maymont La	12	T 23
McAdoo Av	12	U 25
McGuire Rd	19	V 22
Meadow Rd	18	U 22
Meadow Rd W	18	U 22
Meadow Ridge Dr	18	T 21
Meadow View Dr	18	U 22
Meadow Wood Rd	12	U 23
Melrose Av	12	T 24
Merrill Rd	12	T 24
Merrimac Dr	18	T 22
Merritt Blvd	13	V 25
Merritt Pkwy	12	T 24
Merwin	12	T 24
Middlebrooks Av	12	U 23
Midland Rd	13	V 23
Mischa Hill Rd	13	V 24
Misty Wood La	18	U 21
Mitchell Rd	12	T 23
Mohawk Dr	13	V 23
Monitor Hill	18	T 22
Monroe Tpke	18	U 21
Moorland Rd	12	U 24
Moose Hill Rd	19	V 22
Morningside Ter	12	U 24
Morris Av	12	T 24
Mount Pleasant Dr	12	T 24
Mountain Hill	7	V 25
Mountain Hill	13	V 25
Mulberry	12	U 23
Natalie Rd	18	U 22
Newton La	18	T 21
Newtown Tpke	12	T 24
Nichols Av	7	V 25
Nokomis Dr	18	U 22
Normandy Dr	18	T 21
North	13	V 24
North Field Dr	13	V 24
North Green Acres La	19	V 22
North Lynwood Dr	18	U 22
North Stowe Pl	13	V 24
Northwood Rd	13	V 24
Norwood Ter	12	U 24
November La	12	U 23
Nuthatch Hill Rd	19	V 22
Nutmeg Dr	7	V 25
Oakland Dr	18	U 22
Oakridge Rd	12	U 25
Oakview Dr	12	U 24
Ochsner Pl	12	T 24
October La	18	U 22
Old Barn Rd	12	T 23
Old Beardsley Pkwy	12	U 25
Old Broadbridge Rd	12	U 24
Old Church Hill Rd	12	U 23
Old Coach La	18	U 22
Old Dairy Rd	13	V 24
Old Dike Rd	13	V 24
Old Elm Rd	12	T 24
Old Farm Rd	12	T 24
Old Fire Rd	19	V 21
Old Green Rd	13	V 24
Old Hollow Rd	12	U 23
Old Mill Rd	12	U 24
Old Mine Rd	18	U 21
Old Oak Rd	18	T 22
Old Orchard La	13	V 23
Old Pinewood Tr	13	V 24
Old Saw Mill Rd	13	V 24
Old Stream La	13	V 23
Old Town Rd	5	U 25
Old Town Rd	12	T 24
Old Turnpike Rd	18	U 21
Old Village La	18	T 22
Oldfield Rd	13	V 23
Orchard	12	T 24
Oriole Cir	13	V 24
Oriole La	13	V 24
Orleans Dr	19	V 21
Overhill Dr	13	V 24
Overlook Pl	18	U 22
Owl Hill Tr	18	U 21
Oxen Hill Rd	19	V 22
Pachaug Rd	13	V 24
Palisade Av	12	U 23
Palmer Tr	13	V 24
Pam Bar Rd	13	V 22
Par La	12	U 23
Parallel	18	U 22
Park	12	U 24
Park Av	12	S 24
Park La	12	T 23
Parkway Dr	12	T 24
Parkwood Rd	13	V 23
Parkwood Rd N	13	V 23
Parlor Rock Rd	18	U 22
Partridge La	7	V 25
Paugusset Cir	12	U 24
Paulina Pl	12	T 23
Pauline	7	V 25
Peaceful Valley Rd	18	T 22
Pemberton Dr	18	U 22
Penny Av	7	V 25
Pepperidge Rd	12	U 25
Pequonnock Rd	12	U 24
Pequot Ct	12	U 24
Pert	12	U 24
Peters Rd	12	U 24
Petticoat La	19	V 22
Pilgrim La	13	V 23
Pine	12	T 24
Pinehurst	12	U 23
Pinewood Tr	13	V 24
Pioneer Tr	18	U 21
Pitkin Hollow	18	U 22
Placid	12	U 23
Plattsville Rd	12	T 24
Pleasant	12	U 23
Plumb Rd	12	T 24
Plumtree La	12	S 24
Plymouth Av	12	T 24
Pomona Rd	18	U 22
Pond La	18	U 22
Pond View Av	12	T 23
Pondway La	12	U 25
Poplar	12	U 23
Porters Hill Rd	19	V 22
Post Gate Rd	18	T 22
Powder Mill La	13	W24
Preston Rd	18	T 22
Primrose Dr	13	V 24
Priscilla Pl	7	V 25
Prospect Av	12	T 24
Providence Dr	18	U 22
Pumpkin Hill Rd	18	U 22
Puritan Rd	13	V 24
Putting Green Rd	12	U 23
Putting Green Rd N	18	U 22
Quail Tr	7	V 25
Quaker La	13	V 23
Quality	12	U 23
Quarry Rd	12	U 23
Quartz La	18	U 21
Ranch Dr	19	V 22
Randall Dr	18	U 22
Randolph Pl	12	T 23
Rangely Dr	12	T 23
Raven Rd	18	T 22
Raynor Av	12	T 24
Raynor Pl	12	T 24
Reading Rd	18	T 22
Rebecca	12	U 25
Red Barn Rd	18	T 21
Red Fox La	13	W24
Red Maple La	12	T 23
Redcoat La	12	T 23
Regina	12	U 23
Reiner Cir	12	U 25
Reiner Dr	12	U 25
Rempsen	12	U 25
Rennison Rd	13	V 24
Reservoir Av	12	U 25
Revere La	12	T 23
Rexview Cir	12	U 24
Richards Pl	12	U 24
Richfield Rd	12	T 24
Ridgebury Dr	12	T 24
Ridgeview Av	18	U 22
River Bend Rd	12	U 24
River Rd	12	U 25
Riverside Dr	18	U 22
Robinwood Rd	13	V 24
Robinwood Ter	13	V 24
Rockland Cir	12	U 23
Rockland Rd	12	U 23
Rockspring Rd	19	V 22
Rockwell Av	12	U 23
Rocky Hill Rd	12	U 24
Rocky Hill Ter	12	U 25
Rocky Ridge Dr	7	V 25
Rolling Wood Dr	7	V 25
Roosevelt Dr	13	V 23
Rose Ter	12	T 23
Rosebud Dr	12	U 24
Rosellen Dr	12	T 23
Rosemond Ter	12	T 24
Round Hill Rd	7	V 25
Round Ridge Tr	13	V 24
Ruffed Grouse La	13	W24
Russ Rd	12	S 24
Ruth	12	U 24
Rutlee Dr	12	U 24
Sabina Rd	18	U 22
Saint Johns Dr	7	V 25
Salem Rd	18	U 22
Sallyann Dr	18	T 22
Samuel	12	T 24
Sanford Av	18	U 22
Sarenee Cir	18	U 22
Saxony Dr	18	T 21
Saybrook Rd	7	V 25
Scattergood Cir	12	T 23
Scenic Hill Rd	12	U 23
Scenic Hill Rd	13	V 23
Sciortino Rd	18	U 22
Scott La	12	U 24
Seeley Rd	18	T 22
Seminole Tr	18	T 21
Seneca Dr	12	U 24
Sentry Hill	18	T 21
Shadowood La	13	V 24
Shady La	12	T 24
Sharon Rd	18	U 22
Shawnee Rd	12	U 24
Shelbourne Rd	12	T 24
Shelter Rock Rd	13	V 23
Shelton Rd	7	V 25
Shelton Ter	18	U 22
Sherman Av	12	U 23
Silo Cir	13	V 24
Silver La	7	V 25
Skating Pond Rd	18	U 21
Sky Top Dr	12	U 23
Sky View Dr	13	V 24
Smith Dr	12	T 23
Smith Pl	12	T 23
Solar Ridge	18	U 22
Soundview Av	12	T 24
South Edgewood Av	12	U 23
Southgate Rd	13	V 24
Spinning Wheel Rd	13	V 23
Splitrock Rd	13	V 23
Sport Hill Rd	12	T 23
Spring	18	T 22
Spring Hill Rd	18	U 21
Springwood Dr	12	T 24
Spruce	12	T 24
Stag La	19	V 22
State Route 15	12	T 24
State Route 25	12	T 24
State Route 25	18	U 22
State Route 111	12	U 23
State Route 111	18	U 21
State Route 127	12	U 23
Station Hill	18	T 22
Stella	7	V 25
Stemway Rd	18	T 22
Stephanie Cir	12	T 23
Sterling Rd	12	U 23
Stirrup Dr	18	U 22
Stonebridge La	12	U 25
Stonehouse Rd	18	T 22
Stoneleigh Rd	13	V 23
Stones Throw	13	V 24
Stonewall La	12	T 24
Stoney Brook Cir	12	T 23
Stowe Pl	13	V 24
Strobel Rd	13	V 23
Stuart Pl	12	T 24
Sturbridge La	18	T 21
Summit Av	12	U 23
Sunbeam Dr	18	U 22
Sunnycrest Rd	12	U 24
Sunnydale Rd	12	T 24
Sunnyridge Pkwy	12	U 25
Sunrise Av	18	U 22
Sunset Av	12	U 24
Surrey La	18	T 21
Sutton Pl	12	U 24
Suzanne Cir	12	U 24
Sweet Briar Rd	13	V 24
Sycamore	12	T 24
Sylvan Av	12	U 25
Tahoe Cir	18	U 22
Tait Rd	12	U 24
Taits Mill Rd	12	U 24
Tamarack Cir	13	V 24
Tanager La	13	V 24
Tanglewood Rd	18	U 22
Tashua Knolls La	18	U 21
Tashua La	18	U 22
Tashua Pkwy	18	U 21
Tashua Rd	18	T 21
Teeter Rock Rd	13	V 24
Teller Rd	18	U 22
Temple	12	U 23
Thomas	18	U 22
Thorburn Av	12	U 24
Thornapple Pl	12	T 23
Thornwood Pl	18	U 22
Three Trees La	18	T 22
Timberlane Tr	13	V 24
Topaz La	19	V 21
Tory La	13	W24
Towerview Cir	13	V 23
Towerview Dr	13	V 23
Trefoil Dr	18	U 21
Trumbull Quarry Rd	12	U 25
Tuckahoe Rd	12	T 23
Tudor La	18	U 21
Tulip	12	T 24
Tungsten Cir	18	U 21
Tungsten La	18	U 21
Turkey Meadow Rd	13	V 24
Turner Av	12	T 24
Turney Pl	12	U 23
Twelve O'Clock Cir	18	T 22
Twin Brooks Dr	12	U 24
Twin Circle Dr	7	W25
Twisted Oak Cir	12	T 23
Twitchgrass Rd	12	U 24
Under Cliff Rd	12	U 23
Unity Dr	7	V 25
Unity Park Rd	12	U 25
Unity Rd	7	V 25
Val De-Mere Av	12	U 23
Valley Rd	12	U 24
Valley View Rd	12	U 23
Vazzano Pl	7	V 25
Velvet	18	T 21
Vesper Hill	13	V 24
Veterans Cir	18	U 22
Vintage Rd	19	V 22
Vista Pl	12	U 24
Vixen Rd	18	T 22
Wakely	12	T 23
Walker Rd	12	U 23
Waller Rd	12	T 24
Walnut Av	12	T 24
Ward Pl	12	U 24
Wareham Pl	19	V 22
Washington	13	V 24
Wauneta Rd	18	U 22
Wedgewood Rd	18	T 22
Wendover Rd	18	T 22
Wendy Rd	12	S 24
Wesley Dr	12	U 24
West Lake Rd	13	V 24
West Mischa Rd	13	V 24
West Rock Rd	18	U 22
West Wind Rd	12	T 23
Westbrook Rd	12	T 23
Westfield Dr	18	T 22
Westwood Rd	12	T 23
Whalburn Av	12	T 24
Whalley Rd	12	U 24
Wheeler Dr	7	V 25
Whippoorwill La	12	T 24
White Birch Dr	12	U 24
White Oak Rd	12	U 24
White Plains Rd	12	U 24
White Tail La	12	U 23
Whitefield Dr	19	V 22
Whitney Av	18	U 22
Whitney Av	19	V 22
Wildfire La	19	V 22
Wildflower La	13	V 25
Wildwood Dr	18	T 22
Williams Rd	12	T 24
Willow La	13	V 23
Willowbrook Rd	13	V 24
Wilmot Av	12	T 24
Wilson Av	12	U 25
Windmill La	13	V 25
Windy Ridge	12	U 24
Winhall La	19	V 22
Winslow Rd	12	T 24
Wintergreen La	19	V 22
Wintter Cir	18	U 22
Wisteria Dr	13	V 24
Wood Av	12	T 23
Woodcrest Av	7	V 25
Woodfield Dr	18	U 22
Woodhaven Dr	18	U 21
Woodhill Rd	13	V 24
Woodlawn Dr	12	U 23
Woodmere Dr	13	V 23
Woodridge Cir	12	T 24
Woodside Av	12	U 24
Woosley Av	12	U 24
Wordins La	12	U 23
Yorktown Cir	12	T 23
Zephyr Rd	18	U 22

WESTON

STREET	MAP	GRID
Adam's Way	17	O 22
Alwyn La	21	P 21
Arlen Rd	11	O 23
Arrowhead Way	11	O 23
Aspetuck Hill La	17	Q 22
Aspetuck La	17	P 23
Autumn Ridge Rd	17	P 22
Beaver Brook Rd	17	O 22
Benedict La	17	O 22
Bernhard Dr	17	Q 21
Birch Hill Rd	17	O 21
Bittersweet La	17	O 23
Bittersweet Rd	17	P 23
Blue Spruce Cir	21	P 20
Blueberry Hill Rd	17	P 22
Bradley Rd	17	Q 21
Briar Oak Dr	17	N 23
Bridge Rd	17	P 23
Brierbrook Rd	17	P 21
Broad St	17	N 23
Brookwood La	21	O 21
Buck La	17	P 21
Buttonball La	17	O 23
Calvin Rd	17	O 22
Cannondale Rd	21	O 21
Cardinal Rd	17	P 23
Cartbridge Rd	17	P 23
Catbriar Rd	17	P 21
Cavalry Rd	17	N 23
Cedar Hills	17	O 23
Cedar La	17	O 23
Cedar Pond Rd	11	O 24
Christopher Hill Rd	21	O 20
Church La	17	P 21
Cindy La	21	O 21
Codfish La	17	Q 22

STREET	MAP	GRID
Coley Dr	17	O 23
Colony Rd	17	P 22
Covenant La	21	O 20
Crestwood Dr	11	O 24
Cricket La	17	O 22
Cristina La	17	Q 22
Crystal Lake Dr	17	O 23
Curiosity La	17	O 22
Davis Hill Rd	17	P 21
Deepwood Rd	17	P 21
Deer Path Rd	17	O 22
Deer Run Tr	17	P 23
Dillon Pass	17	O 21
Dogwood La	17	P 22
Echo Hill Rd	17	P 21
Eleven O'Clock Rd	17	P 23
Fall Ridge Rd	17	P 22
Fanton Hill Rd	17	P 23
Farrell Rd	17	O 22
Fawn Meadow	17	Q 21
Fern Valley Rd	17	P 22
Forest Rd	17	P 22
Freeborn Rd	17	Q 22
Fresh Meadow Rd	17	Q 23
Garden Rd	17	P 23
Georgetown By-Pass	21	O 20
Georgetown Rd	21	O 20
Glen La	17	O 23
Glenwood Rd	17	O 23
Glory Rd	17	O 21
Godfrey Rd E	21	O 21
Godfrey Rd W	21	O 21
Good Hill Rd	17	O 23
Gosper Rd	21	P 21
Gray Lock Rd	17	N 23
Gray's Farm Rd	17	O 23
Graystone La	17	P 22
Great Hill Rd	17	P 23
Greenfield Dr	17	P 21
Greenlea Ct	17	P 23
Greenlea La	17	P 23
Grindstone Hill Rd	21	P 20
Hackberry Hill Rd	17	P 22
Hart La	17	O 22
Harvest La	17	P 23
Hedgerow Common	17	O 22
Hemlock Ridge Rd	17	P 22
Heritage La	17	O 23
Hickory La	17	O 23
Hidden Hill Rd	17	O 23
Hidden Meadow Rd	17	O 23
High Acre Rd	17	N 23
High Meadow Rd	17	O 23
High Noon Rd	17	P 22
Hill Farm Rd	17	P 21
Hillcrest La	21	P 20
Hillside Rd N	17	O 21
Hillside Rd S	17	O 22
Hilltop La	17	P 21
Hilltop Rd	17	P 23
Homeward La	17	O 23
Huckleberry La	11	O 23
Humble La	17	P 22
Hunt La	17	P 23
Hyde Ridge Rd	17	O 22
Indian Valley Rd	21	O 20
James Ct	17	O 23
Jana Dr	17	Q 23
Joanne La	17	O 23
Katydid La	17	P 22
Kellogg Hill Rd	17	P 22
Kettle Creek Rd	17	O 23
Kettlewold La	17	O 23
Kramer La	21	O 20
Ladder Hill Rd N	21	P 20
Ladder Hill Rd S	21	O 21
Lakeside Dr	17	O 21
Langner La	17	N 21
Laurel Lake E	17	P 21
Laurel Lake W	17	P 21
Laurel Ridge La	21	P 21
Ledgebrook Ct	17	O 23
Ledgewood Dr E	21	P 20
Ledgewood Dr W	21	P 20
Lilac La	17	P 23
Little Brook La	17	O 23
Little Fox La	17	O 22
Logan La	17	P 21
Lords Hwy	17	O 22
Lords Hwy E	17	P 21
Lost Acre La	17	P 22
Lyon Plains Rd	17	P 23
Maple St	21	O 20
Marshall La	17	N 21
Martin Rd	17	P 22
Maureen Dr	21	O 20
Mayflower La	17	Q 22
Meadowbrook La	21	O 20
Merry La	21	O 21
Messex La	17	Q 22
Michaels Way	17	O 21
Mountainview Dr	17	O 21
Narrow Brook Rd	17	P 23
Newtown Tpke	17	O 22
Nimrod Farm Rd	17	O 22
Nordholm Dr	17	P 23
Norfield Rd	17	O 22
Norfield Woods Rd	17	O 23
North Av	11	O 24
North Calvin Rd	17	O 22
November Tr	17	O 21
Oak La	21	P 20
Oakwood Dr	17	P 22
October Dr	17	O 21
Old Easton Tpke	17	P 23
Old Farm Hill Rd	21	O 20
Old Farm Rd	21	O 20
Old Field La	17	O 21
Old Hyde Rd	17	O 22
Old Hyde Rd Ext	17	O 21
Old Kings Hwy	17	P 23
Old Mill Rd	17	N 22
Old Orchard Dr	17	O 21
Old Redding Rd	17	Q 22
Old Rock Rd	17	P 23
Old Rte 57	21	O 20
Old Stagecoach Rd	17	Q 22
Old Weston Rd	17	O 23
Osborne Farm Rd	21	O 20
Overbrook La	17	O 23
Parade Ground Ct	17	O 22
Partridge La	17	P 22
Patchen La	17	P 21
Pent Rd	21	O 21
Pepperbush Rd	21	P 21
Pheasant Hill Rd	17	P 22
Pilgrim La	17	P 23
Pilgrim Tr	17	N 23
Pilot Hill Rd	17	O 21
Pine Field Rd	17	O 21
Pink Cloud La	17	O 23
Powder Horn Hill Rd	21	P 21
Ravenwood Dr	17	P 21
Richmond Hill Rd	17	P 21
Ridge La	17	N 23
Ridge Rd	17	O 23
River Rd	17	O 23
Riverbank Rd	17	P 23
Riverfield Dr	11	O 24
Rogues Ridge Rd	17	O 21
Roscrea Pl	17	O 21
Sachem Rd	17	O 23
Salem Rd	17	O 22
Samuelson Rd	21	O 20
Sasqua Tr	21	O 20
Saugatuck River Rd	17	O 23
Saw Mill Rd	17	P 23
Scatacook Tr	21	O 21
School Path Rd	17	O 22
School Rd	17	O 22
September La	17	O 21
Shinnecock Pl	21	O 21
Silver Ridge Common	17	P 23
Skylark La	17	P 22
Slumber Corners	17	O 23
Smith Farm Rd	17	P 22
Soundview Farm Rd	17	Q 22
Spring Valley Rd	17	O 21
Spruce Hill Rd	21	O 20
Squires La	11	O 23
State Route 53	17	O 22
State Route 53	21	P 20
State Route 57	17	O 23
State Route 57	21	O 20
State Route 105	17	P 22
Steep Hill Rd	17	O 22
Stillwater La	17	O 21
Stone Cliff Rd	17	P 21
Stonehenge Rd	17	P 22
Sunset Dr	17	P 22
Tannery La N	17	P 22
Tannery La S	17	P 22
Ten O'Clock La	17	P 23
Thompson Av	21	P 20
Thorp Dr	17	P 23
Timber Mill La	17	O 23
Timothy Rd	17	O 22
Tobacco Rd	17	O 22
Tower Dr	17	N 23
Trail's End	17	O 21
Treadwell Ct	17	P 21
Treadwell La	17	P 22
Trout Brook La	17	Q 21
Tubbs Spring Ct	17	P 21
Tubbs Spring Dr	17	P 21
Twelve O'Clock Rd	17	P 22
Upper Parish Dr	21	O 20
Valley Forge La	17	P 21
Valley Forge Rd	17	P 22
Valley Forge Rd	21	P 20
Wagon Wheel La	17	P 22
Walden Woods La	21	O 21
Walker La	17	P 21
Walnut La	21	P 21
Wampum Hill Rd	21	N 21
Waterbury St	17	O 22
Weddington La	17	Q 22
Wedges Field	17	O 21
Wells Hills Rd	17	Q 22
West Branch Rd	11	N 24
West Branch Rd E	11	O 24
Weston Rd	17	O 23
Whippoorwill La	21	O 20
White Birch Rd	17	O 23
White Birch Ridge	17	O 23
White Oak La	17	O 21
Wildwood La	17	O 22
Willow Dr	17	O 22
Willow Rd	17	P 23
Wilson Rd	21	O 20
Winslow Rd	17	Q 22
Wood Hill Rd	17	O 22
Wood Rd	21	P 21
Woodchuck Hill Rd	17	O 22
Woodland Way	17	P 23
Woods End La	21	P 21

WESTPORT

STREET	MAP	GRID
Abbott's La	11	O 25
Acorn La	11	O 25
Adams Farm Rd	4	O 26
Allen La	4	N 26
Alpine La	4	P 26
Ambler Rd	4	O 26
Ambler Rd W	4	O 26
Anchor La	11	N 25
Angora Rd	4	O 26
Apache Tr	11	O 24
Appletree Tr	3	M 27
April Dr	11	N 24
Ardara	4	O 27
Arlen Rd	17	O 23
Arrow Head Rd	4	O 27
Aspetuck La	17	P 23
Avery Ct	11	N 25
Avery Pl	11	N 25
Baer Tr	11	N 25
Baker Av	4	N 26
Baldwin Pl	11	P 25
Barbara Pl	4	O 26
Barry La	11	N 24
Bauer Pl	4	O 26
Bauer Pl Ext	4	O 26
Bay	11	N 25
Bay Pl	11	N 25
Bayberry Common	11	O 25
Bayberry La	4	O 26
Bayberry La	11	O 24
Bayberry Ridge Rd	11	P 24
Baywood La	11	O 25
Beachside Av	4	O 27
Beachside Common	4	O 27
Beachside La	4	O 27
Bedford Dr	4	O 26
Beechwood La	4	N 26
Belaire Dr	3	M 26
Belden Pl	11	N 25
Berkeley Hill	11	O 24
Berkeley Pl	11	O 24
Berkeley Rd	11	O 24
Bermuda Rd	3	L 26
Berndale Dr	11	O 25
Beverly Pl	4	O 26
Big Pines Rd	11	O 24
Birch	11	N 25
Birchwood La	10	M 25
Bittersweet La	11	O 24
Black Birch Rd	11	O 25
Blackberry La	4	O 26
Blind Brook Rd	10	M 25
Blind Brook Rd S	10	M 25
Blossom La	4	O 27
Blue Chip La	3	L 26
Blue Coat La	11	O 25
Blue Ribbon Dr	11	O 25
Bluewater Hill	4	N 27
Bluewater Hill S	4	N 27
Bluewater La	4	N 27
Bluff Pt	3	M 27
Bobwhite Dr	17	N 23
Bolton La	11	N 25
Bonnie Brook La	11	O 24
Bonnie Brook Rd	11	O 24
Bowling La	4	O 26
Boyd La	4	N 26
Bradley	3	M 27
Bradley La	3	M 26
Breezy Knoll	11	N 24
Bridge	3	M 26
Brightfield La	4	O 26
Broad	17	N 23
Broadview Rd	11	N 25
Brook La	4	P 26
Brooklawn Dr	11	O 24
Brookside Dr	11	N 25
Brookside Pk	11	N 25
Brookside Pl	11	N 25
Bruce La	11	P 24
Buck Hill Rd	11	N 24
Budner La	4	N 26
Buena Vista Dr	4	N 27
Bulkley Av N	4	P 26
Bulkley Av S	4	P 27
Bumble Bee La	11	N 24
Bumpy La	11	N 24
Burnham Hill	4	N 26
Burr Farms Rd	4	O 26
Burr Rd	11	N 25
Burr School Ct	4	O 26
Burr School Rd	4	O 26
Burritts Landing N	3	M 26
Burritts Landing S	3	M 26
Burying Hill Rd	4	O 27
Bushy Ridge Rd	11	O 24
Butternut La	11	O 24
Caccamo La	11	N 25
Caccamo La Ext	11	N 25
Caccamo Tr	11	N 25
Calumet La	11	N 24
Calumet Rd	11	N 24
Canal	11	N 25
Canal Rd	3	M 27
Canning La	4	O 26
Canterbury Close	4	N 26
Cardinal La	11	P 24
Carlisle Ct	11	N 25
Carolyn Pl	11	N 25
Carriage La	11	N 25
Catamount Rd	11	P 24
Cavalry Rd	17	N 23
Cedar Pond Rd	11	O 24
Cedar Rd	4	O 26
Cedargate La	11	O 25
Center	4	O 26
Chapel Hill Rd	4	O 26
Charbeth La	4	P 26
Charcoal Hill Common	11	O 24
Charcoal Hill Rd	11	O 24
Charcoal La	11	O 24
Charles	3	M 26
Charlotte Pl	3	M 26
Chelsea Ct	4	N 26
Cherry La	3	M 26
Chestnut La	3	N 26
Chic-A-Dee La	11	N 25
Church La	11	N 25
Church N	4	O 26
Church S	4	O 26
Clapboard Hill Rd	4	O 27
Clark Av	11	N 25
Clayton	4	O 27
Clifford La	11	N 25
Clinton Av	11	N 24
Clinton Ter	3	M 26
Clover La	11	O 25
Coach La	11	O 25
Cob Dr	11	O 25
Cobble Hill Rd	10	M 25
Cockenoe Dr	3	M 27
Coleytown Rd	11	O 24
Colonial Rd	4	O 26
Colony Rd	11	O 25
Compo Beach Rd	3	M 27
Compo Hill Av	4	N 27
Compo Mill Cove	4	N 27
Compo Pkwy	3	M 26
Compo Rd N	11	N 25
Compo Rd S	3	M 27
Compo Rd S	4	N 26
Concord La	4	N 26
Connecticut Tpke	4	O 27
Conte Pl	3	M 27
Cooper La	11	N 25
Cottage La	4	O 26
Couch La	4	O 26
Country La	11	N 25
Country Rd	11	N 25
Court of Oaks	4	O 26
Covlee Dr	3	L 26
Cranbury Rd	10	M 24
Crawford Hgts	10	M 24
Crawford Rd	10	M 24
Crescent Park Rd	11	N 25
Crescent Rd	4	N 26
Crestwood Rd	11	O 24
Cricket La	3	M 26
Crooked Mile Rd	17	N 23
Cross	11	N 25
Cross Brook La	11	N 24
Cross Hwy	11	N 25
Cross Way	3	M 27
Crow Hollow La	11	N 24
Crystal Cir	4	N 26
Cunningham Pl	11	N 25
Cypress Pond Rd	10	M 24
Danbury Av	3	M 27
Daniel Ct	11	P 25
Daniel Ct Ext	11	P 25
Darbrook Rd	11	N 25
Davenport Av	3	M 26
Davis La	4	O 27
Dawn Dr	11	P 25
Daybreak La	11	N 24
Debra La	4	P 26
Deepwood La	11	P 24
Deerwood La	11	O 25
Deerwood Rd	11	O 25
Deletta La	4	N 26
Depot Pl	3	M 26
Devon Rd	4	O 27
Dexter Rd	4	P 26
Diamond Hill La	11	O 25
Doctor Gillette Cir	3	M 26
Dogwood La	4	N 26
Donald Dr	4	O 26
Dorchester Dr	4	O 26
Dover Rd	11	N 25
Driftwood Point Rd	3	M 26
Drumlin La	4	N 26
Drumlin Rd	4	N 26
Duck Pond Rd	3	L 26
East Main	11	N 25
Eastmeadow Rd	11	N 25
Easton Rd	11	O 24
Echo La	3	M 26
Edge Hill La	11	N 25
Edge Hill Tr	11	N 25
Edgemarth Hill Rd	4	N 26
Edgewater Commons La	4	N 26
Edgewater Hillside	4	N 26
Edgewater Rd	4	N 26
Elaine Rd	3	M 26
Elizabeth Dr	4	P 26
Ellery La	4	N 26
Elliot La	11	O 24
Elm	11	N 25
Elmstead La	4	O 27
Elmwood Rd	4	O 26
Elwil Dr	11	O 25
Eno La	3	M 26
Evans Ct	4	P 26
Evergreen Av	11	N 25
Evergreen Pkwy	11	N 25
Fairfield Av	3	M 27
Fairport Rd	4	P 26
Fairview Dr	11	P 24
Farmer Rd	4	N 26
Farnham Ct	4	N 26
Fenway, The	11	N 25
Fermily La	17	N 23
Fernwood Rd	11	N 25
Ferry La	3	M 26
Ferry La E	3	M 26
Ferry La W	3	M 26
Fieldcrest Rd	11	O 25
Fillow	11	N 24
Flintlock Ridge	17	N 23
Florian Ct	11	P 24
Flower Farm La	4	O 26
Ford Rd	11	N 24
Forest Dr	4	O 26
Fox Fire La	11	N 25
Fox Run La	11	O 25
Fragrant Pines Ct	11	N 25
Franklin	3	M 26
Franklin Av	4	N 26
Fraser La	17	O 23
Fraser Rd	17	O 23
Fresenius Rd	4	O 26
Garden La	4	O 26
Gault Av	4	N 26
Gault Park Dr	11	O 24
George	4	O 26
Gilbert La	4	O 26
Glen Dr	3	M 26
Glen, The	11	O 24
Glendinning Pl	11	O 24
Glenwood La	4	O 26
Godfrey La	4	P 26
Gonczy Rd	4	N 26
Gordon La	4	O 26
Gorham Av	11	N 25
Gorham Isl Rd	11	N 25
Grand	3	M 27
Grant Av	11	N 25
Gray La	4	O 27
Gray's Farm Rd	17	O 23
Great Marsh Rd	3	L 26
Green Acre La	4	N 26
Greenbrier La	11	O 24
Greenbrier Rd	11	O 24
Greens Farms Hollow	4	N 26
Greens Farms Rd	4	O 27
Greenwood La	4	P 26
Grist Mill La	4	P 26
Grouse Path	17	N 23
Grove Point Rd	4	N 26
Guard Hill Rd	11	N 24
Gudzik Ct	11	N 25
Guilder La	11	N 25
Guyer Rd	4	N 26
Hale	4	N 26
Hales Ct	4	N 26
Hales Rd	4	N 26
Half Mile Common	11	O 25
Harbor Hill	4	N 27
Harbor Rd	3	L 26
Harborview Rd	11	N 25
Harding La	4	N 26
Harvest Commons	4	O 26
Hatchery Brook La	11	N 24
Hawthorn Ter	11	O 25
Hazelnut Rd	11	O 24
Heather Hill	4	N 26
Heathwood La	11	N 24
Hedge Row La	3	M 26
Hedley Farms Rd	4	O 27
Hemlock Hill	11	N 25
Hen Hawk La	11	N 25
Herbert Baldwin Rd	3	M 26
Heritage Ct	3	M 26
Hermit Ct	17	N 23
Hermit La	11	N 24
Heron Lake Rd	11	N 24
Hiawatha La	3	M 26
Hickey Hill	4	O 26
Hickory Dr	4	O 26
Hickory Hill Rd	11	N 25
Hidden Hill	3	M 27
Hide-Away La	4	N 26
High	4	N 26
High Gate Rd	4	O 26
High Point E	11	O 25
High Point Rd	4	O 26
High Point W	11	O 25
Highland La	17	N 23
Highland Rd	11	P 24
Highwood La	17	N 23
Highwood Rd	17	N 23
Hilary Cir	4	O 26
Hillandale La	4	O 26
Hillandale Rd	4	N 26
Hill's La	10	M 25
Hills Point Rd	4	N 26
Hillside Rd	4	N 26
Hilltop Tr	4	O 26
Hillyfields La	10	M 25
Hitchcock Rd	11	O 25
Hockanum Rd	11	O 25
Hogan Tr	3	M 26
Hollin Ct	11	N 24
Hooper Rd	11	O 24
Horseshoe Ct	3	M 26
Horseshoe La	3	M 26
Hubbel's La	11	N 25
Hunt Club La	4	O 26
Hunting La	4	P 26
Hyatt Ct	10	M 25
Hyatt La	11	N 25
Hyde La	4	O 26
Imperial Av	3	M 26
Imperial Landing	3	M 26
Increase La	4	O 27

STREET	MAP	GRID
Indian Hill Rd	3	M 26
Indian Pt La	10	M 25
Indian River Green	3	M 26
Interstate Hwy 95	3	M 26
Interstate Hwy 95	4	O 27
Inwood La	4	N 26
Iris La	4	O 26
Iron Gate Hill	4	N 26
Ivanhoe La	4	N 26
Ivy Knoll	11	N 25
Ivy Ter	4	N 26
Izzo La	11	N 24
Jackie La	3	M 26
James La	11	O 25
Janson Ct	11	N 25
Janson Dr	11	N 25
January La	4	O 26
Jennie La	4	N 26
Jennifer La	11	N 24
Jennings Ct	4	P 26
Jesup Rd	11	N 25
Joann Cir	11	O 25
Jonathan La	3	M 26
Judy Point La	3	M 26
Julian Brodie Rd	3	M 26
Juniper Rd	11	N 25
Keene's Rd	4	O 26
Keller La	4	O 26
Kensington Pl	11	O 25
Ketchum	3	M 26
Keyser Rd	3	M 26
Kimberly Dr	11	O 24
Kings Hwy N	11	N 25
Kings Hwy S	3	M 26
Kirock Pl	4	O 26
Lakeview Rd	4	N 26
Lamplight La	4	N 26
Langdon Rd	3	L 27
Lansdowne Common	4	O 26
Lantern Hill Rd	11	N 25
Larch Tree La	11	N 24
Larry La	11	O 25
Laurel La	4	N 26
Laurel Rd	4	N 26
Lazy Brook La	4	O 26
Ledge Meadow La	4	N 26
Ledgemoor La	11	O 25
Lee's La	11	N 25
Lehn Farm Rd	11	O 25
Leslie La	11	O 25
Lilac La	4	N 26
Lincoln	11	N 25
Linda La	4	O 26
Linden	11	N 25
Linden La	11	N 25
Little Fox La	11	N 24
Little La	11	O 24
Lockwood Cir	11	P 24
Locust La	3	M 26
Lone Pine Ct	11	N 25
Lone Pine La	11	N 25
Long Lots Ct	4	O 26
Long Lots Rd	4	O 26
Longview Rd	3	M 27
Lookout La	4	N 26
Lookout Tr	4	N 26
Loren La	11	N 24
Loretta Ct	4	N 26
Lost Lodge Rd	11	O 25
Lowlyn Dr	11	N 24
Ludlow Rd	11	N 25
Lyndale Ct	11	N 24
Lyndale Pk	11	N 24
Lyons Plains Rd	11	O 24
Madeline Av	3	M 27
Main	11	N 25
Mallard La	4	P 26
Manitou Ct	3	M 26
Manitou Rd	3	M 26
Manor Dr	11	N 24
Mansfield Pl	4	N 26
Maple Av N	4	O 26
Maple Av S	4	O 27
Maple La	4	O 27
Maplegrove Av	4	N 26
Maplewood Av	11	N 25
[illegible]arc La	4	O 26
[illegible]rilane	11	N 24
Marine Av	3	M 27
Marion Ct	10	M 25
Marion Rd	10	M 25
Marsh Ct	3	L 27
Marsh Rd	3	L 27
Marvin Pl	4	N 26
Mary Jane La	11	P 25
Mayfair La	4	N 26
Mayflower Pkwy	3	M 26
McMahon La	11	N 23
Meadow La	4	N 26
Meadow View Dr	11	O 24
Meadow View Dr S	11	O 24
Meadowbrook La	4	O 26
Medwell La	4	N 26
Meeker Rd	11	P 24
Melon Patch La	11	O 25
Melwood La	4	P 26
Merritt La	11	N 24
Merritt Pkwy	11	P 25
Messiello Cir	11	P 25
Mews, The	11	N 25
Mill Bank Rd	11	N 24
Mill Brook Rd	4	N 26
Miller Av	11	N 25
Mills	4	O 26
Mimi La	4	N 26
Minard Dr	3	L 26
Minute Man Hill	3	M 27
Morningside Dr N	4	O 26
Morningside Dr S	4	O 27
Morningside La	4	O 26
Mortar Rock Rd	4	N 26
Moss Ledge Rd	4	O 26
Murvon Ct	3	M 27
Myrtle Av	11	N 25
Mystic La	11	O 24
Nappa Dr	4	N 26
Nappa La	4	N 26
Narrow Rocks Rd	3	M 26
Nash La	10	M 25
Nassau Rd	3	L 27
New Creek Rd	4	O 27
Newtown Tpke	11	N 24
Norport Dr	3	L 26
North Av	11	O 25
North Pasture Rd	11	O 25
North Ridge Rd	11	O 24
North Sasco Common	4	P 26
Northfield Dr	11	O 24
Northgate	11	O 25
Northside La	11	O 24
Norwalk Av	3	M 27
Norwood La	11	N 24
Nursery La	11	N 25
Nutcracker La	11	O 24
Nutmeg La	11	N 25
Nyala Farm Rd	4	N 26
Oak	11	N 24
Oak Ridge Pk	3	M 26
Oak View Cir	4	O 26
Oak View La	4	O 26
Oakwood La	11	N 24
Old Cuttings La	3	M 26
Old Hill Farm Rd	11	N 25
Old Hill Rd	11	N 25
Old Mill Rd	4	N 27
Old Orchard Rd	4	O 26
Onion Hill Rd	11	O 25
Orchard Hill Rd	10	M 25
Orchard La	11	N 25
Ostend Av	3	M 27
Otter Tr	3	M 26
Over Rock La	4	N 26
Overlook Rd	11	N 25
Overridge Rd	3	M 26
Owenoke Pk	3	M 27
Oxbow Rd	11	N 25
Paddock La	4	P 26
Palmieri Rd	4	P 26
Pamela Pl	11	O 25
Pan Handle La	11	N 24
Park	3	M 26
Park La	4	N 26
Parker Harding Plz	11	N 25
Parsell La	4	P 27
Partrick La	11	N 24
Partrick Rd	10	M 24
Peabody La	4	O 26
Peaceful La	4	N 25
Peach Lot Rd	11	O 25
Pebble Beach La	3	L 27
Pequot Tr	10	M 25
Peter's La	4	O 26
Pheasant La	11	P 24
Pier Way Landing	3	M 26
Pilgrim Tr	11	P 24
Pin Oak Ct	11	N 24
Pin Oak La	11	N 24
Pine	11	N 25
Pine Dr	4	N 26
Pine Tree Dr	11	O 25
Pioneer Rd	10	M 25
Placid Lake La	11	O 25
Playhouse Sq	11	N 25
Pleasant Valley La	11	O 25
Plover La	3	L 26
Plumtree La	11	O 25
Plunkett Pl	4	O 26
Pond Edge Rd	4	N 26
Pond Rd	11	N 24
Pondside Dr	3	M 26
Pony La	11	O 24
Poplar Plain Rd	17	N 23
Porter's La	17	P 23
Possum Run	11	N 24
Post Office La	4	O 27
Post Rd E	11	N 25
Post Rd W	10	M 25
Powers Ct	11	N 25
Primrose La	11	P 25
Pritchard La	4	O 26
Promised Rd	3	L 27
Prospect Rd	4	N 26
Pumpkin Hill	11	O 25
Punch Bowl Dr	11	O 25
Quaker La	11	O 25
Quarter Mile Rd	11	N 24
Quentin Rd	3	M 27
Quintard Pl	4	O 26
Rabbit Hill Rd	11	O 24
Railroad Pl	3	M 26
Rainey La	4	O 26
Raphael Way	11	N 25
Rayfield Rd	4	N 26
Raymond Pl	3	M 26
Rebel Rd	17	N 23
Red Coat La	11	N 24
Red Coat Rd	11	N 24
Regents Pk	4	O 26
Reichert Cir	11	N 25
Reimer Rd	11	O 25
Remlin Ct	4	N 26
Renzulli La	10	M 25
Renzulli Rd	10	M 25
Rex La	4	O 27
Rice's La	11	N 24
Richard Dr	4	N 26
Richmondville Av	11	N 25
Ridge Dr	3	M 26
Ridgewood La	11	N 25
Rippling Brook La	4	N 26
Rivard Cres	10	M 25
River Ct	3	M 26
River Knoll	11	N 25
River La	11	N 24
River Oaks La	4	N 26
River Oaks Rd	4	N 26
River View Rd	3	M 26
Riverfield Dr	11	O 24
Riverside Av	3	M 26
Riverside Av	10	M 25
Robert La	3	M 26
Robin Hill Rd	4	P 27
Rockland Pl	3	M 26
Rockwell Pl	4	O 26
Rocky Acres La	11	O 25
Rocky Ridge Rd	4	N 26
Rockyfield Rd	11	O 24
Roosevelt Rd	3	M 27
Rose La	4	N 26
Roseville Rd	4	N 26
Roshab La	4	O 27
Round Pond Rd	4	N 26
Rowland Ct	3	L 27
Rowland Pl	3	L 27
Rumpenmile Av	4	O 26
Rustic La	4	O 27
Ruta Ct	4	O 26
Sachem Tr	3	M 26
Saint George Pl	11	N 24
Saint Johns Pl	11	N 25
Salem La	11	O 25
Salem Rd	11	O 25
Salt Meadow La	3	M 26
Sandhopper Tr	4	N 26
Sandpiper Rd	3	M 27
Sandy Hill Ter	10	M 25
Sasco Creek Rd	4	O 27
Saugatuck Av	3	M 26
Saum Pl	11	O 24
Saviano La	11	N 25
Saxon La	3	M 26
Scherer Ct	10	M 25
Scofield Pl	3	M 27
Scot-Alan La	4	N 26
Sea Spray Rd	3	M 27
Shadbush La	10	M 24
Shadow Lawn Dr	4	O 26
Sharp Turn Rd	11	N 25
Sheila La	11	O 24
Sherman's Way	4	N 26
Sherwood Dr	4	N 27
Sherwood Farms La	4	N 26
Sherwood Isl Connector	4	N 26
Sherwood Isl La	4	N 27
Sherwood Sq	11	N 25
Short	11	N 25
Side Hill Rd	11	N 24
Signal La	4	N 26
Silent Grove N	11	O 25
Silent Grove S	11	O 25
Silver Brook Rd	11	O 24
Sipperley's Hill Rd	11	O 24
Sky Top Rd	4	N 26
Sleepy Hollow	4	O 27
Sleigh Ridge	4	N 26
Smicap La	11	N 25
Smoky La	4	N 26
Sniffen Rd	11	N 24
Snowflake La	11	O 24
Soundview Dr	3	M 27
South Blind Brook Rd	10	M 25
Spicer Ct	4	N 26
Spicer Rd	4	N 26
Spring Hill Rd	11	N 25
Spriteview Av	3	M 27
Spruce	11	N 25
Sprucewood La	4	P 26
Squire La	11	O 25
State Route 15	11	N 24
State Route 33	11	N 24
State Route 57	11	N 24
State Route 136	3	M 26
State Route 136	11	N 25
Sterling Dr	4	N 27
Stone Dr	3	M 26
Stoneboat Rd	11	N 24
Stony Brook Rd	10	M 25
Stony Point Rd	3	M 26
Stony Point W	3	M 26
Stuart La	3	M 27
Sturges Commons	11	P 25
Sturges Hollow	11	P 25
Sturges Hwy	11	P 24
Sue Ter	11	N 25
Summer Hill Rd	4	O 26
Sunny Acres La	4	P 26
Sunny La	11	N 24
Sunnyside La	11	P 24
Sunrise Rd	3	M 26
Surf La	3	L 27
Surf Pt	3	L 27
Surf Rd	3	L 27
Surrey Dr	3	M 26
Swallow La	3	M 27
Sycamore Dr	11	P 25
Sylvan La	10	M 25
Sylvan Rd N	10	M 25
Sylvan Rd S	10	M 25
Tall Trees Dr	11	N 24
Tamarac Rd	11	N 25
Tanglewood La	11	N 25
Tar Rock Rd	3	M 26
Tarone Dr	3	M 26
Taylor La	4	O 26
Taylor La Ext	4	O 26
Taylor Pl	11	N 25
Teregram Pl	11	N 25
Terehune	11	O 25
Thomas Rd	11	N 25
Tierney La	4	O 26
Tiffany La	4	O 27
Timber La	11	O 25
Todd's Way	4	P 26
Tomahawk La	4	P 27
Tower Ridge	11	P 25
Town Crier La	11	O 24
Trailing Rock La	4	O 26
Trails End	11	O 25
Treadwell Av	3	M 26
Tuck La	11	O 24
Tulip La	11	O 25
Tupelo Rd	11	P 24
Turkey Hill Cir	4	O 26
Turkey Hill La	4	O 26
Turkey Hill Rd N	4	O 26
Turkey Hill Rd S	4	O 27
Turtleback La	11	N 25
Twin Bridge Acre Rd	17	N 23
Twin Circle Dr	11	O 25
Twin Falls La	11	N 24
Twin Oaks La	11	N 24
Ulbrick La	4	P 26
Underhill Pkwy	3	M 26
US Hwy 1	4	O 26
US Hwy 1	10	M 25
Valley Field Rd	4	O 26
Valley Hgts Rd	4	N 26
Valley Rd	4	N 26
Vani Ct	3	M 26
Veterans Rd	11	N 25
Victoria La	11	O 25
Viking Green	17	N 23
Village Sq	11	N 25
Vineyard La	11	O 25
Violet La	11	N 25
Virginia La	4	O 26
Vista Ter	3	M 26
Wagon Wheel Tr	4	O 26
Wake Robin Rd	4	N 26
Wakeman Acres	4	N 26
Wakeman Pl	3	M 26
Wakeman Rd	4	N 26
Wakenor Rd	4	O 26
Warnock Dr	11	O 24
Washington Av	11	N 25
Wassell La	11	N 24
Watch Hill	11	N 25
Waterside Ter	3	M 26
Weathervane Hill	11	N 25
Webb Rd	11	N 25
Wedge Wood Rd	11	O 25
Wendy La	11	O 24
West Branch	11	O 24
West End Av	3	M 26
West Parish Rd	4	O 26
Westfair Dr	4	P 26
Westfair Rd	4	P 26
Weston Rd	11	O 24
Westport Av	3	M 27
Westway Rd	4	O 27
Wheeler Gate	4	N 26
Whippoorwill La	11	O 25
White Woods La	10	M 24
Whitehead Ter	4	O 27
Whitney	11	N 25
Whitney Ext	11	N 25
Whitney Glen	11	N 25
Wilcox La	4	N 26
Wild Oak La	10	M 24
Wild Rose Rd	11	N 25
Wildwood La	11	N 25
Willbrook Dr	11	N 24
Willow Walk Rd	11	P 25
Wilton Rd	11	N 24
Wilton Ter	11	N 25
Winding La	11	N 25
Winding La W	11	N 25
Windrush La	11	N 24
Windy Hill Rd	11	O 25
Winkel La	11	N 24
Wisteria La	11	O 24
Witch La	11	N 25
Woodcock La	17	N 23
Woodhill Rd	4	O 26
Woodland Dr	4	N 26
Woods End La	11	P 24
Woods Grove Rd	11	N 25
Woodside Av	10	M 25
Woodside La	10	M 25
Woody La	11	O 25
Wright	11	N 25
Wyfromere La	4	O 26
Yankee Hill Rd	3	M 26

WILTON

STREET	MAP	GRID
Abbot La	20	L 20
Acorn Ridge Rd	16	L 23
Admiral La	11	N 23
Ambler La	17	N 21
Antler La	20	M 19
Appletree La	16	L 23
Arrowhead Rd	16	M 23
Azalea La	16	L 22
Bald Hill Pl	20	L 20
Bald Hill Rd	20	L 20
Banks Dr	17	N 22
Bayberry La	16	L 22
Beechwood La	17	N 23
Belden Hill La	16	M 22
Belden Hill Rd	16	L 22
Berch Ct	21	N 20
Bhasking Ridge Rd	17	N 22
Bittersweet Tr	16	M 23
Black Alder La	17	N 21
Black Birch Dr	21	N 20
Blue Ridge Acres Rd	21	N 20
Blue Ridge La	17	N 23
Blue Ridge Rd	21	N 20
Blueberry Hill Pl	20	L 19
Boas La	21	N 20
Bob White La	16	L 23
Borglum Rd	16	L 23
Bossy La	17	N 23
Boulder Brook Rd	21	N 20
Bramble Hill	16	L 22
Branch Brook Rd	20	M 20
Breeds Hill Pl	20	M 20
Briardale Pl	16	M 21
Bristol Ct	21	N 20
Broad Axe La	16	M 22
Brookside Pl	16	M 23
Bryant's Brook Rd	16	M 21
Buckboard Ridge	16	M 22
Buckingham Ridge Rd	17	N 22
Bunker Hill Rd	21	N 20
Butternut Pl	16	M 22
Calvin Rd	17	N 22
Cannon Rd	21	N 21
Canterbury La	17	N 23
Captain's La	17	N 22
Cardinal La	17	N 23
Carriage Dr	20	L 20
Catalpa Rd	16	M 21
Cavalry Hill Rd	17	N 23
Cavalry Rd	17	N 23
Cedar Rd	17	N 22
Center St	16	M 22
Charter Oak Pl	20	M 20
Cheese Spring Rd	20	L 21
Cherry La	17	N 22
Chessor La	16	M 23
Chestnut Hill Rd	17	N 23
Chicken St	20	M 20
Chipmunk La	16	M 23
Church St	22	O 19
Cider Mill Pl	16	M 21
Clover Dr	16	M 23
Clover Dr Ext	16	M 23
Coachman's Pl	20	L 20
Cobblestone La	17	N 21
Cobblestone Pl	17	N 21
Cobb's Mill Rd	17	N 22
Coley Rd	17	N 22
Collinswood Rd	20	M 20
Comstock Pl	20	L 21
Connery St	21	N 19
Cora La	21	N 19
Cricket La	16	M 22
Crofoot Rd	20	L 20
Cross Way	16	M 22
Crosswicks Ridge Rd	17	N 21
Dark Pond Tr	20	M 19
Davenport Dr	16	M 22
Deacons La	16	M 21
Deepwood Dr	16	L 23
Deer Run Rd	20	M 20
Deerfield Rd	16	M 22
De Forest La	20	L 20
De Forest Rd	20	L 20
Dirksen Dr	16	M 23
Dogwood La	16	M 23
Dorado Ct	21	N 20
Downe La	16	M 23
Drum Hill Rd	16	M 21
Duck Pond Pl	17	N 22
Dudley Rd	16	M 23
Dumplin Hill Rd	21	N 19
East Meadow Rd	17	N 23
Echo La	16	L 21
Edgewater Dr	16	L 22
Edith La	16	M 23
English Dr	20	M 21
Erdmann La	16	M 23
Evans La	16	L 21
Evergreen Av	16	M 22
Exeter Dr	16	M 23
Fairfax Av	16	M 22
Fairview La	21	N 20
Fawn Pl	20	M 19
Fawn Ridge La	10	M 23
Fenwood La	16	L 22
Forest La	20	L 20
Forge Rd	16	L 23
Forge Rd N	16	L 23
Four Winds Dr	17	N 23
Fox Run	20	M 19
Fresh Water La	16	M 23
Friendlee La	17	N 22
Fullin La	20	L 19
Gilly La	20	M 19
Glen Hill La	16	L 21
Glen Hill Rd	16	L 21
Godfrey La	21	N 19
Godfrey Pl	16	M 22
Graenest Rd	16	M 22
Granite Dr	21	N 19
Great Nor La	16	M 23
Greenbriar La	16	M 22
Grey Rocks Rd	20	M 20
Ground Pine Rd	20	L 20
Grumman Av	16	M 23
Grumman Hill Rd	16	M 23
Hanford La	16	M 23
Hawthorne La	17	N 22
Hearthstone La	16	L 22
Heather La	17	N 23
Hemmelskamp Rd	20	M 20
Henry Austin Dr	17	N 22
Heritage Ct	17	N 21
Hickory Hill Rd	20	M 20
Hidden Lake Ridge	16	M 21
High Ridge Rd	17	N 23
High School Rd	16	M 21
Highfields Rd	16	L 23
Highview Dr	16	M 21
Highwood Rd	17	N 23
Hillbrook Rd	20	M 20
Hillcrest Pl	16	L 23
Hollow Tree Pl	16	L 21
Holly Pl	16	M 23
Hollyhock Rd	16	M 23
Honey Hill Rd	21	N 20
Honey Hill Tr	21	N 20
Horseshoe Rd	16	M 22
Hubbard Rd	16	M 22
Huckleberry Hill Rd	16	L 22
Hulda Hill Rd	21	N 20

STREET	MAP	GRID	STREET	MAP	GRID	STREET	MAP	GRID	STREET	MAP	GRID	STREET	MAP	GRID	STREET	MAP	GRID	STREET	MAP	GRID
Hunting Ridge La	16	M21	Mail Coach Ct	16	L23	Old Boston Rd	16	L22	Pilgrim Tr	17	N23	Ryders La	20	M20	Stonecrop Rd	17	N22	Walnut Pl	16	L21
Hurlbutt	17	N22	Mail Coach Dr	16	L23	Old Boston Rd N	16	L22	Pimpewaug Rd	16	M21	Saddle Ridge Rd	16	L23	Sturgess Ridge Rd	17	N22	Wampum Hill Rd	21	N21
Hyland Dr	17	N21	Maple St	16	M22	Old Danbury Rd	16	M21	Pin Oak La	21	N20	Saint Johns Rd	20	M20	Sugar Hollow Rd	21	N19	Warncke Rd	16	M21
Indian Hill Rd	21	N19	Mark's Tr	20	M20	Old Driftway Dr	16	L21	Pine Ridge Rd	17	N22	Salem Rd	16	M23	Sugar Loaf Dr	21	N20	Washington Post Dr	16	M23
Indian Rock Pl	21	N20	Marvin Ridge Pl	16	L21	Old Farm Rd	16	L22	Pipers Hill Rd	20	M20	Saunders Dr	21	N21	Sugarbush Ct	20	L19	Weeburn La	20	M19
Irmgard La	21	N20	Mather St	21	N20	Old Grumman Hill Rd	17	N23	Pond Rd	17	N22	Scarlet Oak Dr	20	L19	Sunset Hill Rd	21	N20	Weir Isl Rd	21	N19
Ivy La	16	M23	Mayapple Rd	21	N20	Old Highway	16	M22	Pond St	17	N22	School Rd N	16	M20	Sunset Pass	21	N19	West Church St	21	N19
Jackson Rd	17	N22	Mayflower Dr	20	L19	Old Huckleberry Rd	16	L21	Poplar Plain Rd	17	N23	School St	21	N19	Surrey Glen	20	M20	West Meadow Rd	17	N23
Juniper Pl	16	L22	McFadden Dr	16	M23	Old Huckleberry Rd W	16	L22	Portland Av #1	21	N19	Scribner Hill Rd	21	N20	Tall Oaks La	21	N19	Westfield Rd	20	L21
Katydid La	16	L22	Merwin's La	16	M21	Old Kingdom Rd	16	L22	Portland Av #2	21	N19	Seeley Rd	21	N21	Tall Trees La	17	N23	Westport Rd	16	M23
Keelers' Ridge Rd	20	L20	Middlebrook Farms Rd	16	M21	Old Kings Hwy	16	L22	Powder Horn Hill Rd	16	M21	Serendipity La	21	N19	Tamarack Pl	21	N20	Whipple Rd	16	M23
Kellogg Dr	20	L19	Miller St	21	N19	Old Lantern	21	N20	Quail Ridge Rd	21	N20	Shadow La	17	N22	Tanner's Dr	20	M20	Whipstick Rd	20	M20
Kelly Ct	16	L21	Millstone Rd	20	M20	Old Lantern Dr	16	M23	Quarry Way	20	M19	Shagbark Pl	20	M20	Teapot Hill Rd	20	M20	White Birch Rd	21	N19
Kennsett Av	16	M23	Mohackemo Dr	16	L23	Old Mill Rd	21	N20	Quiet Lake La	16	L22	Sharp Hill Rd	16	M22	Telva Rd	16	L23	Whitewood La	16	M22
Kennsett Dr	16	M23	Mollbrook Dr	17	N23	Old Nursery Dr	16	L23	Range Rd	16	M23	Sier Hill Rd	16	L23	Thayer Pond La	16	L21	Wick's End La	17	N21
Kent Hills Rd	16	M23	Montville Dr	16	L22	Old Post Office Sq	16	M21	Raymond La	16	M22	Signal Hill Rd N	20	L21	Thayer Pond Rd	16	L21	Wild Duck Rd	16	L21
Kent Rd	16	L23	Morand La	17	N22	Old Ridgefield Rd	16	M21	Read Pl	21	N19	Signal Hill Rd S	20	L21	Thistle La	17	N23	Wildwood Dr	20	L20
Kingdom Ridge Rd	16	L22	Moriarity Dr	16	L22	Old Town Rd	22	N19	Redland Rd	21	N20	Silver Spring Rd	20	L20	Thunder Lake Rd	21	N19	Willow Brook Pl	20	L20
Kings La	16	K22	Mountain Rd	21	N20	Old Wagon Rd	16	M21	Richards La	16	L22	Skunk La	16	M21	Timber Top Tr	21	N20	Wilridge Rd	21	N19
Langner La	17	N21	Musket Ridge Rd	16	L23	Old Westport Rd	17	N23	Richdale Dr	16	M21	Slawson Ct	16	M22	Tito La	20	M20	Wilton Acres #1	16	M23
Laurel La	16	L22	New Canaan Rd	16	L22	Olmstead Hill Rd	20	M20	Ridge La	16	M23	Snowberry La	20	M19	Topfield Rd	17	N22	Wilton Acres #2	16	M23
Laurelwood La	21	N20	New St	21	N20	Orchard Dr	17	N21	Ridgefield Rd	16	M21	South Gaylord Dr	16	M22	Tory Pl	16	L23	Wilton Hills	16	M23
Lavilla Pl	20	M20	New St Ext	21	N20	Orems La	16	M22	Ridgefield Rd	20	L20	Spectacle La	20	M19	Trails End Rd	16	L22	Wilton Station Rd	16	M22
Ledgewood Dr	16	L21	Newsome La	16	L23	Overidge La	17	N22	Ridgewood Rd	17	N22	Spicewood La	17	N23	Turner La	16	M21	Wilton Woods Rd	20	M19
Lee Allen La	17	N21	Newtown Tpke	17	N23	Own Home Av	21	N19	Riding Club Rd	20	M21	Spoonwood Rd	17	N22	Turner Ridge Ct	20	M20	Windy Ridge Pl	16	M22
Lennon La	16	M23	Nod Hill Rd	22	M20	Parish Rd	17	N22	River Gate Woods	17	N22	Spring Brook La	17	N21	Turtleback Rd	20	M19	Winton Ter	16	M23
Liberty St	17	N22	North Gaylord Dr	16	M22	Parting Brook Rd	16	L21	River Rd	16	M22	Spruce Dr	17	N21	Turtlehead Rd	20	M19	Wiston La	17	N23
Linden Tree Rd	20	L20	North Main St	22	O19	Pelham La	20	M19	Rivergate Dr	17	N23	Spruce Meadow Ct	20	M20	Twin Brook La	17	N22	Wolfpit La	16	M22
Little Flower La	20	L19	Norwalk Danbury Rd	16	M22	Pepperidge La	17	N22	Robin La	20	L19	State Route 33	20	L20	Twin Oaks La	16	M21	Wolfpit Rd	16	L22
Little Fox La	17	N22	Norwalk Danbury Rd	21	N20	Pheasant Run Rd	16	L21	Rockhouse Rd	21	N20	State Route 53	17	N23	Twin Ponds La	16	L23	Wood Hill Rd	20	L21
Littlebrook Rd	17	N22	Nutmeg La	20	L20				Rocky Neck Rd	20	L20	State Route 106	16	M21	US Hwy 7	10	M23	Woodchuck La	16	M22
Long Meadows Rd	20	M19	Oakledge La	16	M22				Rolling Ridge Rd	21	N20	Station Rd	16	M21	US Hwy 7	21	N20	Woodland Pl	16	L21
Lords Hill Way	16	L23	Old Belden Hill Rd	16	L23				Rossimur Ct	20	L20	Stewart La	20	M21	Vale View Dr	16	L23	Woods End Dr	16	L22
Loring La	17	N22							Roxbury La	16	M22	Stirrup Pl	17	N23	Vista Rd	20	L20	Woodway Rd	17	N23
Lovers La	16	M21							Ruscoe Rd	20	L20	Stonebridge Rd	17	N22	Wakefield Rd	16	L23	Wren Thicket	20	M20
Lynlee La	20	M19							Rustic Acres Rd	21	N20									

Notes